ADJUDICATING TRADE AND INVESTMENT DISPUTES

Recent trends suggest that international economic treaties and adjudication may be witnessing a renaissance of convergence – both parallel and intersectional. Signs of convergence are of legal, empirical and normative interest but convergence discourse also warrants scepticism. Focusing on dispute settlement, this volume contributes to both the general debate on the fragmentation of international law and the specific discourse concerning the interplay between international trade and investment. Moving beyond broad observations or singular case studies, it provides a wide-reaching assessment of multiple standards, processes, mechanisms and behaviours. Methodologically, a normative stance is largely eschewed in favour of doctrinal, quantitative and qualitative methods. The book finds that there is no bright line or clear yardstick for determining the nature or degree of convergence but that the evidence of it is not especially strong.

SZILÁRD GÁSPÁR-SZILÁGYI is a lecturer in Law at Keele University. He is a former postdoctoral fellow at PluriCourts, University of Oslo. He holds a PhD from Aarhus University (Denmark) and a two-year LLM from Maastricht University. He taught or conducted research at the University of Amsterdam, The Hague University, Michigan Law School and the Centre for EU External Relations Law (TMC Asser Institute, The Hague). He regularly publishes on issues relating to EU and international investment law, EU external relations law, and the domestic application of international law in the EU legal order.

DANIEL BEHN is a senior lecturer in International Dispute Resolution at Queen Mary University of London and Associate Professor II at the PluriCourts Centre of Excellence, Faculty of Law, University of Oslo. He is an associate editor for the *Journal of World Investment & Trade* and Visiting Professor at Penn State Law School. Daniel's scholarship focuses on the interdisciplinary study of international courts and tribunals. He has written extensively about the sociological and normative legitimacy of international tribunals with a specific focus on international arbitration. His work is empirically orientated and applies quantitative social science methodologies to the study of international adjudication.

MALCOLM LANGFORD is a professor of Public Law, University of Oslo and Co-Director of the Centre on Law and Social Transformation, Chr. Michelsen Institute and University of Bergen, and Associate Fellow at the Pluricourts Centre of Excellence. A lawyer and social scientist, his publications span international investment law, human rights, international development, comparative constitutionalism, technology and the politics of the legal profession. He chairs the Academic Forum on Investor-State Dispute Settlement (ISDS) and is a co-editor of the Cambridge University Press book series *Globalization and Human Rights*.

STUDIES ON INTERNATIONAL COURTS AND TRIBUNALS

General Editors
Andreas Føllesdal, University of Oslo
Geir Ulfstein, University of Oslo

Studies on International Courts and Tribunals contains theoretical and interdisciplinary scholarship on legal aspects as well as the legitimacy and effectiveness of international courts and tribunals.

Other books in the series:

Mads Andenas and Eirik Bjorge (eds.) *A Farewell to Fragmentation: Reassertion and Convergence in International Law*

Cecilia M. Bailliet and Nobuo Hayashi (eds.) *The Legitimacy of International Criminal Tribunals*

Amrei Müller with Hege Elisabeth Kjos (eds.) *Judicial Dialogue and Human Rights*

Nienke Grossman, Harlan Grant Cohen, Andreas Follesdal and Geir Ulfstein (eds.) *Legitimacy and International Courts*

Robert Howse, Hélène Ruiz-Fabri, Geir Ulfstein and Michelle Q. Zang (eds.) *The Legitimacy of International Trade Courts and Tribunals*

Theresa Squatrito, Oran Young, Andreas Føllesdal and Geir Ulfstein (eds.) *The Performance of International Courts and Tribunals*

Marlene Wind (ed.) *International Courts and Domestic Politics*

Christina Voigt (ed.) *International Judicial Practice on the Environment: Questions of Legitimacy*

Freya Baetens (ed.) *Legitimacy of Unseen Actors in International Adjudication*

Martin Scheinin (ed.) *Human Rights Norms in 'Other' International Courts*

Shai Dothan *International Judicial Review: When Should International Courts Intervene?*

Szilárd Gáspár-Szilágyi, Daniel Behn and Malcolm Langford (eds.) *Adjudicating Trade and Investment Disputes: Convergence or Divergence?*

ADJUDICATING TRADE AND INVESTMENT DISPUTES

Convergence or Divergence?

Edited by

SZILÁRD GÁSPÁR-SZILÁGYI
Keele University

DANIEL BEHN
Queen Mary University and University of Oslo

MALCOLM LANGFORD
University of Oslo

CAMBRIDGE
UNIVERSITY PRESS

University Printing House, Cambridge CB2 8BS, United Kingdom

One Liberty Plaza, 20th Floor, New York, NY 10006, USA

477 Williamstown Road, Port Melbourne, VIC 3207, Australia

314–321, 3rd Floor, Plot 3, Splendor Forum, Jasola District Centre, New Delhi – 110025, India

79 Anson Road, #06-04/06, Singapore 079906

Cambridge University Press is part of the University of Cambridge.

It furthers the University's mission by disseminating knowledge in the pursuit of education, learning, and research at the highest international levels of excellence.

www.cambridge.org
Information on this title: www.cambridge.org/9781108487405
DOI: 10.1017/9781108766678

© Cambridge University Press 2020

This publication is in copyright. Subject to statutory exception and to the provisions of relevant collective licensing agreements, no reproduction of any part may take place without the written permission of Cambridge University Press.

First published 2020

A catalogue record for this publication is available from the British Library.

ISBN 978-1-108-48740-5 Hardback

Cambridge University Press has no responsibility for the persistence or accuracy of URLs for external or third-party internet websites referred to in this publication and does not guarantee that any content on such websites is, or will remain, accurate or appropriate.

CONTENTS

List of Figures   page ix
List of Tables   x
List of Editors and Contributors   xi
Preface and Acknowledgements   xv

1 Assessing Convergence in International Economic Disputes – A Framework   1
SZILÁRD GÁSPÁR-SZILÁGYI, DANIEL BEHN AND MALCOLM LANGFORD

PART I   DISPUTE SYSTEM DESIGN   19

2 Investment Chapters in PTAs and Their Impact on Adjudicative Convergence   21
SZILÁRD GÁSPÁR-SZILÁGYI AND MAXIM USYNIN

3 The EU Investment Court System and Its Resemblance to the WTO Appellate Body   62
HANNES LENK

4 Entry Rights and Investments in Services: Adjudicatory Convergence between Regimes?   92
MURILO LUBAMBO

PART II   USE OF PRECEDENT ACROSS REGIMES   119

5 Approaches to External Precedent: The Invocation of International Jurisprudence in Investment Arbitration and WTO Dispute Settlement   121
NICCOLÒ RIDI

6 Engagement between International Trade and
   Investment Adjudicators   149
   MICHELLE Q ZANG

   PART III   INTERPRETIVE POWERS AND ADJUDICATIVE
              BEHAVIOUR   165

7 Inherent Powers of the WTO Appellate Body and ICSID
   Tribunals – A Tale of Cautious Convergence   167
   RIDHI KABRA

8 The Use of Object and Purpose by Trade and Investment
   Adjudicators: Convergence without Interaction   190
   GRAHAM COOK

9 Assessing Convergence between International Investment
   Law and International Trade Law through Interpretative
   Commissions/Committees: A Case of
   Ambivalence?   211
   YULIYA CHERNYKH

10 Regime Responsiveness in International Economic
   Disputes   244
   MALCOLM LANGFORD, COSETTE D CREAMER AND
   DANIEL BEHN

                          * * *

11 Epilogue: 'Convergence' Is a Many-Splendored
   Thing   285
   JOSÉ E ALVAREZ

   Index   313

FIGURES

1.1 Rise of investment chapters in free trade agreements   *page* 3
1.2 Evolution of regional trade agreements (1948–2017)   6
2.1 Inclusion of investment chapters and ISDS   32
2.2 MFN and national treatment   37
2.3 Prohibition of expropriation and extra (FET, FPS)   38
2.4 ICSID +   40
5.1 WTO reference to the jurisprudence of other international tribunals   131
5.2 ICJ and PCIJ citation network by investment tribunals   134
5.3 Connection between investment decisions and Iran–US claims Tribunal decisions   136
5.4 Citation of ECtHR decisions by investment tribunals   137
5.5 Citation of WTO decisions by investment tribunals   138
10.1 Yearly estimates for proportion of DSB report statements   261
10.2 Estimated effects on WTO adjudicative responsiveness   265
10.3 Claimant-investor success ratios (by year)   274
10.4 State Mood I – Number of unilateral treaty exits (by year)   276
10.5 State Mood II – Number of new treaties signed (by year)   277
10.6 Predicted outcomes for State Mood I (treaty exits)   281
10.7 Predicted outcomes for State Mood II (new treaties)   281
10.8 Influential state signals and structural breaks   283

TABLES

2.1 Post-NAFTA PTAs and date of signature (end of 2016): North Atlantic   *page* 55
2.2 Post-NAFTA PTAs and date of signature (end of 2016): Asia Pacific   56
2.3 Post-NAFTA PTAs and date of signature (end of 2016): Latin America   58
2.4 Post-NAFTA PTAs and date of signature (end of 2016): Africa   59
2.5 Statistics   60
10.1 Logit regression results for state mood   279
10.2 Summary statistics – fully resolved investor-state arbitration cases   280

EDITORS AND CONTRIBUTORS

Editors

SZILÁRD GÁSPÁR-SZILÁGYI is a lecturer in Law at Keele University. He is a former postdoctoral fellow at PluriCourts, University of Oslo. He holds a PhD from Aarhus University (Denmark) and a two-year LLM from Maastricht University. He taught or conducted research at the University of Amsterdam, The Hague University, Michigan Law School and the Centre for EU External Relations Law (TMC Asser Institute, The Hague). He regularly publishes on issues relating to EU and international investment law, EU external relations law, and the domestic application of international law in the EU legal order.

DANIEL BEHN is a senior lecturer in International Dispute Resolution at Queen Mary University of London and Associate Professor II at the PluriCourts Centre of Excellence, Faculty of Law, University of Oslo. He is an associate editor for the *Journal of World Investment & Trade* and Visiting Professor at Penn State Law School. Daniel Behn's scholarship focuses on the interdisciplinary study of international courts and tribunals. He has written extensively about the sociological and normative legitimacy of international tribunals with a specific focus on international arbitration. His work is empirically orientated and applies quantitative social science methodologies to the study of international adjudication.

MALCOLM LANGFORD is a professor of Public Law, University of Oslo and Co-Director of the Centre on Law and Social Transformation, Chr. Michelsen Institute and University of Bergen, and Associate Fellow at the PluriCourts Centre of Excellence. A lawyer and social scientist, his publications span international investment law, human rights, international development, international investment, comparative constitutionalism, technology and the politics of the legal profession. He chairs the Academic Forum on Investor-State Dispute Settlement

(ISDS) and is a co-editor of the Cambridge University Press book series *Globalization and Human Rights*.

Contributors

JOSÉ E ALVAREZ, currently the Herbert and Rubin Professor of International Law at NYU School of Law, was formerly the Hamilton Fish Professor of International Law at Columbia Law School. He has also held tenured positions at the University of Michigan and George Washington law schools. A former president of the American Society of International Law and special adviser to the first prosecutor of the International Criminal Court, Professor Alvarez was a co-editor in chief of the leading peer-reviewed journal in the field, the *American Journal of International Law,* and is a member of the Institut de Droit International.

YULIYA CHERNYKH holds an LLM from Stockholm University and is a doctoral candidate at the University of Oslo where she is working on contract interpretation in investment arbitration. She has extensive practical experience as an arbitrator, expert and counsel in international commercial arbitration proceedings under a number of European and Asian arbitration rules. Yuliya lectures on international arbitration at various universities including the University of Oslo, Stockholm University, Kiev-Mohyla Academy, and Riga Graduate School of Law. She is a Chartered Arbitrator.

GRAHAM COOK is a counsellor with the Legal Affairs Division of the WTO Secretariat. In that capacity, he serves as a legal advisor to WTO dispute settlement panels. He is the author of various publications on WTO law, including *A Digest of WTO Jurisprudence on Public International Law Concepts and Principles* (Cambridge University Press, 2015). He frequently lectures on WTO dispute settlement as part of the Secretariat's technical assistance activities, and has been a guest lecturer at IELPO (Barcelona), MILE (Bern), and the University of Geneva.

COSETTE D CREAMER is an assistant professor of political science at the University of Minnesota and affiliated faculty at the University of Minnesota Law School. Her research interests rest at the intersection of international and comparative law, politics and the empirical analysis of law. The substantive focus of her research spans trade and economic law, international arbitration and dispute resolution, international business transactions, human rights, criminal law and procedure, the laws of war, and comparative policing practices. She received her PhD from Harvard University (2016), JD from Harvard Law School (2010), MA in international relations from the University of Chicago (2004) and BA in international studies from the University of Chicago (2002).

RIDHI KABRA is an associate at Three Crowns LLP, London. She holds a PhD from the University of Cambridge. Prior to joining Three Crowns, Ridhi was a lecturer in law at the University of Bristol. She also has taught international law courses at the University of Cambridge, the University of Oxford and Anglia Ruskin University.

HANNES LENK is an assistant professor in European Union law at Aarhus University. In 2019 he completed his doctoral thesis on the EU investment court system at the University of Gothenburg. He studied law and European legal studies at the University of Westminster in London and obtained his LLM in European law at the University of Leiden, in 2012. Before commencing his doctoral studies, Hannes worked briefly at the European Commission where he participated in the WTO Trade Policy Review in 2013. His research focuses on the EU as a global actor, as well as international investment law and arbitration.

MURILO LUBAMBO holds a PhD in International Economic Law from University College London. He is a Senior Fellow at UCL Faculty of Laws and teaches LLM and LLB courses in competition law, private international law and international law of foreign investments. His research focuses on the legal convergence between international trade and international investment, with a particular emphasis on trade in services, under a scholarship from the CAPES Foundation (Process 0738-14-0). He was a Visiting Exchange Scholar at Yale University and a Resident Researcher at the World Trade Organization. As a trade policy coordinator for the Ministry of Finance of Brazil, he was part of negotiation teams of investment and trade treaties.

NICCOLÒ RIDI is a lecturer in law at the University of Liverpool, a Postdoctoral Research Fellow and Visiting Lecturer at King's College London. When this chapter was written, he was a Swiss National Science Foundation Research Fellow at the Graduate Institute of International and Development Studies, Geneva. His work deals with the theory of international dispute settlement as well as with the interaction of private and public international law. He holds degrees in law and political science from the Universities of Florence (LLB/MA), Cambridge (LLM), and King's College London (PhD).

MAXIM USYNIN is a PhD fellow at the Centre for Enterprise Liability (CEVIA), University of Copenhagen. Maxim obtained his bachelor degree in law from the Saint Petersburg State University and two master degrees in law from the Russian School of Private Law and the University of Oslo. In 2015–16, Maxim worked in the investment pillar at the PluriCourts Centre of Excellence (University of Oslo).

MICHELLE Q ZANG is a senior lecturer at Victoria University Wellington, Faculty of Law. She was a postdoctoral research fellow at PluriCourts, Centre for the Study of the Legitimate Roles of the Judiciary in the Global Order, University of Oslo. She specializes, publishes and teaches in international economic law and European law. She worked for the Appellate Body Secretariat of the WTO and King & Wood Mallesons, Beijing.

PREFACE AND ACKNOWLEDGEMENTS

The idea of a *unified* international economic law has undergone a renaissance. The rise of investment chapters in multilateral free trade agreements, cross-regime jurisprudential borrowing, and the emergence of trade-like institutions in investment adjudication has given credence to the idea that the once poster child of the fragmentation of international law may be moving towards harmonization.

This book sets out to test this convergence hypothesis in international economic law with a focus on the field of adjudication. Are the regimes moving closely together? Or is it just an epiphenomenon that disguises a deeper divergence? This interdisciplinary book provides the first in-depth study of convergence of adjudication within international economic law, with a focus on dispute settlement design, use of precedent, and interpretive strategy. We hope it provides a valuable resource to scholars and practitioners alike in thinking through the extent of convergence as well as its underlying dynamics and empirical limits, especially given a series of reform efforts to close the gap.

The book draws together scholars and some advocates from a range of disciplines, resulting in a multimethod perspective on convergence and divergence. The methods vary from comparative case design and doctrinal analysis to regression, network and computational text analysis. The origins of the volume lie in a conference organized by the Pluricourts Centre of Excellence, University of Oslo: *Adjudicating International Trade and Investment Disputes: Between Interaction and Isolation*. In the wake of the conference, some papers emerged as chapters while other chapters were solicited. We would like to deeply thank the authors for their willingness to take on the challenge, particularly in uncovering new insights and perspectives, and their patience in dealing with endless questions and queries from the editors.

We would also like to deeply thank Ole Kristian Fauchald, a coordinator at Pluricourts, for supporting the project throughout its duration and Michelle Zang and Geir Ulfstein in helping shape the original conference. We are grateful to the Pluricourts' directors Andreas Føllesdal and Geir Ulfstein, for including the book within their Cambridge University Press book series *Studies on International Courts and Tribunals* and to Laura Letourneau-Tremblay and Maksim Usynin for help with organizing the original conference.

In the production of the book, we are very grateful to Finola O'Sullivan and Tom Randall at Cambridge University Press for their support for the project from its inception, to Becky Jackaman and Podhumai Anban for shepherding the book through its various phases and to Silvia Glick for the painstaking copy editing of the entire manuscript.

SzGSz, DB and ML, September 2019

1

Assessing Convergence in International Economic Disputes – A Framework

SZILÁRD GÁSPÁR-SZILÁGYI, DANIEL BEHN
AND MALCOLM LANGFORD

By the early 2000s, the international trade and investment regimes had become leading symbols of the fragmentation of international law.[1] Despite periods of shared history and focus,[2] these two regimes could not be more different in their approach to the regulation of cross-border economic activity. They offered divergent approaches to the model of state membership (multilateral/bilateral), the construction of state

---

[1] Martti Koskenniemi and Päivi Leino, 'Fragmentation of International Law? Postmodern Anxieties' (2002) 15 *Leiden Journal of International Law* 553–9; Panagiotis Delimatsis, 'The Fragmentation of International Trade Law' (2011) 45(1) *JWT* 87. On fragmentation in other areas of international law, see: Margaret Young (ed.), *Regime Interaction in International Law: Facing Fragmentation* (Cambridge University Press, 2012); Jonathan Charney, 'Is International Law Threatened by Multiple International Tribunals?' (1998) 271 *Recueil des cours* 101; Tomer Broude and Shany Yuval (eds.), *Multi-Sourced Equivalent Norms in International Law* (Hart, 2011); Marjan Ajevski, *Fragmentation in International Human Rights Law: Beyond Conflict of Laws* (Routledge, 2015); Barbara Stark, 'International Law from the Bottom Up: Fragmentation and Transformation' (2013) 34(4) *Pennsylvania JIL* 687.

[2] From the nineteenth century to the mid-twentieth century, both bilateral Friendship, Commerce and Navigation (FCN) Treaties and colonial-era capitulation agreements between European powers and Asian states often dealt with international trade and investment relations in a single document. Disputes that arose in this period relating to trade and foreign investment were largely resolved extra-legally through diplomatic channels or force. Except for claims commissions and a number of state-state arbitrations, this period saw few instances of formal international adjudication. By the mid-twentieth century the increased legalization and judicialization of international trade and investment law became apparent. However, during this period international trade and investment law – while rapidly expanding – developed along very different paths. The international trade regime witnessed the development of the General Agreement on Tariffs and Trade (GATT) 1947 and later the multilateral World Trade Organization (WTO) regime with a permanent dispute settlement mechanism. In comparison, the international regulation of FDI took a different course; it is a regime governed by over 3,500 bilateral treaty relationships that provide for ad hoc investor-state arbitration should a dispute arise.

obligations (degree of specificity), and dispute resolution (permanence of adjudicatory body, standing for private actors, deference to respondent states, and the types of remedies). After the failure to achieve greater convergence in the 1990s through a WTO-based multilateral agreement on foreign investment regulation, and the subsequent explosion of bilateral investment treaties (BITs) and related disputes, fragmentation in international economic law seemed entrenched.[3]

However, recent trends suggest that international economic law may be witnessing a renaissance of convergence – both parallel and intersectional. For a start, recent bilateral and multilateral free trade agreements exhibit a marked tendency to include chapters on investment protection and investor-state dispute settlement (ISDS),[4] representing a spatial merging of the two fields (see the increasing annual proportion of BITs to treaties with investment protection provisions in Figure 1.1 below). This textual clustering of international trade and investment agreements may result in substantive convergence, especially given the shared objectives of these agreements, liberalizing trade and promoting investments and development, and the need to interpret the provisions in the context of these merged agreements.[5]

Institutionally, the two regimes appear to be creeping towards each other. In the wake of its post-Lisbon competences over foreign direct investment (FDI), the EU has promoted standing investment courts in its new generation of trade and investment agreements,[6] as well as the possibility of a Multilateral Investment Court (MIC)[7] with an Appellate Mechanism that may resemble that of the WTO Dispute Settlement

---

[3] See Jürgen Kurtz, *The WTO and International Investment Law: Converging Systems* (Cambridge University Press, 2016), ch 2.

[4] See the Trans-Pacific Partnership (TPP), The Comprehensive Economic and Trade Agreement between the EU and Canada (CETA) and the proposal for the Transatlantic Trade and Investment Partnership (TTIP). Besides investment, these new generation free trade agreements – especially those negotiated by the EU – also include fields that were traditionally not part of trade agreements, such as the liberalization of services, economic development, or the protection of intellectual property rights. See Maxim Usyinin and Szilárd Gáspár-Szilágyi, 'The Rising Trend of Including Investment Chapters into PTAs' (2018) *Netherlands Yearbook of International Law 2017*, ch 9, 267–304.

[5] Art 31, Vienna Convention on the Law of Treaties.

[6] See Arts 8.27 and 8.28 CETA; Arts 12 and 13, Ch II, EU-Vietnam FTA; Arts 9 and 10, Sec 3, TTIP Proposal. See Szilárd Gáspár-Szilágyi, '*Quo Vadis* EU Investment Law and Policy? The Shaky Path towards the International Promotion of EU Rules' (2018) 23(2) *European Foreign Affairs Review* 167.

[7] Council of the European Union, *Negotiating Directives for a Convention Establishing a Multilateral Court for the Settlement of Investment Disputes* (20 March 2018), http://data.consilium.europa.eu/doc/document/ST-12981-2017-ADD-1-DCL-1/en/pdf, accessed 21 June 2018.

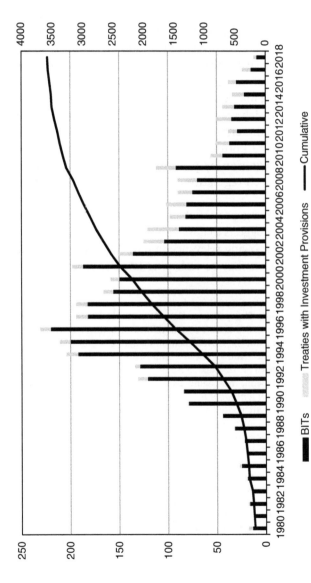

Figure 1.1 Rise of investment chapters in free trade agreements[8]

[8] Source: UNCTAD International Investment Agreement Navigator, http://investmentpolicyhub.unctad.org/IIA/AdvancedSearchBITResults, accessed 21 June 2018.

Understanding (DSU). This attempt could result not only in the creation of a standing, multilateral court, but also in considerable design convergence between the WTO Appellate Body and the MIC's Appeals Mechanism. Even China – a state frequently seen as sceptical about international adjudication – has signalled potential support for an appellate review panel in investor-state disputes.[9]

The adjudicative process also reveals signs of convergence. Investment arbitrators have adopted various interpretive techniques common in trade law, possibly because international investment law is undergoing a legitimacy crisis similar to that experienced by the WTO in its early days.[10] These developments may be also a function of purported broader trends of defragmentation across international courts and tribunals.[11] Adjudicatory convergence is enhanced by a growing use of precedents in investor-state arbitrations, which may evince an attempt to create a more judicial-like regime that is coherent, consistent and hierarchical.[12] This has been reinforced, from the bottom up, by private actors that have accelerated the thematic integration by pushing simultaneous litigation on the same issues (e.g. tobacco regulation,[13] market access, intellectual property[14]) in both regimes.

These diverse claims of convergence are of legal, empirical and normative interest. *Legally*, convergence suggests that the tools and techniques in international trade law may be of growing relevance in international investment law and vice versa. Convergence may be reshaping law and legal doctrine.

---

[9] *United Nations Commission on International Trade Law, Working Group III (Investor-State Dispute Settlement Reform)*, Thirty-fifth session, New York, 23–27 April 2018, Intervention of China on 24 April. See also: 'Possible reform of investor-State dispute settlement (ISDS) - Submission from the Government of China', UN Doc No A/CN.9/WG.III/WP.177 (19 July 2019) and Anthea Roberts and Taylor St. John, 'UNCITRAL and ISDS Reform: China's Proposal', EJIL: Talk!, 5 August 2019.

[10] Malcolm Langford and Daniel Behn, 'Managing Backlash: The Evolving Investment Arbitrator?' (2018) 29(2) *European Journal of International Law* 551.

[11] Mads Andenæs and Eirik Bjørge, *Farewell to Fragmentation: Reassertion and Convergence in International Law* (Cambridge University Press, 2015); Mads Andenæs, 'Reassertion and Transformation: from Fragmentation to Convergence in International Law (2015) 46 (3) *Georgetown JIL* 685; Jed Odermatt, 'A Farewell to Fragmentation; Reassertion and Convergence in International Law' (2016) 14(3) *IJCL* 776.

[12] Alec Stone Sweet and Florian Grisel, *The Evolution of International Arbitration: Judicialization, Governance, Legitimacy* (Oxford University Press, 2017).

[13] See *Philip Morris Asia Limited v. The Commonwealth of Australia*, UNCITRAL, PCA Case No. 2012-12; *Philip Morris Brands Sàrl, Philip Morris Products S.A. and Abal Hermanos S.A. v. Oriental Republic of Uruguay*, ICSID Case No. ARB/10/7.

[14] See *Eli Lilly and Company v. The Government of Canada*, UNCITRAL, ICSID Case No. UNCT/14/2.

Empirically, the discourse has implications for policymaking and adjudication practices. It suggests or reifies a trajectory of reform that would privilege certain policy options and sequences over others. *Normatively*, convergence discourse offers a rebuff to concerns over the legitimacy of international law in general and international economic law in particular. The system is presented as uniform, coherent and stable rather than fragmented, conflicted and chaotic.

Yet, convergence discourse also warrants scepticism. Not all agree that general convergence across international law is as significant as claimed[15] and the identified incidences in international economic law may be both deceptive and misleading. In many cases, the investment chapters of FTAs are cordoned off from the rest of the agreement, with separate rules and procedures for dispute settlement. A single concrete dispute can result in two adjudication processes under the same free trade agreement (FTA), one leading to investor-state arbitration, and the other to a state-state dispute under the agreement's trade rules.[16] Moreover, recent disputes based on investment chapters in FTAs to date (e.g. primarily under the North American Free Trade Agreement (NAFTA) and the Central American-Dominican Republic Free Trade Agreement (DR-CAFTA)) appear to treat the investment chapters as stand-alone agreements with little reference to other sections of these FTAs.[17] In any case, the emergence of a handful of mega-regionals that include both trade and investment chapters[18] does not obviate the reality that the vast majority of trade and investment agreements coexist as separate treaties.

Furthermore, emerging powers such as China and India and the current US administration are signalling their own preferences for the development or even dismantling of various parts of the international economic law regime. International trade law itself is far from being a unified field and we may be witnessing convergence in reverse. The growing spread of bilateral

---

[15] Malcolm Langford, 'The New Apologists: The International Court of Justice and Human Rights' (2015) 48(1) *Retfærd* 49–78.

[16] Roger P. Alford, 'The Convergence of International Trade and Investment Arbitration' (2013) 12 *Santa Clara Journal of International Law* 35, 44–9; Andrea K. Bjorklund, 'Convergence or Complementarity' (2013) 12 *Santa Clara Journal of International Law* 65, 71–3.

[17] See Nicholas DiMascio and Joost Pauwelyn, 'Non-discrimination in Trade and Investment Treaties: Worlds Apart or Two Sides of the Same Coin?' (2008) 102(1) *AJIL* 48–89.

[18] Following the CJEU's *Opinion 2/15* on the competences to conclude the EU-Singapore FTIA, the European Commission decided to split the EU-Singapore FTIA into a separate trade and a separate investment agreement.

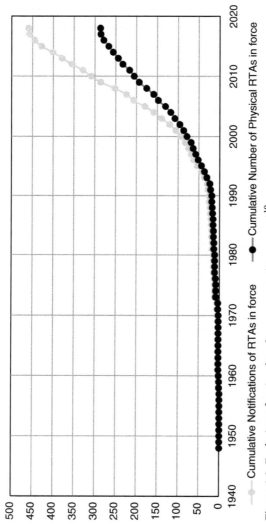

Figure 1.2 Evolution of regional trade agreements (1948–2017)[19]

[19] Source: WTO Secretariat, http://rtais.wto.org/UI/Charts.aspx#, accessed 21 June 2018.

and regional free trade agreements (see Figure 1.2 above) now resembles the diffuse and fragmented web of international investment agreements (IIAs) that has resulted from years of largely bilateral agreements (see Figure 1.1 above). These types of preferential regional free trade agreements often contain their own dispute settlement mechanisms, which all combined may increasingly come into conflict with the monopoly on international trade dispute settlement that the WTO has largely held since its inception. Finally, it is not clear how adjudicatory practices and interpretations have converged: doctrinal variance remains a strong feature of investor-state arbitration and WTO dispute settlement processes make little reference to other regimes, especially international investment law.

This volume therefore aims to contribute to both the general debate on the fragmentation of international law and the particular discourse concerning the interplay between international trade and investment,[20] with a specific focus on dispute settlement.[21] It especially seeks to move beyond broad observations or singular case studies to provide an informed and wide-reaching assessment by investigating multiple standards, processes, mechanisms and behaviours. The topic is also timely, given the new reform processes in international investment law and dispute resolution, the ongoing public backlash against investment law and its recent return in trade law, the proliferation of more complex FTAs, and the continuing impasse of the multilateral trade system in achieving the Doha Round of trade negotiations – in which presumptions about the state of the two systems abound.

---

[20] Kurtz (n. 3); Markus Wagner, 'Regulatory Space in International Trade Law and International Investment Law' (2014–2015) 36(1) *Pennsylvania JIL* 1; Debra P Steger, 'International Trade and Investment: Towards a Common Regime?' in Roberto Echandi and Pierre Sauvé (eds.), *Prospects For International Investment Law and Policy* (Cambridge University Press, 2013), p. 156; R Michael Gadbaw and Robert B Thompson, 'Trade, International Economic Law, and the Challenges of the Global Economy: A Symposium in Honor of John H. Jackson' (2014) 14 *JIEL* 601; Anthea Roberts, 'Clash of Paradigms: Actors and Analogies Shaping the Investment Treaty System' (2013) 107(1) *AJIL* 45; Andrew Mitchell, Elizabeth Sheargold and Tania Voon, 'Good Governance Obligations in International Economic Law: A Comparative Analysis of Trade and Investment' (2016) 17 (1) *JWIT* 7.

[21] Todd Allee and Manfred Elsig, 'Why Do Some International Institutions Contain Strong Dispute Settlement Provisions? New Evidence from Preferential Trade Agreements' (2016) 11(1) *The Review of International Organizations* 89; Alford (n. 16); Bjorklund (n. 16); Joost Pauwelyn, 'The Rule of Law without the Rule of Lawyers? Why Investment Arbitrators are from Mars, Trade Adjudicators from Venus' (2015) 109(4) *AJIL* 761; DiMascio and Pauwelyn (n. 17).

1 Research Design

Comparing adjudication in international trade and investment law, we ask: To what extent has convergence (or divergence) occurred? And, under what conditions does it emerge? In order to provide sufficient focus and an original answer to these questions, the authors concentrate on the *adjudication of disputes* rather than the broader treaty framework. The volume is thus structured around three aspects of adjudication: *design* of the dispute settlement system (Part I), the *conduct* of the adjudicative process (Part II) and the *behaviour* of the adjudicators (Part III). While this limits the potential field of convergence, it is important to remember that much of the controversy around both systems surrounds their adjudicatory dimensions (especially in international investment law).

Methodologically, a normative stance is largely eschewed in favour of a range of 'doctrinal', quantitative and qualitative approaches that are used to address the research questions. However, most authors also take up normative questions in their conclusions – looking ahead to what forms of convergence or divergence might be necessary and desirable. Moreover, divergence might be preferred in some circumstances. Not all convergence may be healthy. For example, the WTO Appellate Body's interpretation of the national treatment obligations under the GATT may not always be appropriate for investor-state arbitration tribunals given different treaty wordings across BITS.

2 Thinking about Convergence and Divergence

In determining the *extent* of convergence, it is important to recognize that there is no bright line or clear yardstick for determining its nature or degree. Signs of 'convergence' for one scholar might be deemed as random, insignificant, secluded or momentary by another. Thus, no strict definition of divergence or convergence is offered in the book, and the authors are free to confine themselves to a singular understanding if so desired.

This is further complicated by the terms themselves. According to the *Oxford Dictionary*, the verb 'to converge' entered the English language in the seventeenth century as a composite Latin word made up of *con* ('together') and *vergere* ('incline'). While the verb implies some form of 'finality' (the meeting of elements from different directions at a certain 'end point'), the noun 'convergence' refers to a process without the need of a 'final point'. Divergence, with *dis* ('in two ways'), denotes the reverse process of drifting apart, moving into different directions – but without connoting a complete dissolution. Both concepts, albeit opposite to one another, denote an *ongoing process*, without the necessity of some form of result. Considering this lack of finality, it is somewhat impossible to establish an endpoint.

While the indeterminate nature of these concepts makes the task methodologically challenging, we can identify four relevant types of convergence (with corresponding divergence), which we use to analyse the volume's results.

- The first is *absolute* convergence or divergence, in which adjudication of international trade and investment disputes occurs under an identical/completely separate framework of rules and processes. It would suggest that the two legal orders are conceptually, structurally and interpretively the same/different with virtually complete overlap/ no overlap. Such convergence or divergence is hard to find in international law, even in nominally similar fields such as human rights.
- The second is *structural*, where the design and structures of dispute settlement mechanisms – under international trade and investment agreements – are separate but similar. Each regime remains distinct, but the dispute settlement processes become increasingly indistinguishable. This has partly occurred with fields such as human rights and international criminal law; although divergence is equally common, particularly with new regional courts in Africa and the Caribbean.[22]
- The third is *sociological*, through which the network and community of actors involved in the adjudication of international trade and investment disputes (parties to disputes, counsel and adjudicators) increasingly converge and engage with each other through judicial or general dialogue, cross-citation and double-hatting across the two regimes.[23]

---

[22] Theresa Squatrito, 'Resourcing Global Justice: The Resource Management Design of International Courts' (2017) 8 *Global Policy* 62.

[23] For an analysis of the actors involved in the different regimes, see Malcolm Langford, Daniel Behn and Runar Lie, 'The Revolving Door in International Investment Arbitration' (2017) 20(2) *JIEL* 301; Marcelo Varella, 'Building International Law from the Inside Out: The Making of International Law by Infra-State and Non-State Actors', https://ssrn.com/abstract=2288209, accessed 21 June 2018; Rachel Cichowski, 'Women's Rights, the European Court, and Supranational Constitutionalism' (2014) 38 *Law and Society Review* 489.

- The final is *epistemic*, with the cross-usage of similar interpretive techniques and methods between trade and investment tribunals. Such interpretive convergence would also suggest that there is learning between the two regimes – whether doctrinally or strategically. Andenæs and Bjørge claim that this is now common between a range of international courts on questions of human rights.[24]

Moreover, we can seek to evaluate the degree, direction and permanence of convergence and divergence. Thus, which field is moving towards the other, to what extent, and for how long? Is investment law moving steadily towards trade law, is it the reverse, or is it mutual? In addition, we can ask what happens in the shadow of convergence – are other less visible areas diverging? As discussed, both concepts – convergence and divergence – albeit opposite to one another, denote an *ongoing process*, without the necessity of some form of result. Various views 'on converging and diverging trends' are constantly put forward in the literature, including studies on harmonization,[25] unification,[26] Europeanization,[27] internationalization[28] and defragmentation.[29]

---

[24] Andenæs and Bjørge (n. 11).

[25] See Larry Catá Backer, *Harmonizing Law in an Era of Globalization: Convergence, Divergence and Resistance* (Carolina Academic Press, 2007); Silvia Fazio, *The Harmonization of International Commercial Law* (Kluwer, 2007); Stephen Weatherill and Stefan Vogenauer (eds.), *The Harmonisation of European Contract Law: Implications for European Private Laws, Business and Legal Practice* (Hart, 2006).

[26] See Alkuin Kölliker, *Flexibility and European Unification: The Logic of Differentiated Integration* (Rowman and Littlefield, 2006); Sacha Prechal and Bertvan Roermund (eds.), *The Coherence of EU Law: The Search for Unity in Divergent Concepts* (Oxford University Press, 2008).

[27] See Francis Snyder (ed.), *The Europeanisation of Law: The Legal Effects of European Integration* (Hart, 2000); Thomas Watkin (ed.), *Europeanisation of Law* (BIICL, 1998); Jan Wouters et al. (eds.), *The Europeanisation of International Law* (Springer, 2011).

[28] Marcelo Varella, *Internationalization of Law: Globalization, International Law and Complexity* (Springer, 2014); Jan Klabbers and Mortimer Sellers (eds.), *The Internationalization of Law and Legal Education* (Springer, 2009); Jens Drolshammer and Michael Pfeifer (eds.), *The Internationalization of the Practice of Law* (Springer, 2001).

[29] Martti Koskenniemi (ed.), 'Fragmentation of International Law: Difficulties Arising from the Diversification and Expansion of International Law' Report of the Study Group of the ILC, Erik Castrén Institute Research Reports (2007); Margaret Young (ed.), *Regime Interaction in International Law: Facing Fragmentation* (Cambridge University Press, 2015); Andrzej Jakubowski and Karolina Wierczyńska (eds.), *Fragmentation Versus the Constitutionalisation of International Law: A Practical Inquiry* (Routledge, 2016); Philippa Webb, *International Judicial Integration and Fragmentation* (Oxford University Press, 2016); Andenæs and Bjørge (n. 11).

We can ask also why there is convergence, divergence, or both. To be sure, any discussion on causation is fraught with danger. Nonetheless, in investigating different types and areas of convergence, it is possible to identify competing explanations and it helps provide a deeper understanding of the nature and permanence of any convergence. For instance, are changing interpretive styles in investor-state arbitration a result of strategic moves by arbitrators to gain legitimacy, an isomorphic shift in the prevailing consensus on interpretation, a legalistic reflection of new treaty standards, or the particular choices by claimants in framing a case? Some authors proceed deductively and test out particular theories for explaining convergence and divergence; the majority move inductively sorting through the reasons that might explain both shifts and stasis, whether drivers or barriers.

3 Structure of the Book

3.1 Dispute System Design

The adjudication of disputes, regardless of the field, needs a mechanism under which the contentious issues that lead to the development of the dispute can be resolved. The WTO has often been praised for its dispute settlement system, especially for the creation of a standing Appellate Body that brought much needed coherence and stability to the system. In turn, investor-state dispute settlement often faces criticism for its ad hoc nature and the lack of a central body that could bring much needed coherence in the jurisprudence. One would thus assume that the two systems could not be further apart. Nonetheless, there is room for convergence. Both dispute settlement systems are remarkably efficient, and the same dispute often can be and is brought before both dispute settlement mechanisms. Furthermore, ISDS mechanisms are increasingly included within FTAs and there is a renewed interest for the creation of a MIC with an Appeals Mechanism. Therefore, the volume reserves Part I for discussions on the 'structures' in which trade and investment disputes take place.

In Chapter 2 Szilárd Gáspár-Szilágyi and Maxim Usynin focus on the first stage in which some level of convergence between the adjudication of trade and investment disputes might be observed: treaty design. After an analysis of 144 preferential trade agreements (PTAs) in fifteen different countries and regional economic integration organizations (REIOs), they conclude that there is a rising trend of including investment chapters with ISDS mechanisms into PTAs. However, this trend is not uniform around the world. Therefore, if structural convergence is to occur between the two adjudicatory mechanisms, due to both being included under the same 'treaty roof', such convergence will not be global, but regional or local. The chapter continues with a discussion of the potential implications of this phenomenon and argues that some level of convergence can still be expected in two areas. First, the broader context and objectives of PTAs with investment chapters can have an influence on the reasoning of investment tribunals. Instead of confining themselves to investment provisions, tribunals can take into consideration the overall purpose of PTAs, such as trade liberalization, promotion of investment, regulatory space, protection of non-economic interests, and general exceptions, when interpreting investment protection provisions. Second, some level of convergence might occur due to the interpretive functions of treaty committees, which oversee all the relevant policy fields covered by PTAs, including trade and investment (a topic further developed by Yuliya Chernykh in Chapter 9). Nonetheless, convergence might be minimal for the following reasons: trade and investment dispute settlement are still served by different epistemic communities; investment chapters often look like stand-alone BITs within a trade agreement; and the recent PTAs with investment chapters require different qualifications for trade and investment dispute settlement decision makers.

Hannes Lenk broadens the view once again in Chapter 3, as he looks at the possibility of multilateralizing investment dispute resolution in EU trade and investment agreements. This chapter discusses the EU's proposed Investment Court System (ICS) in the context of previous attempts to create such a multilateral institution. With the treaty-centred approach as the basis for this development, the chapter analyses the alternative scenarios of how a multilateral investment court could come about, including an assessment of existing international frameworks that are likely to host that institution (e.g. the WTO, OECD, ICSID and UNCITRAL). The author argues that the EU's active engagement in the field could fall victim to its own success – if it ever becomes successful, that is. If the proposed ICS turns out to be effective, efficient and accepted as more legitimate than investor-state arbitration, it might in fact inhibit the efforts of establishing a multilateral investment court. Alternatively, the increasing use of these instruments could result in a creeping multilateralization, creating a quasi-multilateral network of treaty-centred investment courts, a shrine to Western neoliberal values. A glimpse of hope, on the other hand, might come as a spin-off effect of current developments, should existing frameworks such as ICSID, UNCITRAL and the WTO rise to the occasion.

Lastly, Part I looks at the narrower issue of entry rights and investment in services. In Chapter 4 Murilo Lubambo discusses the jurisdiction to adjudicate disputes related to entry rights in services. The chapter initially evaluates whether investor-state arbitration (ISA) can be strategically used to enforce disputes "before the making of an investment". Then, it assesses the potential of state-state dispute settlement mechanisms for investment disputes. This is followed by an evaluation of the jurisdiction of the Dispute Settlement Body (DSB) of the World Trade Organization (WTO), especially when it comes to the enforcement of provisions of the General Agreement for Trade in Services (GATS) concerning mode 3, represented by the commercial presence of an entity in the territory of another WTO member. This panorama sets the ground for explaining the recent innovative approaches taken by the current treaties and negotiations on the subject, illustrated by the services and establishment chapters of the Comprehensive Economic and Trade Agreement between the European Union and Canada (CETA). Finally, the chapter tests the extent to which the interaction in this area provides evidence of a gradual move towards a specific type of enforcement. The chapter concludes that state actors are progressively adopting convergent approaches in adjudication, at least with respect to the entry of investors in services. Evidence of this is the increasing number of IIAs containing establishment rights, but at the same time narrowing down the choices of enforcement of those rights.

3.2 The Use of Precedent across Regimes

Leaving behind the design and structure of the dispute settlement mechanisms, Part II of the book focuses on *network convergence and divergence*, identifying the degree to which the actors involved in the adjudication of international trade and investment disputes engage with each other, via judicial dialogue or cross-citation across the two regimes. More importantly, the contributors look at the types of interactions that exist between the two dispute settlement systems and whether the regimes rely on the jurisprudence of the other.

Chapter 5, written by Niccolò Ridi, looks at the usage of precedents from other fields. The author argues that international adjudicators routinely refer to their own decisions, even though the general unwillingness to grant law-making powers to international judicial bodies is reflected in the orthodoxy on the sources of international law, which sees judicial decisions as 'subsidiary means' for the determination of rules of law. Adjudicators also refer to each other's decisions, and compelling evidence suggests that such 'external precedents' are regarded as equally persuasive. This chapter investigates and compares the attitudes that two different types of dispute settlement bodies dealing with international economic law – investment arbitration tribunals and the WTO Panels and Appellate Body – exhibit towards the decisions of other international adjudicators. This task is accomplished through a mixed quantitative and qualitative methodology. Firstly, all the cases citing external precedents are mapped – employing citation and network analysis techniques – to identify the most cited courts and decisions, and to trace the issue areas that prompt recourse to external precedent. Secondly, the author assesses the importance of different factors in identifying precedents, such as: the legal regime, the factual matrix, the quality of the decision's reasoning, and the reputation of the adjudicators that rendered it. Thirdly, he considers whether the invocation of external precedent might pursue goals going beyond the ones traditionally identified in the literature. Finally, Ridi compares the ways in which external precedents are currently employed by trade and investment adjudicators under a systemic perspective, ultimately considering how different approaches to the issue may affect – and may be affected by – the position of the originating regime in relation to general international law and other regimes.

In Chapter 6, Michelle Zang broadens the discussion. She introduces the term 'judicial engagement' to conceptualize the interaction between different international courts. Judicial engagement occupies a large middle ground on the continuum between resistance and convergence, highlighting the willingness of the participating adjudicators to consider external sources in the appropriate case, denoting a commitment to judicial deliberation but openness to an outcome of either harmony or dissonance. This chapter focuses on two specific research questions. The first concerns the normative grounds for this adjudicative behaviour, and the author identifies the elements that support it, as well as those that render 'cross-judging' impossible. The second question relates to the possible function and contribution of engagement between trade and investment tribunals. The ultimate enquiry concerns whether we should or should not promote this adjudicative behaviour. If so, what would its benefits be? The discussion in this regard investigates the possible function of judicial engagement in light of the legitimacy challenges currently faced, and the role of governance currently performed, by the tribunals involved.

3.3 Interpretive Powers and Adjudicative Behaviour

Part III of the book focuses attention on the powers that the adjudicative and interpretive bodies possess, as well as adjudicative behaviour. As mentioned, interpretive convergence would suggest that there is an increasing amount of cross-use of interpretive techniques and methods between trade and investment tribunals on the interpretation of comparatively similar substantive and procedural rules

In Chapter 7 Ridhi Kabra looks at the 'inherent powers' of the WTO Appellate Body and ICSID Tribunals. She argues that the key to the exercise of the international judicial function is the principle of inherent powers. Inherent powers are conferred upon judicial bodies to safeguard the judicial function. Yet, for the WTO Appellate Body (AB) and ICSID tribunals (collectively, the tribunals), it is often assumed that while ICSID tribunals have broad inherent powers, the AB's inherent powers are restricted. She asks the question whether this means that these tribunals are fragmented in the exercise of their judicial function, and consequently their inherent powers, and if so, what factors contribute to such fragmentation. This chapter answers the above questions by examining the way the AB and ICSID tribunals perceive their authority to exercise inherent powers through the examples of (a) objections to admissibility of a case; and (b) amicus curiae submissions. Using these examples, this chapter challenges absolutist assumptions about the inherent powers of the AB and ICSID tribunals. Instead, it develops a nuanced understanding of the scope of the inherent powers of these tribunals through a study of their respective judicial functions. This involves a close study of the meaning of 'international judicial function', analysis of convergences in the judicial functions of the AB and ICSID tribunals, and an identification of the factors that contribute to the adoption of divergent judicial policies. The particular approaches of these tribunals towards their inherent powers is then rationalized by highlighting the unique interplay between, and balancing of, the international judicial function and the structural and institutional limitations of these tribunals. In doing so, the chapter highlights the converging nature of the judicial function of these tribunals and dispels the notion that these tribunals are responsible for fragmenting the law on inherent powers.

Finally, by drawing on the divergences in the judicial framework of the tribunals, this chapter cautions against promoting convergence at the cost of carefully structured differences in the functioning of these tribunals.

Graham Cook, in Chapter 8, compares instead the practice of trade and investment adjudicators in relation to the requirement to interpret a treaty 'in the light of its object and purpose'. The author begins by identifying a range of issues and choices that adjudicators are confronted with in this regard, and the practical barriers to any significant degree of judicial interaction or cross-fertilization between trade and investment adjudicators. He then shows that notwithstanding the absence of judicial interaction, there is a remarkable degree of convergence in the legal reasoning of trade and investment adjudicators on diverse issues. Among these issues, he includes the basis for identifying a treaty's object and purpose, the need to balance competing objectives, the recognition of some of the limitations of purposive reasoning, and even standard forms of consequentialist arguments. The final section argues that such convergence is most easily explained by the theory that many aspects of legal reasoning and treaty interpretation derive not from knowledge of prior precedent and judicial practices, but from common sense and the nature of the judicial function in the context of international dispute settlement.

Chapter 9, written by Yuliya Chernykh, leaves tribunals and courts behind, and instead focuses on treaty committees that share interpretative functions with adjudicative bodies. She argues that the trend to restrict the tribunals' interpretative powers by allowing treaty committees (ITCs) to provide binding interpretations of the underlying treaty is not new. Since NAFTA, special arrangements for the binding interpretation of the ITCs have been introduced in a number of FTAs and BITs concluded by Canada, the United States and Mexico. Some other non-NAFTA countries began to use similar provisions in their treaty practice as well. Nonetheless, the first interpretation ever generated by an ITC – the NAFTA Interpretative Note of 2001 – has posed serious procedural questions, such as when is an interpretation a genuine interpretation and not an amendment and who has the power to decide whether the document presented is an amendment or a genuine interpretation. This chapter aims to explore whether, and to what extent, joint interpretative commissions/committees are in fact signs of convergence between international investment law and international trade law. The author addresses convergence through the following four dimensions: spatial, temporal, ideological and functional. She concludes that a deeper convergence can be found in the ideological dimension than in the spatial and temporal perspectives, namely through the introduction of a new epistemic community into the field of international investment. Furthermore, the functional dimension shows lasting similarities and differences between the fields. Nevertheless, the author's deeper analysis shows complexity in reconciling the dual role of states as both respondents and interpreters in pending proceedings, and this is where convergence meets resistance.

Malcolm Langford, Cosette Creamer and Daniel Behn in Chapter 10, focus on adjudicative behaviour. How do trade and investment adjudication regimes respond to the prevailing mood of states and other stakeholders? This question is not only relevant to the study of convergence between the regimes, but it is central in current UNCITRAL Working Group III debates over establishing a court system and appellate review mechanism for investor-state dispute settlement. In order to understand the extent of adjudicative responsiveness in both systems, this chapter examines adjudicator behaviour during periods of backlash by states. There are strong rational choice and discursive-based reasons for thinking that WTO and investor-state dispute settlement mechanisms would self-correct and bend towards the arc of enhanced sociological legitimation. However, competing legalistic and attitudinal factors may dampen responsiveness and legitimation incentives may be weak in decentralized investor-state arbitration as compared to the WTO. Comparing and contrasting prior empirical work on both regimes, the authors find evidence that adjudicators are responsive to negative and positive signals from states, especially influential, developed and vocal states. However, the effects are much stronger in the WTO regime. This suggests that efforts to move investor-state dispute settlement towards a more centralized system may produce more state-sensitive outcomes.

In the concluding Epilogue of the book, José Alvarez opens with the observation that many international law 'scholars would prefer, all else being equal, to find evidence of structural or substance convergence' and points to institutional legitimation and professional self-preservation as two important reasons for converge discourse. This is followed by a reflection on the conclusions of the contributors to the edited volume and he points to strong evidence of divergence across the many chapters. Based on his prior analysis of 395 ISDS rulings and how they reference WTO law and European human rights law, he proceeds to throw cold water on the proposition that the trade and investment regimes, which some see as wrongly separated at birth, are converging around substantive common principles, standards or rules. Firstly, if significant trade-investment law convergence exists, it is not occurring through explicit reliance on WTO law by ISDS arbitrators. Secondly, the references to WTO law that he finds were narrow not only with respect to the numbers of IIAs involved; they were narrow with respect to the kinds of issues on which trade law was deemed relevant. Alvarez furthermore acknowledges the limitations of citation studies, such as the ones conducted by him, as the two regimes may engage in other ways, apart from what happens at the final public stage of formal dispute settlement.

PART I

Dispute System Design

2

Investment Chapters in PTAs and Their Impact on Adjudicative Convergence

SZILÁRD GÁSPÁR-SZILÁGYI AND MAXIM USYNIN[*]

1 Introduction

The breakdown of the multilateral WTO talks has led to the proliferation of bilateral and regional preferential trade agreements (PTAs).[1] From the mid-1990s onwards PTAs began including non-trade related fields, covering not only labour standards, human rights, intellectual property or environmental protection, but also investment protection.[2] Following the coming into force of the North American Free Trade Agreement (NAFTA, 1994) investment protection standards and investor-state dispute settlement (ISDS), traditionally the domain of bilateral investment treaties (BITs), have come under the ambit of a growing number of PTAs.[3] More recent mega-regionals, such as the Trans Pacific

---

[*] This work was partly supported by the Research Council of Norway through its Centres of Excellence funding scheme, project no. 223274, and the Danish Council for Independent Research. We thank Geir Ulfstein, Andreas Føllesdal, Ole Kristian Fauchald, Malcolm Langford, Daniel Behn, Taylor St John and Theresa Squatrito for their useful comments. Parts of this chapter appear in an earlier publication: Maksim Usynin and Szilárd Gáspár-Szilágyi, 'The Growing Tendency of Including Investment Chapters in PTAs' (2018) 48 *Netherlands Yearbook of International Law* 267.

[1] See Sébastien Miroudot, 'Investment' in Jean-Christophe Maur, Jean-Pierre Chauffour (eds.), *Preferential Trade AgreementPolicies for Development: A Handbook* (World Bank Publications 2011); Steve Lee, 'The United States-Korea Free Trade Agreement' in Simon Lester, Bryan Mercurio and Lorand Bartels (eds.), *Bilateral and Regional Trade Agreements* (2nd ed., CUP, 2015), pp. 7–9; Pamela Apaza Lanyi, Armin Steinbach, 'Promoting Coherence between PTAs and the WTO through Systemic Integration' (2017) 20(1) *JIEL* 61.

[2] See Henrik Horn, Petros C. Mavroidis, André Sapir, 'Beyond the WTO? An Anatomy of EU and US Preferential Trade Agreements' (2012) 33 *The World Economy* 1565.

[3] For a brief overview of the evolution of IIAs see Daniel Behn, 'Performance of Investment Treaty Arbitration' in Andreas Follesdal et al. (eds.), *The Performance of International Courts and Tribunals* (Cambridge University Press, 2018), pp. 82–6.

Partnership (TPP), the 'frozen' Transatlantic Trade and Investment Agreement (TTIP) or the EU-Canada Comprehensive Economic and Trade Agreement (CETA)[4] also include investment chapters.

Over the years, several large-scale academic projects have focused on the proliferation of PTAs. In 2011, Baccini et al. set up a database comprised of over 600 PTAs,[5] while in 2016 Allee and Elsig compared the complete texts of 378 PTAs to analyse the extent to which treaties 'copy-paste' existing or model treaties.[6] The 2017 project of Alschner et al. used text-data analysis methods to map 447 PTAs.[7]

Studies have also focused separately on the dispute settlement mechanisms of BITs and PTAs. As is well known, the traditional mechanism of dispute settlement found in BITs is ISDS, most often in the form of investor-state arbitration. This mechanism gives standing to private actors to challenge state measures. Allee and Peinhardt's 2010 study of 1,500 BITs identified systematic variation in legal delegation to the International Centre for the Settlement of Investment Disputes (ICSID). In the case of trade disputes, the dispute settlement mechanism of choice has been some form of state-to-state mechanism. In the multilateral context the WTO's Dispute Settlement Mechanism (DSM) reigns supreme, while in the case of PTAs Allee and Elsig's 2015 study of nearly 600 PTAs paints a much more varied picture.[8] They found that

---

[4] See Chin L. Lim, Deborah K. Elms and Patrick Low (eds.), *The Trans-Pacific Partnership: A Quest for a Twenty-first Century Trade Agreement* (Cambridge University Press, 2012); James Mathis, 'Multilateral Aspects of Advanced Regulatory Cooperation: Considerations for a Canada-EU Comprehensive Trade Agreement (CETA)' (2012) 39(1) *LIEI* 73; Ingo Venzke, 'Investor-State Dispute Settlement in TTIP from the Perspective of A Public Law Theory of International Adjudication' (2016) 17(3) *JWIT* 374; Luca Pantaleo, Wybe Douma and Tamara Takács, 'Tiptoeing to TTIP: What Kind of Agreement for What Kind of Partnership?' CLEER Working Papers 2016/1 (2016), www.asser.nl/media/3005/cleer16-1_complete_web.pdf, accessed 31 March 2019.

[5] Leonardo Baccini, Andreas Dür, Manfred Elsig and Karolina Milewicz, 'The Design of Preferential Trade Agreements: A New Dataset in the Making' (2011) WTO Staff Working Paper ERSD, No 2011-10, www.academia.edu/2918412/The_design_of_preferential_trade_agreements_A_new_dataset_in_the_Makin, accessed 31 March 2019.

[6] Todd Allee and Manfred Elsig, 'Are the Contents of International Treaties Copied-and-Pasted? Evidence from Preferential Trade Agreements' (2016) WTI Working Paper No. 8, Aug 2018.

[7] Wolfgang Alschner, Julia Seiermann and Dmitriy Skougarevskiy, 'Text-as-Data Analysis of Preferential Trade Agreements: Mapping the PTA Landscape' (2017) UNCTAD Research Paper No. 5. UNCTAD/SER.RP/2017/5, https://unctad.org/en/pages/PublicationWebflyer.aspx?publicationid=1838, accessed 31 March 2019.

[8] Todd Allee and Manfred Elsig, 'Dispute Settlement Provisions in PTAs. New Data and Concepts' in Andreas Dür and Manfred Elsig (eds.), *Trade Cooperation: The Purpose, Design and Effects of Preferential Trade Agreements* (Cambridge University Press, 2015).

83 per cent of PTAs include some form of mechanism to settle disputes arising under the agreements (not including the specialized DSMs for investment protection or intellectual property protection), and this number rises to 97 per cent if one considers only PTAs concluded after 2000.[9] According to this study, PTAs provide for several mechanisms of trade dispute settlement, such as consultations, mediation, arbitration, standing courts and references to external bodies, such as the WTO DSM, the outliers being African PTAs, which mostly do not provide for DSMs. They conclude that there is considerable overlap between these mechanisms, in the sense that a PTA will normally provide for several methods of dispute settlement.

Unlike ISDS clauses, which have resulted in a surge of cases in the last two decades,[10] 'the apparent paradox of [PTA] DSMs is that, despite the creation of increasingly elaborate mechanisms to resolve disputes ..., these mechanisms do not appear to be used very often'.[11] One explanation is that consultations are often behind closed doors, while according to another, a number of PTAs refer to WTO DSM, and the WTO mechanism already handles disputes arising under PTAs.

The specific study of ISDS mechanisms in PTAs, however, has garnered less attention in large-scale studies, with the exception (up to 2018) of Kotschwar's 2009 mapping of investment provisions in fifty-three Regional Trade Agreements (RTAs), which provides a comparative analysis of the investment provisions included in RTAs.[12]

Our analysis differs from existing literature in several ways. Firstly, this chapter has a narrower aim; it builds upon and further investigates the

---

For an older study that used a dataset of PTAs from 1957 to 2008, see Hyeran Jo and Hyun Namgung, 'Dispute Settlement Mechanisms in Preferential Trade Agreements: Democracy, Boilerplates, and the Multilateral Trade Regime' (2012) 56(6) *Journal of Conflict Resolution* 1041.

[9] Allee and Elsig 2015 (n. 8) 324.

[10] See PITAD database, available at https://pitad.org/index#welcome, accessed 31 March 2018.

[11] Robert McDougall, 'Regional Trade Agreement Dispute Settlement Mechanisms: Modes, Challenges and Options for Effective Dispute Resolution' (2018) IDB and ICTSD Issue Paper, 10.

[12] Barbara Kotschwar, 'Mapping Investment Provisions in Regional Trade Agreements: Towards an International Investment Regime?' in Antoni Estevadeordal, Kati Suominen and Robert Teh (eds.), *Regional Rules in the Global Trading System* (Cambridge University Press, 2009), pp. 373–5. Since this project began, a very recent study has also touched upon this issue on a broader dataset; see Jo-Ann Crawford and Barbara Kotschwar, 'Investment Provisions in Preferential Trade Agreements: Evolution and Current Trends' (2018) WTO Staff Working Paper ERSD-2018-14, 14 December 2018.

assumption that combining trade and investment provisions – be they substantive provisions or DSMs – in the same agreement might lead to convergence in the context of adjudicating trade and investment disputes. Secondly, since the trade dispute–settlement mechanisms of PTAs have already been the object of large-scale studies, we focus instead on the PTA provisions relating to investment protection and ISDS, questioning their potential outreach to other provisions of PTAs. Thirdly, the PTAs are organized in such a way as to reflect regional or country-specific trends instead of global ones.

The first part of the chapter is descriptive and draws on the data gathered for our previous study on the drivers behind the inclusion or non-inclusion of investment provisions into PTAs.[13] We look at 144 post-NAFTA PTAs concluded by fifteen countries and regional economic integration organizations (REIOs) from 'all four corners' of the Earth in order to ascertain whether including investment chapters into PTAs is a global phenomenon. Qualitatively, the analysis also looks at the types of investment protection standards that appear in the PTAs and whether ISDS is present, and if so under which rules. The study finds that the practice of including investment provisions into PTAs is not uniform and the countries/REIOs analysed can be placed into three groups: (1) those that conclude PTAs that regularly include investment chapters; (2) those whose investment policies are evolving and their newer PTAs include investment provisions; and (3) those whose PTAs do not include investment chapters. Thus, if one assumes that the inclusion of investment chapters into PTAs can foster convergence between investment and trade dispute settlement, such convergence will not be uniform around the globe, but will have regional or country-specific features.

The second part of the chapter is analytical and discusses whether the inclusion of investment chapters into PTAs might result in some level of convergence in the process of adjudicating trade and investment disputes. We rely on both the findings from the first part of the chapter as well as academic literature dealing with the relationship between trade and investment law. It is important to distinguish between the areas in which convergence might occur: structural convergence due to the institutional consolidation of dispute settlement mechanisms; convergence between the various epistemic communities of decision

---

[13] Maksim Usynin and Szilárd Gáspár-Szilágyi, 'The Growing Tendency of Including Investment Chapters in PTAs' (2018) 48 *Netherlands Yearbook of International Law* 267.

makers; convergence in the reasoning used by the interpretative committees set up by the treaties; and convergence because of the usage of standards developed in the other field. We argue that, despite being included into PTAs, the investment chapters resemble standalone BITs and have an existence of their own in the agreements, which hampers convergence.

2 The Inclusion of Investment Chapters into PTAs

While not as numerous as BITs, the number of PTAs is also rising, and the PTA landscape is becoming an increasingly fragmented one. The assumption that the inclusion of investment chapters into the text of PTAs will lead to some level of convergence between investment and trade dispute settlement needs to be nuanced. If the inclusion of investment chapters with ISDS is a global phenomenon, then it is to be expected that convergence could occur on a wider geographical scale.[14] However, if this is more of a local or regional trend, then a global-wide convergence between investment and trade dispute settlement is more difficult to achieve, and convergence will occur rather locally or regionally.

This part begins with a description of the methodology used in gathering the data, followed by an empirical analysis of two interrelated issues. Firstly, we look at whether the inclusion of investment chapters with ISDS is a global phenomenon, or a regional one. Secondly, we look at the types of investment protection clauses used, be they various substantive standards, ISDS or both. The last section is reserved for interim conclusions.

2.1 Dataset and Selection Criteria

For this study, the dataset includes 144 individual post-NAFTA PTAs (see Annex 1) selected from the WTO Regional Trade Agreement Information System (RTA-IS), UNCTAD's International Investment Agreements Navigator,[15] and the official websites of state governments

---

[14] See Chapter 9 by Yuliya Chernykh, who also looks at the spatial and temporal dimensions of convergence.

[15] UNCTAD's classification of 'Treaties with Investment Provisions' includes also PTAs that only mention investment promotion in a cursory manner. See http://investmentpolicyhub.unctad.org/IIA, accessed 31 March 2019.

and REIOs. The number rises to 162 if we count the PTAs of the individual countries/REIOs, as some agreements appear in two or more groups (marked with grey in Annex 1). The starting point is the entry into force of NAFTA (1994) – since this was the first agreement to merge under one roof comprehensive trade and investment provisions[16] and can thus be regarded as a 'trend-setter'[17] – until early 2017 when this study was concluded. The number of PTAs selected represents close to half of all PTAs (pre- and post-NAFTA) registered in the WTO RTA-IS that have entered into force.[18] Besides the treaty texts and policy documents, model agreements and academic literature were also consulted.[19]

The dataset (see Annex 1) includes thirteen PTAs for the USA (twelve trade agreements concluded between 2000 and 2007, plus NAFTA),[20] fourteen for Canada,[21] nineteen EU PTAs concluded

[16] Ling Ling He and Razeen Sappideen, 'Investor-State Arbitration under Bilateral Trade and Investment Agreements: Finding Rhythm in Inconsistent Drumbeats' (2013) 47 *Journal of World Trade* 215, 232; Kotschwar (n. 12) 366. The pre-NAFTA 1989 Canada-USA FTA, which was subsequently replaced by NAFTA, dedicated Chapter Sixteen to investment. The Agreement included two standards of treatment (national treatment and the prohibition of expropriation), but omitted MFN, FET, FPS and ISDS. See also Filippo Fontanelli and Giuseppe Bianco, 'Converging towards NAFTA: An Analysis of FTA Investment Chapters in the European Union and the United States' (2014) 50(2) *Stanford Journal of International Law* 211, 219.

[17] See Fontanelli and Bianco (n 16); Céline Lévesque, 'Influences on the Canadian FIPA and the US Model BIT: NAFTA Chapter 11 and Beyond' (2006) 44 *Canadian YIL* 249; Alschner et al. (n. 7) at 19–20 conclude that many South-South PTAs also included NAFTA language.

[18] Almost 300 regional trade agreements have been notified by WTO members, WTO RTA Database (2017), http://rtais.wto.org/UI/PublicAllRTAList.aspx, accessed 31 March 2019. 'Due to its growing size and complexity, the PTA universe has become increasingly difficult to navigate.' See Alschner et al. (n. 7) 3.

[19] See the various sources mentioned in Part 3. Examples include: Fontanelli and Bianco (n. 16); Henning G Ruse-Khan and Chantal Ononaiwu, 'The CARIFORUM-EU Economic Partnership Agreement' in Lester et al. (n. 1); EU Commission, Investment in TTIP and Beyond – The Path to Reform, Concept Paper (2015), http://trade.ec.europa.eu/doclib/docs/2015/may/tradoc_153408.PDF, accessed 31 March 2019; 2004 Canadian Model Foreign Investment Protection Agreement (FIPA).

[20] Office of the United States Trade Representative, https://ustr.gov/trade-agreements/free-trade-agreements, accessed 31 March 2019. The statistics also include NAFTA, while the two mega-regionals (TPP and TTIP) were excluded due to their uncertain future for the USA.

[21] Government of Canada (2017) Canada's Free Trade Agreements, www.international.gc.ca/trade-commerce/trade-agreements-accords-commerciaux/agr-acc/index.aspx?lang=eng, accessed 31 March 2019. There is also an increasing number of agreements under negotiations for which final texts are not available. There are also

CONVERGENCE IN PTAS WITH INVESTMENT CHAPTERS 27

after the Lisbon Treaty entered into force,[22] nineteen for India,[23] thirteen for China, six for ASEAN,[24] fifteen Japanese Economic Partnership Agreements (EPAs),[25] eleven for Australia,[26] three for Brazil, fourteen for Chile,[27] twelve for MERCOSUR, four for CARICOM,[28] six bi- and plurilateral trade agreements for South

---

several older Trade and Investment Cooperation (TICA) Agreements and Trade and Economic Cooperation Arrangements (TECA) that functioned more as initiators for further collaboration or set a framework for cooperation. These agreements have not been included in the study since they do not provide clear trade liberalization commitments.

[22] These are: FTAs and FTIAs with Korea (2009), Singapore (not signed), Canada (CETA, 2016), Vietnam (not signed), Colombia and Peru (2013, from 2016 also Ecuador); AAs that include DCFTAs with Georgia (2014), Moldova (2014), Ukraine (2014), Central America (2012), SAA with Kosovo (2015); PCA with Iraq (2012); Enhanced PCAs with Kazakhstan (2015); Interim Partnership Agreements with Papua New Guinea and Fiji (2009); EPAs with ECOWAS (not signed), EAC (not signed) and SADC (2016); interim EPA with Cameroon (2009), Ghana (2016) and Madagascar (2009). See EU's Treaty Office Database, http://ec.europa.eu/world/agreements/default.home.do, accessed 31 March 2019.

[23] Department of Commerce, Government of India, http://commerce.gov.in/#, accessed 31 March 2019. Two trade agreements, two framework agreements and four short bilateral trade agreements with African countries were excluded from the analysis due to an absence of substantive legal commitments to liberalize trade.

[24] ASEAN has specific agreements with all the other countries analysed from the Asia-Pacific region, which were considered together with other ASEAN treaties in order to avoid double counting.

[25] Japan is also negotiating EPAs with Canada, Colombia, the Golf Cooperation Council, the EU and South Korea. See Ministry of Foreign Affairs of Japan, www.mofa.go.jp/policy/economy/fta/, accessed 31 March 2019.

[26] Includes ten post-NAFTA FTAs with investment chapters and the Protocol on Investment to the Australia-New Zealand FTA of 1983 (e.i.f. 2013). The FTAs with the US, China, Japan and ASEAN also appear in the parts of the chapter presenting those countries' sections. See Australian Government, Department of Foreign Affairs and Trade, http://dfat.gov.au/trade/agreements/pages/trade-agreements.aspx, accessed 31 March 2019.

[27] The treaty with MERCOSUR (1996) will be presented below together with other regional treaties, while PTAs with Canada (1996), India and USA (both 2003), China (2005), Japan (2007) and Australia (2008) are reviewed together with these countries respectively. The Chile-EU Association Agreement that includes a comprehensive FTA (2003) was concluded before the Lisbon Agreement and therefore excluded from the analysis.

[28] The PTA with the EU was counted as an EU agreement. See Ruse-Khan and Ononaiwu (n. 19) pp. 146–9. A number of other agreements (CARICOM-Central American Integration System, PTIAs with MERCOSUR and USA) are under negotiation without draft texts being available. The PTA with Canada was not included since negotiations broke down between the parties. The draft text, however, includes both investment protection provisions and broad access to ISDS.

Africa,[29] six trade agreements for Morocco,[30] and seven African plurilaterals.[31]

Some further explanations are warranted for the EU and the African dataset. With regard to the EU, firstly, the analysis does not include EU PTAs signed prior to 1 December 2009, because the EU had acquired the competence to conclude international agreements that cover foreign direct investment (FDI) after the entry into force of the Lisbon Treaty.[32] Secondly, while EU member states could conclude BITs prior to 2009[33] and under certain conditions can do so after Lisbon as well,[34] they could not solely conclude PTAs, since this field was/is covered by the EU's Common Commercial Policy (CCP). Thirdly, the EU can conclude agreements with trade components under multiple policy areas, such as the EU's CCP, the EU's Neighbourhood Policy (ENP) and others.[35] Therefore, some of these agreements are called free trade agreements, while others association agreements (AAs) that include deep and comprehensive trade agreements (DCFTAs), partnership and cooperation

---

[29] Concluded either as a sole entity or as a member of a regional organization, such as the South African Customs Union (SACU) or the South African Development Community (SADC). 'Trade Agreements' (Department of Trade and Industry of the Republic of South Africa), www.thedti.gov.za/trade_investment/ited_trade_agreement.jsp, accessed 31 March 2019. The TIFA and TIDCA between South Africa and the USA were not included due to their hortatory and exploratory character. Neither were two non-reciprocal trade agreements.

[30] Concluded six trade agreements with countries and REIOs from the North-Atlantic Area (EU) or North Africa/the Middle East (Pan-Arab Free Trade Area).

[31] The SADC Agreement (1996), the East African Community Agreement (EAC, 1999), the SACU Agreement (2002), the Agreement on the West African Economic and Monetary Union (WAEMU, 1994), the Tripartite Agreement (2015) between EAC, COMESA and SADC, the Revised Cotonou Agreement (2010) with the EU, and the ECOWAS Protocol on Energy concluded in 2003, but not yet in force. The main ECOWAS agreement (1993) and the Agreement on the Common Market for Eastern and Southern Africa (COMESA, 1993) were not included in the statistics because they were concluded before NAFTA.

[32] Treaty on the Functioning of the European Union (TFEU), Article 207. See Robert Basedow, 'A Legal History of the EU's International Investment Policy' (2016) 17(5) JWIT 743; Szilárd Gáspár-Szilágyi (2018), 'Quo Vadis EU Investment Law and Policy? The Shaky Path Towards the International Promotion of EU Rules', 23(2) European Foreign Affairs Review 167.

[33] See Pantaleo et al. (n. 4); Fontanelli and Bianco (n. 16) 215–18.

[34] See Regulation No. 1219/2012 establishing transitional arrangements for bilateral investment agreements between EU member states and third countries, OJ L 351/40, Articles 7–11.

[35] See Colin M Brown and Jeremy Record, 'EU-Korea Free Trade Agreement' in Lester et al. (n. 1) 42; Bart Van Vooren and Ramses Wessel, EU External Relation Law (Cambridge University Press 2014), ch 15.

agreements (PCAs), economic partnership agreements (EPAs) or stabilization and association agreements (SAAs).

Researching African PTAs also posed some challenges. Firstly, the PTAs between African and non-African countries often follow the model agreements of a more economically powerful partner. Thus, such agreements cannot be counted as truly 'African'.[36] Secondly, compared to other regions, the number of PTAs analysed is quite low (seventeen PTAs), often due to difficulties obtaining the treaty texts. Most notably, the analysis excludes twenty-seven Kenyan PTAs[37] the texts of which could not be found in online databases.[38] Thirdly, a number of post-NAFTA intra-regional and inter-regional PTAs deserve special attention, as they cover a significant number of African countries. Considering these limitations, the conclusions for the African region are rather tentative.

Regarding the selection criteria, some parameters were taken into consideration when selecting the data. Firstly, the determining factor in the selection of the treaties was not their name but their contents. The agreements had to include clear obligations and legal commitments to liberalize trade between the parties and not just hortatory or promissory language, common for so-called framework agreements.[39]

Secondly, the sample includes both bi- and plurilateral agreements (the latter being popular among African and Asian countries) for which a final version of the text exists. Treaties that are being negotiated at the moment of writing are generally excluded from the statistics; however, they are discussed if they carry a high normative force, such as TTIP or if a text already exists.

---

[36] A contrasting example of novel drafting technique between the two African states is the Morocco-Nigeria BIT; see Tarcisio Gazzini, 'Nigeria and Morocco Move Towards a "New Generation" of Bilateral Investment Treaties' (*EJIL: Talk!*, 8 May 2017), ejiltalk.org/nigeria-and-morocco-move-towards-a-new-generation-of-bilateral-investment-treaties/, accessed 31 March 2019.

[37] 'EPC Kenya – Trade Agreements' (*Export Promotion Council of Kenya*, 11 September 2017), http://epc.go.ke/index.php/component/sppagebuilder/39-faqs, accessed 31 March 2019.

[38] The Government of Kenya's website only includes the names of the agreements, not their texts. The WTO RTA Database does not include RTAs with Kenya. The UNCTAD database under 'Treaties with Investment Provisions' (TIPs) only includes agreements to which Kenya is a party via its membership to REIOs, such as COMESA.

[39] Examples of promissory language include the 1999 US-South Africa Trade and Investment FA (TIFA), Article 1(2) 'The Parties *will seek* to: (2) take appropriate measures to *encourage* and *facilitate* the exchange of goods and services'; and the India – Mauritius Trade Agreement (2002), Article II 'The Contracting Parties shall *encourage* and *facilitate* contacts between their natural and juridical persons' (emphasis added). See also Henry Gao, 'China-New Zealand Free Trade Agreement' in Lester et al. (n. 1) p. 80.

Thirdly, we selected fifteen countries and REIOs from around the world, namely: the USA, Canada, the EU, China, India, Japan, ASEAN, Australia, Brazil, Chile, MERCOSUR, CARICOM, Morocco, South Africa and several inter-African regional agreements. When selecting the representative countries/REIOs various factors were considered, including the number of PTAs concluded, the ability of a country/REIO to be a rule-maker, its economic might and the need to have a balanced geographical representation. For example, when selecting the USA or the EU, one must account for the normative force exerted by their agreements,[40] and their sheer economic power. Similar factors were also taken into consideration when choosing Japan, China and India. For the latter two, recent academic discussions on the goal of China and India to become rule-makers and not rule-takers were also consulted.[41]

It was also necessary to ensure an adequate geographical and ideological balance, as well as a balance between countries and REIOs. Therefore, for the Latin American region Chile, a country with an open investment policy, and Brazil, a country known for its aversion towards mainstream investment law and policy, were chosen.[42] Two REIOs, MERCOSUR and CARICOM, were also added to the Latin American region. In Africa (beyond some difficulties in gathering the data, see *supra*), the study covered the major inter-African REIOs and considered a representative from sub-Saharan Africa (South Africa) and one from Northern Africa (Morocco). Furthermore, the traditional North-South/capital exporting-capital importing type of agreements have now given way to a more complex scene that also includes agreements between traditionally capital importing or exporting countries.[43]

Fourthly, the qualitative side of the analysis focuses on investment protection provisions that traditionally appear in BITs, and excludes the services chapters of PTAs (see Chapter 4); the latter, in essence do not deal with investment protection standards and ISDS.[44] The study

---

[40] See Fontanelli and Bianco (n. 16).
[41] Guiguo Wang, 'China's FTAs: Legal Characteristics and Implications' (2011) 105 *AJIL* 493; Prabhash Ranjan, 'Comparing Investment Provisions in India's FTAs with India's Stand-Alone BITs: Contributing to the Evolution of New Indian BIT Practice' (2015) 16 *JWIT* 899.
[42] See Part 2.2.
[43] Smitha Francis, 'Foreign Direct Investment Concepts: Implications for Negotiations' (2010) 45(2) *Economic and Political Weekly* 31, 35–6; Alschner et al. (n. 7) 25.
[44] For similar approaches see Kotschwar (n. 12) 370; Miroudot (n. 1); James Mathis and Eugenia Laurenza, 'Services and Investment in the EU-South Korea Free-Trade Area: Implications of a New Approach for GATS V Agreements and for Bilateral Investment

examines the occurrence of the following core standards of investment protection: national treatment (NT), most-favoured nation treatment (MFN), prohibition of expropriation, and other standards including fair and equitable treatment (FET), full protection and security (FPS) and protection from civil strife. Furthermore, it looks at whether ISDS is included, and if so, whether the agreements provide a choice between multiple arbitral rules.

2.2 A Global or a Local/Regional Phenomenon?

As discussed in Chapter 1 to this edited volume, one can speak of *structural* convergence, 'where the design and structures of dispute settlement mechanisms under international trade and investment agreements are separate but similar'. One could argue that the inclusion of investment chapters with ISDS into PTAs could enhance structural convergence between the two dispute settlement systems. However, as Figure 2.1 indicates, the inclusion of investment chapters with ISDS into PTAs does not portray a uniform pattern throughout the world. Thus, if structural convergence is to occur, it will do so in a more localized and fragmentary fashion rather than a global one.

According to the data, the selected countries/REIOs can be split into three groups.

The first group includes the USA, Canada, Japan, Australia, ASEAN and CARICOM. According to the country-specific data in Figure 2.1 and Annex 2, most PTAs (approx. 65–100 per cent) concluded by these countries/REIOs include investment chapters with investment protection standards and ISDS. In these countries (except for Australia) the way in which trade agreements have been concluded has been fairly static in the last fifteen years or so.

Countries and REIOs belonging to the second group (EU, India, China and Chile) have a higher number of PTAs (approx. 65–85 per cent) that do not include investment chapters. Nevertheless, their trade and investment policies are evolving, and an increasing number of their recent PTAs include investment chapters.

Treaties' (2012) 13 *JWIT* 157; Eric De Brabandere, 'Co-existence, Complementarity or Conflict? Interaction Between Preferential Trade and Investment Agreements and Bilateral Investment Treaties' in Christian J Tams, Stephan W Schill, and Rainer Hoffmann (eds.), *Preferential Trade and Investment Agreements: From Recalibration to Reintegration* (Nomos 2013), pp. 40–41; Fontanelli and Bianco (n. 16) 213.

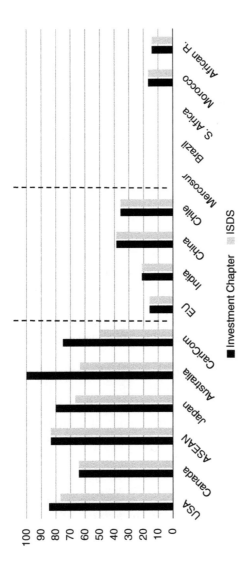

Figure 2.1 Inclusion of investment chapters and ISDS

The third group includes countries/REIOs in which almost all PTAs lack investment chapters. Countries, such as Brazil, and REIOs influenced by these countries, such as MERCOSUR,[45] often have an adverse position towards mainstream investment protection/ISDS, which is reflected in the lack of such provisions in PTAs. The African Regionals, as well as Moroccan and South African PTAs, often defer the inclusion of investment protection to future negotiations.

Some further observations are also warranted. Firstly, NAFTA had a tremendous influence on the design of subsequent US trade agreements with investment chapters, either directly or by influencing the 2004/2012 US Model BITs, which in turn affected the design of investment chapters in subsequent trade agreements.[46] Like their US counterparts, the investment chapters of Canadian PTAs follow the templates set up by the 2004 Canadian Model Foreign Investment Protection Agreement (FIPA), which in turn had been influenced by Chapter 11 NAFTA and investment cases brought under it.[47] The Japanese experience is similar to the US and Canadian ones. The conclusion of Economic Partnership Agreements (EPAs) with investment chapters started in the early 2000s, following the same model.

Secondly, Indian and Chinese PTAs are going through a process of reformation. The practice of including investment protection standards into Indian bilateral PTAs is a more recent phenomenon that began with the India-Singapore Comprehensive Economic Cooperation Agreement (2005), followed by the agreements with South Korea (2009), Malaysia (2010) and Japan (2011). The investment chapters of more recent Indian PTAs depart from the 2003 Model BIT and are considered more balanced, since they include broader substantive coverage and reserve more regulatory space for the state.[48] Chinese treaty practice is also not uniform: two agreements include links to the relevant existing BITs

---

[45] See Facundo P Aznar and Henrique C Moraes, 'The MERCOSUR Protocol on Investment Cooperation and Facilitation: Regionalizing and Innovative Approach to Investment Agreements' (2017) EJIL Talk, www.ejiltalk.org/the-mercosur-protocol-on-investment-cooperation-and-facilitation-regionalizing-an-innovative-approach-to-investment-agreements, accessed 31 March 2019.

[46] See David A Gantz, 'The Evolution of FTA Investment Provisions: From NAFTA to the United States-Chile Free Trade Agreement' (2004) 19(4) *American University ILR* 679, 680 and 711 on the influence of NAFTA case law on subsequent agreements. See also Fontanelli and Bianco (n. 16) 218.

[47] Lévesque (n. 17) 250–1 and 254.

[48] Ranjan (n. 41) 928–9.

between the same parties,[49] one free trade agreement (FTA) was designed in co-existence with an active BIT,[50] while another bilateral FTA has reserved place for the investment chapter upon the negotiation of a regional FTA.[51] The scope of investment provisions has expanded over time, as China was calibrating its position in the multilateral trade system.[52]

Thirdly, in the case of US, CARICOM, Japanese and Australian PTAs, the number of agreements that include investment chapters is higher than of those that include ISDS, as not all investment chapters include ISDS. The US FTAs with Jordan and Bahrain do not include an investment chapter, since the United States had previously concluded BITs with these countries,[53] while the US-Australia BIT does not provide for ISDS, even though it includes standards of investment protection (Article 11.6). The apparent reason for the US-Australia FTA not including ISDS[54] was the 'robust' legal systems of the two countries for resolving disputes.[55] Furthermore, in 2011 the Gillard Government vowed to exclude ISDS from future Australian trade agreements.[56] This is why the FTAs with Japan (2014), Malaysia (2012) and the Protocol to the ANZCERTA (2013), negotiated and concluded in this period, do not include ISDS.[57] Nevertheless, this policy towards ISDS changed following the instatement of a new government in late 2013, reflecting the Australian policy from the early 2000s. In the case of the Japan-Philippines EPA, the government of the Philippines had specifically asked Japan not to include ISDS,[58] while

---

[49] 2010 China-Costa Rica, Article 89, linking to 2007 China-Costa Rica BIT; 2013 China-Iceland, Article 92, linking to 1994 China-Iceland BIT.
[50] 2015 China-Australia, Article 9.9(2).
[51] 2008 China-Singapore, Article 84, referring to the ongoing negotiations of the ASEAN-China Investment Agreement.
[52] Wang (n. 41) 497.
[53] 1999 US-Bahrain BIT; 1997 US-Jordan BIT.
[54] Still, Article 11.6 does envisage the possibility of setting up an ISDS in the future.
[55] Kyla Tienhaara and Patricia Ranald, 'Australia's Rejection of Investor-State Dispute Settlement: Four Potential Contributing Factors' (*Investment Treaty News*, 2011), www.iisd.org/itn/2011/07/12/australias-rejection-of-investor-state-dispute-settlement-four-potential-contributing-factors, accessed 31 March 2019; Jurgen Kurtz and Luke Nottage, 'Investment Treaty Arbitration "Down Under": Policy and Politics in Australia' (2015) 30 *ICSID Review – Foreign Investment Law Journal* 465, 469.
[56] See Luke Nottage, 'Throwing the Baby Out with the Bathwater: Australia's New Policy on Treaty-Based Investor-State Arbitration and Its Impact in Asia' (2013) 37 *Asian Studies Review* 253, 255–8; He and Sappideen (n. 16).
[57] Australia does not have pre-existing BITs with these countries. See Australian BITs, http://investmentpolicyhub.unctad.org/IIA/CountryBits/11, accessed 31 March 2019.
[58] Kurtz and Nottage (n. 55) 466.

the Japanese EPA with Australia was concluded after the Gillard Government came to power.

Lastly, the reasons for not including investment chapters in PTAs vary. None of the PTAs concluded by Brazil and MERCOSUR (of which Brazil is a member) include investment chapters. Brazil is known for not ratifying its BITs and refraining from undertaking international investment commitments that emulate widely used standards.[59] Nevertheless, lately Brazil has been concluding cooperation and facilitation investment agreements (CFIAs) and has even come up with a new Model BIT, all of which diverge significantly from the mainline of IIA drafting.[60] However, the latter do not include preferential trade arrangements, and are thus beyond the scope of this chapter. Furthermore, they still refrain from including investor-state arbitration. Similarly, the MERCOSUR PTAs do not contain investment chapters, but in a few cases the agreements mention the need to promote and encourage investments or conclude BITs in the future, without further elaboration.[61]

Another reason for not including investment chapters is the existence of previous BITs between the contracting parties, such as in the case of the Canadian PTAs with Jordan, Costa Rica and Ukraine[62] or the Japanese EPAs with Vietnam and Peru.[63] Furthermore, most African PTAs do not include the traditional standards of investment protection or ISDS. A similar conclusion, but for trade-related state-to-state arbitration, was reached by Allee and Elsig, who noted that only two out of thirty-five African PTAs analysed included arbitration.[64] With regard to PTAs with non-African states a possible explanation might be the abundance of existing BITs between these parties. As regards the regional trade agreements there are two explanations. Firstly, most countries that share membership in at least one regional organization have concluded

---

[59] Leany B Barreiro and Daniela Campello, 'The Non-Ratification of Bilateral Investment Treaties in Brazil: A Story of Conflict in a Land of Cooperation' (2013) SSRN, https://papers.ssrn.com/sol3/papers.cfm?abstract_id=2243120, accessed 31 March 2019, at 13 et seq.
[60] Katia F Gómez and Catherine Titi, 'International Investment Law and ISDS: Mapping Contemporary Latin America' (2016) 17(4) JWIT 522–4; Joaquim de Paiva Muniz and Luis Peretti, 'Brazil Signs New Bilateral Investment Treaties with Mozambique and Angola: New Approach to BITs or "Toothless Lions"?', Global Arbitration Review, https://globalarbitrationnews.com/20150407-brazil-signs-new-bilateral-investment-treaties/, accessed 31 March 2019.
[61] 1996 Chile-MERCOSUR, Article 41; 1996 Bolivia-MERCOSUR, Articles 35–36; 2005 MERCOSUR-Peru, Articles 29–30; 2010 Egypt-MERCOSUR, Article 23.
[62] Preceded by the FIPAs with Jordan (2009), Costa Rica (1998) and Ukraine (1994).
[63] Preceded by the BITs with Vietnam (2003) and Peru (2009).
[64] Allee and Elsig 2015 (n. 8) 327.

separate BITs between each other.[65] Secondly, regional organizations such as COMESA, ECOWAS or SADC have signed either a regional protocol, some regional regulation related to investment, or are developing model regional investment agreements.

The most recent Chilean bilateral PTAs or the Japanese EPA with ASEAN show a tendency of putting investment chapters aside during the original negotiations, while leaving an anchor clause for further consultations.[66] This approach might shorten the time needed to negotiate FTAs, while Chile's strong domestic protection of foreign investment can provide adequate protection to foreign investors until subsequent BITs are concluded.[67]

In the case of the EU, most of the post-Lisbon Association Agreements, DCFTAs and Partnership Agreements follow similar design patterns that do not include investment chapters. Nevertheless, they all include 'review' or 'rendez-vous' clauses under which the contracting parties undertake to carry out further negotiations or cooperation on investment protection.[68] Furthermore, following the Court of Justice of the EU's *Opinion 2/15* concerning the conclusion of the EU-Singapore FTA, the investment chapter has been split from the trade agreement and the EU-Singapore FTA shall be concluded as a separate EU-only agreement. This ruling has influenced the conclusion of subsequent FTAs, such as the one with Japan.[69]

2.3 What Types of Investment Protection Provisions are Included?

The previously mentioned three groups of countries/REIOs also exist when looking at the types of substantive investment protection clauses included in the PTAs and the rules under which ISDS can be used.

As Figures 2.2 and 2.3 illustrate, the same countries that include investment chapters into their PTAs will also include the four/five traditional

---

[65] Laura Páez, 'Bilateral Investment Treaties and Regional Investment Regulation in Africa: Towards a Continental Investment Area?' (2017) 18 *JWIT* 379, 389.
[66] See Chilean FTAs between Chile and Turkey (2009), Malaysia (2010), Vietnam (2011), Hong Kong, China (2012) and Thailand (2013); Japan-ASEAN EPA, Article 51.
[67] Gómez and Titi (n. 62) 530; Jacopo Tavassi, 'The Regime of International Investments within the EC-Chile Association Agreement: Towards a Possible Renegotiation?' (2013) 14 *JWIT* 352, 366.
[68] EU-ECOWAS, Article 106(2)e; EU-East African Community, Article 3(b)ii; 2014 EU-Georgia, Article 80(2); 2014 EU-Moldova, Article 206(2); 2014 EU-Ukraine, Article 89(2); 2012 EU-Central America, Article 168; 2013/2016 Colombia-Peru-Ecuador, Article 166.
[69] See Szilárd Gáspár-Szilágyi, 'A Follow-up to the EU Commission's Decision to 'Split' Trade and Investment Protection' (2018) *International Economic Law and Policy Blog*, 14 Sept 2017.

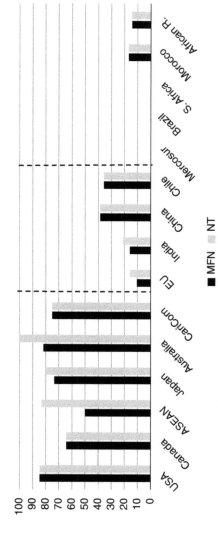

Figure 2.2 MFN and national treatment

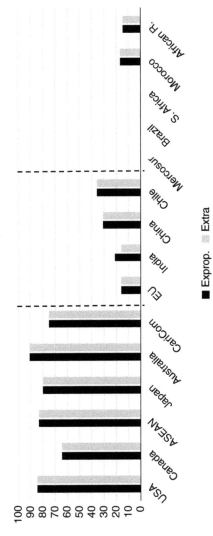

Figure 2.3 Prohibition of expropriation and extra (FET, FPS)

standards of investment protection: national treatment (NT), most-favoured-nation treatment (MFN), the prohibition of expropriation without compensation and other standards, such as fair and equitable treatment (FET) and full protection and security (FPS). Nevertheless, some agreements do not include all four standards.

As Figure 2.2 illustrates, in EU, ASEAN, Japanese and Australian PTAs the number of MFN clauses is lower than national treatment clauses. One could call this the 'Singapore exception'. The EU-Singapore FTA (since 2018 a separate investment agreement) does not include an MFN clause; this has been characterized as a REIO exception clause.[70] In a fashion similar to the EU-Singapore FTA, the Japan-Singapore EPA lacks an MFN provision, while MFN treatment is missing from the Australian FTAs with Singapore and ASEAN (a member of which is Singapore). In Africa, only the ECOWAS Energy Protocol includes the core standards of investment protection.

It is also interesting to note that, as Allee and Elsig observe in their 2016 study, 'copy-pasting' seems to be quite prevalent in agreements based on a model agreement. In the case of the US FTAs with Colombia,[71] CAFTA-DR, Morocco, Panama and Peru, even the number of the articles on NT, MFN and the minimum standards of treatment match between these agreements. Furthermore, some US agreements also include an extra clause on protection during civil strife and armed conflict,[72] while Japanese EPAs include provisions on 'access to courts of justice', 'general treatment' or 'minimum standards of treatment', instead of FPS or FET.

Concerning the rules under which ISDS is to be conducted, as Figure 2.4 illustrates, in the overwhelming number of PTAs that provide for ISDS, the rules do not only include the ICSID Arbitration Rules, but also allow for the use of other rules such as the UNCITRAL Arbitration Rules, the ICSID Additional Facility Rules or other rules agreed upon by the disputing parties (marked as 'ICSID+' in Figure 2.4).[73] The three exceptions are some PTAs of China, Australia and CARICOM. The China-Pakistan FTA only includes the ICSID Arbitration Rules. Following this FTA, Chinese

---

[70] Miroudot (n. 1) 316.
[71] See K William Watson, 'United States-Colombia Trade Promotion Agreement' in Lester et al. (n. 1).
[72] 2006 US-Peru, Article 10.6; 2007 US-Panama, Article 10.6.
[73] It is also interesting to note that several Canadian FTAs do not accord the parties the right to agree on arbitral rules; see 2010 Canada-Panama, Article 9.23; 1996 Canada-Chile, Article G-023(2).

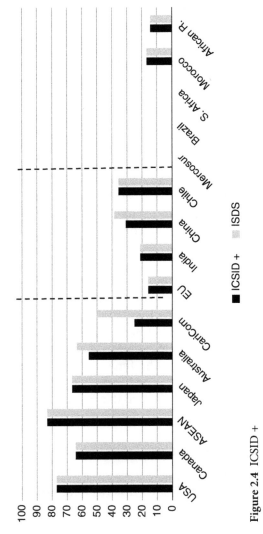

Figure 2.4 ICSID +

PTAs have expanded the choice for ISDS by including ICSID arbitration, ICSID Additional Facility arbitration, UNCITRAL arbitration and any other arbitration agreed to by the parties.[74] The second exception is the Australia-Thailand FTA. Australian FTAs that include ISDS mostly provide for the ICSID Arbitration Rules, the ICSID Additional Facility Rules and the UNCITRAL Arbitration Rules. The FTA with Thailand, however, provides for only two options for ISDS: domestic judicial/administrative venues or UNCITRAL arbitration (Article 917).

Several CARICOM agreements provide the third exception. The FTA with the Dominican Republic lacks ISDS provisions and includes only domestic dispute settlement procedures.[75] The FTA with Cuba contains a rather unique reference to an 'international arbitrator' or UNCITRAL arbitration.[76] The inclusion of the Washington-based ICSID would have probably turned problematic given the past tensions between the USA and Cuba. The subsequent FTA with Costa Rica (2004) contains an investment chapter with a full set of observed guarantees and broad access to ISDS.

2.4 Interim Conclusions

Just as the global network of BITs are forming an ever-expanding web, so is the number and complexity of PTAs. As the data indicates, several REIOs and countries are including investment chapters with ISDS into their PTAs, others are changing their policy and increasingly do so, while others do not include them at all. Therefore, one cannot talk about a global pattern of including investment chapters into PTAs, but rather of regional or country-specific patterns. This means that if some form of structural convergence between trade and investment dispute settlement in PTAs is to occur, this will be country or region specific.

Furthermore, even the PTAs of those countries/REIOs that regularly include investment chapters do not always include ISDS. As we have seen, sometimes this might be due to political or legal reasons in the partner country or due to the existence of prior BITs between the contracting parties. Such is the case of the US PTAs with Bahrain and Jordan, the Canadian PTAs with Jordan, Costa Rica and Peru as well as the

---

[74] See 2009 China-Peru, Article 139; 2009 ASEAN-China Agreement on Investment, Article 14; 2015 China-Australia, Article 9.12(4).
[75] CARICOM-DR, Annex III, Article VIII.
[76] CARICOM-CUBA, Annex A, Article XII.

Japanese EPAs with Vietnam and Peru. Furthermore, as we have argued elsewhere,

> states/REIOs can choose to include investment chapters into their PTAs in order to *replace or reform an existing investment agreement* between them. For example, the China-New Zealand FTA (2008) included investment protection provisions that were meant to replace the outdated standards of the China-New Zealand Investment Protection and Promotion Agreement of 1998.[77]

The number of PTAs analysed that are preceded by existing BITs is quite low, as we have seen. Nonetheless, the 'ease' with which investment chapters are sometimes left out of PTAs – due to one of the contracting parties' objections or due to domestic legal impediments – suggests that contracting parties rather view them as separate parts of PTAs that can be detached from the main agreement if needed, instead of viewing them as integral parts of PTAs. In other words, investment chapters in PTAs function more like stand-alone BITs. Such an 'attitude' of states can affect whether structural convergence between trade and investment dispute settlement under the umbrella of one agreement is possible or desired by the contracting parties.

In the next part we examine whether despite these findings, some level of convergence might be expected when including investment chapters into PTAs.

3 Could the Inclusion of Investment Chapters into PTAs Still Facilitate Convergence?

As previously concluded, when investment chapters are included into PTAs, they seem to function as separate parts of the main agreement; as stand-alone BITs and not as integral parts of the agreement. This in turn could affect any possible convergence between the trade and investment DSMs. Nevertheless, in this part we look at whether the inclusion of investment chapters into the text of PTAs could still result in some level of convergence between the adjudication of trade and investment disputes. For this purpose, we also rely on academic discussions on the relationship between trade and investment law.

The inclusion of investment protection into PTAs leads to changes in the institutional frameworks of the treaties. For example, a number of these PTAs create two types of international bodies: various treaty

---

[77] See Usynin and Gáspár-Szilágyi (n. 13) 289.

bodies/committees charged with the power to interpret[78] or supervise the implementation of the international agreements,[79] and various mechanisms to solve disputes arising out of the various fields covered by the agreements.

These developments in the treaty architecture suggest that convergence may occur in several ways. Firstly, the inclusion of trade and investment provisions under the same treaty may lead to some form of structural convergence via the institutional consolidation of the various dispute settlement bodies (DSBs).[80] Secondly, convergence might occur between the various epistemic communities of decision makers. Thirdly, one could also expect convergence in the way in which various treaty bodies/committees interpret the agreements. Fourthly, convergence could occur due to direct borrowings and the usage of standards of treatment across different chapters of the agreements, and through the cross-usage of jurisprudence between the two disciplines. The present section discusses the viability of these suggestions and identifies those factors that might hamper convergence and propagate existing divergent paths.

3.1 Structural Convergence of Dispute Settlement Bodies?

In the previous part we concluded that if structural convergence – in the sense that the design and structures of DSMs under the two regimes are separate but similar – between investment and trade dispute settlement is to occur due to the inclusion of investment chapters into PTAs, this will happen on a regional- or country-specific scale and not on a global one. Even so, how is one to assess structural similarities on this narrower scale between the two methods of DSM in PTAs? Should one look at the

---

[78] See Birgit Schlütter, 'Aspects of Human Rights Interpretation by the UN Treaty Bodies' in Geir Ulfstein and Helen Keller (eds.), *UN Human Rights Treaty Bodies: Law and Legitimacy* (Cambridge University Press, 2012) p. 261.

[79] Geir Ulfstein, 'Treaty Bodies and Regimes' in Duncan B Hollis (ed.), *The Oxford Guide to Treaties* (Oxford University Press 2012) pp. 429–30. For a classification of treaty bodies (commissions or committees) see Henry G Schermers and Niels M Blokker, *International Institutional Law: Unity Within Diversity, Fifth Revised Edition* (Martinus Nijhoff Publishers, 2011) pp. 421–31, who classify them into functional, consultative, ad hoc advisory, procedural and regional commissions. See also Szilárd Gáspár-Szilágyi, 'Binding Committee Interpretations in the EU's New Free Trade and Investment Agreements' (2017) 2 *European Investment Law and Arbitration Review* 90–134.

[80] Not to be confused with the WTO Dispute Settlement Body.

institutional set-up of the DSMs, the parties who have standing before them, the procedural rules used, or their actual usage?

The institutional set-up of the trade and investment DSMs under PTAs with investment chapters could not be more different. As Allee and Elsig have concluded, state-to-state mechanisms are the preferred choice in PTAs. Thus, with the rising inclusion of investment chapters into PTAs one would have expected that any disputes – be they trade, or investment related – arising under these 'hybrid' agreements would be handled by the same, state-to-state dispute settlement mechanism. Nevertheless, as previously discussed (Figure 2.1 *supra*), the vast majority of PTAs that include investment chapters provide for their own, separate dispute settlement mechanism, ISDS; more specifically investor-state arbitration.

The treaty parties also limit the jurisdiction of investor-state tribunals to the provisions of investment chapters[81] and in most cases allow the arbitration to be conducted under multiple arbitration rules (Figure 2.4 *supra*). In other words, the old institutional and procedural differences between trade and investment law's dispute settlement methods are kept in the PTAs that we have analysed, making any level of structural convergence of the DSBs highly unlikely.

Furthermore, not even the trade DSMs in PTAs can be said to follow the same patterns. Allee and Elsig have shown that the trade-related DSM methods range from consultations, to arbitration, standing courts, and external bodies, with various degrees of overlap. In other words, the preferred trade-related DSM methods differ among the treaties, making any discussion about large-scale structural convergence between investment and trade DSMs in PTAs more difficult. One could argue that there is one aspect in which the two DSMs are similar: most PTAs include not just arbitration – be it investor-state or state-to-state – but other alternatives, such as conciliation and mediation.

If one considers standing, then the differences are obvious. Investment-related DSMs allow investors, as private parties, to launch dispute settlement proceedings, while the trade-related DSMs only allow states to initiate proceedings. The same differences are also kept at the procedural level, the ISDS provisions overwhelmingly allowing for ICSID and other investment arbitration venues (Figure 2.4 *supra*), further propagating the differences between the two methods of dispute settlement.

---

[81] See Art 8.18(5) CETA; Art 76(1) Japan-Mexico.

When discussing large-scale structural convergence, one also needs to consider whether the same PTAs offer both trade and investment DSM. As we concluded, not all countries or REIOs include investment chapters into their PTAs, and of those that include investment chapters not all include ISDS. Conversely, Elsig and Allee conclude that an overwhelming majority (97 per cent) of post-2000 PTAs include some form of trade-related DSM.

Two further factors can also hamper structural convergence between the two dispute settlement mechanisms. Firstly, as mentioned, in the PTAs that we have analysed, both trade- and investment-related DSBs function separately, according to separate institutional and procedural rules. This in itself would not be entirely problematic, if some form of central dispute settlement body existed, such as in the case of treaty committees, that supervised the work of both trade and investment dispute settlement mechanisms. However, no such central DSBs exist that could offer some form of institutional oversight. Secondly, one also needs to consider the practical usage of the two DSMs under the PTAs. As McDougall notes, the PTAs' trade-related DSMs are very rarely used.[82] Contrast this to the high usage of ISDS mechanisms under PTAs, not just BITs. According to the newest statistics from the PITAD database, of the more than 1,100 pending and concluded investment treaty arbitrations, approximately 10 per cent were brought under the investment chapters of PTAs.[83]

In conclusion, structural convergence between the trade and investment DSMs included in PTAs might be hampered by the continued existence of different mechanisms for trade and investment disputes, their different usage in practice and the lack of a central dispute settlement body to offer some form of oversight.

3.2 Epistemic Convergence?

Then there is the question of convergence between the epistemic communities that are involved in trade and investment disputes. We need to separate between two communities: those that design the DSMs and those that are the adjudicators sitting on the DSMs.

---

[82] McDougall (n. 11).
[83] We thank Runar Hilleren Lie for providing us with these statistics from the PluriCourts Investment Treaty Arbitration Database (PITAD).

Firstly, it matters who designs and negotiates the PTAs with investment chapters. The fields of trade and investment are served by two, largely divided epistemic communities; lawyers and policy advisers will mostly be experts in either trade or investment.[84] During the negotiation and drafting of PTAs with investment chapters, contracting parties must ensure that both trade and investment are adequately represented. Otherwise, they would risk not fully grasping the implications of some of the commitments they enter into.

This is not only an issue for less developed states, but also for developed states/REIOs such as the EU or the USA. In the case of developing countries, the risk is that a certain government department might not have sufficient expertise in both trade and investment. Even in the EU, following the extension of EU competences over foreign direct investment, the European Parliament called on the EU Commission 'to invest in terms of its personnel and its material resources' in the negotiation and conclusion of investment agreements.[85] In the USA, issues arose not because of a lack of personnel, but because the primary authority over investment agreements was transferred from the State Department to the Office of the US Trade Representative in the 1980 reorganization of the Executive Branch.[86] It follows that the negotiators of PTAs with investment chapters 'need more negotiating expertise due to the likelihood of interaction and cross-chapter application of rules in such treaties'.[87] Therefore, combining trade and investment provisions under the roof of a single agreement does not yet guarantee convergence between the two dispute settlement mechanisms.

Secondly, some level of convergence could still be achieved if the two DSMs shared the same adjudicators or at least were selected from the same rosters. Arbitration under the two types of DSMs is possible, and most often it is to be conducted by ad hoc panels of

---

[84] Christian J Tams, Stephan W Schill and Rainer Hoffmann (eds.), *Preferential Trade and Investment Agreements: From Recalibration to Reintegration* (Nomos, 2013) p. 15.

[85] European Parliament, 'Resolution of 6 April 2011 on the Future European International Investment Policy', P7-TA(2011) 0141, www.europarl.europa.eu/sides/getDoc.do?pubRef=-//EP//NONSGML+TA+P7-TA-2011-0141+0+DOC+PDF+V0//EN, point 16. Currently, Unit B2 under DG Trade is tasked with investment matters.

[86] Kenneth J Vandevelde, *United States Investment Treaties: Policy and Practice* (Kluwer, 1992) p. 30.

[87] Freya Baetens, 'Preferential Trade and Investment Agreements and the Trade/Investment Divide: Is the Whole More than the Sum of Its Parts?' in Christian J Tams, Stephan W Schill and Rainer Hoffmann (eds.), *Preferential Trade and Investment Agreements: From Recalibration to Reintegration* (Nomos, 2013) p. 101.

three panellists.[88] Thus, one could say that this is an important structural similarity. However, trade and investment arbitrators are not selected from the same rosters and it is well discussed in the literature that trade and investment DSMs are served by decision makers that belong to different epistemic communities.

The differences between trade and investment disputes require specialized knowledge by the decision makers, which conditions low levels of cross-disciplinary participation and expertise. Joost Pauwelyn anecdotally coined these differences as 'investment arbitrators are from Mars', while 'trade adjudicators are from Venus'.[89] In other words, state-to-state, trade-related arbitration will require arbitrators with a different background and expertise than those in investor-state arbitration.

From a legal perspective, the striking differences between these two epistemic communities of decision makers can explain the impeded convergence between WTO and ISDS case law and the lack of cross-fertilization between the two fields.[90] It shall be noted that the recent EU FTAs (to be split into separate trade and investment agreements following *Opinion 2/15*) also follow this tradition and separate the decision-making communities into arbitrators of government-to-government dispute settlement panels and 'judges' of the Investment Court System, with different qualification requirements.[91] Arbitrators of trade disputes need to have specialized knowledge and experience of law and international trade,[92] while judges in investment disputes have to show broader and much more specialized competences in various fields, such as public international law, international investment law and international trade law together with qualifications 'required in their respective countries for appointment to judicial office, or be jurists of recognized competence'.[93]

---

[88] McDougall (n. 11).
[89] Joost Pauwelyn, 'The Rule of Law without the Rule of Lawyers? Why Investment Arbitrators Are from Mars, Trade Adjudicators from Venus' (2017) 109(4) *AJIL* 761.
[90] Ibid. at 800.
[91] For trade DSB, see 'European Union's Initial Proposal for Legal Text on "Dispute Settlement (Government to Government)" in TTIP' (European Commission 2015), http://trade.ec.europa.eu/doclib/docs/2015/january/tradoc_153032.pdf, accessed 31 March 2019. For ISDS, see 'European Union's Proposal for Investment Protection and Resolution of Investment Disputes in the Transatlantic Trade and Investment Partnership' (European Commission 2015), http://trade.ec.europa.eu/doclib/docs/2015/november/tradoc_153955.pdf, accessed 31 March 2019.
[92] Article 29.8 CETA; Article 15.23.3 EU-Vietnam FTA; Article 14.20.4 EU-Singapore FTA.
[93] Article 8.27 CETA; Article 3.9.4 EU-Singapore Investment Promotion Agreement (IPA); Article 3.23.3 EU-Vietnam IPA. When the data was originally gathered the EU-Singapore

3.3 Converging Interpretations of the Treaty Bodies/Committees?

Some level of convergence might occur due to the interpretive functions of treaty bodies – such as various committees and commissions – that oversee the relevant policy fields covered by PTAs, including trade and investment. Since Chernykh explores this question in more detail in Chapter 9 using four dimensions (spatial, temporal, ideological and functional) only a short discussion is provided here.

Several PTAs with investment chapters set up a central treaty body that supervises their implementation, and which can also adopt binding interpretations of the agreements. Depending on their functions and relationship to other treaties, subsidiary bodies and a secretariat may also be established.[94] For example, the recent EU FTAs (now split into separate trade and investment agreements) provide for central Joint/Trade Committees[95] and specialized subcommittees, handling various policy areas covered by the agreements, such as trade in goods and customs[96] or services and investment.[97] Canadian and US FTAs provide for Joint/Free Trade Commissions/Committees,[98] subcommittees[99] and even secretariats to provide administrative assistance[100] or free trade agreement coordinators tasked with developing agendas for further cooperation.[101] Japanese EPAs set up Joint Committees[102] and often include the various specialized subcommittees in the chapters dealing with a specific policy field.[103]

It can be argued that the inclusion of investment protection in PTAs, among other policy areas such as trade in goods, services or IP rights,

---

and EU-Vietnam IPAs were an integral part of the trade agreements. They were subsequently split following *Opinion 2/15* of the CJEU.

[94] Ulfstein (n. 79) 430.
[95] Article 26.1 CETA. For a further discussion, see Gáspár-Szilágyi (n. 79).
[96] Article 26.2 CETA; Article16.2.1 EU-Singapore FTA; Article 17.2.1 EU-Vietnam FTA.
[97] Article 26.2(b) CETA, 'Committee on Services and Investment'; Article 16.2.1(d) EU-Singapore FTA, 'Committee on Trade in Services, Investment and Government Procurement'; Article 17.2.1(d) EU-Vietnam FTA, 'Committee on Services, Investment and Government Procurement'.
[98] Article 20.1 Canada-Korea; Article 21.1 Canada-Honduras; Article 21.01 Canada-Panama; Article 20.1 US-Colombia; Article 19.2 US-Oman; Article 19.1 CAFTA-DR.
[99] Annex 20-A Canada-Korea; Article 21.1.7 Canada-Honduras; Annex 21.01 Canada-Panama; Article 20.1.3 US-Colombia; Article 19.1.3 CAFTA-DR.
[100] Article 21.3 Canada-Honduras.
[101] Article 21.02 Canada-Panama; Article 20.2 US-Colombia; Article 19.2 CAFTA-DR.
[102] Article 165 Japan-Mexico; Article 13 Japan-Malaysia.
[103] Articles 19, 37, 103, 117 Japan-Mexico; Articles 14, 25, 49, 58, 65, 70, 93, 110, 129, 134, 143 Japan-Malaysia.

might lead to more coherence and convergence in the implementation and interpretation of these rules when they are handled under one institutional roof. Even though specialized subcommittees handle the implementation and interpretation of the different policy fields, the chances of conflict or overlap between them are lowered because their overall supervision is ensured by one central body. Conversely, as previously explained, such a central, supervisory body does not exist for trade and investment DSBs.

The power of treaty committees to interpret the provisions of these agreements does raise questions as to where the power of dispute settlement bodies to interpret the agreements ends and where the same power of treaty committees begins.[104] Giving interpretative powers to the treaty parties risks politicizing potential disputes. For example, according to the EU Commission the 'binding interpretations' clause in EU agreements is meant to ensure that the contracting parties are 'to control and influence the interpretation of the agreement, and correct errors by the tribunals'.[105] The moment when the interpretations are delivered can also raise concerns of fairness, due process and party equality, if the contracting parties issue such an interpretation during dispute settlement proceedings to which they are parties.[106]

Furthermore, agreeing on an interpretation that is acceptable by both/all the treaty parties might pose further practical challenges that depend on the internal, constitutional constraints of the contracting parties and their willingness to reach a consensus in the treaty committees. For example, experience with NAFTA shows that treaty committee interpretations are an underutilized mechanism. The same holds true for WTO law as well.[107]

---

[104] See Charles H Brower II, 'Why the FTC Notes of Interpretation Constitute a Partial Amendment of NAFTA Article 1105' (2005) 46 *Virginia Journal of International Law* 347; Gabrielle Kaufmann-Kohler, 'Interpretive Powers of the Free Trade Commission and the Rule of Law' in Emmanuel Gaillard & Frédéric Bachand (eds.), *Fifteen Years of NAFTA Chapter 11 Arbitration* (JurisNet, 2011).

[105] See Gáspár-Szilágyi (n. 79) 101.

[106] Gáspár-Szilágyi (n. 79) 127; see also André Nollkaemper, 'International Adjudication of Global Public Goods: The Intersection of Substance and Procedure' (2012) 23(3) *EJIL* 770, 782 on the issue of procedural fairness and Jan Paulsson, 'Unlawful Laws and the Authority of International Tribunals' (2008) 23 *ICSID Rev – Foreign Investment LJ* 215.

[107] Gáspár-Szilágyi (n. 79) 129–30; see art IX(2) WTO Agreement and Claus-Dieter Ehlermann and Lothar Ehring, 'The Authoritative Interpretation Under Article IX:2 of the Agreement Establishing the World Trade Organization: Current Law, Practice and Possible Improvement' (2005) 8(4) *JIEL* 803.

In conclusion, the presence of treaty committees with interpretative powers might foster some convergence when it comes to the interpretation of an agreement's provisions on trade and investment. However, the power of these committees can politicize trade and investment disputes, and so far, the interpretative powers of such treaty bodies are under-utilized in practice.

3.4 Convergence in the Use of Jurisprudence and the Cross-Usage of Standards?

One could argue that the inclusion of various policy areas in one agreement may lead to a more holistic reading and interpretation of the treaty in dispute settlement proceedings. International trade law has been traditionally perceived as an authoritative source for the interpretation of investment treaties,[108] especially in the context of NT and MFN provisions.[109] As we have seen, the investment chapters analysed included the standards of protection traditionally found in BITs, such as MFN, NT, prohibition of expropriation, and full protection and security. Similarly, the trade parts of PTAs will often include a national treatment and an MFN clause. However, any type of convergence that might be initiated by the dispute settlement bodies needs to be treated with caution.

From the perspective of investment DSBs, one first needs to consider that they are to handle disputes arising *only* under the investment chapter. Thus, they will interpret the aforementioned standards of investment protection, but not other standards from the rest of the agreement. It has been suggested that the interpretation of the investment chapters in PTAs may be influenced by the 'surrounding treaty context', leading to a somewhat different application of investment protection standards in PTAs from stand-alone BITs.[110] These have been characterized as 'conceivable theoretical problems' since 'there is virtually no case law addressing this

---

[108] For a comprehensive review of literature, see Tams, Schill and Hoffmann (n. 84) p. 15 fn. 23.

[109] Rudolf Dolzer and Christoph Schreuer, *Principles of International Investment Law* (Oxford University Press, 2012) pp. 204–6; Peter Muchlinski, 'The Role of Preferential Trade and Investment Agreements in International Investment Law: From Unforeseen Historical Developments to an Uncertain Future' in Tams, Schill and Hoffmann (n. 84) pp. 220–1.

[110] Baetens (n. 87) 96.

issue'.[111] However, questions of mutual interference between different chapters have actually appeared in jurisdictional decisions of NAFTA tribunals, showing the lack of any consistent approach to trade and investment matters within a single agreement.[112]

For instance, in two cases filed by the exporters of sweeteners against Mexico,[113] the investment tribunals had no problems accepting the claims for damages incurred by the local companies under the NAFTA's investment chapter. However, they had different opinions as to whether the claimants could recover damages for the products produced in the USA and exported to Mexico, subject to additional taxation. Export activities are a matter of international trade in goods, regulated elsewhere in NAFTA. In one case, the investment tribunal declined jurisdiction over these claims arguing that they fell outside of the territorial scope of the investment chapter.[114] In another case, the investment tribunal decided that the inability of the parent company to export products negatively affected the investment in Mexico and accepted the claim.[115]

It may nevertheless be suggested that the broader context of PTAs with investment chapters can have an influence on the reasoning of investment tribunals. Instead of confining themselves to investment provisions, tribunals can take into consideration the overall purpose of the agreement (trade liberalization, promotion of investment, regulatory space, protection of non-economic interests, and general exceptions) when interpreting investment protection provisions. Like the discussion in Section 3.3, only a short discussion is provided here, as Cook in Chapter 8 discusses in more detail the usage of treaty object and purpose by trade and investment adjudicators.

Taking into consideration the overall purpose of the PTA could create a more balanced approach towards the goal of trade and investment

---

[111] Ibid; Eric De Brabandere, 'Co-Existence, Complementarity or Conflict? Interaction between Preferential Trade and Investment Agreements and Bilateral Investment Treaties' in Tams, Schill and Hoffmann (n. 84) pp. 65–6.

[112] For an overview of cases see Céline Lévesque, 'Inconsistency in Investor-State Awards and the Role of State Interpretations: The Example of the Mexican Sweetener Trio of Cases under NAFTA' in Andrea K Bjorklund (ed.), *Yearbook on International Investment Law and Policy, 2013–2014* (Oxford University Press, 2015) pp. 376–86.

[113] *Archer Daniels Midland Company and Tate & Lyle Ingredients Americas, Inc v. The United Mexican States*, ICSID Case No. ARB (AF)/04/5, Award (21 November 2007) (Cremades, Rovine, Sequeiros); *Cargill, Incorporated v. United Mexican States*, ICSID Case No. ARB(AF)/05/2, Award (18 September 2009) 167 (Pryles, Caron, McRae).

[114] *ADM v. Mexico (Award)* (n. 113) paras. 270–274.

[115] *Cargill v. Mexico (Award)* (n. 113) paras. 519–526.

liberalization, than just having a short BIT. At the same time, some tribunals might still only focus on those provisions that concern their respective areas of jurisdiction, neglecting the rest of the agreement. For example, NAFTA arbitral practice 'contains mixed conclusions as to whether the inclusion of an investment chapter in a PTA would indeed substantially change the scope and character of both its trade and investment provisions'.[116]

From the perspective of trade-related DSBs the situation is slightly different. These bodies are often charged with the interpretation and application of the whole agreement, including the investment chapter.[117] Thus, one could argue that a state could initiate a claim against another state for the latter's failure to abide by the investment protection standards included in the investment chapter. Due to the wide scope of jurisdiction, the claim may include both trade and investment provisions, leading to a potential overlap at the dispute settlement stage. For instance, a home state of the investor can plead a breach of anti-discrimination provisions in both trade and investment chapters. As a result, the DSB will have to apply two different – yet relevant – standards to one factual situation and may draw interpretative linkages between them. While this is a possibility, in practice investors prefer to take the lead and initiate proceedings under the investment chapters themselves, without the need for home states to step in.

In conclusion, while it is likely that arbitration tribunals (both trade and investment) may consider the overall purpose of a PTA with an investment chapter when interpreting either the trade or the investment parts of the agreement, convergence might be hampered by the rare usage of state-state arbitration for trade-related matters and the jurisdictional limitations of the two types of DSMs.

4 Conclusions

This chapter has addressed the assumption that combining trade and investment provisions in the same agreement might lead to convergence between trade and investment dispute settlement.

The empirical findings lead us to conclude that if *structural* convergence is to occur, such convergence will not be uniform around the globe, but will occur on a regional or country-specific level. While there is

---

[116] Tillmann Rudolf Braun, 'Investment Chapters in Future European Preferential Trade and Investment Agreements: Two Universes or an Integrated Model?' in Tams, Schill and Hoffmann (n. 84) pp. 138–41.

[117] See for example Article 22.4 US-Korea FTA.

a growing tendency to include BIT-like investment chapters into PTAs, this practice is not uniform around the globe and the countries/REIOs analysed can be classified into three groups. Most of the PTAs concluded by the USA, Canada, Japan, ASEAN and CARICOM include comprehensive investment chapters, which in turn contain detailed investment protection standards and ISDS. Most of the PTAs concluded by China, India, the EU and Chile do not include investment chapters. Nevertheless, their trade and investment policies are changing, and an increasing number of recent PTAs include investment chapters. PTAs concluded by Brazil and MERCOSUR do not include investment chapters, while most of the African Regionals, as well as Moroccan and South African PTAs, often defer the inclusion of investment protection to further negotiations. Furthermore, even when investment chapters are included into PTAs, they have their own, separate existence within the agreement, possibly hampering convergence.

Some level of convergence between trade and investment dispute settlement might still be possible when both trade and investment appear under the same 'roof'. On the structural level, convergence is likely to be minimal, due to the inclusion of different mechanisms of dispute settlement for trade-related and investment-related disputes under the same agreement. One could speak of a potential convergence of trade and investment provisions at the dispute resolution stage under those PTAs that allow trade-related dispute settlement bodies to apply and interpret the investment chapters. In that case, the state can combine claims under both trade and investment chapters under one roof, enticing dispute settlement bodies. Nevertheless, the practical relevance of such a scenario remains low, as the trade-related dispute settlement mechanisms found in PTAs are under-utilized.

Furthermore, epistemic convergence might also be minimal due to the different epistemic communities of decision makers in trade and investment law. Some level of convergence could occur when interpreting and implementing the various trade- and investment-related provisions of the PTAs, given the presence of different treaty bodies charged with the implementation and interpretation of the PTAs' investment and trade provisions, but which are supervised by one central body/committee. Furthermore, when interpreting treaty provisions, the various arbitral tribunals – both trade and investment – might be influenced by the broader treaty context, which includes both trade liberalization and investment protection.

ANNEX 1

Post-NAFTA PTAs and date of signature (end of 2016)

I *North Atlantic*

	United States			Canada			EU (post-Lisbon)	
1	NAFTA	1992	1	NAFTA	1994	1	Korea	2009
2	Jordan	2000	2	Israel	1996	2	Cameroon	2009
3	Chile	2003	3	Chile	1996	3	East. and South. Africa	2009
4	Singapore	2003	4	Costa Rica	2001	4	Papua NG and Fiji	2009
5	Australia	2004	5	Colombia	2008	5	Iraq	2012
6	Bahrain	2004	6	EFTA	2008	6	Central America	2012
7	CAFTA-DR	2004	7	Peru	2008	7	Colombia, Peru, Ecuador	2013(6)
8	Morocco	2004	8	Jordan	2009	8	Georgia	2014
9	Colombia	2006	9	Panama	2010	9	Moldova	2014
10	Oman	2006	10	Honduras	2013	10	Ukraine	2014
11	Peru	2006	11	Korea	2014	11	Kosovo	2015
12	Korea	2007	12	Ukraine	2016	12	Kazakhstan	2015
13	Panama	2007	13	TPP	2016	13	SADC	2016
			14	CETA	2016	14	CETA	2016
						15	Ghana	2016
						16	Singapore	N.S.
						17	Vietnam	N.S.
						18	ECOWAS	N.S.
						19	EAC	N.S.

II *Asia Pacific*

	India			China			Japan	
1	South Africa	1994	1	Hong Kong	2003	1	Mexico	2005
2	Mongolia	1996	2	Macau	2004	2	Malaysia	2006
3	Seychelles	1998	3	Chile	2005	3	Singapore	2006
4	Sri Lanka	1999	4	Asia – Pacific TA (Bangkok)	2005	4	The Philippines	2006
5	Liberia	1999	5	Pakistan	2006	5	ASEAN	2007
6	Tanzania	2000	6	New Zealand	2008	6	Chile	2007
7	Botswana	2001	7	Singapore	2008	7	Thailand	2007
8	Swaziland	2002	8	Peru	2009	8	Indonesia	2007
9	Chile	2003	9	ASEAN	2009	9	Brunei	2008
10	Afghanistan	2003	10	Costa Rica	2010	10	Switzerland	2009
11	SAFTA	2004	11	Switzerland	2013	11	Vietnam	2009
12	MERCOSUR	2004	12	Ireland	2013	12	India	2011
13	Singapore	2005	13	Australia	2015	13	Peru	2011
14	Bangladesh	2006	14	Korea	2015	14	Australia	2014
15	Bhutan	2006				15	Mongolia	2015
16	Nepal	2009						
17	Korea	2009						
18	Malaysia	2010						
19	Japan	2011						
20	ASEAN	2014						

	ASEAN			Australia	
1	Japan	2008	1	Singapore	2003
2	Korea	2009	2	Thailand	2003
3	China	2009	3	US	2004
4	AANZFTA	2009	4	Chile	2008
5	Compr. Inv. Agreement	2009	5	AANZFTA	2009
6	India	2014	6	Malaysia	2012
			7	Protocol on Invest. w NZ	2013
			8	Korea	2014
			9	Japan	2014
			10	China	2015
			11	TPP	2016

III *Latin America*

	Brazil			MERCOSUR			Chile	
1	Guyana	2001	1	Chile	1996	1	Mexico	1998
2	Mexico	2002	2	Bolivia	1996	2	Central America	1999
3	Suriname	2005	3	South Africa	2000	3	Korea	2003
			4	Mexico	2002	4	EFTA	2003
	CARICOM		5	India	2004	5	Trans-Pacific SEPA	2005
1	Colombia	1994	6	SACU PTA	2004	6	Panama	2006
2	Dominican R	1998	7	Peru	2005	7	Peru	2006
3	Cuba	2000	8	Israel	2007	8	Colombia	2006
4	Costa Rica	2004	9	Jordan	2008	9	Turkey	2009
5	EU	2008	10	SACU FTA	2008	10	Malaysia	2010
			11	Palestine	2010	11	Vietnam	2011
			12	Egypt	2010	12	Hong Kong	2012
						13	Thailand	2013
						14	Pacific Alliance	2014

IV *Africa*

	South Africa			Morocco			Plurilaterals	
1	Zimbabwe	1996	1	EU	1996	1	WAEMU	1994
2	EU TDCA	1999	2	Pan Arab FTA	1997	2	SADC	1996
3	SACU	2002	3	US	2004	3	East African Community	1999
4	EFTA-SACU	2006	4	Agadir Agr	2004	4	SACU	2002
5	SACU-MERCOSUR	2008	5	EFTA	1997	5	ECOWAS Energy Prot.	2003
6	SADC-EU	2016	6	Turkey	2004	6	EU (Revised Cotonou)	2010
						7	Tripartite Agreement: COMESA, EAC, SADC	2015

ANNEX 2

Statistics

States/REIOs	PTA	Standards of investment protection										ISDS								No ISDS	
		NT		MFN		Exprop.		Extra		Just ICSID		ICSID +		No ISDS	
		No.	%	No.	%	No.	%	No.	%	No.	%	No.	%	No.	%
USA	13	11	84.6	11	84.6	11	84.6	11	84.6	0	–	10	76.9	3	23.1
Canada	14	9	64.3	9	64.3	9	64.3	9	64.3	0	–	9	64.3	5	35.7
EU	19	3	15.8	2	10.5	3	15.8	3	15.8	0	–	3	15.8	16	84.2
India	19	4	21.1	3	15.8	4	21.1	3	15.8	0	–	4	21.1	15	78.9
China	13	5	38.5	5	38.5	4	30.8	4	30.8	1	7.7	4	30.8	8	61.5
ASEAN	6	5	83.3	3	50	5	83.3	5	83.3	0	–	5	83.3	1	16.7
Japan	15	12	80	11	73.3	12	80	12	80	0	–	10	66.7	5	33.3
Australia	11	11	100	9	81.8	10	90.9	10	90.9	0	–	6	55.5	4	36.6
Brazil	3	0	–	0	–	0	–	0	–	0	–	0	–	3	100
Chile	14	5	35.7	5	35.7	5	35.7	5	35.7	0	–	5	35.7	9	64.3
MERC.	12	0	–	0	–	0	–	0	–	0	–	0	–	12	100
CARI.	4	3	75	3	75	3	75	3	75	0	–	1	25	2	50
S. Africa	6	0	–	0	–	0	–	0	–	0	–	0	–	6	100
Morocco	6	1	16.7	1	16.7	1	16.7	1	16.7	0	–	1	16.7	5	83.3
Regionals	7	1	14.3	1	14.3	1	14.3	1	14.3	0	–	1	14.3	6	86.7

3

The EU Investment Court System and Its Resemblance to the WTO Appellate Body

HANNES LENK

1 Introduction

Investment treaty arbitration, which for a long time remained the domain of a small group of legal practitioners and scholars, has attracted much public attention in recent years. Indeed, the proliferation of bilateral investment treaties (BITs) throughout the 1990s, and the increasing tendency to embrace investor-state dispute settlement (ISDS) provisions as standard features of these agreements, has led to a significant increase in investor-state disputes since the mid-1990s.[1]

This quasi-privatization of dispute resolution revolving around 'public issues with economic and political consequences'[2] has brought investor-state arbitration under intense public scrutiny and provoked criticism that gravitates around a lack of legitimacy affecting both the arbitrator and the process of arbitration.[3] Although a number of commonly reiterated narratives (such as pro-investor bias, or a structural bias against developing countries) are unsupported by empirical findings,[4] other – often

---

[1] Daniel Behn, 'The Performance of Investment Treaty Arbitration' in Theresa Squatrito, et al. (eds.), *The Performance of International Courts and Tribunals* (Cambridge University Press, 2018), pp. 77–113, 84.

[2] Susan D Franck, 'The Legitimacy Crisisin Investment Treaty Arbitration: Privatizing Public International Law through Inconsistent Decisions' (2005) 73(4) *Fordham Law Review* 1521–1625, 1521–22.

[3] For an overview of the criticism, see UNCTAD, *Reform of investor-state dispute settlement: in search of a roadmap*, IIA Issue Note No. 2, June 2013.

[4] Note that empirical evidence does not appear to support all of these claims: on pro-investor bias, see Daniel Behn, 'Legitimacy, Evolution, and Growth in Investment Treaty Arbitration: Empirically Evaluating the State-of-the-Art' (2015) 46 *Georgetown Journal of International Law* 372–3; Susan D Franck, 'Empirically Evaluating Claims about Investment Treaty Arbitration' (2007) 86 *North Carolina Law Review* 1–87, 50; on bias against developing countries, see Susan D Franck, 'Conflating Politics and Development?

institutionally or structurally embedded features – raise legitimate concerns. These include the possibility of arbitrators to act as arbitrator and counsel in similar proceedings,[5] and an unpredictability that results from the incoherent and inconsistent interpretation and application of investment protection standards to similar factual scenarios arising out of different agreements, despite their often identical wording.[6]

The criticism against investor-state arbitration and the public opposition to the inclusion of ISDS provisions into trade and investment agreements has sparked a variety of policy responses.[7] Whereas some states decided to terminate their BITs,[8] others decided to exit the International Centre for the Settlement of Investment Disputes (ICSID) – the leading forum for investor-state arbitration[9] – and have more generally demonstrated a desire to exert greater control over the process of dispute resolution.[10] Most recently, governments decided in UNCITRAL that multilateral ISDS reform is needed.[11]

Examining Investment Treaty Arbitration Outcomes' (2014) 55(1) *Virginia Journal of International Law* 13–71; Susan D Franck, 'Development and Outcomes of Investment Treaty Arbitration' (2009) 50 *Harvard International Law Journal* 435–89.

[5] Malcolm Langford, Daniel Behn and Runnar Lie, 'The Revolving Door in International Investment Arbitration' (2017) 20(2) *Journal of International Economic Law* 301–32.

[6] Franck (n. 2) 1586.

[7] Malcolm Langford, Daniel Behn and Ole Kristian Fauchald, 'Backlash and State Strategies in International Investment Law' in Thomas Gammeltoft-Hansen and Tanja E Aalberts (eds.), *The Changing Practices of International Law: Sovereignty, Law and Politics in a Globalising World* (Cambridge University Press, 2018) pp. 70–102; For an overview, see Louis T Wells, 'Backlash to Investment Arbitration: Three Causes' in Michael Waibel et al. (eds.), *The Backlash against Investment Arbitration: Perceptions and Reality* (Wolters Kluwer, 2010), pp. 341–52.

[8] See most recently the termination of all BITs by India following its new Model BIT of 2015, which makes access to ISDS conditional on the exhaustion of local remedies.

[9] Bolivia, Ecuador and Venezuela denounced the ICSID Convention in accordance with Article 71 of the Convention respectively in 2007, 2009 and 2012; for a discussion see Christoph Schreuer, 'Denunciation of the ICSID Convention and Consent to Arbitration' in Michael Waibel et al. (eds.), *The Backlash against Investment Arbitration* (Wolters Kluwer, 2010) pp. 353–68.

[10] Martins Paparinskis, 'Masters and Guardians of International Investment Law: How to Play the Game of Reassertion' in Andreas Kulick (ed.), *Reassertion of Control Over the Investment Treaty Regime* (Cambridge University Press, 2016), pp. 30–52; Michael Waibel, 'Arbitrator Selection: Towards Greater State Control' in Andreas Kulick (ed.), *Reassertion of Control Over the Investment Treaty Regime* (Cambridge University Press, 2016) pp. 333–55.

[11] For an overview over the multilateral reform initiative in the context of UNCITRAL, consider the papers under discussion during the 36th Session of Working Group III, accessible at www.uncitral.org/uncitral/en/commission/working_groups/3Investor_State.html.

Another concrete response to public pressure is the EU Investment Court System (ICS), which was first introduced in the context of the proposed EU-US Transatlantic Trade and Investment Partnership (TTIP) Agreement.[12] The ICS has since been adopted for all post-Lisbon investment agreements (i.e. the Comprehensive Economic and Trade Agreement (CETA) with Canada, the EU-Singapore Investment Protection Agreement and the EU-Vietnam IPA),[13] and has developed into a building block of the Union's foreign investment policy.[14]

---

[12] European Commission Press Release, 'Commission proposes new Investment Court System for TTIP and other EU trade and investment negotiations' (16 September 2015), accessed on 13 September 2017 at http://europa.eu/rapid/press-release_IP-15-5651_en.htm; an informal text of the proposal dated 16 September 2015 is available at trade.ec.eu/doclib/docs/2015/november/tradoc_153955.pdf.

[13] OJ L11/23, 14 January 2017, Comprehensive Economic and Trade Agreement between Canada, of the one part, and the European Union and its Member States, of the other part (CETA), Chapter 8; EU-Singapore Investment Protection Agreement, accessible at http://trade.ec.europa.eu/doclib/press/index.cfm?id=961, Chapter 3 (EUSIPA); EU-Vietnam Investment Protection Agreement, accessible at http://trade.ec.europa.eu/doclib/press/index.cfm?id=1437, Chapter 3 (EUVIPA); the modernization of the EU-Mexico FTA is also envisaged to include the ICS but this is not further considered in this analysis; the draft text of the dispute settlement chapter is accessible at http://trade.ec.europa.eu/doclib/docs/2018/april/tradoc_156814.pdf.

[14] In the aftermath of Opinion 2/15 the Commission excluded investment protection and ISDS from its recommendation to open FTA negotiations with Australia and New Zealand; see Commission Communication, 'A balanced and progressive trade policy to harness globalization', 13 September 2017, COM(2017) 492 final, accessible at https://publications.europa.eu/en/publication-detail/-/publication/4a4b13f2-e3a6-11e7-9749-01aa75ed71a1/language-en/format-PDF; European Commission, 'Recommendation for a Council Decision authorising the opening of negotiations for a Free Trade Agreement with Australia', 13 September 2017, COM(2017) 472 final, accessible at https://eur-lex.europa.eu/legal-content/EN/TXT/?uri=COM:2017:472:FIN; European Commission, 'Recommendation for a Council Decision authorising the opening of negotiations for a Free Trade Agreement with New Zealand', 13 September 2017, COM(2017) 469 final, accessible at https://eur-lex.europa.eu/legal-content/EN/TXT/?uri=COM:2017:469:FIN; note, however, that the impact assessments on Australia and New Zealand emphasized the need for a uniform system of investment protection and a modernization of ISDS; see European Commission, 'Commission Staff Working Document – Impact assessment accompanying the document recommendation for a Council Decision authorising the opening of negotiations for a Free Trade agreement with Australia ' (SWD(2017) 293 final) 13 September 2017, accessible at https://eur-lex.europa.eu/legal-content/EN/TXT/PDF/?uri=CELEX:52017SC0293&from=EN, 7 and 10; European Commission, 'Commission Staff Working Document – Impact assessment accompanying the document recommendation for a Council Decision authorising the opening of negotiations for a Free Trade agreement with New Zealand' (SWD(2017) 289 final) 13 September 2017, accessible at https://ec.europa.eu/transparency/regdoc/rep/10102/2017/EN/SWD-2017-289-F1-EN-MAIN-PART-1.PDF, 7 and 10; more recently the Council concluded that future negotiations should separate exclusive from shared competences, unless the nature of agreements would dictate its conclusion as a mixed agreement, which is the case for

The institutional design of the ICS is influenced by the dispute settlement system of the World Trade Organization (WTO), and in particular the WTO Appellate Body (AB).[15] The present study contributes to the ongoing debate on ISDS reform, exploring whether, and to what extent, the ICS converges with or diverges from the WTO dispute settlement system. A comparison of these two systems is useful because even if the ICS remains unsuccessful it will undoubtedly define the Commission's policy preferences for a multilateral reform initiative.[16]

Section 2 places the bilateral ICS initiative into the wider context of ISDS reform and introduces its core institutional and procedural features. Section 3 compares the ICS with the WTO dispute settlement system, focusing in particular on the available remedies (Section 3.1), core operational principles (Section 3.2.), the adjudicator selection (Section 3.3), and the appeals mechanism (Section 3.4). For the purpose of the present analysis, the ICS initiative is presumed to be a reaction to public opposition to traditional investor-state arbitration. It should be

---

association agreements; see European Council, 'Draft Council conclusions on the negotiation and conclusion of EU trade agreements' (ST 8622 2018 INIT), accessible at http://data.consilium.europa.eu/doc/document/ST-8622-2018-INIT/en/pdf, paras. 3 and 4; this explains why ISDS is an element in the modernization of the EU-Mexico association agreement; see Council of the European Union, 'Directives for the negotiation of a Modernised Association Agreement with Chile', 13553/17 ADD 1, accessible at www.consilium.europa.eu/media/32405/st13553-ad01dc01en17.pdf, both the EU-Singapore and EU-Vietnam FTAs have since Opinion 2/15 been divided into an FTA and a parallel IPA; see Council of the European Union, 'Decision (EU) 2018/1676 of 15 October 2018 on the signing, on behalf of the European Union, of the Investment Protection Agreement between the European Union and its Member States, of the one part, and the Republic of Singapore, of the other part', 15 October 2018, OJ L 279/1, accessible at https://eur-lex.europa.eu/legal-content/EN/TXT/?uri=CELEX:52018PC0693; and European Commission, 'Proposal for a Council Decision on the conclusion of the Investment Protection Agreement between the European Union and its Member States, of the one part, and the Socialist Republic of Viet Nam, of the other part', 17 October 2018, COM(2018) 693 final, accessible at https://eur-lex.europa.eu/legal-content/EN/TXT/?uri=CELEX:52018PC0693; note also that the EU-Japan EPA does not include investment protection or ISDS as the parties could not agree to the ICS, OJ L330/3, 27 December 2018, Agreement between the European Union and Japan for an Economic Partnership.

[15] European Commission, 'Commission proposes new Investment Court System for TTIP and other EU trade and investment negotiations', 16 September 2015, accessible at http://europa.eu/rapid/press-release_IP-15-5651_en.htm.

[16] A challenge against the ICS is currently pending before the CJEU; see OJ C 369/2, 30.10.2017, Opinion 1/17: Comprehensive Economic and Trade Agreement [the Opinion has been delivered since the time of writing].

noted at the outset, however, that this chapter does not attempt to normatively assess the ICS in light of the criticism against investor-state arbitration. Rather, this study focuses primarily on the comparison of the ICS with the WTO dispute settlement system.

2 The EU Investment Court System

2.1 The ICS in the Context of Institutional ISDS Reform

The emergence of the modern investment treaty regime is largely built on bilateralism, apart from a few regional and plurilateral efforts. This must be understood against the backdrop of a long line of unsuccessful attempts to establish a multilateral framework for the regulation of foreign investment.[17] The United States in particular lobbied strongly for the inclusion of investment measures in the Havana Charter,[18] and later reiterated their position to extend the GATT non-discrimination provisions to foreign investment in the process leading up to the Uruguay round of GATT negotiations in 1986.[19] In 2001, the Doha round negotiations included investment on their agenda. Well known is also the OECD negotiation for a Multilateral Agreement on Investment (MAI) in the mid-1990s.[20] The ambitious scope underlying these initiatives was, however, only matched by the fierce political resistance they had to face.[21] The Havana Charter was never ratified by the United

---

[17] Muchlinski differentiates between attempts to conclude an investment protection regime (incl. the MAI), and attempts to establish a framework that balances investor rights and state interests (incl. the Havana Charter); see Peter T Muchlinski, 'The Rise and Fall of the Multilateral Agreement on Investment: Where Now?' (2000) 34(3) *The International Lawyer* 1033–53, 1034.

[18] Riyaz Dattu, 'A Journey from Havana to Paris: The Fifty-Year Quest for the Elusive Multilateral Agreement on Investment'(2000) 24(1) *Fordham International Law Journal* 275–316, 287.

[19] Stefan D Amarasinha and Juliane Kokott, 'Multilateral Investment Rules Revisited' in Peter Muchlinski, Federico Ortino and Christoph Schreuer (eds.), *The Oxford Handbook of International Investment Law* (Oxford University Press, 2008), pp. 119–51, 125

[20] OECD, *A Multilateral Agreement on Investment*, Report by the Committee on International Investment and Multinational Enterprises / and the Committee on Capital Movements and Invisible Transactions, 5 May 1995, (DAFFE/CMIT/CIME(95) 13/FINAL). For a background on the MAI negotiations, see Riyaz Dattu (n. 18) 295–303; Rainer Geiger, 'Regulatory Expropriation in International Law: Lessons from the Multilateral Agreement on Investment' (2002) 11(1) *New York University Environmental Law Journal* 94–109; Peter T Muchlinski (n. 17).

[21] The author discussed the political causes for the failure to establish a multilateral investment regime elsewhere; see Hannes Lenk, 'Something Borrowed, Something New: The TTIP Investment Court: How to Fit Old Procedures into New Institutional Design' in

States, among other countries, because of diverging views over the right balance between the protection of investors' rights and the regulatory interests of the state.[22] Due to the strong opposition from developing countries, the GATT and later WTO members were never able to agree on anything more comprehensive than the Agreement on Trade-Related Investment Measures.[23] Indeed, foreign direct investment was dropped from the Doha round negotiation agenda in 2003, never to return.[24] The MAI, besides unfortunate timing, fell prey to political resistance from developed[25] and developing countries alike, and faced strong opposition from civil society.[26]

Notably, both the Havana Charter and the MAI explicitly addressed the issue of dispute settlement,[27] although only the OECD initiative included reference to ISDS. Indeed, the possibility of a permanent investment tribunal and appellate mechanism was briefly floated in the MAI negotiations, but was swiftly rejected by the majority of delegations.[28] Without any signs that a consensus could be reached on the multilateral level, some states reacted to the growing criticism against ISDS in domestic legislation and bilateral negotiations. The US Trade Promotion Authority Act of 2002 in particular provided political impetus for the creation of bilateral appeals mechanisms in investment arbitration.[29] As a result,

---

Elaine Fahey (ed.), *Institutionalisation beyond the Nation State* (Springer International, 2018) pp. 129–47, 134–7.

[22] Riyaz Dattu (n. 18) 288; on the US policy perspective on reasons behind the non-ratification of the Havana Convention, see Todd S Shenkin, 'Trade-Related Investment Measures in Bilateral Investment Treaties and the GATT: Moving Toward a Multilateral Investment Treaty' (1994) 55(2) *University of Pittsburgh Law Review* 541–606, 556–8.

[23] Stefan D Amarasinha and Juliane Kokott (n. 19) 125; Riyaz Dattu (n. 18) 295, for a comprehensive discussion of investment-related negotiations in the GATT / WTO context, see 288–95.

[24] To this date, the WTO working group on trade and investment remains inactive and without a specific mandate; see Stefan D Amarasinha and Juliane Kokott (n. 19)128–9.

[25] In light of the first NAFTA awards against Canada (e.g. *Ethyl Corporation v. Canada*, UNCITRAL, Award on Jurisdiction of 24 June 1998), developed countries started to perceive ISDS as a procedural mechanism to challenge regulatory policy choices; see ibid. at 101.

[26] Rainer Geiger (n. 20) 97–102; Peter T. Muchlinski (n. 17) 1037–48.

[27] *United Nations Conference on Trade and Employment – Final Act and Related Documents* (1948) Chapter VIII.

[28] Rainer Geiger (n. 20) 106.

[29] As a principal trade negotiating objective, the United States shall provide for 'an appellate body or similar mechanism to provide coherence to the interpretations of investment

programmatic treaty language committing to the establishment of a treaty-centred appeals mechanism started to appear in the US Model BITs of 2004 and 2012, and in all US FTAs and investment agreements adopted on this model.[30] The most concrete example was the Dominican Republic-Central America-United States FTA (CAFTA-DR) that envisaged, within three months of entry into force of the agreement, the formation of a negotiating group charged with the task of developing an internal appeals mechanism for investor-state disputes.[31] Similar commitments have since frequently been included in bilateral[32] and regional agreements[33] (see Chapter 2).

Stressing the risk of further fragmentation, the ICSID Secretariat proposed a number of amendments to the ICSID Regulations and Rules, and the ICSID Additional Facility Rules,[34] including the creation of an ICSID Appeals Facility with wide jurisdictional privileges.[35] Accordingly, the ICSID Appeals Panel would consist of fifteen members with different nationalities, elected by the ICSID Administrative Council (featuring one representative of all states participating in ICSID). Individual cases were to be heard in a division of three. As grounds for appeal, the discussion paper envisaged 'clear error of law', narrowly defined instances of serious factual errors, as well as any of the five grounds for annulment in Article 52 ICSID.[36] The appeals tribunal, as proposed, would have had the power to uphold, modify, reverse or annul the initial award in part or *in toto*.[37] Notably, the proposed Appeals

---

provisions in trade agreements'; see Trade Promotion Authority Act of 2002, P.L. 107-210, sec 2102(b)(3)(g)(iv), 19 U.S.C § 3802(b)(3)(G)(iv).

[30] See, for instance, Singapore-US FTA of 2003, Art15.19(10); Chile-US FTA of 2004, Article 10.19(10); Uruguay-US BIT of 2005, Article 28(10); US Model BIT of 2004, Article 28(10); US Model BIT of 2012, Article 28(10).

[31] Dominican Republic-Central America-United States FTA of 2004, Article 10.20(10).

[32] See, for instance, Canada-Korea FTA of 2014, Annex 8-E; Australia-China FTA of 2014, Article 9.23; Australia-Korea BIT of 2014, Article 11.20.13 and Annex 11-E; Korea-New Zealand FTA of 2015, Article 10.26.9.

[33] See, for instance, Trans-Pacific Partnership Agreement, Article 9.22(11).

[34] ICSID Secretariat Discussion Paper, *Possible improvements of the framework for ICSID arbitration*, October 2004.

[35] For an overview of the proposed amendments, see Gabrielle Kaufmann-Kohler, 'In Search of Transparency and Consistency: ICSID Reform Proposal' (2005) 2(5) *Transnational Dispute Management* 1–8; Antonio Parra, 'The New Amendments to the ICSID Regulations and Rules and Additional Facility Rules' (2004) 3(2) *The Law & Practice of International Courts and Tribunals* 181–8.

[36] Annex to the ICSID Secretariat Discussion Paper, *Possible improvements*, para. 7.

[37] Ibid., para. 9.

Facility Rules would have been applicable to awards rendered under ICSID and the ICSID Additional Facility Rules. Furthermore, the Appeals Facility Rule would have also extended to UNCITRAL and other arbitration rules, subject to the inclusion of the appeals mechanism into the underlying investment treaty.[38] However, as it transpired that the treaty language in BITs – such as the CAFTA-DR – amounted to little more than 'declarations of intent',[39] the ICSID initiative was dropped from the reform agenda for being 'premature'.[40] More recently, the multilateralization of ISDS has gained new momentum, as UNCITRAL has taken up talks over a possible reform agenda in 2017.[41]

The Lisbon Treaty, which endowed the European Union (EU) with far-reaching competences for the negotiation of investment agreements, is also notable in the context of institutional ISDS reform.[42] On the one hand, in its post-Lisbon investment agreements the EU commits to finding a multilateral solution to the challenges faced by ISDS,[43] and actively participates in the UNCITRAL initiative to that end.[44] Together with Canada, the EU presented a co-sponsored discussion paper at the

[38] Ibid., paras. 2–3; notably, the contractual nature of its inclusion is furthermore considered to provide a workable solution to circumvent the restrictions of Article 53(1) ICSID, i.e. the explicit exclusion of any appeal against awards rendered under ICSID.

[39] Gabrielle Kaufmann-Kohler and Michele Potestà, 'Can the Mauritius Convention serve as a model for the reform of investor-State arbitration in connection with the introduction of a permanent investment tribunal or an appeal mechanism? – Analysis and roadmap' (CIDS Research Paper, 3 June 2016, commissioned by UNCITRAL), 22–3.

[40] Working Paper of the ICSID Secretariat, *Suggested changes to the ICSID Rules and Regulations*, May 2005, para. 4; for an overview of the 2006 ICSID amendments, see Aurélia Antonietti, 'The 2006 Amendments to the ICSID Rules and Regulations and the Additional Facility Rules' (2006) 21(2) *ICSID Review* 427-48; Antonio R Parra, 'Advancing Reform at ICSID' (2014) 11(1) *Transnational Dispute Management* 1.

[41] The status of the UNCITRAL discussion, including audio recordings of the meetings, can be accessed at www.uncitral.org/uncitral/en/commission/working_groups/3Investor_State.html.

[42] For a comprehensive overview of the evolution of an EU foreign investment policy, see Szilárd Gáspár-Szilágyi, 'Quo vadis EU Investment Law and Policy? The Shaky Path towards the International Promotion of EU Rules' (2018) 23(2) *European Foreign Affairs Review* 167–86.

[43] Article 12 of the TTIP proposal; Article 29 of CETA; Article 3.12 of the EUSIPA; Article 3.41 of the EUVIPA; the Commission published recommendations for a Council decision authorizing the opening of negotiations for a Convention establishing a multilateral court for the settlement of investment disputes, including a draft negotiating mandate (COM (2017) 493 final, 13 September 2017).

[44] Working Group III United Nations Commission on International Trade Law, 'Possible reform of investor-State dispute settlement (ISDS): Submission from the European Union' (A/CN.9/WG.III/WP.145) 23–27 April 2018.

UNCTAD World Investment Forum in Nairobi in July of 2016[45] and more recently at the World Economic Forum in Davos.[46] On the other hand, the European Commission advocates the ICS as a response to public and political pressure over the lack of legitimacy in traditional investor-state arbitration.[47] These two strands of the reform agenda are mutually reinforcing. Whereas endorsing the ICS as a pillar of the Union's foreign investment policy acknowledges the difficulties involved in multilateral reform, it also creates a momentum for multilateral negotiations to avoid further fragmentation of the investment treaty system.[48] The present chapter focuses exclusively on the ICS and its institutional features.

2.2 Institutional and Procedural Features of the ICS

In an attempt to address criticism over the lack of coherence and predictability in ISDS and calls for the establishment of an appeals mechanism,[49] the ICS establishes a two-tier judicial system featuring

---

[45] Co-sponsored discussion paper of the Government of Canada and the European Commission, 'Reforming investment dispute settlement: Considerations on the way towards a multilateral investment dispute settlement mechanism', 17–21 July 2016, accessed on 13 September 2017 at http://trade.ec.europa.eu/doclib/ docs/2017/january/ tradoc_155266.07.13%20Non-paper%20on%20multilateral%20investment%20court% 20(rev2)(clean).pdf.

[46] Co-sponsored discussion paper of the Government of Canada and the European Commission, 'The case for creating a multilateral investment dispute settlement mechanism', 20 January 2017, accessed on 13 September 2017 at http://trade.ec.europa.eu/doclib/ docs/2017/january/tradoc_155264.pdf.

[47] Cecilia Malmström, 'Proposing an Investment Court System', blog post of 16 September 2015, accessed on 13 September 2017 at https://ec.europa.eu/commis sion/commissioners/2014-2019/malmstrom/blog/proposing-investment-court-system_en; European Commission Press Release, 'Commission proposes new Investment Court System for TTIP and other EU trade and investment negotiations' of 16 September 2015, accessed on 13 September 2017 at http://europa.eu/rapid/press-release_IP-15-5651_en.htm.

[48] The lack of visible political commitment to implement treaty-centered appeals mechanisms explains the failure of the ICSID Appeals Facility; see Antonio R Parra (n. 40) 9.

[49] Naboth van Den Broek and Danielle Morris, 'The EU's Proposed Investment Court and WTO Dispute Settlement: A Comparison and Lessons Learned' (2017) 2(1) *European Investment Law and Arbitration Review* 35–89, 49; for a comprehensive discussion of the Union's ICS initiative, see also Catharine Titi, 'The European Union's proposal for an international investment court: Significance, innovations and challenges ahead' (2017) *Transnational Dispute Management*; Elsa Sardinha, 'Party-Appointed Arbitrators No More' (2018)17(1) *The Law & Practice of International Courts and Tribunals* 117–34; and Luca Pantaleo, 'Lights and shadows of the TTIP Investment Court System' in Luca

CONVERGENCE IN THE DESIGN OF THE EU ICS 71

a tribunal of first instance (the Tribunal)[50] and an Appeal Tribunal.[51] The number of Tribunal members and Appeal Tribunal members varies across the agreements, with fifteen Tribunal members under CETA,[52] nine under the EU-Vietnam IPA[53] and as little as six Tribunal members under the EU-Singapore IPA.[54] Two thirds of the Tribunal members are nationals of the Contracting Parties, whereas the remaining third is composed of third-country nationals. Accordingly, using the example of CETA, five Tribunal members are EU nationals, five Tribunal members are Canadian nationals, and the remaining five Tribunal members are third-country nationals. As to the Appeal Tribunal, both the EU-Singapore IPA and the EU-Vietnam IPA provide for an initial six-member strong Tribunal, including nationals of the Contracting Parties and third-country nationals.[55] CETA makes no explicit stipulation but leaves the number of members and the composition of the Appeal Tribunal to be decided by the CETA Joint Committee.[56] Notably, the affiliation of ICS members is a matter of appointment rather than nationality.[57] The EU-Singapore IPA no longer makes any reference to nationality in this respect, other than that the third-country members of the ICS may indeed not have the nationality of either Singapore or the EU.[58] It is perhaps also noteworthy that, unlike the early TTIP negotiating proposal, neither CETA nor the IPAs with Singapore and Vietnam in their current versions refer to members of the Tribunal as 'judges'.[59]

Pantaleo, Wybe Douma and Tamara Takács (eds.), *Tiptoeing to TTIP: What kind of agreement for what kind of partnership?*, CLEER Papers 2016/1 (2016) 77–92; for an assessment of the ICS system from a Union law perspective, see Szilárd Gáspár-Szilágyi, 'A Standing Investment Court under TTIP from the Perspective of the Court of Justice of the European Union' (2016) 17(5) *The Journal of World Investment & Trade* 701–42.

[50] Both CETA (Article 8.27(1)) and the EUVIPA (Article 3.38(1)) employ the term 'Tribunal', whereas the EUSIPA (Article 3.9(1)) uses 'Tribunal of First Instance'.
[51] CETA (Article 8.28(1)) employs the term 'Appellate Tribunal', whereas the EUSIPA (Article 3.10(1)) and the EUVIPA (Article 3.39(1)) refer to the second instance tribunal as 'Appeal Tribunal'.
[52] Article 8.27(2) CETA.
[53] Article 3.39(2) of the EUSIPA.
[54] Article 3.38(2) of the EUVIPA.
[55] Article 3.10(8) of the EUSIPA; Article 3.39(2) of the EUVIPA.
[56] Article 8.28(7)(f) CETA.
[57] Footnote 11 to Article 8.27(2) CETA; and footnotes to Articles 3.38(2) and 3.38(2) of the EUVIPA.
[58] Articles 3.9(2)(c) and 3.10(2)(c) of the EUSIPA.
[59] Notably, whereas Article 9 of the textual proposal for the Chapter on Trade in Services, Investment and E-Commerce in TTIP of 12 November 2015, Section 3, Sub-Section 5

Under CETA and the agreement with Vietnam it is the respective trade committee that is responsible for the appointment of the members of the Tribunal and Appeal Tribunal.[60] The Committee, comprised of representatives of the Contracting Parties and co-chaired by the responsible trade minister and the EU Trade Commissioner,[61] takes decisions by mutual consent.[62] In the case of the EU-Singapore ICS, even though the respective trade committee adopts the formal decision to appoint the ICS members, the national members are directly nominated by the respective Contracting Parties.[63] Hence, whereas the composition of ICS formations in CETA and the EU-Vietnam IPA are subject to a politically brokered compromise, the EU-Singapore ICS endows the EU and Singapore with direct influence over the appointment of their affiliated ICS members and thereby, as will be discussed shortly, the panels. This important difference is reiterated in the relevant footnotes to the agreements in CETA and the EU-Vietnam IPA, which allow the Contracting Parties to 'propose' those members of the Tribunal and Appeal Tribunal that are affiliated to them.[64]

Members are appointed to tribunal divisions by the respective presidents of the ICS tribunals[65] on a rotating basis, ensuring that the composition of the divisions is random and unpredictable, while giving equal opportunity to all members to serve.[66] This is remarkable from the point of view of party autonomy,[67] which is central to investor-state arbitration.[68] Indeed, the attempt to remove the direct influence of parties over the panel formations is supported by the fact that all ICS

[hereinafter referred to as 'TTIP proposal'] refers to Judges on the Tribunal, Article 10 on the Appeal Tribunal refers to Members of the Appeal Tribunal.

[60] Articles 3.27(2), 8.28(3) and (7) CETA; Articles 3.38(2) and 3.29(3) of the EUVIPA.
[61] Article 26.1(1) CETA; Article 4.1(2) of the EUVIPA.
[62] Article 26.3(3) CETA; Article 4.2(3) of the EUVIPA.
[63] Articles 3.9(2) and 3.10(2) of the EUSIPA.
[64] Footnote 11 to Article 8.27(2) CETA; and footnotes to Articles 3.38(2) and 3.38(2) of the EUVIPA.
[65] For who is selected among the third-party national members, see Article 8.27(8); Articles 3.9(6) and 3.10(6) of the EUSIPA; Articles 3.38(8) and 3.39(6) of the EUVIPA.
[66] Article 8.27(7) CETA; Articles 3.9(8) and 3.10(8) of the EUSIPA; Articles 3.38(7) and 3.39(8) of the EUVIPA.
[67] For some context on the removal of party-appointments from the ICS structure, see Elsa Sardinha (n. 49) 122–4.
[68] Naboth van Den Broek and Danielle Morris (n. 49) 41; more generally on party autonomy in international arbitration, see Emmanuel Gaillard, *Legal Theory of International Arbitration* (Martin Nijhoff, 2010) p. 110.

tribunal divisions are chaired by a third-country national member.[69] Consequently, even though all parties to the proceedings are formally removed from the arbitrator selection process, the design of the ICS places Member States in a position to indirectly influence tribunal divisions as they retain direct influence over the nomination of members to the ICS tribunals.[70] In the case of CETA and the agreement with Vietnam, this is effectively exercised through the Contracting Parties' participation in the respective trade committees, whereas under the EU-Singapore IPA the Contracting Parties exert a direct influence over the nomination of their affiliate members. It is notable in this context that the general composition of tribunal divisions reflects the tri-partite representation that fundamentally characterizes the composition of the ICS tribunals.[71] In other words, two out of the three tribunal members are affiliated with the Contracting Parties.

Another core feature of the ICS is its heightened professional and ethical standards. Members of the ICS must not only be competent to be appointed to judicial office in their respective countries, or be jurists of recognized competence,[72] but must also demonstrate expertise in a number of areas, including public international law, international trade law, international investment law and international dispute resolution. Additionally, upon appointment, members refrain from acting in any other conflicting position, i.e. counsel, party-appointed expert, or witness in any other dispute.[73]

Although the ICS purports to establish a permanent, quasi-judicial ISDS institution, it functions within the constraints of existing arbitration rules. All ICS formations thus far refer to ICSID, the ICSID Additional Facility Rules, the UNCITRAL arbitration rules, and any other rules as agreed to by the disputing parties.[74] This poses a number of legal challenges, from both the internal perspective of Union law as

---

[69] Article 2.27(6) CETA; Articles 3.9(7) and 3.10(7) of the EUSIPA; Articles 3.38(6) and 3.39(8) of the EUVIPA.

[70] For criticism of the ICS with respect to the appointment of members to individual divisions, see Elsa Sardinha (n. 49) 128–32.

[71] With the exception of the CETA Appellate Tribunal division, which is composed of three 'randomly appointed' members; see Article 8.28(5) CETA.

[72] Article 8.28(4) CETA; Article 3.9(4) of the EUSIPA; Article 3.38(4) of the EUVIPA. Members of the Appeal Tribunal under the IPAs with Singapore and Vietnam shall fulfil the requirements to be appointed to the highest judicial office in their respective countries; see Article 3.10(4) of the EUSIPA; Article 3.39(7) of the EUVIPA.

[73] Article 8.30 CETA; Article 3.11(1) of the EUSIPA; Article 3.40(1) of the EUVIPA.

[74] Article 8.23(2) CETA; Article 3.6(1) of the EUSIPA; Article 3.33(2) of the EUVIPA.

well as the wider international law perspective,[75] not least with respect to the challenge and enforcement of awards.[76] As the present analysis is not concerned with a critical appraisal of the institutional design of the ICS, suffice it to acknowledge that the procedural framework is governed by established arbitration rules.

Perhaps the most relevant institutional feature of the ICS is its appeals mechanism. Accordingly, both parties are eligible to appeal the provisional awards of the Tribunal(s) if it is alleged that the latter has erred in the interpretation and application of the applicable law, or manifestly erred in the appreciation of facts, including the appreciation of relevant domestic law.[77] Additionally, the grounds for appeals also include the reasons for annulment under ICSID, by reference to Article 52 of the ICSID Convention.[78] The Appeal Tribunal may uphold, modify or reverse the award.[79] With respect to the power to refer a matter back to the Tribunal, all three agreements demonstrate significant differences. Under the EU-Singapore IPA, the Appeal Tribunal shall refer all cases

---

[75] The author developed on these aspects in more detail elsewhere; see Hannes Lenk (n. 21) 141–3.

[76] On the modification of the ICSID convention and its effects on the enforcement of ICS awards, see August Reinisch, 'Will the EU's Proposal Concerning an Investment Court System for CETA and TTIP Lead to Enforceable Awards?—The Limits of Modifying the ICSID Convention and the Nature of Investment Arbitration' (2016) 19 *Journal of International Economic Law* 761, in particular 779–80; with respect to the UNCITRAL arbitration rules, under post-Lisbon Union IIAs the appellate review is mandatory, imposing an obligation on the disputing parties not to submit the dispute to any other kind of review, setting aside procedure, or other challenges (e.g. Articles 8.27(9)(b) and (e) in combination with Article 8.41(3) CETA), whereas the UNCITRAL rules are specifically tailored for the involvement of the domestic courts and for that purpose require the determination of a seat of arbitration (Articles 3(3)(g) and 18 of the UNCITRAL Arbitration Rules); see Joel Dahlquist, 'Place of arbitration in the proposed "Investment Court" scenario: An overlooked issue?', Kluwer Arbitration Blog, 23 March 2017, accessed at http://kluwerarbitrationblog.com/2017/03/23/joel-booked/; notably, only few domestic arbitration laws allow for the right to post-award challenges to be waived by the parties (e.g. Belgium (Article 1717(4) of the Belgian Judicial Code), France (Article 1522 of the French Code of Civil Procedure), Sweden (Article 51 of the Swedish Arbitration Act), Switzerland (Article 192(1) of the Swiss Private International Law Act), for a discussion see Daniella Stirk, 'Growing number of countries allowing exclusion agreements with respect to annulment warrants greater scrutiny of arbitration clauses', Kluwer Arbitration Blog, 11 January 2012, accessed at http://arbitrationblog.kluwerarbitration.com/2012/01/11/growing-number-of-countries-allowing-exclusion-agreements-with-respect-to-annulment-warrants-greater-scrutiny-of-arbitration-clauses/.

[77] Notably, CETA does not specify whether both parties are eligible to submit appeals.

[78] Article 8.28(2) CETA; Article 3.19(1) of the EUSIPA; Article 3.54(1) of the EUVIPA.

[79] Article 8.28(1) CETA; Article 3.19(3) of the EUSIPA; Article 3.54(3) of the EUVIPA.

back to the Tribunal, which must revise the provisional award in accordance with the findings of the Appeal Tribunal. On the contrary, the EU-Vietnam Appeal Tribunal is furnished with extensive powers to conclude the legal analysis, and may refer cases back to the Tribunal only if the facts established by the Tribunal are insufficient to apply its own legal findings.[80] CETA does not explicitly provide for the power to remand the case, but allows the CETA Joint Committee to decide on such procedures at a later point.[81] Notably, neither CETA nor the EU-Singapore formation of the Appeal Tribunal are explicitly established on a permanent basis, which supports the view that the Union's primary ambition is to pursue multilateral ISDS reform.[82] It remains to be seen whether only awards or also separate decisions on jurisdiction or other matters are subject to review.[83]

3 Comparing the EU ICS and the WTO Dispute Settlement System: Convergence or Divergence for the Adjudication of Trade and Investment Disputes?

The institutional design of the ICS is undoubtedly inspired by features of the WTO dispute settlement system, and in particular the WTO Appellate Body (AB).[84] The Dispute Settlement Understanding (DSU)[85] has been praised as an exemplary effort to 'transform, in a highly pragmatic manner over a period of five decades, what was initially a rudimentary, power-based system for settling disputes through diplomatic negotiations into an elaborate, rules-based system for settling disputes through adjudication'.[86] The present section attempts to compare the WTO dispute settlement

---

[80] Article 3.19(3) of the EUSIPA.
[81] Article 3.54(4) of the EUVIPA.
[82] Elsa Sardinha, 'Towards a New Horizon in Investor-State Dispute Settlement? Reflections on the Investment Tribunal System in the Comprehensive Economic Trade Agreement (CETA)' (2017) 54 *The Canadian Yearbook of International Law* 311–65, 326.
[83] Sardinha points out that it is unclear from the drafting of the ICS whether separate decisions on inter alia jurisdiction are also subject to review; see ibid.
[84] European Commission Press Release, 'Commission proposes new Investment Court System for TTIP and other EU trade and investment negotiations' of 16 September 2015, http://europa.eu/rapid/press-release_IP-15-5651_en.htm, accessed on 13 September 2017.
[85] Annex II to the WTO Agreement, Understanding on rules and procedures governing the settlement of disputes.
[86] Peter Van den Bossche and Werner Zdouc, *The Law and Policy of the World Trade Organization*, 3rd ed., (Cambridge University Press, 2013) p. 159.

system with the proposed ICS in an attempt to single out similarities and differences, and assess whether the image of the WTO dispute settlement system as a poster child of effective international dispute settlement is transferable to the investor-state context. Rather than engaging in a comprehensive analysis of the WTO dispute settlement system and the extensive body of decisions it produced, this section focuses on core institutional features. The principal areas of comparison for the ensuing analysis are the aims and objectives (Section 3.1), core operational principles (Section 3.2), the adjudicator selection (Section 3.3) and the appeals mechanism (Section 3.4).

3.1 Between Damages and Compliance: Divergences in the Available Remedies under the WTO Dispute Settlement System and the EU ICS

In the context of the WTO, dispute settlement has the primary objective of assuring the effective implementation of the WTO agreements and aims to that end at 'providing security and predictability to the multilateral trading system'.[87] This is exemplified by, on the one hand, the available remedies in the WTO dispute settlement system and, on the other hand, the characteristics of measures that form the subject of complaints. First, the primary remedy in cases where a measure amounts to the nullification of a benefit accruing under a WTO agreement, or presents an impediment of such benefit or to the attainment of objectives under that agreement,[88] is the cessation or modification of the contested measures.[89] Monetary compensation, on the other hand, fulfils a secondary purpose, and is offered on a voluntary and temporary basis only where a panel report cannot be implemented in a timely manner.[90] Neither WTO panels nor the AB award compensation for a loss that a private party has suffered as a result of the contested measure.[91] Rather, through their adjudicative role, WTO panels and the AB carry a systemic

---

[87] Article 3.2 DSU; see also *US – Final Anti-dumping Measures on Stainless Steel from Mexico*, Appellate Body Report (20 May 2008), WT/DS344/AB/R, para. 160.
[88] Article 23.1 DSU; see also Article XXIII:1 GATT 1994.
[89] Articles 3.7 and 19.1 DSU.
[90] Articles 3.7 and 22.1 DSU; see also Marco Bronckers and Naboth van Den Broek, 'Financial Compensation in the WTO: Improving the Remedies of WTO Dispute Settlement' (2005) 8(1) *Journal of International Economic Law* 101–26, 103.
[91] Although private parties do not actively participate in WTO proceedings they play an important role behind the scenes, for a detailed account see Gregory C Shaffer, *Defending Interests: Public-Private Partnerships in WTO Litigation* (Brookings Institute Press, 2003).

responsibility to maintain a balance of rights and obligations for all WTO members.[92]

The WTO dispute settlement system allows for complaints to be brought against a regulation 'as such' – that is to say in the absence of a particular applied measure that would lead to a concrete violation of the WTO agreements,[93] and under certain circumstances facilitates complaints against a continued measure in successive cases.[94] At the same time, measures that have already been terminated can only be challenged if they continue to have adverse effects on the complainant party.[95] Dispute settlement plays in this context an important role in assuring the overall successful operation of the WTO agreements, as it provides the 'security and predictability needed to conduct future trade'.[96]

In comparison, the fundamental purpose of the ICS is to provide compensation for investors with respect to any losses suffered as a result of a wrong committed by the host state. Regulatory measures can only be challenged if the claimant investor is able to demonstrate damages caused by a concrete violation of any of the substantive standards of investment protection; for otherwise there will be no remedy.[97] In certain circumstances of expropriation, restitution might be available to aggrieved investors, but the underlying objective remains to remedy the individual investors for the losses they incurred at the hand of the host state. Indeed, damages in lieu of restitution are available upon request of the respondent state.[98] Although investment awards might have an impact on the future regulatory conduct of a state,[99] an investor

---

[92] Article 3.3 DSU.
[93] *United States – Sunset Review of Anti-Dumping Duties on Corrosion-Resistant Carbon Steel Flat Products from Japan*, Appellate Body Report (15 December 2003) WT/DS244/AB/R, paras. 81–82; *United States – Sunset Review of Anti-Dumping Measures on Oil Country Tubular Goods from Argentina*, Appellate Body Report (29 November 2004), WT/DS268/AB/R, AB, para. 172.
[94] *US – Continued Existence and Application of Zeroing Methodology*, Appellate Body Report (4 November 2009, WT/DS350/AB/R, paras. 179–81 and 185.
[95] *US – Subsidies on Upland Cotton*, Appellate Body Report (3 March 2005), WT/DS267/AB/R, paras. 261–62.
[96] *US – Corrosion-Resistant Carbon Steel Sunset Review* (n. 93) para. 82.
[97] Article 8.18(1) CETA; Article 3.1(1) of the EUSIPA; Article 3.27(1) of the EUVIPA.
[98] Article 8.39(1)(b) CETA; Article, 3.18(1)(b) of the EUSIPA; Article 3.53(1)(b) of the EUVIPA.
[99] For a discussion on the impact of investor-state dispute settlement on the regulatory policy of states, see Christian Tietje and Freya Baetens, *The Impact of Investor-State-Dispute Settlement (ISDS) in the Transatlantic Trade and Investment Partnership*, Study for the Ministry of Foreign Affairs, The Netherlands (2014), http://media.leidenuniv.nl

cannot challenge regulatory measures 'as such' for the purpose of having them withdrawn or modified.

The two systems thus have diverging aims and objectives. The system of remedies under the DSU is prospective in that the adjustment of non-compliant state conduct facilitates a continuous implementation of the WTO agreements. The primary function of the ICS is reactive in that it is exclusively concerned with providing relief to an injured investor in concrete cases.

3.2 Converging Operational Principles? Comparing the Workings of the WTO Dispute Settlement System and the EU ICS

The WTO dispute settlement operates under a number of central operational principles. As such, it presents a single and integrated system – an adjudicative umbrella institution – for all covered WTO agreements.[100] It is essentially designed as a state-to-state dispute settlement system to which only WTO members have access, at the exclusion of individuals and corporate entities.[101] This is perhaps the single most apparent difference between the ICS and the WTO framework. In this context it is noteworthy that special procedural provisions in individual WTO agreements are, as far as possible, to be read as complementing, rather than replacing the general provisions under the DSU.[102] With this in mind, while it appears possible to implement the access of individuals to the WTO dispute settlement system, it nonetheless represents a significant break from the underlying state-to-state paradigm. The dispersed network of the investment treaty regime, which is based on thousands of bilateral and regional agreements, and the bilateral nature of the ICS stand in harsh conflict with the idea of a coherent and integrated system.

As it now stands, the ICS is designed as a treaty-centred system. To entertain the argument that the ICS could lead to a 'single and integrated' system for the settlement of investor-state disputes accepts the premise

/legacy/the-impact-of-investor-state-dispute-settlement-isds-in-the-ttip.pdf, accessed 10 September 2017.

[100] Article 1.2 DSU; see also *Guatemala – Anti-Dumping Investigation Regarding Portland Cement from Mexico*, Appellate Body Report (2 November 1998), WT/DS60/AB/R, paras. 64–66.

[101] *United States – Import Prohibition of Certain Shrimp and Shrimp Products*, Appellate Body Report (12 October 1998), WT/DS58/AB/R, para. 101.

[102] *Guatemala – Anti-Dumping Investigation Regarding Portland Cement from Mexico*, Appellate Body Report (25 November 1998), WT/DS60/AB/R, paras. 65 and 66.

that the ICS can be 'multilateralized', i.e. that the various ICS formations can be coordinated so as to harness efficiency benefits through the sharing of resources. The two-tier judicial system of such a 'multilateralized' ICS would indeed resemble the WTO system.[103] Whereas this would require that the procedural and institutional features of all ICS formations are compatible (if not identical), the three existing ICS formations already demonstrate significant variations. To view the ICS as a stepping-stone towards a multilateral investment court is, therefore, an attractive but entirely unrealistic argument. Although the two-tier judicial system indeed resembles the institutional set-up of the WTO dispute settlement system, the ICS is more likely to hamper than further multilateral ISDS reform. Rather than leading towards a more WTO-like system, the treaty-centred ICS is likely to entrench institutionalized ISDS on an agreement-by-agreement basis that might make it more difficult to implement a multilateral solution.

WTO jurisdiction is compulsory, exclusive and contentious. Just as it is the case for the ICS, the WTO has no competence to render advisory opinions. Although Article 3.2 of the DSU stipulates that the WTO dispute settlement system serves to 'clarify the existing provisions of those agreements', neither a WTO panel nor the AB will engage in these questions outside the context of a particular dispute,[104] or on the basis of hypothetical assumptions.[105] Another similarity with the ICS is the compulsory nature of dispute settlement. WTO members have explicitly consented to WTO dispute settlement in a general fashion by way of Article 6.1 of the DSU. A general consent to the jurisdiction of the ICS is incorporated into the post-Lisbon EU IIAs in a similar fashion.[106]

The question remains to what extent the jurisdiction of the ICS can be seen to be *exclusive*. Indeed, this is arguably the main difference in the core operational principles between the WTO and the ICS. WTO members are by virtue of Article 23.1 of the DSU prevented from bringing an action alleging the violation of a WTO agreement before any judicial body outside the WTO dispute settlement system; and they are precluded from taking unauthorized unilateral actions.[107] The ICS, on the other

---

[103] Naboth van Den Broek and Danielle Morris (n. 49) 54.
[104] *US – Measures Affecting Imports of Woven Wool Shirts and Blouses from India*, Appellate Body Report (25 April 1997), WT/DS33/AB/R, para. 19.
[105] *EC – Measures Affecting Trade in Commercial Vessels*, WTO Panel Report (22 April 2005), WT/DS/301/R, para. 7.30.
[106] Article 8.25 CETA; Article 3.6(2) of the EUSIPA; Article 3.36(1) of the EUVIPA.
[107] *EC – Commercial Vessels* (n. 105) para. 7.193.

hand, presents a procedural alternative to domestic litigation;[108] a standing invitation, which investors are welcome, but not bound, to accept.[109] Be that as it may, an investor who wishes to initiate a claim before the ICS is prevented from seeking recourse to the domestic judiciary, and, in fact, the ICS requires the investor to withdraw any currently pending proceedings over the same alleged violation from the domestic judiciary.[110] Against this backdrop, the jurisdiction of the ICS is best described as of a conditional exclusive nature to the extent that its operation is conditioned on the exclusion of other judicial fora over the same dispute.

Furthermore, WTO panels and the AB serve to clarify the provisions of the WTO agreements 'in accordance with customary rules of interpretation of public international law'.[111] Similar to the approach taken by investment tribunals,[112] this has been interpreted by the WTO AB to be a reference to Articles 31 and 32 of the Vienna Convention on the Law of Treaties (VCLT), which has thus been endorsed as reflecting the position of customary international law.[113] The WTO AB has attached particular weight to contextual analysis, taking into account the object and purpose of WTO agreements.[114] Investment tribunals have also displayed a tendency to heavily rely on preambular language in pursuit of extensive investor-friendly interpretations of substantive standards of investment.[115]

---

[108] Kenneth J Vandevelde, *Bilateral Investment Treaties: History, Policy and Interpretation* (Oxford University Press, 2010) p. 457 et seq.

[109] Christoph Schreuer, 'Consent to Arbitration' in Peter Muchlinski, Federico Ortino and Christoph Schreuer (eds.), *The Oxford Handbook of International Investment Law* (Oxford University Press, 2008) pp. 831–66, especially 836–7.

[110] Article 3.22(1)(f) CETA; Article 3.7(1)(f) of the EUSIPA; Article 3.34(4)(a) of the EUVIPA; generally on the issue of parallel proceedings in investor-state proceedings, see Hanno Wehland, 'The Regulation of Parallel Proceedings in Investor-State Disputes' (2016) 31(3) *ICSID Review* 576–96; and Katia Yannaca-Small, 'Parallel Proceedings' in Peter Muchlinski, Federico Ortino and Christoph Schreuer (eds.), *The Oxford Handbook of International Investment Law* (Oxford University Press, 2008) pp. 1008–48.

[111] Article 3.2 DSU.

[112] E.g. *Mondev International Ltd. v. United States of America*, ICSID Case No. ARB(AF)/99/2, Final award of 11 October 2002, para. 43; *Aguas del Tunari SA v. Republic of Bolivia*, ICSID Case No. ARB/02/3, Decision on Respondent's Objections to Jurisdiction of 21 October 2005, para. 91.

[113] *US – Standards for Reformulated and Conventional Gasoline*, Appellate Body Report (29 April 1996) WT/DS2/AB/R, paras. 15–16; *Japan – Taxes on Alcoholic Beverages*, Appellate Body Report (4 October 1996) WT/DS8/AB/R, para. 104.

[114] Isabelle Van Damme, 'Treaty Interpretation by the WTO Appellate Body' (2010) 21(3) *European Journal of International Law* 605–48, 621 et seq., especially 635 and 639.

[115] Generally on the role of preambles in investment treaty arbitration, see Max H Hulme, 'Preambles in Treaty Interpretation' (2016) 164 *University of Pennsylvania Law Review* 1281–1343, 1312 et seq.

Whether or not the ICS will develop a common method of interpretation akin to the level of institutional integrity of the WTO dispute settlement system remains to be seen. Indeed, the applicable law provisions of all post-Lisbon EU IIAs make explicit reference to the VCLT.[116] However, as the ICS is treaty-centred, this is unlikely to prevent diverging approaches to treaty interpretation and applications of the provisions of the VCLT in similar factual circumstances under different agreements.[117] A coherent interpretative approach may well emerge, but is institutionally secured only within the context of every individual agreement. Consequently, the operational principles of the ICS converge with the WTO dispute settlement system, although its bilateral nature prevents the ICS from merging into a 'single and integrated' system with a common method of treaty interpretation.

3.3 WTO Panels and Tribunals of the EU ICS: Close Enough, or Miles Apart? Comparing the Adjudicator Selection Process and the Composition of Panels

The WTO dispute settlement system provides for a two-tier system with much significance accorded to the appellate mechanism. Indeed, the ICS has taken a similar approach. However, while the AB exhibits the characteristics of a permanent international tribunal, WTO panels are established on an ad hoc basis.[118] This goes against the ambition of the ICS, which establishes both the First Instance Tribunal and the Appellate Tribunal as permanent institutions with appointed members that are subject to strict eligibility criteria. Whereas ICS Tribunal members are prevented from being affiliated with any government, and are otherwise

---

[116] Article 8.31(1) CETA; Article 3.13(2) of the EUSIPA; Article 3.42(3) of the EUVIPA.

[117] These divergences also exist in investment treaty arbitration. In *Plama Consortium Ltd v. Bulgaria* (ICSID Case No. ARB/03/24, Decision on Jurisdiction of 8 February 2008) the tribunal rejected the claimant's argument, which emphasized the relevance of the object and purpose of the Bulgaria-Cyprus BIT for interpreting the most-favoured nation treatment so as to extend to consent to arbitration provided in another agreement. In *Aguas del Tunari SA v. Republic of Bolivia* (ICSID Case No. ARB/02/3, Decision on Respondent's Objections to Jurisdiction of 21 October 2005). On the other hand, the tribunal came to the conclusion, in interpreting the definition of 'corporate nationality', that a literal interpretation of the term 'control' would be incompatible with the object and purpose of the Netherlands-Bolivia BIT. Note, however, that even in rejecting the relevance of object and purpose of the BIT for the interpretation of the MFN clause in that agreement, the tribunal did not adhere to textual interpretation as such, but rather justified its conclusion by reference to the parties' intentions (para. 199).

[118] Article 8.5 DSU.

severely restricted in their professional activities, the selection of WTO panellists is governed only by general conflict-of-interest and impartiality provisions.[119] Panellists are often high-level government officials,[120] a practice that is explicitly encouraged in the DSU.[121] Conversely, ICS Tribunal members must be eligible for the appointment to judicial office in their respective countries. In light of the above, it is clear that the selection criteria of the ICS Tribunal caters to a different professional community than panellists in the WTO dispute settlement system.

WTO members exert a direct influence over the composition of panels.[122] Although panellists are nominated upon the proposal of the WTO Secretariat, this is subject to agreement by the disputing parties.[123] The WTO Secretariat's list of panellists is in this respect merely indicative – an instrument to facilitate rather than control the selection processes.[124] The disputing parties can only oppose the proposed nominees for 'compelling reasons'.[125] In the absence of an agreement with the disputing parties, the Director-General of the WTO will, in consultation with the Dispute Settlement Board (DSB) and the disputing parties, determine the composition of the panel. Consequently, the WTO members that are parties to the dispute are involved at every stage of the selection process. Section 2.2 demonstrated that the ICS removes the direct influence of the disputing parties over the composition of Tribunal divisions.[126] Instead, members are selected on the basis of rotation, randomly and in an unpredictable manner, a standard also adopted by the AB[127] but not applied to WTO panels.[128]

---

[119] Article 8.9 DSU.
[120] Naboth van Den Broek and Danielle Morris (n. 49) 66.
[121] Article 8.8 DSU; for the qualification of panellists see Article 8.1: 'Panels shall be composed of well-qualified governmental and/or non-governmental individuals, including persons who have served on or presented a case to a panel, served as a representative of a Member or of a contracting party to GATT 1947 or as a representative to the Council or Committee of any covered agreement or its predecessor agreement, or in the Secretariat, taught or published on international trade law or policy, or served as a senior trade policy official of a Member.'
[122] Naboth van Den Broek and Danielle Morris (n. 49).
[123] Article 8.6 DSU.
[124] Article 8.4 DSU.
[125] Article 8.6 DSU.
[126] This is notwithstanding the indirect influence that contracting states exert over the composition of ICS Tribunal and Appeal Tribunal divisions through the nomination of members to the ICS; see *supra* Section 2.2.
[127] Article 8.27(7) CETA; Article 3.9(8) of the EUSIPA; Article 3.38(7) of the EUVIPA.
[128] Rule 6.2 Working Procedure for Appellate Review, adopted on 16 August 2010, WT/AB/WP/6.

In the WTO context, states pursue both defensive and offensive interests because, over the course of time, they are likely to be involved in disputes as both complainant and respondent and can therefore be expected to have a systemic interest in the development and predictability of the multilateral trading system more generally.[129] This is not the case for the ICS, where states are merely involved as respondents to disputes. Although it cannot be assumed outright that states would pursue only defensive interests in their selection of members to the ICS[130] – clearly home states have an offensive interest in protecting their investors abroad – there is obviously a different dynamic at play compared to the WTO. Influence over the composition of WTO panels is exercised by both disputing parties, whereas the ICS establishes a de facto imbalance in favour of the respondent state that maintains indirect influence over the composition of tribunal divisions while at the same time shutting the investor out of the selection process. In addition, the DSU warrants the impartiality of the panel by means of precluding nationals of either of the disputing parties from acting as panellists.[131] This is not the case for the ICS where the equal representation of the national affiliation of the disputing parties – subject to the above-mentioned 'random and unpredictable' criterion – constitutes a fundamental institutional characteristic. WTO panels, thus, operate under a fundamentally different paradigm.

3.4 Designing an Appeals Mechanism: The Principle Element of Institutional Convergence between the EU ICS and the WTO Dispute Settlement System?

Discrepancies in institutional design between the WTO dispute settlement system and the ICS are least pronounced on the appellate level. Both the AB and the ICS Appeal Tribunal aspire to a permanent status and operate in a similar manner. Members of the AB are appointed for a term of four years, renewable once, by the DSB. The indirect influence

---

[129] Donald McRae, 'The WTO Appellate Body: A Model for an ICSID Appeals Facility?' (2010) 1(2) *Journal of International Dispute Settlement* 371–87, 378.
[130] For a discussion of the risk that the ICS judge-selection process may be captured by state interests, see Stephen S Kho et al., 'The EU TTIP Investment Court Proposal and the WTO Dispute Settlement System: Comparing Apples and Oranges?' (2017) 32(2) *ICSID Review* 326–45, 340 and 343.
[131] Article 8.3 DSU.

and political process[132] underlying the selection of AB members are therefore similar to the role of trade committees in CETA and the EU-Vietnam IPA. The strict eligibility criteria and ethical standards of the ICS also resemble those imposed on AB members. Accordingly, members of the AB may not accept any employment or pursue any professional activity during their term of office that is inconsistent with their duties and responsibilities.[133] The AB hears disputes in a division of three with members being assigned to disputes on the basis of rotation in accordance with 'the principles of random selection, unpredictability and opportunity for all Members to serve regardless of their national origin'.[134] It is considered that the principle of unpredictability in this context assures that the disputing parties cannot exercise any influence over the composition of the division in a concrete case and, thus, safeguards the operational impartiality and procedural legitimacy of the AB.[135]

It was already touched upon in Section 3.3 that this appointment mechanism has clearly inspired the selection process of ICS members to individual tribunal divisions. Notably, the ICS versions differ with respect to the Appeal Tribunal. The EU-Singapore IPA and EU-Vietnam IPA reflect the same selection process on both the level of first instance as well as the appeal. Thus, both of them endorse the requirement that members of Appeal Tribunal divisions are to be selected randomly and unpredictably, giving all members an equal opportunity to serve – subject only to the principle of equal representation of national affiliation. Conversely, CETA merely requires a composition of 'three randomly appointed Members' and leaves matters of procedure to be adopted by the CETA Joint Committee at a later stage.[136] It is nonetheless clear that unlike the WTO AB, which disregards the nationality of its members, the ICS is firmly built on the equal representation of the nationality of the disputing parties.

---

[132] The political dimension is well illustrated by the current crisis of the AB that was triggered by the USA blocking the reappointment of South Korean Appellate Body member Seung Wha Chang; see Naboth van Den Broek and Danielle Morris (n. 49) 68–9.

[133] Rules 2.2 and 2.3 Working Procedure for Appellate Review, para. II(1) Rules of Conduct.

[134] Rule 6.2 Working Procedure for Appellate Review.

[135] Robert W Schwieder, 'TTIP and the Investment Court System: A New (and Improved?) Paradigm for Investor-State Adjudication' (2016) 55(1) *Columbia Journal of Transnational Law* 202.

[136] Articles 8.27(5) and (7) CETA.

Furthermore, being a member of the ICS Appeal Tribunal is not envisaged as a full-time position,[137] nor was this initially the case for AB members.[138] The initial ICS negotiating proposal for the TTIP clearly followed the model of the AB with respect to the retainer fee for members of the ICS Appeal Tribunal.[139] Neither CETA, nor the agreements with Singapore or Vietnam, make explicit stipulations in this respect. Although the text is clear that a retainer fee is to be paid, the amount is to be determined by the respective trade committee later. As far as the daily fee is concerned, however, the ICS refers to the ICSID fee schedule for Tribunal Members,[140] and leaves the remuneration paid to members of the Appellate Tribunal to be determined by the respective trade committee.[141]

In order to assure the effective operation of the AB, Article 17.7 of the DSU stipulates that it shall be provided with appropriate administrative and legal support. In practice, the AB is supported by its own secretariat, whose role is invaluable to the AB members[142] and which contributes in this respect to the objective of the WTO dispute settlement system, i.e. the uniform, coherent and predictable interpretation and application of the WTO treaties.[143] The ICS, on the other hand, leans heavily on the

---

[137] Members of the Tribunal shall ensure their availability at all times and are for that purpose paid a retainer fee (Article 8.27(11) CETA; Articles 3.9(12) and 3.10(11) of the EUSIPA; Articles 3.38(14) and 3.39(14) of the EUVIPA). Although CETA is silent with respect to the members of the Appellate Tribunal, the EU-Vietnam ICS proposal suggests that the same structure will be applied also to the Appellate Tribunal. The respective trade committees have the power to transform fee structure into a regular salary (Article 8.27(15) CETA; Articles 3.9(15) and 3.10(13) of the EUSIPA; Articles 3.38(17) and 3.39(17) of the EUVIPA).

[138] Claus-Dieter Ehlermann, 'Six Years on the Bench of the "World Trade Court": Some Personal Experiences as Member of the Appellate Body of the World Trade Organization' (2002) 36(4) *Journal of World Trade* 605–39, 614.

[139] Indeed, an earlier version of the TTIP ICS proposal explicitly referred to a retainer fee equivalent to that paid to AB members (ibid. at 609). CETA and the IPAs with Singapore and Vietnam are less explicit and leave this question to be determined by their respective bilateral committees (Articles 8.27(11) and 8.28(7)(d) CETA; Articles 3.9(12) and 3.10(11) of the EUSIPA; Articles 3.38(14) and 3.39(14) of the EUVIPA).

[140] Article 8.27(15) CETA; Article 3.9(14) of the EUSIPA; Article 3.38(16) of the EUVIPA.

[141] Article 8.28(7)(d) CETA; Article 3.10(11) of the EUSIPA; Article 3.39(14) of the EUVIPA.

[142] Catharine Titi (n. 49) 10.

[143] Although the Appellate Body has outgrown initial expectations; see Claus-Dieter Ehlermann (n. 138) 613; note also that Rule 4 of the Rules of Procedure provides for all Appellate Body members to participate in the deliberations to avoid diverging interpretations. For a discussion of the significance of collegiality for the operation of the WTO AB, see Donald McRae (n. 129) 373.

administrative support of the ICSID Secretariat.[144] In the context of a bilateral ICS the administrative outsourcing is certainly unsurprising, as the establishment of a permanent secretariat would appear to be the least cost-effective solution. A multilateral ICS, on the other hand, would benefit from the support of a standing secretariat that is deeply involved in the dispute settlement processes.[145] Reliance on the administrative and legal support of the ICSID Secretariat ultimately impedes the establishment of an institutional memory that is instrumental in attaining coherence and predictability.[146] This illustrates the divergence between the systemic objectives of the WTO dispute settlement system, and the adjudicative function of the ICS.

In light of the above, it appears that the establishment of an appeals mechanism is likely leading to a greater level of coherence in the bilateral context. That is to say that the CETA ICS Appellate Tribunal contributes to the consistent application of CETA investment provisions just as much as the Appellate Tribunal in the EU-Singapore or EU-Vietnam formation improves consistency in the application of their respective agreements.[147] On the multilateral level, on the other hand, the establishment of an appeals mechanism would not logically lead to more coherence and consistency. Indeed, a multilateral ICS would have to adjudicate disputes in relation to a multitude of investment agreements, without strong regime-internal reference points.[148] Despite some important commonalities across the large network of bilateral investment agreements,[149] it is unlikely that under these conditions an appeals mechanism would improve coherence and predictability beyond the level achieved through cross-fertilization of interpretative approaches applied by investment tribunals today.[150]

---

[144] Article. 8.27(16) CETA, leaving the administrative support for the Appellate Tribunals to be decided by the CETA Joint Committee Article 8.28(7)(a) CETA; Articles 3.9(16) and 3.10(14) of the EUSIPA; Articles 3.38(18) and 3.39(18) of the EUVIPA.

[145] Claus-Dieter Ehlermann (n. 138) 612–13.

[146] Naboth van Den Broek and Danielle Morris (n. 49) 57; note that the appointment of ICS members, which prevents the entire roster from being replaced at once, demonstrates an intention to build an institutional memory; see Elsa Sardinha (n. 82) 322.

[147] Donald McRae (n. 129) 387.

[148] Stephen S Kho et al. (n. 130) 344, 383.

[149] Stephan W Schill, *The Multilateralization of Investment Law* (Cambridge University Press, 2009).

[150] Ibid. at 357 et seq.; the problem that the fragmentation of the investment treaty regime poses for the role of an appellate mechanism is also recognized by McRae; see Donald McRae (n. 129).

The jurisdiction of the WTO AB is limited to issues of law and legal interpretations developed by the panel.[151] The question over what amounts to an issue of law is more controversial than it would appear, particularly where the case requires an appreciation of domestic law. Indeed, the AB observed that domestic law becomes relevant either as evidence of state practice and, thus, a matter of fact, or as evidence of compliance with WTO obligations,[152] which requires an examination of the domestic law.[153] This 'legal characterization' of facts falls within the jurisdiction of the AB as an issue of law, within the meaning of Article 17.6 DSU.[154] The consideration of domestic law by the AB as a matter of law is viewed critically, and has been singled out as being in urgent need of reform.[155] In a recent concept paper on WTO reform, the European Commission addressed this point, proposing a clarification of Article 17.6 of the DSU in order to declare domestic law explicitly a matter of fact.[156] Notable in this respect is that the ICS also unequivocally declares domestic law a matter of fact.[157] The design of the ICS appeal mechanism is, thus, not only inspired by the WTO AB but draws on experiences within the WTO dispute settlement context, demonstrating a positive trend towards convergence of the two systems.

Domestic law may also come before the AB in accordance with its Article 11 DSU jurisdiction, i.e. by means of determining whether the

---

[151] Article 17.6 DSU.
[152] *India – Patent Protection for Pharmaceutical and Agricultural Chemical Products*, Appellate Body Report (17 December 1997) WT/DS50/AB/R, para. 65.
[153] Ibid., para. 66; *United States – Anti-Dumping Measures on Certain Hot-Rolled Steel Products from Japan*, Appellate Body Report (23 August 2001) WT/DS184/AB/R, para. 200.
[154] *United States – Section 211 Omnibus Appropriations Act of 1998*, Appellate Body Report (2 January 2002) WT/DS176/AB/R, para. 105; *China – Measures Affecting Imports of Automobile Parts*, Appellate Body Report (15 December 2008) WT/DS339/AB/R, WT/DS340/AB/R and WT/DS342/AB/R, para. 225.
[155] Jan Bohanes and Nicolas Lockhart, 'Standard of Review in WTO Law' in Daniel Bethlehem et al. (eds.), *The Oxford Handbook of International Trade Law* (Oxford University Press, 2009) pp. 378–436, 421. The USTR recently remarked that '[T]he Appellate Body consistently asserts that it can review the meaning of a Member's domestic measure as a matter of law rather than acknowledging that it is a matter of fact and thus not a subject for Appellate Body review'; see US Trade Representative, *2018 Trade Policy Agenda and 2017 Annual Report of the President of the United States on the Trade Agreements Program*, 28.
[156] European Commission, 'Concept Paper on WTO modernisation' 18 September 2018, part iv of the reform proposals regarding the WTO Appellate Body.
[157] Article 8.31(2) CETA; Footnote 7 to Article 3.13(2) of the EUSIPA; Articles 3.42(2) and (3) of the EUVIPA.

WTO panel employed the requisite standard of carrying out an objective factual assessment.[158] The standard of review is in this respect very high. The AB in *EC-Hormones* clarified that a failure to provide an objective assessment implies more than 'simply an error of judgment in the appreciation of evidence but rather an egregious error that calls into question the good faith of the panel.'[159] Although the ground for review resembles Article 11 DSU, it is unclear whether the Appeal Tribunal will apply the 'manifest' standard as a similarly high threshold for the review of facts.[160] While the language of the ICS is clear to prevent de novo reviews, the Appeal Tribunal could apply the 'manifest' standard to the correctness of appreciation of facts, which presents a significantly more extensive jurisdiction over factual review as compared to the WTO AB.[161]

Lastly, the WTO AB has the power to uphold, modify or reverse the legal findings and conclusion of the panel.[162] The AB has also observed that it has the power to complete the WTO panel's analysis[163] on issues that were raised in the complaint but have not been decided by the panel,[164] as long as the panel report provides sufficient evidentiary information.[165] Unlike the WTO dispute settlement system, the permanent nature of the ICS allows the Appeal Tribunal to refer matters back to the Tribunal. This is particularly pronounced in the EU-Singapore ICS formation where in principle all final awards are issued by the Tribunal, including awards revised in accordance with the Appeal Tribunal's findings.[166] The EU-Vietnam ICS formation, on the other hand, is more akin to the WTO dispute settlement system. Accordingly, the EU-Vietnam Appeal Tribunal will only refer the matter back to the Tribunal where the established facts do not allow the Appeal Tribunal to complete

---

[158] Naboth van Den Broek and Danielle Morris (n. 49) 68.
[159] *European Communities – EC Measures Concerning Meat and Meat Products (Hormones)*, Appellate Body Report (16 January 1998) WT/DS26/AB/R and WT/DS48/AB/R para. 133.
[160] Naboth van Den Broek and Danielle Morris (n. 49) 70.
[161] Similar problems arise when compared with the high threshold over factual review by the ICSID annulment committee; see Elsa Sardinha (n. 82) 328–9.
[162] Article 17.13 DSU.
[163] *Hormones* (n. 159) para. 222; *Canada – Certain Measures Concerning Periodicals*, Appellate Body Report (30 June 1997) WT/DS31/AB/R, para. 469.
[164] *Australia – Measures Affecting Importation of Salmon*, Appellate Body Report (20 October 1998) WT/DS18/AB/R, paras. 117–18.
[165] For an example of circumstances where the AB will and will not complete the legal analysis, see *US – Section 211 Appropriations Act* para. 343.
[166] Article 3.19(3) of the EUSIPA.

the analysis.[167] CETA provides no details on the applicable procedure for referral.

4 Conclusions

The institutional design of the ICS is undeniably inspired by the WTO dispute settlement system, and in particular by structural features of the WTO AB. Four levels of convergence between the WTO dispute settlement system and the ICS can be identified. Firstly, 'structural convergence' occurs where ICS features reflect the DSU. This is visible in the appointment of members, which in the context of the WTO AB is a highly politicized matter. The appointment of ICS members is likewise subject to political compromise, exercised through the relevant trade committees. Another example can be found in the high level of ethical and professional standards for all ICS members that are similar to those imposed on WTO AB members. Additionally, the DSU adopts a similar procedure for the selection of AB members to panels hearing individual disputes in order to guarantee a random selection and equal opportunities for all AB members. Unlike the WTO dispute settlement system, the ICS establishes two permanent tribunals. It is not surprising, therefore, that structural inspirations are drawn from the WTO AB, rather than the organization of WTO panels. Secondly, 'judicial practice convergence' occurs where the ICS consolidates WTO AB praxis. A clear example of this type of convergence is the explicit power of the EU-Vietnam Appeal Tribunal's power to complete the legal analysis. A third level of convergence, 'prospective convergence', is evident where the design of the ICS reflects WTO reform initiatives, or more broadly, notions of how the WTO AB ought to function. This is illustrated by the attempt to limit the scope of review over factual issues, which is a contentious issue in AB praxis and where the ICS reflects the EU's concept paper on WTO reforms. The fourth level of potential convergence is exemplified by the adoption of the 'manifest' standard, which may be developed as restrictively as it is applied by the WTO AB, but which also allows the Appeal Tribunal to ascertain broader powers over the review of facts or, alternatively, draw on ICSID awards rather than WTO AB reports.

There are, however, also three levels of divergence that can be identified. First, an 'objectives divergence' is visible if the systemic objectives of

---

[167] Article 3.54(4) of the EUVIPA.

the WTO dispute settlement system are compared to the adjudicative functions of the ICS. Unlike the WTO dispute settlement system, the ICS is not tailored to achieve compliance but merely to indemnify private parties for losses caused by the host state's conduct. Damages are in this respect a calculable element of a cost-benefit assessment for non-compliance with investment standards, whereas no such option is provided for within the WTO. A second level may be termed 'political impact divergence'. Whereas the influence of WTO members on the AB is limited to the appointment of AB members (albeit a very important function as exemplified by the recent opposition of the United States to the appointment of new WTO AB members), the trade committees under the EU IIAs have significant influence over many aspects of the Appeal Tribunal, including composition, appellate procedure and the effect of Appellate Tribunal findings. This is particularly pronounced in CETA, which lacks details on the Appeal Tribunal and instead furnishes the CETA Joint Committee with extensive powers to decide on these issues later. This is in line with the generally observed backlash to investor-state arbitration but is hardly reminiscent of the WTO dispute settlement system. Another example of 'political impact divergence' is the institutionally embedded representation of the Contracting State's nationality on ICS divisions, which is irreconcilable with the WTO dispute settlement system. Third, 'procedural divergence' occurs in as far as the procedural pedigree of the ICS is based on existing arbitration rules. The ICS does not, therefore, completely give up traditional investor-state arbitration but incorporates procedural design features by reference to ICSID, the ICSID Additional Facility Rules and UNCITRAL arbitration rules, and inherits procedural limitations and idiosyncrasies that may inhibit the ICS from growing into a single and unified system à la WTO.

The bilateral ICS as well as multilateral ISDS reform efforts stand much to gain from institutional comparisons with established adjudicative institutions. The above analysis demonstrated that although the ICS is inspired by the WTO AB it is no copy-paste exercise. This is not a weakness, and divergence is not in this respect fraught with a normative judgment of failure to create a WTO AB-like judicial structure for the settlement of investor-state disputes. Indeed, it is sometimes argued that the two systems are complementary, with the WTO dispute settlement system ensuring compliance and harnessing overall benefits for economies at large, whereas ISDS offers relief to private investors that have suffered losses at the hands of states.[168] This functional divergence needs to be imprinted in the institutional DNA of the ICS tribunals. Comparison of these two systems, however, provides some insight into what involved actors perceive to be desirable features and where convergence can be achieved through future reform.

[168] Naboth van Den Broek and Danielle Morris (n. 49).

4

Entry Rights and Investments in Services: Adjudicatory Convergence between Regimes?

MURILO LUBAMBO

> *Will your grace command me any service to the world's end? I will go on the slightest errand now to the Antipodes that you can devise to send me on; I will fetch you a tooth-picker now from the furthest inch of Asia, bring you the length of Prester John's foot, fetch you a hair off the great Cham's beard, do you any embassage to the Pigmies . . . .*
>
> Much Ado About Nothing *II.1*

1 Introduction

Not long ago, the Chinese government imposed certain requirements that affected foreign companies willing to invest in the provision of electronic payment services in China. It granted certain privileges to domestic companies related to the issuing and marketing of credit cards and the operation of terminal equipment in specific transactions. The measures affected renminbi[1] payment card transactions with bank cards issued or used in China, changing the conditions of competition to the detriment of foreign providers, especially American companies. As a result, not only did the foreign companies have less access to the market but they also had their presence severely limited in certain operations in Hong Kong and Macao. On the one hand, there was the right of the Chinese government to control investments and set conditions for foreign investors; on the other, there was the interest of Chinese consumers to have access to a broader supply of services and innovative facilities.

In another part of the globe, the United States used to ban Mexican companies that operated trucking services from establishing operations in the United States. Mexican companies were even prohibited from

---

[1] The official currency of the People's Republic of China, also known as CNY (Chinese yuan) and yuan.

owning or investing in US companies providing those services. Canadian companies, on the other hand, were not subject to those restrictions. The argument was that safety and environmental requirements were not sufficiently high for Mexican businesses. Two decades later, Mexican-owned trucking companies can now apply to operate international long-haul trucking services and establish operations in the United States. Some attribute the prior ban and the delay to the heavy lobbying of US trucking associations.

Not far away, Canadian investors proposed the construction of a pipeline to transport gas from Canada to the southern US states. Several other pipelines ran throughout the United States, some of them already operated by the Canadian investors. The cross-border aspect of the project required authorization by the US president. After seven years of deliberations and public acrimony, the US government decided to deny the investment, justifying its denial by asserting its need to be coherent with its environmental policies. Later, the new US administration invited the company to resubmit the application and swiftly gave the green light to the project.

These three situations gave rise to cases that were decided in different fora. The first one (Chinese measures concerning renminbi payments) was brought to the World Trade Organization (WTO) dispute settlement mechanism. It resulted in a report adopted by the Dispute Settlement Body (DSB).[2] The other two situations were litigated under the North American Free Trade Agreement – NAFTA.[3] Mexico brought a state-state arbitration claim against the United States that was decided in 2001, under NAFTA Chapter 20.[4] A Canadian investor, TransCanada, brought an investor-state arbitration case against the United States (discontinued in January 2017) claiming damages for the denial of the Keystone Pipeline XL, under NAFTA Chapter 11.[5] Whereas the exact outcome of the cases is not the object of this chapter, the point here is to show the

---

[2] WTO, 'China: Certain Measures Affecting Electronic Payment Services – Report of the Panel' (31 August 2012) WT/DS413/R.
[3] North American Free Trade Agreement (adopted 17 December 1992) 32 ILM 289, 605 (1993) (NAFTA). NAFTA is to be replaced by the United States-Mexico-Canada Agreement (signed 30 November 2018, pending ratification) (USMCA).
[4] *In re Cross-Border Trucking Services (Mexico v. United States)*, Case No. USA-MEX-98-2008-01 North America Free Trade Agreement Chapter 20 Arb Trib Panel Decision, Final Report, 2 (6 February 2001), available at www.nafta-sec-alena.org/DesktopModules/NAFTA_DecisionReport/pdf.ashx?docID=18355& lang=1.
[5] *TransCanada Corporation & TransCanada PipeLines Limited v. United States of America* – Request for Arbitration (24 June 2016) ICSID Case no. ARB/16/21.

connections of these apparently unrelated situations. Despite being raised in different international courts and arbitral tribunals, all the cases share a common aspect: they relate to an investor's entry into a particular state.

Hence, in order to evaluate whether and how states can enforce the rights and obligations associated with the entry of investments, this chapter will tackle the issue through the lenses of treaty interpretation and application. It will be structured as follows. First, it will analyse the role of treaty-based investor-state arbitration (ISA). Next, it will describe and assess state-state investment arbitration as a possible alternative to investor-state arbitration. It will then evaluate the WTO mechanism and the cases brought in that forum. Finally, it will assess if this framework shows signs of adjudicatory convergence between the regimes. For the purposes of this analysis, convergence means 'a predicted *increase in the legal and systemic characteristics shared by the two regimes* and a predicted *reduction in non-shared characteristics*.'[6] Therefore, the idea of adjudicatory convergence will refer to a progressive move to similar enforcement mechanisms with the same systemic characteristics.

2   Entry Rights and Investor-State Arbitration: Possibilities and Uses

2.1   Context

The analysis of adjudicatory convergence requires the presentation of the general characteristics of the different mechanisms. To set the context, it is useful to introduce briefly the international substantive rules on the issue.

Entry rights are granted by international treaties regulating access for investments; in the absence of treaties, there is wide sovereign control over whether and how investments can be made in a country. In other words, international treaties reduce the host state's policy space regarding entry in exchange for more investments in the state.[7] This takes place

---

[6] Jurgen Kurtz, *The WTO and International Investment Law: Converging Systems* (Cambridge University Press, 2016) p. 24 (emphasis added).

[7] For a political economy take on why entry rights have been initially excluded from treaties, see the argument of 'nationalism behind the liberal facade' in Kenneth J. Vandevelde, 'The Political Economy of a Bilateral Investment Treaty' (1998) 92 *American Journal of International Law* 621, 635.

whenever international investment agreements (IIAs)[8] – including bilateral investment treaties (BITs) and regional economic agreements with investment provisions (see Chapter 2) – cover the process of admission of investments or provide for national or most-favoured-nation treatment in the establishment phase.[9] They confer what are called 'entry rights' i.e., the permission for unrestricted entry or entry under specific conditions set out in international commitments.[10] IIAs, including some under negotiation, increasingly encompass these situations.[11]

Moreover, the WTO also regulates the issue. While other agreements touch on investments in one way or another – for example, TRIMS[12] and ASCM[13] in relation to local content requirements and TRIPS[14] in relation to intellectual property – it is in the General Agreement on Trade in Services (GATS)[15] that a major part of this regulation is found.[16] This is

---

[8] Unless otherwise noted, all IIAs and model BITs, and all investment decisions, mentioned here are available at the UNCTAD database and Italaw, respectively, http://investmentpolicyhub.unctad.org/IIA and www.italaw.com, both accessed 18 March 2019.

[9] Martín Molinuevo, *Protecting Investment in Services: Investor-State Arbitration versus WTO Dispute Settlement* (Kluwer Law International, 2012) p. 87; Ignacio Gómez-Palacio and Peter Muchlinski, 'Admission and Establishment' in Federico Ortino, Peter Muchlinski and Christoph H Schreuer (eds.), *The Oxford Handbook of International Investment Law* (Oxford University Press, 2008) pp. 229-30; Thomas Pollan, *Legal Framework for the Admission of FDI* (Eleven International Pub, 2006) p. 54.

[10] Murilo Lubambo, 'How Does International Economic Law Regulate the Right of Entry of Investments in Services?' (Social Science Research Network 2016) SSRN Scholarly Paper ID 2801925 15; 20, http://papers.ssrn.com/abstract=2801925, accessed 13 September 2016.

[11] To illustrate, there are more than 2,300 BITs in force, of which more than 1,200 involve members of the European Union, according to the UNCTAD database at http://investmentpolicyhub.unctad.org/IIA . The new EU model, which is likely to contain investment liberalization commitments, will lead to the re-negotiation of those BITs, resulting in wider coverage of the world market.

[12] Agreement on Trade-Related Investment Measures (15 April 1994) Marrakesh Agreement Establishing the World Trade Organization Annex 1A 1868 UNTS 186.

[13] Agreement on Subsidies and Countervailing Measures (15 April 1994) Marrakesh Agreement Establishing the World Trade Organization Annex 1A 1869 UNTS 14.

[14] Agreement on Trade-Related Aspects of Intellectual Property Rights (15 April 1994) Marrakesh Agreement Establishing the World Trade Organization Annex 1C 1869 UNTS 299.

[15] General Agreement on Trade in Services (15 April 1994) Marrakesh Agreement Establishing the World Trade Organization Annex 1B 1869 UNTS 183 [hereinafter GATS].

[16] Bart De Meester and Dominic Coppens, 'Mode 3 of the GATS: A Model for Disciplining Measures Affecting Investment Flows?' in Zdenek Drabek and Petros Mavroidis (eds.), *Regulation of Foreign Investment*, vol 21 (World Scientific, 2013) p. 99; Martín Molinuevo, 'Foreign Investment in Services and the DSU' in Marion Panizzon,

because the GATS regulates the provision of services by the constitution of commercial presence (mode 3), which is equivalent to one form of investment.[17]

Therefore, acts that discriminate between foreign investors are not allowed by the GATS, whenever the international investment takes place in the service sector. In addition, discrimination in favour of national investors is prohibited or restrained if the countries have undertaken specific commitments. Restrictions that affect the so-called market access (GATS Article XVI) for investments are evaluated under an absolute standard, that is, they dispense with a discrimination analysis.[18] There are nonetheless general and security exceptions (respectively, GATS Article XIV and XIV *bis*) aimed at safeguarding the legitimate regulation of entry.[19]

Finally, there is perhaps an indication of some convergence of both the WTO law and investment law regimes in the common aim of the anti-discrimination standard represented by national treatment: to guarantee a level of equality and ensure the same competitive opportunities.[20] This is more evident when it comes to granting entry rights. In fact, entry rights are an aspect of investment liberalization, also a key component of the GATS, that are given prominence in the new treaties.[21] In fact, some recent BITs and investment chapters in trade treaties are progressively incorporating entry rights.[22] Moreover, investment chapters in trade

---

Nicole Pohl and Pierre Sauvé (eds.), *GATS and the Regulation of International Trade in Services* (Cambridge University Press, 2008) p. 319; Rudolf Adlung, 'International Rules Governing Foreign Direct Investment in Services: Investment Treaties versus the GATS' (2016) 17 *Journal of World Investment & Trade* 47.

[17] GATS art. 1 (2) c and XXVIII (d).
[18] Molinuevo (n 9) 84; Martín Molinuevo and Panagiotis Delimatsis, 'Article XVI' in Rüdiger Wolfrum, Peter-Tobias Stoll and Clemens Feinäugle (eds.), *WTO-Trade in Services* (Martinus Nijhoff Publishers, 2008) p. 377.
[19] Jorge A Huerta-Goldman, 'Cross-Cutting Observations on National Treatment' in Jorge A Huerta-Goldman, Antoine Romanetti and Franz X Stirnimann (eds.), *WTO Litigation, Investment Arbitration and Commercial Arbitration* (Kluwer Law International, 2013) pp. 265-71.
[20] Kurtz (n 6) 84-5.
[21] Sergio Puig, 'The Merging of International Trade and Investment Law' (2015) 33 *Berkeley Journal of International Law* 1, 12; see also Pierre Sauvé, 'Chapter 14 – Investment Liberalization in GATS' in Pierre Sauvé (ed.), *Trade Rules Behind Borders: Essays on Services, Investment and the New Trade Agenda* (Cameron May, 2003) pp. 335-65.
[22] Lubambo (n 10) 30-4; Filippo Fontanelli and Giuseppe Bianco, 'Converging towards NAFTA: An Analysis of FTA Investment Chapters in the European Union and the United States' (2014) 50 *Stanford Journal of International Law* 211.

treaties (for instance, the new European Union agreements, as will be seen) include GATS-type language regarding market access.[23]

When it comes to enforcement, it is known that the international adjudication of disputes, that is, the determination of outcomes of cases by a third party – for example, an arbitral tribunal or an international court – is a way to interpret legal norms and solve conflicts in the international arena.[24] As enforcement through adjudication depends on the existence of jurisdiction given to a specific entity, the different paths to jurisdiction regarding entry rights are explored in the following sections.

2.2 Investor-State Treaty Arbitration

2.2.1 Jurisdictional Clauses

Treaty-based investor-state arbitration (ISA) is triggered with the acceptance by the investor of the consent expressed by the host state in investment treaties. This consent gives an investor the right to bring a claim directly against the host state. The investor-state jurisdictional clause is the clause that defines the scope and extent of this right. The clause also sets out the mechanisms of dispute settlement that will be used and defines general rules on the composition and functioning of the arbitral tribunal.

To find out whether the ISA jurisdictional clause covers issues related to entry rights, it is necessary to check whether it covers the substantive clauses in IIAs that generally confer these rights. As emphasized above, IIAs grant and expand entry rights through several means. They may use the most-favoured-nation obligation, the obligation of national treatment related to establishment or provisions of market access in investment and trade treaties. Thus, if the jurisdictional clause is broad and general or if it explicitly mentions, or refers to, any of these provisions, a prospective investor could foresee the possibility of bringing a claim for a treaty violation.

---

[23] Panagiotis Delimatsis, 'The Evolution of the EU External Trade Policy in Services – CETA, TTIP, and TiSA after Brexit' (2017) 20 *Journal of International Economic Law* 583, 596; for a classic analysis in the context of the European Union, see Piet Eeckhout, 'Constitutional Concepts for Free Trade in Services' in Joanne Scott and Gráinne De Búrca (eds.), *The EU and the WTO: Legal and Constitutional Aspects* (Hart, 2001) p. 216.

[24] Yuval Shany, *Questions of Jurisdiction and Admissibility before International Courts* (Cambridge University Press, 2016) p. 7.

However, it is possible that the jurisdictional clause contains exceptions. More specifically, even though entry rights are protected by the treaty, ISA will not be available in situations where there are substantive or procedural carve-outs. For example, no matter how widely national treatment is covered, the clause may exclude ISA when the dispute relates to establishment. In fact, in the context of the recent critiques against ISA, this is an aspect of the movement towards a more careful drafting of those provisions in order to limit access to the mechanism.[25]

Some recent treaty practice reflects the aforementioned changes. For example, in the Comprehensive Trade and Economic Agreement (CETA) – currently under ratification – there is a general exception that excludes any dispute related to establishment. To illustrate, Article 8.18 of the CETA provides:

> 1. Without prejudice to the rights and obligations of the Parties under Chapter Twenty- Nine (Dispute Settlement), an investor of a Party may submit to the Tribunal constituted under this Section a claim that the other Party has breached an obligation under:
>
> (a) *Section C, with respect to the expansion, conduct, operation, management, maintenance, use, enjoyment and sale or disposal of its covered investment; or*
> (b) Section D:
>
> where the investor claims to have suffered loss or damage as a result of the alleged breach. (emphasis added)

Hence, by implication, CETA excludes entry rights from the jurisdiction of ISA. This is evident by the omission of the word 'establishment' and 'acquisition' in CETA Article 8.18(1)(a). The provisions on market access (CETA Article 8.4) and performance requirements (CETA Article 8.5) are also excluded, since they are part of Section B of the treaty, which is not mentioned. The EU-Singapore Agreement[26] does not provide for investment arbitration in relation to establishment or expansion, which is mentioned in a separate part of the agreement.[27] In the same way, the

---

[25] UNCTAD, 'World Investment Report' (United Nations 2016) UNCTAD/WIR/2016 111–113.

[26] Concluded in October 2014, entered into force 21 November 2019. Available at http://trade.ec.europa.eu/doclib/press/index.cfm?id=961, accessed 18 March 2019.

[27] Compare Sec C (Establishment) of Ch. 8 to Art. 9.2 of Ch. 9: 'This Chapter shall apply to covered investors and *covered investments made in accordance with the applicable law*, whether such investments were made before or after the entry into force of this Agreement' (emphasis added).

EU-Vietnam Agreement[28] only offers investment arbitration in relation to the operation of investments, not for establishment and admission.[29]

Another way to exclude entry rights from the ISA is to impose conditions for processing claims, that is, *procedural impediments*. If the treaty only offers monetary compensation as a remedy or requires that the investor prove injury to its investments, a frustrated investor, whose main interest is accessing the territory of the state, will not be able to use ISA. The arbitral tribunal will not admit the claim. The US model BIT, for instance, requires that the investor suffer loss or damage as a condition of permitting ISA.[30] This was introduced in the 2004 model version, apparently to prevent the submission of disputes that are not yet ripe.[31] In addition, there must be a link between the breach and the loss. The initial notice of the claim requires the exposition of the relief sought and the approximate amount of damages.[32] The Comprehensive and Progressive Transpacific Partnership (CPTPP), like the US model BIT, provides that in order to use the investor-state system, the investor must show not only a breach of an obligation (or of an investment authorization or agreement) but also loss or damage due to the breach.[33]

ISA case law suggests that the loss must take place within the territory of the host state.[34] However, the claimant does not need to know in advance the specific amount, if it is uncertain.[35] An ISA award can be limited to restitution of property or monetary damages.[36] This reveals to some extent that the ISA option is less attractive or even unavailable to investors that want to enter a host state and have not yet suffered quantifiable losses. In turn, a case for damages based on lost market

---

[28] Signed 30 June 2019, it is in the process of ratification. Available at http://trade.ec.europa.eu/doclib/press/index.cfm?id=1437, accessed 18 March 2019.

[29] See Art. 1 of Sec 3 [Resolution of Investment Disputes] of Ch. 8 [Trade in Services, Investment and E-commerce].

[30] US Model BIT (2012), Article 24 (1)(a)(ii) and Article 24 (1)(b)(ii).

[31] Kenneth J Vandevelde, *US International Investment Agreements* (Oxford University Press, 2009) p. 598.

[32] US Model BIT (2012), Article 24(2)(d).

[33] See art. 9.19 1(a)(ii), Ch. 9 of CPTPP, signed 8 March 2018. Available at https://ustr.gov/sites/default/files/TPP-Final-Text-Investment.pdf, accessed 18 March 2019.

[34] *United Parcel Service of America Inc.* v. *Government of Canada*, UNCITRAL, Award on Jurisdiction (22 November 2012) para. 121.

[35] *Continental Casualty Company* v. *The Argentine Republic*, ICSID Case No. ARB/03/9 Decision on Jurisdiction (22 February 2006) para. 92.

[36] US Model BIT (2012), Article 34 and NAFTA Article 1135.

opportunities could possibly be envisaged, but this is subject to a high degree of speculation.

The draft text of the EU proposal to the Transatlantic Trade and Investment Partnership (TTIP) – the failed EU-US megaregional negotiations – was also illustrative:

Section 3 – Resolution of Investment Disputes and Investment Court System

SUB-SECTION 1: SCOPE AND DEFINITIONS

Article 1 – Scope and Definitions

1. This Section shall apply to a dispute between, on the one hand, a claimant of one Party and, on the other hand, the other Party concerning treatment alleged to breach Section 2 [Investment Protection] or Article 2-3(2) [National Treatment] or Article 2-4(2) [Most-Favoured Nation] of Section 1 [Liberalisation of Investments], which breach allegedly *causes loss or damage* to the claimant or its locally established company. (emphasis added)

Not only did the draft provision require loss or damage, but it also restricted ISA to the breach of articles that deal with already established investments. This is because there was no mention of TTIP Article 2-3(1) or Article 2-4(1) of the EU proposal, respectively national treatment and MFN for establishment.[37] In the light of this treaty practice, one might ask what the role for ISA is in these cases. This is what Section 2.2.2 deals with.

2.2.2 The Case for ISA to Prospective Investors

It is fair to say that if the treaty does not provide for any special qualification whatsoever in relation to ISA, no immediate procedural impediment to the claim exists. Nevertheless, according to Zachary Douglas, there are no published awards concerning the breach of an obligation at the 'pre-investment stage', in BITs following the pre-entry (establishment) model.[38] At least in theory, a prospective investor that

---

[37] TTIP Art. 2-3 National Treatment 1. 'Each Party shall accord to investors of the other Party and to their investments, *as regards the establishment of an enterprise in its territory,* treatment no less favourable than the treatment it accords, in like situations, to its own investors and their investments.'; TTIP Art. 2-4 Most-Favoured-Nation Treatment 1. 'Each Party shall accord to investors of the other Party and to their investments *as regards the establishment of an enterprise in its territory,* treatment no less favourable than the treatment it accords, in like situations, to investors and investments of any non-Party' (emphasis added).

[38] Zachary Douglas, *The International Law of Investment Claims* (Cambridge University Press, 2009) pp. 140–1.

fits the treaty definition could opt for this kind of adjudication. However, the question is: what would ISA offer to the prospective investor? The hypothesis here is that using the investor-state mechanism in IIAs may not offer much to address problems faced by those investors. If this is true, then the treaty practice observed above is nothing more than an adjustment of the jurisdiction clause to the lack of usefulness of this alternative. On the other hand, if there is a residual role for ISA, then the change is an obvious limitation to the investor.

Some aspects of the IIAs might explain the absence of litigation concerning prospective investors. First, many treaties require that a claim is brought with reference to a breach of a standard that applies to an 'investment' or a 'covered investment'. However, prospective investors have yet to make an investment. Furthermore, ISA adjudicatory institutions – the ICSID, for instance, established by the ICSID Convention[39] – can also set limitations for prospective investors. Article 25(2) of the ICSID Convention clearly states that 'the jurisdiction of the Centre shall extend to any legal dispute arising directly out of an investment'. Hence, a full analysis of an ISA's jurisdiction must take into account not only clauses in the original IIA but also those related to the rules of the chosen dispute settlement mechanism. This problem will not arise if the issue is brought to the ICSID Additional Facility, the Stockholm Chamber of Commerce (SCC) or arbitration institutions and ad hoc arbitrations using the UNCITRAL rules. These cases will not rely on the language of an institutional treaty but on rules drafted or chosen by the parties or the institutions themselves.

Second, as shown, the IIA may require that in order to use ISA, losses must have occurred. This generally translates into monetary damages. A host state decision that denies an investment or imposes conditions contrary to international commitments constitutes a barrier to investment. The kind of losses arising from the impossibility of making an investment are different from those occurring when an investment is already made. In the case of the former, there is harm to business plans and investment strategies, something not easily translated into the language of compensation or restitution.

Third, most investment restrictions to entry affect a group of investors; for example, an ownership restriction on land that affects all prospective

---

[39] Convention on the Settlement of Investment Disputes between States and Nationals of Other States (ICSID Convention), adopted 18 March 1965, entered into force 14 October 1966, 575 UNTS 159.

foreign projects on tourist services, such as hotels and restaurants. Such prospective investors would need to coordinate themselves to characterize the situation as resulting in collective losses/injury. However, some jurisdictional or institutional rules may restrict the possibility of bringing class claims. It is true that there have been cases where class claims were accepted,[40] but this was not without controversy.[41]

Finally, the long duration of the disputes[42] and the consequences of an ISA claim might affect investors' incentives to trigger the mechanism. If the interest of the investor is to have access to a country in the short term, it will think twice before bringing a claim against the host state. The claim might strain their relationship with the host state even more and diminish the prospects for entry. However, a large investor may be able to use the threat of litigation as an effective stick. In any case, a protracted claim may be costly for the investor and the practical result – actual entry – may not be achieved. Hence, engaging in ISA may not compensate in the end.

Thus, there is possibly a trend to design more narrowly the jurisdictional and admissibility requirements for the claims. Seemingly, this is a response to the critiques against procedural aspects of investor-state arbitration. In CETA, apart from what was mentioned in Section 2.2.1, Canada has explicitly drafted a carve-out related to investment screening.[43] It provides:

> **Annex 8-C Exclusions from Dispute Settlement**
>
> A decision by Canada following a review under the Investment Canada Act, R.S.C. 1985, c. 28 (1st Supp.), *regarding whether or not to permit an investment that is subject to review, is not subject to the dispute settlement*

---

[40] *Abaclat and Others v. Argentine Republic*, ICSID Case No. ARB/07/5, Decision on Jurisdiction and Admissibility (4 August 2011); *Giovanni Alemanni and Others v. The Argentine Republic*, ICSID Case No. ARB/07/8, Decision on Jurisdiction and Admissibility (17 November 2014).

[41] See Dissenting Opinion by George Abi-Saab, in *Abaclat* (n. 40).

[42] UNCTAD, 'Investor-State Disputes: Prevention and Alternatives to Arbitration' (United Nations 2010) UNCTAD/DIAE/IA/2009/11 18.

[43] A similar provision had been included in the Canada-China BIT: Annex D.34 'Exclusions 1. A decision by Canada following a review under the *Investment Canada Act*, an Act respecting investment in Canada, with respect to whether or not to: (a) initially approve an investment [For Canada, the concept of "initially approve an investment" in paragraph 1 means all decisions made with respect to whether or not to permit an investment under the *Investment Canada Act*] that is subject to review; or (b) permit an investment that is subject to national security review; *shall not be subject to the dispute settlement provisions under Article 15 and Part C of this Agreement*' (emphasis added). In the new USMCA (n. 3), breaches of MFN and national treatment related to establishment and acquisition are also not subject to investor-state disputes, according to Annex 14-D, art 3(1)(a)(i)(A).

provisions under Section F, or to Chapter Twenty-Nine (Dispute Settlement).' (emphasis added)

One may think first that this is some sort of clarification, since these acts have never been arbitrable. A more convincing explanation comes from the contrary argument: when such a carve-out is absent with reference to an ISA clause, investment screening measures may be challenged without impediment.[44] Therefore, the clarification was deemed to be essential and constitutes perhaps a movement towards more sovereign control. In any case, the idea that there might be a residual role for ISA is reinforced in the analysis of expansion in Section 2.2.3.

2.2.3 ISA and the Expansion of Investments

In fact, a more nuanced analysis should be made when the investment is an *expansion* of a current one. This is also the case when a subsequent investment that does not amount to an 'expansion' is nevertheless somewhat linked to a previously made investment. These situations may provide channels to evade the procedural impediments. The investor can easily bring a claim related to the denial of access to licenses to an expansion arguing that the case arises out of an existing investment.

This seems to have been the case in the NAFTA arbitration in *Clayton v. Canada*.[45] The decision involved the procedure of application for an environmental authorization to carry out quarrying activities. The denial of licenses to new quarrying rights, after the review from a joint panel in a Canadian province, gave rise to a claim of fair and equitable treatment against Canada. The majority found that both the minimum standard of treatment (NAFTA Article 1105) and national treatment (NAFTA Article 1102) were breached.[46]

Since the claim was brought under the UNICTRAL rules, the jurisdictional requirement of an existing 'investment' was not an issue. As shown, NAFTA applies in a broad manner and does not require the existence of an investment, given that NAFTA Article 1102 also relates to

---

[44] Cf. *Global Telecom Holding S.A.E.* v. *Canada* Procedural Order n. 1 (13 June 2017) ICSID Case No. ARB/16/16 pending. Some details are available at www.iareporter.com/articles/canada-hit-by-first-legal-blowback-under-its-bits-with-developing-countries-as-egyptians-telecoms-giant-launches-arbitration/, accessed 18 March 2019.

[45] *William Ralph Clayton, William Richard Clayton, Douglas Clayton, Daniel Clayton and Bilcon of Delaware Inc* v. *Government of Canada*, UNCITRAL, PCA Case No. 2009-04, Award on Jurisdiction and Liability (17 March 2015) and Award on Damages (10 January 2019).

[46] For a critique of the decision, see Cory Adkins and David Singh Grewal, 'Democracy and Legitimacy in Investor-State Arbitration' (2016) 126 *Yale Law Journal Forum* 57.

establishment and acquisition. However, the arbitral award affirmed, without further discussion, that the claim was related to an investment, apparently the original one. This was done notwithstanding the fact that the case dealt with a newly proposed activity.[47] One wonders whether the case led to the inclusion of CETA Article 8.18 (2), which reads:

> 2. Claims under subparagraph 1(a) with respect to the expansion of a covered investment may be submitted only to the extent the measure relates to the existing business operations of a covered investment and the investor has, as a result, incurred loss or damage with respect to the covered investment.

The provision permits a claim concerning expansion provided that the measures relate to existing operations. A contrario, measures related to other aspects of an expansion cannot be challenged. This limits jurisdiction in line with the trend to narrow down the possibilities of ISA. On the other hand, such carve-outs are absent from the previous Canada-Korea Free Trade Agreement[48] and from the recent Canada-Mongolia BIT,[49] both of which cover establishment and expansion. In the Canada-China BIT[50] – since its national treatment clause does not include establishment but only expansion – it was necessary to include a substantive carve-out to expansion whenever approvals are needed. Article 6 of the BIT states:

> 3. The concept of 'expansion' in this Article applies only with respect to *sectors not subject to a prior approval* process under the relevant sectoral guidelines and applicable laws, regulations and rules in force at the time of expansion. The expansion may be subject to prescribed formalities and other information requirements. (emphasis added)

Finally, there is the case when an investor is already investing in a sector different from the sector which it seeks to enter in. Should the fact that the investor is already present in a country matter when the investment is in a completely different activity? This situation is rather unclear: depending on how the new investment is structured, the barrier to ISA could be circumvented to some extent. An investor that is already present in the host state can argue that the new investment in a different sector is an expansion. In addition, it can try to prove that the denial of this expansion affects the value and prospects of its existing operations, at

---

[47] *Clayton Bilcon* (n. 45) – Memorial of the Investor, paras. 408–411.
[48] Signed 22 September 2014, entered into force 1 January 2015.
[49] Signed 08 September 2016, entered into force 24 February 2017.
[50] Signed 10 February 2016, entered into force 06 September 2016.

least financially. An investor from outside the host state cannot put forward those arguments and will not have access to ISA.

To sum up, there is recent treaty practice that sets further limits to the use of ISA for the enforcement of entry rights by including various jurisdictional and admissibility hurdles. One can also note a restriction of the indirect ways to bring claims affecting new investments, such as framing the investment as an expansion. In this latter case, the ISA might have some residual role. This suggests, as will be later argued, a reduction in the non-shared characteristics between the investment and trade regimes. One could then observe some signs of convergence between the two adjudicative mechanisms. Whether this is a welcome development depends on the analysis of the possibilities to resort to other mechanisms, handled below in Section 3.

3 Entry Rights and State-State Arbitration: Alternative Enforcement

3.1 State-State Investment Arbitration

3.1.1 General Concepts

It is natural then to proceed to a description of state-state arbitration in foreign investment disputes (SSIA) under the current practice of international law.[51] This provides the framework to discuss if it is an available alternative to enforce establishment rights granted by investment provisions. The introduction of ISA has substituted the recourse to diplomatic protection to a large extent.[52] However, state-state dispute settlement mechanisms persist in IIAs. In fact, one should note the existence of state-state jurisdictional clauses in virtually all the BITs. In addition, recent state-state cases may indicate a resurgence of the practice in the area.[53]

---

[51] For a more extensive account and for an understanding of the reluctance of states to sue each other, see Murilo Lubambo, 'Is State-State Investment Arbitration an Old Option for Latin America?' (2016) 34 *Conflict Resolution Quarterly* 225.

[52] *Ahmadou Sadio Diallo (Republic of Guinea v. Democratic Republic of the Congo)* (Preliminary Objections, Judgment) [2010] ICJ Rep p. 36 para. 88; *CMS Gas Transmission Company v. Argentina*, Case No. ARB/01/8 Decision of the Tribunal on Objections to Jurisdiction para. 45.

[53] *Peru v. Chile* arbitration related to the preliminary objections in the *Empresas Lucchetti, S. A. and Lucchetti Peru, S.A. v. The Republic of Peru*, ICSID Case No. ARB/03/4; *Italian Republic v. Republic of Cuba*, ad hoc State-State Arbitration Award (1 Jan 2008); *Republic of Ecuador v. United States of America* (PCA Case No. 2012-5).

The analysis of jurisdictional clauses in IIAs providing consent to SSIA is a good starting point. In the current practice, a typical state-state clause in an IIA, this one from the Argentina-Qatar 2016 BIT,[54] reads:

> **ARTICLE 15 – Settlement of Disputes between the Contracting Parties**
>
> 1. The two Contracting Parties shall strive with good faith and mutual cooperation to reach a fair and quick settlement of *any dispute arising between them concerning interpretation or application of this Treaty*. In this connection the two Contracting Parties hereby agree to enter into direct objective negotiations to reach such settlement.
>
> If the disagreement has not been settled within a period of six months from the date on which the matter was raised by either Contracting Party, *it may be submitted at the request of either Contracting Party to an Arbitral Tribunal* composed of three members and under the UNCITRAL Arbitration Rules (2013), which shall apply except as otherwise mutually agreed by the disputing parties.
>
> ...
>
> 7. [...] *Such award shall be final and binding on both Contracting Parties*. (emphasis added)

One can observe that the language is generally broad, concerning either the interpretation or application of the agreement. Either party gives the consent for the other party to submit a request for arbitration. Moreover, the final award is binding on both states. Having briefly set the context, the next step is to analyse how SSIA can be used to enforce entry rights.

3.1.2 Entry Rights and Declaratory Claims

The first immediate possibility for adjudication under SSIA is the case of merely interpretative claims, especially in declaratory requests. International courts can be called upon to resolve merely interpretive questions without claims of treaty violations and can recognize jurisdiction to make declaratory awards on the correct interpretation of a provision.[55] The request for a declaratory decision by the home state will be within the mandate of most SSIA jurisdiction clauses, since this generally involves an exercise of the power to interpret or apply the treaty.

---

[54] Signed on 6 November 2016.
[55] See *Rights of the National of the United States of America in Morocco (France v. United States of America)* (Judgment) [1952] ICJ Rep p. 179; *Right of Passage over Indian Territory (Portugal v. India)* (Judgment on Merits) [1960] ICJ Rep; *Dispute Regarding Navigational and Related Rights (Costa Rica v. Nicaragua)* (Judgment) [2009] ICJ Rep pp. 270-1 para. 156.

State-state arbitration in a BIT seems to be an adequate avenue for home states to ask for declaratory decisions that can affect entry rights. The context is one of interpretation and application of the provisions related to entry, such as national treatment and MFN on the establishment of an investment and market access, as well as to the non-conforming measures and schedules of liberalization, highlighted before. Home states may be interested in ensuring that their negotiated bargains to open up investment sectors were not in vain. This is particularly relevant in the context of prospective entry, since the home state may be seeking the correct interpretation of a treaty commitment without claiming a breach regarding one of its investors.

In this vein, a provision in the Australia-China trade agreement states: 'For greater certainty, the State to State Dispute Settlement mechanism in Chapter 15 (Dispute Settlement) of this Agreement applies to this Chapter *including pre-establishment obligations* under Article 9.3.'[56] This is an example of a clarification that the SSIA clause applies to entry rights. It is an option when there are several unnamed potential investors which may not have even decided to invest. SSIA would be the only option of redress in disputes concerning the abstract interpretation of provisions.

In addition, the home state could argue that a tribunal has jurisdiction to accept a declaratory claim concerning the application of the treaty to a concrete situation affecting a prospective investor.[57] While in an investor-state context prospective investors could fear reactions of the host state,[58] through the SSIA path the tensions are arguably filtered. Declaratory relief using SSIA could involve the power of the tribunal to make recommendations, but not orders, to cease certain conduct or carry out measures to achieve compliance.[59] In any case, a declaratory award

---

[56] Footnote of art. 9.12 of the Investment Chapter (emphasis added).

[57] A declaratory claim related to a concrete measure towards an investor, despite its resemblance with diplomatic protection, may also involve direct rights of the parties; see Martins Paparinskis, 'Investment Arbitration and the Law of Countermeasures' (2009) 79 *British Yearbook of International Law* 264, 314.

[58] Theodore R Posner and Marguerite C Walter, 'The Abiding Role of State-State Engagement in the Resolution of Investor-State Disputes' in Jean E Kalicki and Anna Joubin-Bret (eds.), *Reshaping the Investor-State Dispute Settlement System: Journeys for the 21st Century* (Brill Nijhoff, 2015) pp. 383, 392.

[59] Nathalie Bernasconi-Osterwalder, 'State–State Dispute Settlement in Investment Treaties' (International Institute for Sustainable Development 2014) 14, www.iisd.org /sites/default/files/publications/best-practices-state-state-dispute-settlement-investment -treaties.pdf, accessed 23 July 2015.

related to a specific situation may be useful redress for some investors, such as the American, Mexican and Canadian investors involved in the examples raised in the introduction of this chapter.

3.1.3 Entry Rights and Diplomatic Protection

The traditional possibility would be to resort to SSIA in the context of diplomatic protection. Diplomatic protection has been described as involving the use of diplomatic action or any other means of dispute settlement by a state in response to an injury to its in face of a wrongful act of another state.[60]

It is well established that the admissibility of a claim to determine state responsibility in the context of diplomatic protection requires the fulfilment of certain criteria. These are the nationality of claims and the exhaustion of local remedies.[61] The latter is an important principle of international law but the possibility of its explicit waiver by treaty is widely recognized.[62] In the absence of an investment treaty with consent to ISA, or other regional trade agreements, the recourse to diplomatic protection remains the sole international alternative.[63]

In a treaty context, the obligations owed to another state and its investors in an IIA may constitute the primary obligations, the breaches of which can be the grounds for a diplomatic protection claim.[64] Furthermore, in this context, the state-state clause of a treaty may constitute the jurisdictional basis on which the diplomatic protection will further proceed.[65] Hence, a SSIA can ultimately deal with a diplomatic

---

[60] Frank Berman, 'The Relevance of the Law on Diplomatic Protection in Investment Arbitration' in Federico Ortino et al. (eds.), *Investment Treaty Law: Current Issues II, Nationality and Investment Treaty Claims; Fair and Equitable Treatment in Investment Treaty Law* (British Institute of International and Comparative Law, 2007) p. 68.

[61] See art. 44 of the ILC, 'Draft Articles on Responsibility of States for Internationally Wrongful Acts, with Commentaries' (2001) UN Doc A/CN.4/SER.A/2001/Add.1 (Part 2) [hereinafter ARSIWA].

[62] Also, while a waiver is not to be presumed, this is rebuttable, so the possibility of an implicit waiver should not be excluded. See 'ILC Draft Articles on Diplomatic Protection' [hereinafter ILCDP] in ILC, 'Report of the International Law Commission on the Work of its 58th Session' (2006) UN Doc A 61/10, Commentary on Article 15(e), paras. 16 p. 85. See also James Crawford, 'The ILC's Articles on Diplomatic Protection' (2006) 31 *South African Yearbook of International Law: Suid-Afrikaanse Jaarboek Vir Volkereg* 29, 48–9.

[63] See *Elettronica Sicula SPA. (ELSI) (United States of America v. Republic of Italy)* (Judgment) [1989] ICJ Rep 15.

[64] ILCDP (n. 62) Commentary on Article 1, para 4, pp. 25–6.

[65] *ELSI case* (n. 63) para. 48.

protection claim; the ad hoc arbitration *Italy* v. *Cuba* is instructive in this regard.[66]

While diplomatic protection claims may take place without any publicity and are generally underreported, prospective frustrated investors can and do request protection from their home state. If there is SSIA jurisdiction, a claim can be brought. A reported diplomatic protection initiative involving the establishment of investors was taken by Italy. It was a dispute between Italy and Switzerland in the early 1990s about the right of Italians to acquire property in the Swiss territory. A Swiss measure restraining foreign control of land affected Italian landowners and investors. Italy argued that a treaty with Switzerland granted rights of establishment and property acquisition equal to those of Swiss nationals, under reciprocal conditions.[67] Italy intervened on behalf of its nationals and the case was settled.[68]

The SSIA decision can have a declaratory nature and provide the basis for future ISA claims. It is sometimes the case that the financial burden of bringing a claim is a barrier for an investor, especially if it is an individual or a small company. In this case, resorting to its state may be the most appropriate conduct,[69] even in the presence of investor-state provisions. Furthermore, the possibility of settlements may safeguard some interests of the home state.[70] In any case, a diplomatic protection claim may fit well with the interests of those prospective investors.

3.1.4 Entry Rights and General Measures

A specific feature of declaratory claims is that they can focus on measures of general application. This would encompass a scenario with different

---

[66] See (n. 53); also, Michele Potestà, 'Republic of Italy v. Republic of Cuba' (2012) 106 *American Journal of International Law* 341.

[67] See Establishment and Consular Convention of 1868 between Italy and Switzerland (signed 22 July 1868, entered into effect 1 May 1869), available at http://itra.esteri.it/vwPdf/wfrmRenderPdf.aspx?ID=45862, accessed 18 March 2019.

[68] For a full description of the case, see Giorgio Sacerdoti and Matilde Recanati, 'Approaches to Investment Protection Outside of Specific International Investment Agreements and Investor-State Settlement' in Marc Bungenberg et al. (eds.), *International Investment Law* (Nomos Hart, 2015) pp. 1843–7.

[69] Anthea Roberts, 'State-to-State Investment Treaty Arbitration: A Hybrid Theory of Interdependent Rights and Shared Interpretive Authority' (2014) 55 *Harvard International Law Journal* 1, 14; Berman (n. 60) 71–2.

[70] Matilde Recanati, 'Diplomatic Intervention and State-to-State Arbitration as Alternative Means for the Protection of Foreign Investments and Host States' General Interests: The Italian Experience' in Giorgio Sacerdoti et al. (eds.), *General Interests of Host States in International Investment Law* (Cambridge University Press, 2014) pp. 430, 440.

characteristics compared to diplomatic protection and the mere interpretation of treaty provisions.

In fact, generalized practices or policies denying entry rights to foreign investors may constitute a general situation without a specific injury to an investor but affecting a whole class of investors.[71] They can be, on their own, breaches of an international obligation. To illustrate, according to Douglas, 'one contracting State might seek a *declaration from an international tribunal on the compatibility of domestic legislation* enacted by another contracting State with the minimum standards of investment treatment in the BIT'.[72] It might make more sense, when one considers the effectiveness of the remedy, for the treaty parties to address the situation using the interstate settlement provision.[73]

The rank of the measure in the state's legal order does not matter. The highest measure one could think of would be a general restriction contained in the state's constitution that violates international entry commitments. The reservation by law of specific sectors to domestic providers could also be a breach of national treatment. This scenario can very well occur: the reversal of privatization measures of a former government by a newly elected one and the re-establishment of a monopoly are the immediate examples. While the limitation of foreign investments in a certain sector depends on the priorities of each country, the mere adoption of an investment-restrictive measure might constitute a breach of an international obligation.[74] This could go against market access provisions.

Another possible case is a general measure (such as a law, decree or ministerial regulation) that discriminates against prospective investors based on their origin, which would breach the national treatment standard under the IIA. When restrictive regulations (such as foreign ownership limitations and conditions to investments) or administrative hurdles (e.g. licensing delays) are present, it is possible that other investors are facing the same situation.[75] The main objective of a claim would

---

[71] Berman (n. 60) 72.
[72] Douglas (n. 15) 189 (emphasis added).
[73] Berman (n. 60) 72.
[74] See the commentaries to the ARSIWA (n. 61), Article 12 para. 12, p. 57: 'The question often arises whether an obligation is breached by the enactment of legislation by a State, in cases where the content of the legislation *prima facie conflicts with what is required by the international obligation*, or whether the legislation has to be implemented in the given case before the breach can be said to have occurred.... Certain obligations may be *breached by the mere passage of incompatible legislation*' (emphasis added).
[75] Posner and Walter (n. 58) 392.

then be the repeal of the discriminatory or restrictive norms and not compensation for damages.[76] This would arguably fit into the jurisdiction of a state-state jurisdictional clause, as seen above.

The NAFTA arbitration involving Mexican investments in the United States,[77] referred to in the introduction of this chapter, is an example of a state-state arbitration directly dealing with general measures affecting entry. The tribunal decided that the United States had breached the national treatment obligation towards Mexican investors by passing legislation restricting their presence in US territory, which conflicted with the scheduled obligations of the United States set forth in NAFTA.

A more nuanced approach is taken when the breach concerns the way in which the general measure is implemented.[78] Another example would be the imposition by decree of burdensome requirements for entry that were not present in the non-conforming measures or negative lists in IIAs. In fact, much of the litigation is likely to focus on the interpretation of non-conforming measures.[79] With the incorporation of establishment rights, an array of international legal issues may be expected to relate to those negative lists. This litigation tends to explore the differences between investment treaty commitments and GATS commitments, as will be seen.

Nevertheless, it is possible that entry rights are completely excluded from any dispute settlement provision. The concept of 'legal inflation', defined by Horn, Mavroidis and Sapir,[80] may be helpful to describe this situation. The term refers to the phenomenon of introducing non-clear or non-enforceable obligations in trade agreements.[81] It is a case of non-justiciability of rights. While it seems that vagueness of treaty language is not an issue, legal inflation would occur if some substantial entry rights

---

[76] Wolfgang Alschner, 'The Return of the Home State and the Rise of "Embedded" Investor-State Arbitration' in Shaheeza Lalani and Rodrigo Polanco Lazo (eds.), *The Role of the State in Investor-State Arbitration* (Brill, 2014) p. 331.

[77] *Mexico v. United States*; see n. 4.

[78] See the commentaries to the ARSIWA (n. 60), Article 12, para. 13, p. 57.

[79] In that regard, see *Mobil Investments Canada Inc and Murphy Oil Corporation v. Canada*, ICSID Case No. ARB(AF)/07/4. The arbitrators had to look at whether the non-conforming measures included the restriction under analysis.

[80] Henrik Horn, Petros C Mavroidis and André Sapir, 'Beyond the WTO? An Anatomy of EU and US Preferential Trade Agreements' in David Greenaway (ed.), *The World Economy: Global Trade Policy 2010* (Blackwell Publishing, 2011).

[81] Cf. Jose E Alvarez, 'The Return of the State' (2011) 20 *Minnesota Journal of International Law* 223, 235–8, arguing that the recalibration of BITs expanded the language but shrunk the obligations of host states.

were excluded even from state-state dispute settlement, as shown in the Canadian practice.[82]

Overall, the mere presence of SSIA clauses means that they must be given meaning and purpose. SSIA can be useful to home states to enforce entry rights with a broader scope than, but not excluding, diplomatic protection. In addition, it may serve as a complement to ISA, in the face of procedural impediments to the latter. In sum, the limitation of the possibility of direct claims from prospective investors in this area might make the investment regime closer to the regime for the enforcement of international trade rules, as will be seen. This is perhaps a move towards adjudicatory convergence in the sense adopted in this chapter.

3.2 International Trade Law Dispute Settlement and Entry of Investments

3.2.1 WTO Dispute Settlement: Main Features

The dispute settlement system of the WTO is an interstate system, whereby a WTO member can bring a dispute against other members. No private parties or investors can invoke the mechanism, even if they are directly affected by certain measures. The question must always be framed as a matter of rights and obligations of the members. In this sense, despite important differences,[83] the mechanism shares much more characteristics with SSIA than with ISA. It is regulated by the Dispute Settlement Understanding (DSU),[84] to which all WTO members are a party. Therefore, there is no opt-out from the DSU and this characteristic makes it attractive.

According to the DSU, the WTO mechanism has exclusive jurisdiction over disputes arising from the agreements.[85] The mechanism is activated

---

[82] See (n. 43).
[83] For example, in the composition of the adjudicators in both the trade and investment regimes, which affects the effectiveness of international tribunals, as shown in Joost Pauwelyn, 'The Rule of Law Without the Rule of Lawyers? Why Investment Arbitrators Are from Mars, Trade Adjudicators from Venus' (2015) 109 *American Journal of International Law* 761. See also Kurtz (n. 6) 229–78.
[84] Dispute Settlement Rules: Understanding on Rules and Procedures Governing the Settlement of Disputes (15 April 1994) Marrakesh Agreement Establishing the World Trade Organization Annex 2 1869 UNTS 401 [hereinafter DSU].
[85] DSU arts. 2.1 and 3.2, except perhaps for the resort to DSU art. 25, which provides for arbitration by the parties to solve clearly defined issues. In fact, this provision may offer an interim solution to the current blockage of appointments of Appellate Body members by the United States. Amiti Sen, 'WTO Members to Work on Alternative Mechanism for

without the need for further consent.[86] Within certain limits, panels have jurisdiction to entertain the matter: they shall make an objective assessment and identify the WTO applicable law. The Appellate Body (AB), which reviews the legal issues of the cases, has ultimate responsibility for making the decisions secure and predictable.[87] If decisions are not complied with, members must request the authorization of countermeasures. In this regard, the WTO system has been described as an opt-out from the regime of international responsibility (*lex specialis*).[88]

To the extent that the regulation of the establishment of investments in services (mode 3) is covered by the GATS, it is subject to the DSU. For the dispute settlement to be invoked there must be a violation or breach of an obligation or the nullification or impairment of benefits.[89] Therefore, if a WTO member has violated an obligation affecting investors in services or if the benefits of the GATS were impaired or nullified, a member has the possibility of invoking the DSU and requesting a panel to rule on the issue.

How do these characteristics of the WTO dispute settlement mechanism affect the issues discussed in this chapter? It is probable that the interested party is the home state of the investors that are subject to the measure contrary to the GATS. In any case, a member does not need to show that it is connected to an investor or investments (in the form of a mode 3-type of services provision) affected by the breach. Nor does it need to show, in the face of a violation, that local remedies were exhausted or that the affected investor has the nationality of that member state. In the specific case here, the GATS will be the applicable WTO law. If the violation relates to market access or national treatment, the scheduling of commitments is naturally part of the applicable law. Thus, mode 3 commitments that states have undertaken are most likely to be considered by the panels in their task to interpret and apply the WTO agreements.

As suggested above, obligations similar to those included in the GATS can also be expressed in investment treaties, though in a different language. A positive commitment in the GATS to give national treatment to

---

Dispute Settlement' *The Hindu – Businessline* (New Delhi, 13 March 2018), www.thehindubusinessline.com/news/world/wto-members-to-work-on-alternative-mechanism-for-dispute-settlement/article23229585.ece, accessed 18 March 2019.

[86] DSU arts. 6.1 and 23(2).
[87] DSU art. 3.2.
[88] Piet Eeckhout, 'Remedies and Compliance' in Daniel Bethlehem et al. (eds.), *The Oxford Handbook of International Trade Law* (Oxford University Press, 2009) p. 457.
[89] DSU arts. 3.5 and 10.4.

a mode 3-type of service supply (commercial presence) can be equivalent to national treatment under an IIA, which is provided to establishment without the exception of non-conforming measures. The same situation could result in adjudication before parallel forums if it constitutes a breach of more than one treaty with equivalent norms. When a treaty provides jurisdiction for a claim similar to that arising from the WTO agreement, there is conflict of jurisdiction.[90] The possibility to bring the same case in these two forums is a factor of convergence between the regimes.[91]

The idea of enforcing an equivalent obligation in another regime has been described as inter-regime shifting, whereby parties experiment with cross-enforcement between trade and investment.[92] A relevant question concerning this section is whether the WTO jurisdiction is affected by the fact that the same situation is being analysed in another forum. Some argued that the WTO panel seized of the matter could decline its jurisdiction if it considers that the WTO obligation was superseded by bilateral obligations.[93] However, the WTO AB in *Peru-Agricultural Products* suggested that WTO obligations cannot be modified between the parties.[94] In any case, currently there is no solution for the coordination of overlapping jurisdictions, short of institutional reforms. A possible solution comes from the references in the new megaregionals to the prominence of the forum first seized, such as in CETA Article 29.3. Therefore, if a GATS provision is considered substantially equivalent to an investment obligation under the CETA, the party must opt for one of the mechanisms. This interesting but overarching question goes beyond the scope of this chapter.

3.2.2 Entry Rights and GATS Commitments

Both panel and AB reports have had the opportunity to deal with issues related, in some way or another, to the entry of investors, the *China –*

---

[90] Isabelle Van Damme, 'Jurisdiction, Applicable Law, and Interpretation' in Daniel Bethlehem et al. (eds.), *The Oxford Handbook of International Trade Law* (Oxford University Press, 2009) p. 303.
[91] Kurtz (n. 6) 13–15 and 229–78.
[92] Sergio Puig, 'International Regime Complexity and Economic Law Enforcement' (2014) 17 *Journal of International Economic Law* 491, 503.
[93] Gabrielle Marceau, 'Conflicts of Norms and Conflicts of Jurisdictions: The Relationship between the WTO Agreement and MEAs and Other Treaties' (2001) 35 *Journal of World Trade* 1081, 1130.
[94] WTO, *Peru: Additional Duty on Imports of Certain Agricultural Products – Report of the Appellate Body* (31 March 2015) WT/DS457/AB/R para. 5.111–5.113.

Electronic Payments case referred to in Section 1 being one example.[95] Most of the cases involved the interpretation of schedules, focusing on general measures taken by the state that go against their commitments.[96]

An unsettled issue is whether concrete measures affecting a specific investor – or a group of investors – in services are under the jurisdiction of the WTO dispute settlement mechanism. Put differently, could a state request the initiation of a panel claiming that an individual measure affecting an investor in services is against a GATS commitment? This is the case, for example, in investment screening activities, whereby a governmental decision denies, imposes conditions for or authorizes an investment. Could the individual decision to allow or deny the establishment of a financial institution in the territory of a state be challenged?

As seen above, since the GATS is a covered agreement, the matter is under the WTO dispute settlement jurisdiction if it concerns GATS rights and obligations. The response to the question will initially involve an evaluation of whether the decision is a 'measure' which possibly violates the GATS or impairs its benefits. In this regard, not only is the expression 'measure' very broad, but also the term 'decision' is present in the definition of measures in GATS Article XXVIII(a). Thus, the GATS potentially covers individual and specific situations such as screening procedures.[97] This would be prima facie sufficient for a case to be under the DSB jurisdiction.

The assessment of a violation by the panels would have to go through all the well-known stages. In this regard, the fact that the expression 'service suppliers' is used in plural in the market access provision (GATS Article XVI) does not mean that a decision concerning *a* service supplier is not covered; it can be the prominent or the only supplier of that service.[98] In any case, screening decisions for investments could arguably violate national treatment under the GATS if the imposed conditions were not likewise applied to a domestic service supplier.[99] This is relevant

---

[95] See n. 2.
[96] WTO, *Argentina: Measures Relating to Trade in Goods and Services – Report of the Panel* (30 September 2015) WT/DS453/R and *Report of the Appellate Body* (14 April 2016) WT/DS453/AB/R; WTO, *China: Certain Measures Affecting Electronic Payment Services – Report of the Panel* (31 August 2012) WT/DS413/R; WTO, *China: Publications and Audiovisual Products – Report of the Appellate Body* (19 January 2010) WT/DS363/AB/R; WTO, *European Communities: Regime for the Importation, Sale and Distribution of Bananas – Report of the Appellate Body* (09 September 1997) WT/DS27/AB/R.
[97] Meester and Coppens (n. 16) 112.
[98] Ibid. at 117.
[99] Ibid. at 120.

if states have undertaken national treatment commitments in mode 3, which could be a breach of the GATS actionable under the DSU. Likewise, if there are discriminatory criteria between foreigners, a case could be put forward for a breach of the MFN provision, irrespective of commitments.

3.2.3 Challenges of Effective Enforcement

One of the facets of the WTO regime is that the remedies available for the breach of obligations are generally prospective in nature. This means that whenever a violation is determined in a panel or an AB report, and adopted by the DSB, the usual determination is to bring the measures into conformity.[100]

For the purposes of the situations analysed here, the remedy for the breach of GATS provisions related to mode 3 would generally be the withdrawal of the measure or its adaptation to eliminate the aspects found to be in breach of the agreement. For example, if the WTO DSB deems a measure to be unjustifiably restraining access to investments, the state must change the measure to provide for that access. On the other hand, SSIA would not have that limitation: there is in theory a wider scope of remedies that can be taken, as seen in the previous sections.

The question worth discussing is whether the state-state system is adequate for situations where there is a lack, or limitation, of access of investments and investors. In fact, in the cases where these kinds of measures were challenged in the WTO, the respondent states changed their practices. For example, China complied – without appeal – with the panel report in *China-Electronic Payments* and changed its domestic measures in the agreed time frame.[101] In *China-Audiovisuals* there was an appeal, but in the end, the country complied with the ruling by amending its measures within the time limits.[102] These two cases illustrate an effective use of the interstate framework to tackle investment restrictions.[103]

---

[100] Article 11, Article 19(1) and Article 22.1.
[101] Implementation notified by China on 23 July 2013; see WTO, *China: Certain Measures Affecting Electronic Payment Services – Status Report by China* (14 June 2013) WT/DS413/9.
[102] Implementation notified by China on 24 May 2012; see WTO, *China: Publications and Audiovisual Products – Status Report by China – Addendum* (13 April 2012) WT/DS363/17/Add.15.
[103] 'China Opens Door for Visa and MasterCard to Challenge UnionPay', *Financial Times* (31 May 2015), available at https://next.ft.com/content/6a71b148-0764-11e5-a58f-00144feabdc0, accessed 18 March 2019.

Nevertheless, one must ask a question. Why – in the case of multi-sourced equivalent obligations – would an investor ask its home state to activate the WTO system instead of resorting to state-state arbitration under an IIA, the latter having broader powers? The reason for triggering the WTO mechanism instead of using SSIA may be related to the existence in the WTO of a centralized system of collective pressure. In other regimes, parties have fewer incentives to adjudicate their claims and more incentives to engage in unilateral retaliation.[104] This is because in the WTO members can ask – as a last resort – for retaliation to be authorized by the DSB,[105] as part of this special collective surveillance mechanism. This actually happened in cases involving the GATS: in *EC-Bananas*, for instance, which also dealt with GATS mode 3 commitments, claimants resorted to retaliation since the EU did not abide by the decision.[106] This also took place in *US-Gambling*.[107]

In any case, both alternatives share interstate characteristics and to the extent that parties decide to exclude ISA to entry rights, this shows signs of adjudicatory convergence between the regimes. It is true that one could view this as an indication of divergence since whereas the trade regime has been quite stable on entry rights, international investment law is moving away from the issue. However, this would assume that the latter is only about ISA, which is untrue due to the availability of SSIA, although it is rarely used.

4 Conclusion

Based on the foregoing analysis, there are indications that the effectiveness of investor-state arbitration, as currently implemented in IIAs, is limited in cases of entry. This is because access disputes generally relate to measures affecting several potential investors or to individual decisions denying or limiting an investment to be made. However, the international investment regime is not only about investor-state arbitration. It

---

[104] Geraldo Vidigal, 'Why Is There So Little Litigation under Free Trade Agreements? Retaliation and Adjudication in International Dispute Settlement' (2017) 20 *Journal of International Economic Law* 927, 937–45.

[105] DSU art. 22(3).

[106] WTO, *European Communities: Regime for the Importation, Sale and Distribution of Bananas – Recourse to Article 21.5, Report of the Appellate Body* (26 November 2008) WT/DS27/AB/RW/USA; WT/DS27/AB/RW2/ECU.

[107] WTO, *US: Measures Affecting the Cross-Border Supply of Gambling and Betting Services – Recourse to Arbitration by the United States under Article 22.6 DSU – Decision by the Arbitrator* (7 April 2005) WT/DS285/ARB.

also encompasses state-state mechanisms even if they are rarely used. In fact, state-state investment arbitration appears to address adequately some of the market access concerns of investors. In these cases, investors and their home states will generally be more focused on the withdrawal of measures or on the declaration that a specific internal measure is a violation of treaty provisions.

Recent treaty practice has narrowed down the jurisdiction of investor-state arbitration, thus leaving the adjudication of entry rights only within the scope of state-state dispute settlement systems. The rights and obligations related to entry can be enforced by resorting to different mechanisms, such as ad hoc state-state investment arbitration under BITs, the Dispute Settlement Understanding of the World Trade Organization or the state-state systems of the new mega-regionals. Each of the mechanisms differ in relation to the processes, scope of jurisdiction and criteria for admissibility, but they share the common patterns of state-state third-party mechanisms.

In sum, to the extent that parties decide to limit or exclude investor-state arbitration for entry rights, there is a reduction in the number of non-shared characteristics between the international trade and international investment law regimes. One could interpret this as a sign of adjudicatory convergence between the regimes when it comes to entry. The exclusion of one mechanism may nonetheless lead to a situation of under-enforcement of those rights. While the WTO offers a centralized system of authorized retaliation, the BITs and regional systems will probably rely on the general law of countermeasures in the absence of more specific rules. It will be interesting to observe how the new treaty-making initiatives will develop the issue.

PART II

Use of Precedent across Regimes

5

Approaches to External Precedent: The Invocation of International Jurisprudence in Investment Arbitration and WTO Dispute Settlement

NICCOLÒ RIDI

1 The Problem of Precedent in International Dispute Settlement

It is commonplace to affirm that there is no such thing as a doctrine of precedent in international law. In order to do so, the skilled international lawyer is advised to invoke the authority of Articles 38(1)(d) and 59 of the Statute of the International Court of Justice and proclaim that judicial decisions are confined to the status of 'subsidiary means for the determination of rules of law', and that decisions have 'no binding force except between the parties and in respect of that particular case'.[1] Then comes the observation of reality: citations to precedents from the same or other jurisdictions are a matter of routine. The incongruence between their purported 'subsidiary' status and their actual use has been sometimes denounced rather vocally: '[t]he worst kept secret in international law is that international tribunals rely on precedent',[2] so why not just 'come clean' and end the hypocrisy?[3]

---

[1] Articles 38 and 59 of the ICJ Statute are considered to have general applicability in international adjudication insofar as they reflect the exclusion of a strict rule of granting binding force to previous decisions (stare decisis). However, compelling and authoritative arguments have been made for some time that the purpose of Article 59 was not to exclude *any* precedential force of judicial decisions. On this point, see Mohamed Shahabuddeen, *Precedent in the World Court* (Cambridge University Press, 2007) pp. 99–100.

[2] Harlan Grant Cohen, 'Finding International Law, Part II: Our Fragmenting Legal Community' (2011) 44 *NYUJ Int'l L. & Pol.* 1049, 1079.

[3] Raj Bhala, 'Power of the Past: Towards De Jure Stare Decisis in WTO Adjudication (Part Three of a Trilogy)' (2000) 33 *Geo. Wash. Int'l L. Rev.* 873, 875.

Looking at this tension from a historical standpoint, one may recall that states conceived – and to considerable extent still conceive – of international law as emanating 'from the free will of sovereign independent States': a 'highly contentious metaphysical proposition' perhaps, but one that informed the development of the modern international dispute settlement system.[4] Simply put, there was no desire to grant a court a say in the matter[5] and aspirations for a more structured system of precedent were frustrated since a very early age.[6]

Yet, the idea of precedential force of a past decision can be independent of a formal sanction. By way of example, Arthur Goodhart tackled the question in 1934 and had no hesitation in interrogating himself on how the newly created Permanent Court of International Justice (PCIJ) would tackle the issue of precedent as a matter of some significance.[7] Most importantly, he did not view the issue as a 'yes-no' question, but rather an 'either-or' proposition: '[w]hich method of precedent – English or Continental – is the more likely to be followed by the Permanent Court of International Justice in the development of international law?'[8] To the Oxford scholar, not only was precedent an inevitable tenet of judicial practice; it was also to be welcomed as a technique to be employed to further develop an international law 'still so vague and uncertain that some authorities, even at the present day, deny to it the name of law'.[9] Goodhart's curiosity might have been driven by his interest in the doctrine of precedent in general, and he was not an international lawyer. He was, however, very familiar with the finest of his era. He quoted at length Hersch Lauterpacht's *The Function of Law in the International Community*, which had highlighted the fundamental role of the jurisprudence of international tribunals as a cure for 'the scarcity and indefiniteness of substantive

---

[4] James L Brierly, 'The Lotus Case' (1928) 44 *LQ REV.* 154, 155.
[5] See generally Permanent Court of International Justice, Advisory Committee of Jurists, *Procès-Verbaux of the Proceedings of the Committee, June 16th–July 24th, 1920*.
[6] With reference to the International Prize Court, which never came to exist, see Lassa Oppenheim, 'The Science of International Law: Its Task and Method' (1908) *American Journal of International Law* 313, 332.
[7] The ICJ Statute mirrors that of its predecessor with minor changes.
[8] Arthur I Goodhart, 'Precedent in English and Continental Law' (1934) 50 *Law Quarterly Review* 40, 64. Emphasis added.
[9] Goodhart (n. 8) 64.

rules of international law as the result of the comparative immaturity of the system'.[10]

The relevance of precedents has progressively increased as the judicialization effort proceeded forward. This has been the case since the appearance of international adjudicatory bodies in general.[11] However, the proliferation of international courts and tribunals has brought about an increase in the mass and diversity of the normative output of the international judiciary – alongside, it bears repeating, an increasing risk of 'fragmentation' of the international legal system. Decisions of international courts have risen to the status of crucial materials in the study of international law and its practice,[12] serving as more developed and useful, as well as more neutral, statements of the rules of international law.[13]

Eighty years after Goodhardt's and Lauterpacht's observations, it would be difficult to argue that reliance on precedent has yielded nothing. Even leaving behind the general question of development of the law, reliance on prior decisions has been seen as a miracle cure for fragmentation anxieties and the like. Alternatively, it has been welcome as a remedy to curb the potentially excessive discretion of decision makers who happen to find themselves in a position of almost unconstrained power and in the midst of a legitimacy crisis.[14] Of more immediate relevance, reliance on precedent remains an observable phenomenon: even calling it 'the worst kept secret in international law' is an exercise in understatement.[15]

This is not to say that the use of precedent is wholly unproblematic; rather, the contrary is true. Far from a philosophical discussion on the

---

[10] Hersch Lauterpacht, *The Function of Law in the International Community* (Oxford University Press, 2011) p. 78.

[11] John Bassett Moore, 'General Introduction' (1929) 1 *International Adjudications: Ancient and Modern History and Documents*vii, lxxxix.

[12] Benedict Kingsbury, 'International Courts: Uneven Judicialisation in Global Order' in James Crawford, Martti Koskenniemi and Surabhi Ranganathan (eds.), *The Cambridge Companion to International Law* (Cambridge University Press, 2012) p. 219.

[13] Fuad Zarbiyev, 'Judicial Activism in International Law—A Conceptual Framework for Analysis' (2012) 3 *Journal of International Dispute Settlement* 247, 268.

[14] Susan D Franck, 'The Legitimacy Crisis in Investment Treaty Arbitration: Privatizing Public International Law through Inconsistent Decisions' (2005) 73 *Fordham Law Review* 1521; Tai-Heng Cheng, 'Precedent and Control in Investment Treaty Arbitration' (2007) 30 *Fordham International Law Journal*; Charles N Brower and Stephen W Schill, 'Is Arbitration a Threat or a Boom to the Legitimacy of International Investment Law?' (2008) 9 *Chi. J. Int'l L.* 471.

[15] Cohen (n. 2) 1078.

extent to which anything should be defined by its past, the problem of precedent lies on a perilous fork in the road, where we might be asked to strike a balance between a need for like cases to be decided alike, and a recognition that doing so may be in tension with cases being decided incorrectly or unjustly.[16] We may wonder whether it is fair for precedents to be invoked to ward off criticism when other elements should be taken into account, 'almost as if they were passages from the Holy writ'.[17] Or we may wonder if the fact that international adjudicators have 'succeeded to such a large degree in portraying their interpretations to stand unsoiled and above the dirty business of politics' might conceal some hidden trickery after all.[18]

This chapter, part of a larger research project on the role of precedent in international dispute settlement, aims at investigating how investment tribunals and the WTO Appellate Body have approached the problem of the 'precedential' value – the inverted commas being the operative diacritical marks – to be granted to decisions of other international adjudicators.

2 Objectives and Methodology

2.1 On the Word 'Precedent'

The term 'precedent' has been employed rather liberally here, but this is not generally the case in the literature, as the term is often perceived as a charged one. It may have been avoided in that it appears to imply that a single decision issued by an international adjudicator may propagate effects to the future rights or obligations of non-parties to the original dispute,[19] or because the word is not

---

[16] Thomas Schultz, 'Against Consistency in Investment Arbitration' in Zachary Douglas, Joost Pauwelyn and Jorge E Viñuales (eds.), *The Foundations of International Investment Law: Bringing Theory into Practice* (Oxford University Press, 2014) pp. 301–2.

[17] Robert Y Jennings, 'The Role of the International Court of Justice' (1998) 68 *The British Year Book of International Law* 1, 41.

[18] Ingo Venzke, *How Interpretation Makes International Law: On Semantic Change and Normative Twists* (Oxford University Press, 2012) p. 144.

[19] This is an important point that also hinges on the distinction between precedent and res judicata, very clear in practice, but 'not so easy in a particular case' (RY Jennings, 'The Judiciary, International and National, and the Development of International Law' (1996) 45 *The International and Comparative Law Quarterly* 1, 7). The clearest discussion of the issue is probably that of Alain Pellet; see *'Decisions of the ICJ as Sources of International Law?'*, in *Gaetano Morelli Lectures Series*, 2nd edition (Research Centre for European Law, 2015) pp. 11–16.

understood to properly reflect the nature of reliance by an adjudicator on decisions of its counterparts.[20]

This short contribution is not the place to engage in theoretical discussions of this kind, but it is submitted here that the use of the word may be justified on the basis of its widespread use (in the context of international adjudication and elsewhere),[21] which is no less prominent when 'precedential resources' extend beyond the cases of the jurisdiction considered.[22] It is further submitted that the notion of precedent lends itself to describe those deferential approaches that international adjudicators, by distinguishing rather than outright rejecting, often display.[23] If a definition of precedent must be offered, it can be very broad. For our purposes, we may borrow Barton Legum's, according to whom a precedent is 'any decisional authority that is likely to justify the award to the principal audience for that award' from the perspective of the decision maker.[24] Similarly, we can define 'external precedent' as any decision

---

[20] Consider these differences in terminology: Valentina Sara Vadi, 'Towards Arbitral Path Coherence & Judicial Borrowing: Persuasive Precedent in Investment Arbitration' (2008) 3 *Transnational Dispute Management (TDM)*; Erik Voeten, 'Borrowing and Nonborrowing among International Courts' (2010) 39 *The Journal of Legal Studies* 547; Yonatan Lupu and Erik Voeten, 'Precedent in International Courts: A Network Analysis of Case Citations by the European Court of Human Rights' (2012) 42 *British Journal of Political Science* 413.

[21] For example, Mohamed Shahabuddeen, *Precedent in the World Court* (Cambridge University Press, 1996) (most notably); Zachary Douglas, 'Can a Doctrine of Precedent Be Justified in Investment Treaty Arbitration?' (2010) 25 *ICSID Review* 104; Florian Grisel, 'The Sources of Foreign Investment Law' in Zachary Douglas, Joost Pauwelyn and Jorge E Viñuales (eds.), *The Foundations of International Investment Law* (Oxford University Press, 2014) pp. 213–34.

[22] Shahabuddeen (n. 21) 32; Michele Taruffo, 'Institutional Factors Influencing Precedent', in D Neil MacCormick, Robert S Summers and Arthur L Goodhart (eds.), *Interpreting Precedents: A Comparative Study* (Routledge, 2016) pp. 247, 249.

[23] Alain Pellet, 'The Case Law of the ICJ in Investment Arbitration' (2013) 28 *ICSID Review* 223, 229.

[24] Barton Legum, 'The Definitions of "Precedent" in International Arbitration', in Emmanuel Gaillard, Yas Banifatemi and International Arbitration Institute (eds.), *Precedent in International Arbitration* (Juris Publishing, Inc 2008) pp. 5, 13. Note that this definition is directed at identifying what decision makers perceive as the value of precedent, to be contrasted with other, similarly result-oriented definitions of counsel's idea of precedent. A similar approach is shared by Alec Stone Sweet and Florian Grisel, who define precedent as 'that stream of normative materials, issuing from past awards, that (a) parties plead in submissions, and (b) tribunals rely upon when they justify either their awards or their approach to decision-making' Alec Stone Sweet and Florian Grisel, *The Evolution of International Arbitration: Judicialization, Governance, Legitimacy* (Oxford University Press, 2017) p. 119.

satisfying these conditions that was issued by a jurisdiction different from the one that cites it.

2.2 International Economic Law: Objective Equivalence and System Centrality

As we said, there are many reasons to follow precedent, and the same applies to external precedent; indeed, Article 38(1)(d) of the ICJ Statute, the starting point of any discussion on precedent in international law, does not make any such distinction. Intuitively, one may observe that *external* precedent is a form of judicial borrowing. Nonetheless, one must not forget that there is a fundamental, if subtle, difference between reliance on precedential authority and the invocation of 'borrowed' law. Without engaging in more in-depth theoretical discussions, it may be noted that they differ in the extent to which they represent a reason for action or to which they curb – in an authoritative manner – the discretion of the decision maker. Be that as it may, references to case law of other jurisdictions tend to occur where problems or objectives have some similarity. This is certainly the case for international investment law and international trade law, which, in both their substantive and procedural aspects, have been progressing 'on parallel tracks headed in the same direction'.[25]

This contiguity explains why it is possible to play the analogy game when considering investment tribunals and the WTO dispute settlement mechanism. While speaking of functional equivalence might be an overstatement, they do 'essentially share the same functions by settling international disputes in accordance with international economic law' and 'are asked to strike a balance between economic and non-economic concerns'.[26] Further, they are relatively young fora compared to the traditional pillars of international adjudication such as, for example, the International Court of Justice, which has from its inception dropped into a niche left by its predecessor. As systems of more recent vintage, they are also comparable in that they are – as a matter of ideal representation – similarly 'peripheral', that is to say, equidistant from an ideal core

---

[25] Roger Alford, 'The Convergence of International Trade and Investment Arbitration'(2013) 12 *Santa Clara Journal of International Law* 35, 60.

[26] Valentina Vadi, *Analogies in International Investment Law and Arbitration* (Cambridge University Press, 2015) pp. 61, 210; José E Alvarez, '"Beware: Boundary Crossings" – A Critical Appraisal of Public Law Approaches to International Investment Law' (2016) 17 *The Journal of World Investment & Trade* 171, 217.

represented by the International Court of Justice, seen by some as the chief body administering general international law and the system's centre of gravity.[27] It follows that a comparison between the two jurisdictions and, specifically, one that looks at the way they rely on case law originating outside their jurisdiction, is appropriate because of their intended goals and the contingencies related to their development. Any such observation, however, is liable to exceed its purpose and instigate confirmation bias; accordingly, methodological concerns will be addressed in the following section.

2.3 Methodology

This analysis starts from the premise that, in the international context as well as in the domestic ones, there exist multiple reasons to follow precedents, regardless of their formal status in a doctrine of sources. Rather than discussing them head-on, it approaches the topic in a more agnostic fashion. Accordingly, it will first look at how the chosen jurisdictions have dealt with the authority of external precedent, later considering which theoretical models – if any – provide the best representation.[28] This much will be achieved by identifying and mapping the cases citing external precedent – with the aid of citation analysis techniques – to establish which courts and decisions are most commonly cited and which issue areas prompt recourse to external precedent.

---

[27] For the origin of the expression and a discussion, see James Crawford, *Chance, Order, Change: The Course of International Law, General Course on Public International Law* (Martinus Nijhoff Publishers/Brill Academic, 2014) p. 204; Mads Andenas and Eirik Bjorge (eds.), *A Farewell to Fragmentation: Reassertion and Convergence in International Law* (Cambridge University Press, 2015) p. 6. For arguments on the centrality of the Court see Pierre-Marie Dupuy, 'The Danger of Fragmentation or Unification of the International Legal System and the International Court of Justice' (1998) 31 *NYU Journal of International Law and Politics* 791, 791; Gilbert Guillaume, 'Advantages and Risks of Proliferation: A Blueprint for Action' (2004) 2 *Journal of International Criminal Justice* 300; Rosalyn Higgins, 'A Babel of Judicial Voices? Ruminations from the Bench' (2006) 55 *International & Comparative Law Quarterly* 791, 791; Geir Ulfstein, 'International Courts and Judges: Independence, Interaction, and Legitimacy' (2014) 849 *NYU Journal of International Law and Politics* 14. For an empirical assessment of this claim, see Damien Charlotin, 'The Place of Investment Awards and WTO Decisions in International Law: A Citation Analysis' (2017) 20 *Journal of International Economic Law* 279.

[28] Consider also Chapter 11 in this volume by José E Alvarez.

In order to map the issue in the field of investment arbitration, I have employed the online database Investor State Law Guide.[29] While some decisions have yet to be included, it provides an accessible and workable outlook into a sizeable sample. WTO cases have been mapped by taking advantage of the WTO dispute settlement portal and basic data extraction techniques to point to the various target jurisdictions in order to identify the reports citing decisions from other international courts and tribunals. Due to the comparatively small number of cases, it has been possible to ignore those invocations that only appeared in the arguments of the parties or their summaries, which, while purposely labelled as false positives and beyond the scope of this chapter, surely warrant further study.

Broadly speaking, there are two ways to go about investigating precedent in international adjudication. At the cost of serious oversimplification, one involves the collection of citations; the other requires reading cases and trying to make sense of any such citations. Both methodologies have their merits and shortcomings, which have in turn been addressed with a variety of correctives.[30] This chapter is based on citation analysis.[31] I record the number of citations of decisions of international courts and tribunals – their own as well as those of other jurisdictions – mapping them through the use of social network analysis software.[32] Citations occurring in the summaries of the arguments of the parties are excluded, as are those referring to the original decision in the case of interpretation judgments or annulment procedures in such a way that suggest the intention of reconstructing the history of the dispute. This is a valuable and useful exercise as it allows for the graphic representations of the citation patterns of the international adjudicators examined in this study. For example, it may show the network centrality of specific decisions, and thus their overall systemic importance. It may also shed light on the

---

[29] Jurisprudence Citator: InvestorStateLawGuide.com, www.investorstatelawguide.com/ResearchTools/JurisprudenceCitators?id=11&type=ninv, accessed 26 July 2016.

[30] Citation analysis of this kind is an efficient strategy for the investigation of large amounts of data and has been found to be quite accurate. Qualitative analysis is, in principle, more exact in that it allows for a closer look at the reasoning leading to a citation. It is, however, far more time-consuming and does not always lead to more precise results.

[31] For a discussion of the limits of focusing on citations, see Chapter 11 in this volume by José E Alvarez.

[32] I have employed the software Gephi. See Mathieu Bastian, Sebastien Heymann and Mathieu Jacomy, 'Gephi: An Open Source Software for Exploring and Manipulating Networks' (2009) 8 *ICWSM* 361.

evolution of citation patterns over time, and on the differences between the citation patterns of different courts.[33]

3 Analysis

3.1 Citation of External Authorities in WTO Dispute Settlement

The role of precedent in WTO dispute settlement has been a matter of debate in the literature for quite some time. The Dispute Settlement Training Module – a guide published on the WTO website for the purpose of providing basic information on the dispute settlement mechanism – even devotes one subsection to it.[34] Discussion of the topic, however, has generally been devoted to the precedential or persuasive values of prior reports, be they issued by panels or – more attractively – the Appellate Body.[35] A discussion of reference to precedent *as external authorities* has not been addressed in depth.[36]

The theoretical and practical appeal of precedent is wholly unsurprising in this field, as the following of precedent is usually deemed coherent with the goals of consistency and predictability espoused by the WTO

[33] Christopher S Gibson and Christopher R Drahozal, 'Iran-United States Claims Tribunal Precedent in Investor-State Arbitration' (2006) 23 *Journal of International Arbitration* 521; James H Fowler and Sangick Jeon, 'The Authority of Supreme Court Precedent' (2008) 30 *Social Networks* 16 (on the US Supreme Court); Erik Voeten, 'Borrowing and Nonborrowing Among International Courts' (2010) 39 *Journal of Legal Studies* 547; Lupu and Voeten (n. 20); Wolfgang Alschner and Damien Charlotin, 'The Growing Complexity of the International Court of Justice's Self-Citation Network: Institutional Achievement or Access-to-Justice Concern?' (Social Science Research Network 2016) SSRN Scholarly Paper ID 2832148, https://papers.ssrn.com/abstract=2832148, accessed 27 February 2017.

[34] 'WTO | Disputes – Dispute Settlement CBT – Legal Effect of Panel and Appellate Body Reports and DSB Recommendations and Rulings – Legal Status of Adopted/Unadopted Reports in Other Disputes – Page 1,' www.wto.org/english/tratop_e/dispu_e/disp_settlement_cbt_e/c7s2p1_e.htm, accessed 8 July 2016.

[35] Raj Bhala, 'The Myth about Stare Decisis and International Trade Law (Part One of a Trilogy)' (1998) 14 *Am. U. Int'l L. Rev.* 845; David Palmeter and Petros C Mavroidis, 'The WTO Legal System: Sources of Law' (1998) 92 *AJIL* 398, 399–400 Raj Bhala, 'Precedent Setters: De Facto Stare Decisis in WTO Adjudication (Part Two of a Trilogy) (1999) 9 *J. Transnat'l L. & Pol'y* 1; Raj Bhala, 'Power of the Past: Towards De Jure Stare Decisis in WTO Adjudication (Part Three of a Trilogy)' (2000) 33 *Geo. Wash. Int'l L. Rev.* 873. See also Rachel Brewster, 'The System of Precedent(or the Lack Thereof) at the WTO', in Carl Baudenbacher and Simon Planzer (eds.), *International Dispute Resolution: The Role of Precedent* (German Law Publishers, 2011).

[36] For example, Graham Cook considers discussions of the public international law relating to the subsidiary sources of international law: *A Digest of WTO Jurisprudence on Public International Law Concepts and Principles* (Cambridge University Press, 2015) p. 253.

dispute settlement mechanism and the WTO as a whole.[37] As Pauwelyn observes, however, a choice in favour of de facto reliance on precedent has important implications. First, as far as litigation strategies are concerned, 'no one can successfully engage in WTO dispute settlement without knowing previous Appellate Body case law'.[38] Second, one must be mindful that the rule refinement performed by the Appellate Body in its adjudication is most commonly triggered by disputes involving a minority of states. In this regard Pauwelyn's findings confirm the significance of prior research by Pelc on the strategic value of precedent setting in WTO adjudication, whereby powerful states initiate disputes of little economic value with a view to obtaining a rule gain.[39]

The use of external authority in WTO dispute settlement, instead, remains very much an open issue. A quantitative analysis of the data paints an interesting picture (Figure 5.1 below).[40] WTO panels and the Appellate Body routinely refer to the jurisprudence of other international tribunals, though to a significantly lesser extent than investment tribunals. The most cited judicial authorities are – by far – the decisions of the ICJ/PCIJ. Even then, however, the citation networks are quite scattered and patterns difficult to establish. Overall, an analysis of the network shows panel and Appellate Body reports are more likely to appear as hubs (marked in dark grey in Figure 5.1) than ICJ/PCIJ decisions, few of which have been cited more than once or twice.[41]

Similar patterns also apply to the citation of other external authorities. Investment tribunals have also been cited sparingly, with three awards or decisions in total[42] being cited in just two WTO reports.[43]

---

[37] DSU Article 3.2.
[38] Joost Paulwelyn, 'Minority Rules: Precedent and Participation before the WTO Appellate Body' in Joanna Jemielniak (ed.), *Establishing Judicial Authority in International Economic Law* (Cambridge University Press, 2016).
[39] Krzysztof J Pelc, 'The Politics of Precedent in International Law: A Social Network Application' (2014) 108 *American Political Science Review* 547.
[40] The sample includes all the Appellate Body and Panel Reports available as of August 2016.
[41] *Case Concerning Military and Paramilitary Activities in and Against (Nicaragua v. United States)*, 1986 ICJ Rep 14, 82–86 (cited six times); *Corfu Channel (United Kingdom of Great Britain and Northern Ireland v. Albania)*, 1949 ICJ Rep 15 (cited three times).
[42] *Saipem SpA v. The People's Republic of Bangladesh*, Decision on Jurisdiction and Recommendation on Provisional Measures, ICSID Case ARB/05/07 (2007); *MTD Equity Sdn Bhd and MTD Chile SA*, Award on Merits, ICSID Case No. ARB/01/7; *Saluka Investments BV v. The Czech Republic*, Partial Award, 17 March 2006 (PCA).
[43] *China – Measures Related to The Exportation of Rare Earths, Tungsten, and Molybdenum*, WT/DS431/R WT/DS432/R WT/DS433/R; *United States – Final Anti-dumping Measures on Stainless Steel from Mexico*, WT/DS344/AB/R.

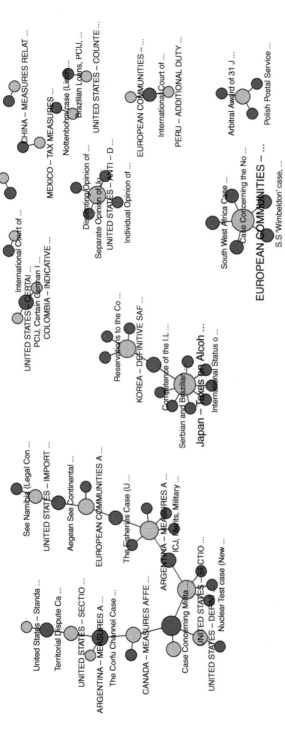

Figure 5.1 WTO reference to the jurisprudence of other international tribunals

3.2 Citation of External Authorities in Investment Arbitration

The issue of precedent has been discussed at length in the field of international investment arbitration, and with excellent reason. With some approximation, the literature discussing the topic has concentrated on a variety of sub-problems reflecting – broadly – the tension between the constitutions of formally independent tribunals, operating on different – and, sometimes, rather dissimilar – treaty bases and the systemic values at stake.[44] Precedent following is generally considered to underscore the rule of law dimension of investment law and arbitration by increasing its consistency, which in turn contributes to enhancing the credibility of the system and its appeal to its users.[45]

To be sure, there is ample room for disagreement. Once it is settled that predictability is but an illusion,[46] one might ask whether precedent following really helps pursue this goal. Alternatively, one may question whether consistency is just a mediocre objective when compared to the higher value of coherency with its objectives in its development,[47] or a poor value when it leads to the preservation of rules that make more harm than good.[48] One may even go so far as to say that, in light of other, more fateful features of the system, the association of investment arbitration with the concept of the rule of law may come across as highly problematic.[49] Yet, there is hardly any doubt that the role of arbitrators and the way they relate to precedent has an impact on the development of international investment law and arbitration. Both contribute to the texture of the legal system and, as it has been argued following the model proposed by David Easton,[50] may be seen as a part of the output of investment arbitration considered as a political system.[51]

---

[44] See generally W Michael Reisman, '"Case Specific Mandates" versus "Systemic Implications": How Should Investment Tribunals Decide?: The Freshfields Arbitration Lecture' (2013) 29 *Arbitration International* 131.

[45] Gabrielle Kaufmann-Kohler, 'Arbitral Precedent: Dream, Necessity or Excuse?: The 2006 Freshfields Lecture' (2007) 23 *Arbitration International* 357, 378.

[46] Jan Paulsson, 'Indirect Expropriation: Is the Right to Regulate at Risk?', DM 2 (2006), www.transnational-dispute-management.com.

[47] Douglas (n. 21) 109.

[48] Schultz (n. 16).

[49] Gus Van Harten, 'Investment Treaty Arbitration, Procedural Fairness, and the Rule of Law' in Stephan W Schill (ed.), *International Investment Law and Comparative Public Law* (Oxford University Press, 2010) p. 629, www.oxfordscholarship.com/view/10.1093/acprof:oso/9780199589104.001.0001/acprof-9780199589104-chapter-20, accessed 26 July 2016.

[50] David Easton, 'An Approach to the Analysis of Political Systems' (1957) 9 *World Politics* 383.

[51] Cédric Dupont and Thomas Schultz, 'Towards a New Heuristic Model: Investment Arbitration as a Political System' (2016) 7 *Journal of International Dispute Settlement* 3, 7.

On the contrary, the same degree of scholarly attention has not been drawn to the phenomenon of external precedent in international investment arbitration.[52] At this point it is worth noting that while it would be possible to stick to the idea of international investment tribunals as strictly independent[53] and isolated from any institutional framework and to claim that any precedent is an external precedent, the strong institutionalization of investment arbitration and the deep connections between its main actors all militate against such a construction.[54]

Overall, tribunals settling investment disputes have resorted to the jurisprudence of other judicial bodies.[55] In this context, we will consider the jurisprudence of the International Court of Justice and its predecessor, the Permanent Court of International Justice; the Iran-US Claims Tribunal; the European Court of Human Rights; and the WTO panels and Appellate Body.

ICJ and PCIJ decisions are the obvious winners, with pinpoints or general references easily in the thousands. The graph in Figure 5.2 represents ICJ and PCIJ cases and weighs them by the number of times they are cited by decisions of investment tribunals.[56] It shows that citations are frequent, with many decisions referring to multiple authorities, several among which are landmarks (for example, *ELSI*, *Factory at Chorzów*, and *Barcelona Traction*).[57] In terms of the number of citations within the same decisions, a pattern emerges whereby more cases are often cited when one of the arbitrators is a member or former member of the International Court – a finding that should not surprise in the least.[58]

---

[52] But see Pellet (n. 23); Gibson and Drahozal (n. 30); Stephan W Schill and Katrine R Tvede, 'Mainstreaming Investment Treaty Jurisprudence' (2015) 14 *Law & Practice of International Courts and Tribunals* 94; Vadi, *Analogies in International Investment Law and Arbitration* (n. 26).

[53] *AES Corporation v. Argentine Republic*, ICSID Case No. ARB/02/17, Decision on Jurisdiction (26 April 2005), para. 30.

[54] Pellet (n. 23) 228.

[55] I consider all decisions hosted on Investor-State Law Guide that were decided between 1995 and 2015.

[56] For the sake of simplicity, the graph does not account for the number of times a citation has been repeated within the same decision, and does not implement edge-weighing.

[57] See *Case concerning Elettronica Sicula SpA (ELSI)* (United States/Italy), Judgment (20 July 1989) (cited in eighty cases), [1989] ICJ Reports 15; *Factory at Chorzów* (Claim for Indemnity) (Merits) (Germany/Poland), Judgment (13 September 1928), PCIJ (Ser. A) No. 17 (sixty-seven mentions); *Barcelona Traction, Light and Power Company, Ltd.* (Belgium/Spain), Judgment (5 February 1970), [1970] ICJ Reports 3 (forty-eight mentions).

[58] See *Ambiente Ufficio S.P.A. and Others (Case formerly known as Giordano Alpi and Others) v. Argentine Republic*, ICSID Case No. ARB:08:9, Decision on Jurisdiction and Admissibility, 8 February 2013 (with Bruno Simma as President).

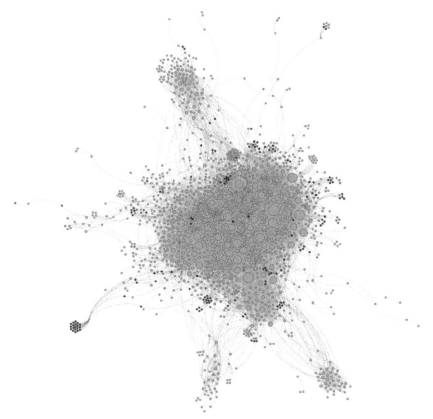

Figure 5.2 ICJ and PCIJ citation network by investment tribunals

The ICJ/PCIJ citation network (Figure 5.2) also reveals that investment tribunals have had few reservations in citing minority opinions, with some among these ranking among the most-cited authorities.[59] Furthermore, advisory opinions tend to feature heavily in the decisions of investment tribunals.[60] Unsurprisingly, the recognized continuity

---

[59] For example, *Case concerning Oil Platforms (Islamic Republic of Iran v. United States of America)*, Separate Opinion of Judge Higgins (12 December 1996), [1996] ICJ Reports 847 (cited thirty-nine times); *Ambatielos Case (Greece/United Kingdom)*, Joint Dissenting Opinion by Sir Arnold McNair, President, and Judges Basdevant, Klaestad and Read (19 May 1953), [1953] ICJ Reports 25 (cited eight times).

[60] See, for example, *Interpretation of Peace Treaties (Bulgaria, Hungary and Romania)*, Advisory Opinion (30 March 1950), [1950] ICJ Rep 65 (cited six times); *Legal*

between the activity of the PCIJ and the ICJ[61] is reflected in the significant number of references to the jurisprudence of the predecessor of the current World Court.[62]

Investment tribunals have also been inclined to cite the jurisprudence of the Iran-US claims tribunals, with a total of 244 unique citations of 76 decisions. The graph in Figure 5.3 (highlighted bottom right quadrant) shows the connections between investment and Iran-US Claims Tribunal decisions.[63] Some cases have proved exceedingly popular authorities,[64] while others have been cited sparsely or only once.[65] Minority opinions have only been cited four times, though at least one such opinion scores six hits in the network.[66] Unsurprisingly, most of the decisions cited were issued between 1982 and 1989, when the Tribunal completed most of its large-scale commercial claims.[67]

Consequences of the Construction of a Wall in Occupied Palestinian Territory, Advisory Opinion (9 July 2004), 2004 ICJ Rep 136 (cited seven times).

[61] Mohamed Shahabuddeen, *Precedent in the World Court* (Cambridge University Press, 2007) pp. 22 ff.

[62] Decisions of the PCIJ have been referred to forty-one times. See, in particular, *Factory at Chorzów (Claim for Indemnity) (Merits) (Germany/Poland)*, Judgment (13 September 1928), PCIJ Ser A No. 17, with a grand total of seventy-six citations.

[63] The size of the network nodes reflects the number of times they have been cited – a measure known as 'in-degree centrality' in network analysis.

[64] See, for example, *Tippets, Abbett, McCarthy, Stratton v. TAMS-AFFA Consulting Engineers of Iran, et al.*, Award (29 June 1984), Award No. 141-7-2 (cited twenty-six times); *American International Group, Inc. v. Iran*, Award (19 December 1983), Award No. 93-2-3 (cited twenty-four times); *Starrett Housing Corporation, et al. v. Iran, et al.*, Award (19 December 1983), Award No. ITL 32-24-1 (cited twenty-two times); *Phillips Petroleum Co. Iran v. Islamic Republic of Iran*, Award (29 June 1989), Award No. 425-39-2 (cited seventeen times).

[65] See, for example, *Aram Sabet et al. v. Iran – Bonyad E. Mostazafan*, Partial Award No. 593-815/816/817-2 (30 June 1999); *Paul Donin de Rosiere, et al. and Iran, et al.*, Interim Award No. ITM 64-498-1 (14 December 1986). These findings show an evolution since the analysis conducted ten years ago by Gibson and Drahozal (n. 30) 544 ff.

[66] *Sylvania Technical Systems Inc. v. The Government of Iran*, Case No. 64, Award No. 180-64-1, Separate Opinion of Howard M. Holtzmann on Awarding Costs of Arbitration (27 June 1985). It should be observed, however, that three such citations refer to the Yukos arbitration, thus affecting their statistical relevance; see *Veteran Petroleum Limited (Cyprus) v. Russian Federation*, PCA Case No. AA 228, Final Award, 18 July 2014; *Hulley Enterprises Limited (Cyprus) v. Russian Federation*, PCA Case No. AA 226, Final Award, 18 July 2014; *Yukos Universal Limited (Isle of Man) v. Russian Federation*, PCA Case No. AA 227, Final Award, 18 July 2014.

[67] David D Caron and John R Crook, *The Iran-United States Claims Tribunal and the Process of International Claims Resolution: A Study by the Panel on State Responsibility of the American Society of International Law* (Transnational Publishers, 2000) 477; John R Crook, 'The U.S. and International Claims and Compensation Bodies' in Cesare PR Romano (ed.), *The Sword and the Scales: The*

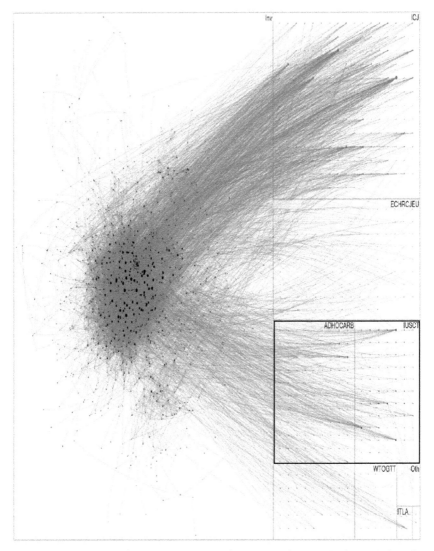

Figure 5.3 Connection between investment decisions and Iran-US Claims Tribunal decisions
* ADHOCARB = Ad hoc arbitration; IUSCT = Iran-US Claims Tribunal

United States and International Courts and Tribunals (Cambridge University Press, 2009) p. 304.

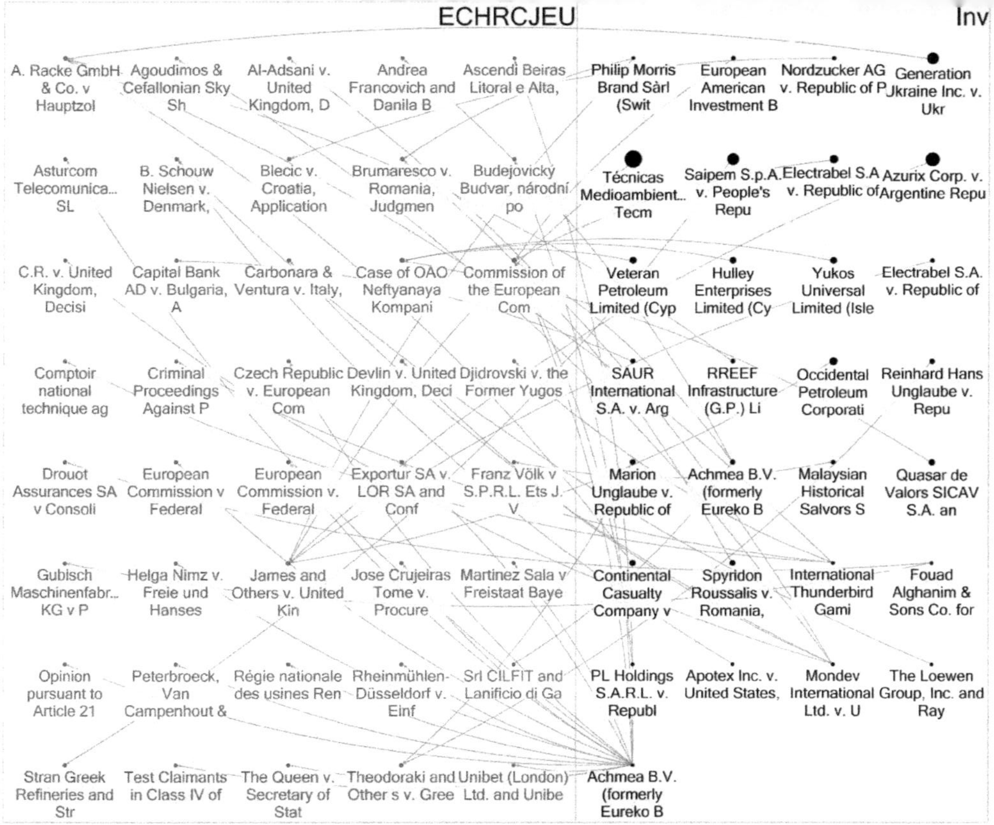

Figure 5.4 Citation of ECtHR decisions by investment tribunals

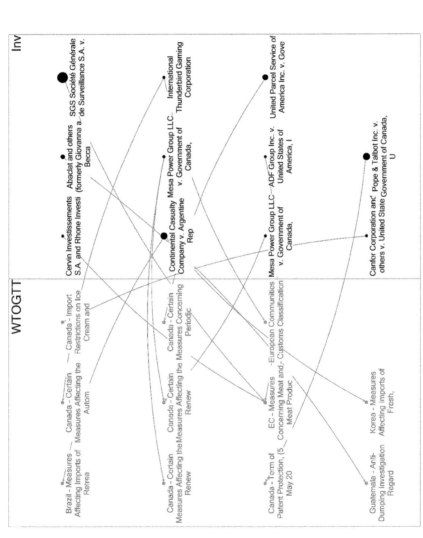

Figure 5.5 Citation of WTO decisions by investment tribunals

EXTERNAL PRECEDENT IN TRADE AND INVESTMENT CASES 139

Different yet is the case of the citation of European Court of Human Rights (ECtHR) jurisprudence.[68] In total, eighty-two decisions issued by the ECtHR were cited. However, the graphic representation in Figure 5.4 shows that citing decisions are more likely to serve as a 'hub'. In other words, the more scattered appearance of the graph is due to the fact that citations of ECtHR case law by investment tribunals are comparatively rare, though, on average, quite scrupulous, with arbitral decisions usually pointing at several court cases.[69] While the reverse is less common, reports of the WTO panels and Appellate Body have also constituted a significant source of jurisprudence for investment tribunals. An analysis of the corresponding citation network (Figure 5.5) shows that such decisions have been cited twenty-nine times by tribunals constituted under the UNCITRAL rules, twenty-seven times by ICSID tribunals, five by PCA tribunals, and once by LCIA tribunals. It bears noting, however, that approximately half of these citations occur in minority opinions.[70]

4 Areas and Objectives Prompting Recourse to External Authority

4.1 WTO Dispute Settlement

As we have seen, WTO panels and the Appellate Body refer to external authorities. The analysis of the data presented above allows us to identify certain patterns. First, while the claim that external authority is never invoked 'to interpret WTO law' is perhaps a bit extreme,[71] it is true that such authority is generally employed to address matters that have a broader significance in general international law. For example,

---

[68] See also Chapter 11 in this volume by José E Alvarez.
[69] See *Mondev International Ltd.* v. *United States of America*, ICSID Case No. ARB(AF)/99/2, Final Award, 11 October 2002 (thirteen references); *Víctor Pey Casado and President Allende Foundation* v. *Republic of Chile*, ICSID Case No. ARB/98/2, Award, 8 May 2008 (eleven references).
[70] *Garanti Koza LLP* v. *Turkmenistan*, ICSID Case No. ARB/11/20, Dissenting Opinion of Laurence Boisson de Chazournes, 3 July 2013, citing *Japan – Taxes on Alcoholic Beverages* (4 October 1996), WTO Doc. WT/DS8/AB/R, WT/DS10/AB/R, WT/DS11/AB/R (Appellate Body Report); *S.D. Myers, Inc.* v. *Government of Canada*, UNCITRAL, Separate Opinion by Dr Bryan Schwartz, Concurring Except with Respect to Performance Requirements, in the Partial Award of the Tribunal, 12 November 2000, citing *Indonesia – Certain Measures Affecting the Automobile Industry* (2 July 1998), WTO Doc. WT/DS54/R, WT/DS55/R, WT/DS59/R, WT/DS64/R (Panel Report).
[71] Voeten (n. 30).

reference has been made to the jurisprudence of the ICJ/PCIJ to address questions of treaty interpretation (even for the purposes of interpreting the WTO agreement),[72] the status and significance of municipal law,[73] the customary status of certain rules of international law,[74] evidence,[75] the status of general principles,[76] procedural[77] and law-ascertaining powers,[78] and even questions relating directly to the administration of disputes under the Dispute Settlement Understanding (DSU).[79]

---

[72] *United States – Section 211 Omnibus Appropriations Act of 1998*, WT/DS176/R, citing *Corfu Channel Case* (1949) ICJ Rep and *Territorial Dispute Case (Libyan Arab Jamahiriya v. Chad)* (1994) ICJ Rep; *Argentina – Measures Affecting The Importation Of Goods*, WT/DS438/R, WT/DS444/R, WT/DS445/R, citing *United States Diplomatic and Consular Staff in Tehran (United States v. Iran)* (1980) ICJ Rep; ICJ, Merits, *Military and Paramilitary Activities In and Against Nicaragua (Nicaragua v. United States of America)* (1986) ICJ Rep; *Fisheries Jurisdiction (United Kingdom v. Norway)* (1951) ICJ Rep; *Armed Activities on the Territory of the Congo (Democratic Republic of the Congo v. Rwanda)*, Jurisdiction of the Court and Admissibility of the Application (2006) ICJ Rep; *Frontier Dispute (Burkina Faso v. Mali)*, Judgment (1986) ICJ Rep.

[73] *Colombia – Indicative Prices and Restrictions on Ports of Entry*, WT/DS366/R; *United States – Certain Measures Affecting Imports of Poultry from China*, WT/DS392/R, both citing *Certain German Interests in Polish Upper Silesia* (1926) PCIJ Rep, Ser A No. 7.

[74] On nationality: *European Communities – Protection of Trademarks and Geographical Indications for Agricultural Products and Foodstuffs*, WT/DS174/R, citing *Nottenbohm (Liechtenstein v. Guatemala)* (second phase) ICJ Reports (1955) 4.

[75] *Argentina – Measures Affecting the Export of Bovine Hides and The Import of Finished Leather*, WT/DS155/R, WT/DS155/R, citing *Corfu Channel*, 1949 ICJ Rep.

[76] For the principle *nemo ex propria turpitudine commodum capere potest*, see *Mexico – Tax Measures on Soft Drinks and Other Beverages*, WT/DS308/AB/R, citing *Factory at Chorzów (Germany v. Poland)* (Jurisdiction) (1927) PCIJ Ser A No. 9.

[77] *United States – Anti-Dumping Act of 1916*, WT/DS136/AB/R,. WT/DS162/AB/R, referring to *Administration of the Prince von Pless* (Preliminary Objection) (1933) PCIJ Ser A/B No. 52, 15; *Anglo-Iranian Oil Co Case* (Preliminary Objection) (Individual Opinion of President McNair)(1952) ICJ Rep 116; *Certain Norwegian Loans*, Separate Opinion of Judge Lauterpacht (1957) ICJ Rep 43; *Interhandel Case* (Preliminary Objections) Dissenting Opinion of Judge Lauterpacht (1959) ICJ Rep 104.

[78] On *iura novit curia*, see *European Communities – Conditions for the Granting of Tariff Preferences to Developing Countries*, WT/DS246/AB/R, citing *Nicaragua* (1986) ICJ Rep; on equity, see *China – Measures Related to the Exportation of Rare Earths, Tungsten, and Molybdenum*, WT/DS431/R, WT/DS432/R, WT/DS433/R, citing *Continental Shelf (Libya v. Malta)* (1982) ICJ Rep.

[79] For example, regarding the concept of standing, see *European Communities – Regime for The Importation, Sale And Distribution Of Bananas*, WT/DS27/AB/R, citing *Northern Cameroons*, ICJ Rep 1963. See also Joost Pauwelyn, *Conflict of Norms in Public International Law: How WTO Law Relates to Other Rules of International Law* (Cambridge University Press, 2003) 81.

Second, reference to the case law of other bodies has sometimes been made for the same purposes.[80] However, in most cases, the citation of external authorities has served the goal of supporting certain practices – if not inherent powers – of the WTO Dispute Settlement Body (DSB). For example, to buttress the practice of relying on prior decisions, reliance has been placed on the jurisprudence of the ECtHR[81] and investment tribunals.[82] Only in one dispute was an investment decision invoked to shed light on the Appellate Body's discussion of the 'even-handedness' requirement arising from Article XX(g) GATT.[83]

Finally, no panel or Appellate Body report has devoted much discussion to the question of the precedential role of external decisions, rather restricting themselves to justifying their citations with the occasional observation on the practice of international judicial bodies.

4.2 Investment Arbitration

Investment tribunals have been particularly active in invoking external authorities. This section briefly considers some aspects of this citation practice.

First, contrary to standard WTO practice, investment tribunals have sometimes felt the need to justify their reliance on precedents by external authorities, though the arguments have often been a little confusing. One of the most interesting justifications remains the one espoused in *Tulip Real Estate*, where a claimed hierarchical relationship between the International Court of Justice and other judicial bodies was purposely not addressed, though the tribunal accepted that 'though not bound by such citations, ... as a matter of comity, it should have regard to earlier

---

[80] *United States – Standards for Reformulated and Conventional Gasoline*, WT/DS2/AB/R, citing the ECtHR case *Golder v. United Kingdom*, ECHR, Ser A (1995) no. 18 (on customary status of VCLT rules); *United States – Anti-Dumping Act of 1916* WT/DS136/AB/R, WT/DS162/AB/R, citing Iran-United States Claims Tribunal, *Marks & Umman v. Iran*, 8 Iran-United States CTR (Award No. 53-458-3) (on Kompetenz-Kompetenz).

[81] *China – Measures Related to the Exportation of Rare Earths, Tungsten, and Molybdenum*, WT/DS431/R, WT/DS432/R, WT/DS433/R, citing *Cossey v. United Kingdom*, 1990 Ser A (1990).

[82] *United States – Final Anti-Dumping Measures on Stainless Steel from Mexico*, WT/DS344/AB/R, citing *Saipem SpA v. The People's Republic of Bangladesh*, Decision on Jurisdiction and Recommendation on Provisional Measures, ICSID Case No. ARB/05/07 (2007).

[83] *China – Measures Related to the Exportation of Rare Earths, Tungsten, and Molybdenum*, WT/DS431/R, WT/DS432/R, WT/DS433/R, citing, *MTD Equity Sdn. Bhd. and MTD Chile SA*, ICSID Case No. ARB/01/7, Award on Merits.

decisions of courts (particularly the ICJ)'.[84] Other tribunals have instead justified reliance on external precedent on the basis of the need for ensuring consistency and the development of investment law,[85] though the opinion is not universally shared.[86] Such statements of deference are, as a rule, normally reserved to the ICJ.

Second, tribunals have relied extensively on external precedent when it was conducive, from the point of view of the arbitrators, to improving the effectiveness of the regime. The well-known fortune in investment jurisprudence of the ICJ dictum in *LaGrand*[87] on the question of the binding character of interim measures is emblematic, and shows the readiness of international tribunals to refer to the reasoning of an authoritative court to increase their powers, going beyond – and according to some, even against – the relevant normative framework.[88]

Third, citation of specialized dispute settlement bodies does not always – or even often, for that matter – reflect the need to refer to their special expertise. This is the case, in particular, of citations of specialized judicial bodies for discussion of matters of general international law such as interpretation,[89] good faith,[90] conflict between treaties and norms,[91]

---

[84] *Tulip Real Estate Investment and Development Netherlands B.V. and Republic of Turkey*, ICSID Case No. ARB/11/28, Decision On Bifurcated Jurisdictional Issue, 5 March 2013.

[85] *Burlington Resources Inc. v. Republic of Ecuador*, ICSID Case No. ARB/08/5, Decision on Liability, 14 December 2012, para. 187.

[86] See also the position of Brigitte Stern in the same case. See also *Total S.A. v. Argentine Republic*, ICSID Case No. ARB/04/1, Concurring Opinion by Luis Herrera Marcano, 27 December 2010, para. 9.

[87] *LaGrand (Germany v. United States of America)* (Judgment) 2001 ICJ Rep 502.

[88] *Victor Pey Casado and President Allende Foundation v. Republic of Chile*, ICSID Case No. ARB/98/2, Decision on Provisional Measures, 25 September 2001, para. 17; *Cemex Caracas Investments BV and Cemex Caracas II Investments BV v. Venezuela*, ICSID Case No. ARB/08/15, IIC 423, Decision on Provisional Measures, 3 March 2010; *Perenco Ecuador Limited v. Ecuador and Empresa Estatal Petróleos del Ecuador (Petroecuador)*, ICSID Case No. ARB/08/6, IIC 375, Decision on Provisional Measures, 8 May 2009.

[89] For examples of references to WTO case law on matters of treaty interpretation, see *Garanti Koza LLP v. Turkmenistan*, ICSID Case No. ARB/11/20, Dissenting Opinion of Laurence Boisson de Chazournes, 3 July 2013, citing WTO case law on questions relating to the VCLT; *Pope & Talbot Inc v. Government of Canada*, UNCITRAL, Award on the Merits of Phase 2, 10 April 2001, fn. 68; *Poštová banka, as. and ISTROKAPITAL SE v. Hellenic Republic*, ICSID Case No. ARB/13/8, Award, 9 April 2015, para 293. On the 'object and purpose' of a treaty, see *ADF Group Inc. v. United States of America*, ICSID Case No. ARB(AF)/00/1, Award, 9 January 2003, para. 147.

[90] *Venezuela Holdings B.V. and others v. Bolivarian Republic of Venezuela*, ICSID Case No. ARB/07/27, Decision on Jurisdiction, 10 June 2010, para. 170.

[91] *European American Investment Bank AG (Austria) v. Slovak Republic*, PCA Case No. 2010-17, Award on Jurisdiction, 22 October 2012, para. 218, fn. 231.

EXTERNAL PRECEDENT IN TRADE AND INVESTMENT CASES 143

questions relating to the burden of proof in interpreting jurisdictional exceptions,[92] retroactive application of domestic law,[93] self-judging clauses,[94] exhaustion of local remedies,[95] jurisdiction *ratione temporis*,[96] provisional measures[97] or the obligation to issue reasoned decisions.[98]

Of course, this is not always the case: citation of WTO case law has been greater for questions within the WTO law's area of expertise, for example with regard to discriminatory measures and national treatment.[99] Some of these cases, however, have attracted criticism. *Continental* v. *Argentina*, in particular, has prompted polarized reactions,[100] only assuaged in part by the – hardly conclusive – refusal on the part of the ad hoc committee to annul the award on the grounds of manifest excess of powers.[101] Similarly, the case law of the ECtHR has been cited with reference to general[102] or

---

[92] *Canfor Corporation v. United States of America, Tembec Inc. et. al. v. United States of America and Terminal Forest Products Ltd. v. United States of America*, UNCITRAL, Decision of Preliminary Question, 6 June 2006, fn. 184.
[93] *Mondev International Ltd. v. United States of America*, ICSID Case No. ARB(AF)/99/2, Final Award, 11 October 2002, para. 138.
[94] *El Paso Energy International Company v. Argentine Republic*, ICSID Case No. ARB/03/15, Award, 31 October 2011, para. 598.
[95] *Achmea B.V. (formerly Eureko B.V.) v. Slovak Republic* [I], PCA Case No. 2008-13, Award on Jurisdiction, Arbitrability and Suspension, 26 October 2010.
[96] *Nordzucker AG v. Republic of Poland*, UNCITRAL, Partial Award (Jurisdiction), 10 December 2008.
[97] *Perenco Ecuador Limited v. Republic of Ecuador and Empresa Estatal Petróleos del Ecuador*, ICSID Case No. ARB/08/6, Decision on Provisional Measures, 8 May 2009, para. 70.
[98] *Tulip Real Estate and Development Netherlands B.V. v. Republic of Turkey*, ICSID Case No. ARB/11/28, Decision on Annulment, 30 December 2015, para. 152.
[99] *Pope & Talbot Inc. v. Government of Canada*, UNCITRAL, Award on the Merits of Phase 2, 10 April 2001, para. 68; *United Parcel Service of America Inc. v. Government of Canada*, UNCITRAL, Separate Statement of Dean Ronald A. Cass, 24 May 2007, para. 120; *Continental Casualty Company v. Argentine Republic*, ICSID Case No. ARB/03/9, Award, 5 September 2008.
[100] José E Alvarez, '"Beware: Boundary Crossings" – A Critical Appraisal of Public Law Approaches to International Investment Law' (2016) 17 *The Journal of World Investment & Trade* 194 ff.; Jürgen Kurtz, 'The Use and Abuse of WTO Law in Investor–State Arbitration: Competition and Its Discontents' (2009) 20 *European Journal of International Law* 749; Federico Ortino, 'Legal Reasoning of International Investment Tribunals: A Typology of Egregious Failures' (2012) 3 *Journal of International Dispute Settlement* 31.
[101] Valentina Vadi, *Analogies in International Investment Law and Arbitration* (Cambridge University Press, 2016) p. 216.
[102] *Víctor Pey Casado and President Allende Foundation v. Republic of Chile*, ICSID Case No. ARB/98/2, Award, 8 May 2008, para. 609.

specific questions of expropriation,[103] shareholders' rights,[104] state immunity[105] and the concept of 'acquired rights'.[106]

5 Reputation, Self-Empowerment and Legitimacy: A Functionalist Paradigm

Prior literature investigating the use of external precedent has generally focused on two aspects of the issue. Some look back to the cited decisions and seek to identify the distinguishing features of a precedent worth following. For example, Brian King and Rahim Moloo's study on international arbitration measures the importance of the originating regime, the factual matrix at issue, the reputation of the adjudicator or arbitrator, and the quality of the reasoning.[107] For Cohen, other elements must be added to the 'checklist', some of them being internal to the decision (for example, the interpretation's adherence to prior interpretations and its fitting within a broader legal regime) and some external (such as its public availability and the frequency of citation).[108] Others have considered a more forward-looking dimension of following and borrowing precedent; that is, the objectives pursued and the results accomplished by following precedent. For example, Slaughter and Helfer have argued that unremitting reliance on internal and – to a considerable degree – external precedent is, along with the excellence of their reasoning and the virtually absolute compliance with their rulings, at the basis of the success

---

[103] With reference to the loss of value of shares in a public company, see *RREEF Infrastructure (G.P.) Limited and RREEF Pan-European Infrastructure Two Lux S.à r.l. v. Kingdom of Spain*, ICSID Case No. ARB/13/30, Decision on Jurisdiction, 6 June 2016; on whether a judicial decision may amount to an expropriation, see *Saipem S.p.A. v. People's Republic of Bangladesh*, ICSID Case No. ARB/05/07, Decision on Jurisdiction and Recommendation on Provisional Measures, 21 March 2007, para. 132.

[104] *Azurix Corp. v. the Argentine Republic*, ICSID Case No. ARB/01/12, Decision on the Application for Annulment of the Argentine Republic, 1 September 2009, para. 128.

[105] *Mondev International Ltd. v. United States of America*, ICSID Case No. ARB(AF)/99/2, Final Award, 11 October 2002, para. 598.

[106] *International Thunderbird Gaming Corporation v. United Mexican States*, UNCITRAL, Separate Opinion, 01 December 2005, para. 27.

[107] See, for example, Rahim Moloo and Brian King, 'International Arbitrators as Lawmakers' (2014) 46 *New York University Journal of International Law and Politics (JILP)*, http://papers.ssrn.com/sol3/ Papers.cfm?abstract_id=2504628, accessed 6 May 2015.

[108] Harlan Grant Cohen, 'Theorizing Precedent in International Law' in Andrea Bianchi, Daniel Peat and Matthew Windsor (eds.), *Interpretation in International Law* (Oxford University Press, 2015) p. 275.

and the high perceived legitimacy of the Court of Justice of the European Union and the ECtHR.[109]

An appraisal of the data tells us a number of things. First, ICJ and PCIJ rulings outnumber any other external judicial authority in both WTO dispute settlement and investment arbitration. Of course, the World Court is, for most, 'de toutes les juridictions celle qui se situe à l'échelon suprême'.[110] No international adjudicator is unfamiliar with the Court's prestige and reputation, which, as difficult as they may be to quantify, 'are nonetheless obvious and real'.[111] This reputation is also extended to the individual members of the Court, which means that their minority opinions enjoy a high number of citations.[112] Furthermore, decisions of the Court are normally extensively reasoned and offer solid support for the building of arguments. Finally, there is merit to the claim that the ICJ acts as a centre of gravity for international law, under both descriptive and normative perspectives.[113]

Similarly, the output of the WTO dispute settlement system appears to enjoy a positive reception. In particular, with regard to the Appellate Body, consistency, balance and self-restraint in its activity, a strong degree of compliance, and the overall high quality of the reasoning make its jurisprudence respected and perceived as worth citing.[114] In other words, it appears that the WTO DSB does not need to engage in the same exercises as investment tribunals to move, quoting Schill and Tvede, 'from the periphery towards the center of the communicative network in which international adjudicative bodies operate'.[115] Overall, the receptiveness of investment tribunals to external authority is largely

[109] Anne-Marie Slaughter and Laurence R Helfer, 'Toward a Theory of Effective Supranational Adjudication' (1997) 107 *Yale Law Journal* 273, 308–24.
[110] *Application for Revision and Interpretation of the Judgment of 24 February 1982 in the case concerning the Continental Shelf* (Tunisia/Libyan Arab Jamahiriya), 1985 ICJ Rep, Oral Pleadings, 187.
[111] Robert Kolb, *The International Court of Justice* (Bloomsbury Publishing, 2013) p. 67.
[112] See *Pulp Mills on the River Uruguay*, 2006 ICJ Rep, Joint dissenting opinion of Judges Al-Khasawneh and Simma.
[113] See Andenas and Bjorge (n. 27); Dupuy (n. 27) 798.
[114] Christian Joerges, 'Compliance Research in Legal Perspectives' in Michael Zürn and Christian Joerges (eds.), *Law and Governance in Postnational Europe: Compliance Beyond the Nation-State* (Cambridge University Press, 2005) p. 240; Giorgio Sacerdoti, 'From Law Professor to International Adjudicator' in David D Caron et al. (eds.), *Practising Virtue* (Oxford University Press, 2015) pp. 212–13.
[115] Stephan W Schill and Katrine R Tvede, 'Mainstreaming Investment Treaty Jurisprudence: The Contribution of Investment Treaty Tribunals to the Consolidation and Development of General International Law' (2015) 14 *The Law & Practice of International Courts and Tribunals* 94.

unparalleled; whether the 'mainstreaming' of investment jurisprudence is (barring *Diallo*)[116] actually producing significant results is a problem that lies beyond the scope of this chapter.

I submit that the key to understanding the use of external precedent is a functionalist approach based on the regime's strength and need of effectiveness. In the case of WTO dispute settlement, reference to external authority is generally scant, and it is not always clear how much this is due to worries about the applicable law and the obligation not to diminish the rights of WTO members under Articles 3.2 and 19.2 of the DSU.[117] However, reference to external authority is noticeably higher when it can be employed to enhance the WTO's effectiveness and procedural legitimacy.[118] In this regard, the DSB's citation patterns confirm Simma and Pulkowski's analysis. The WTO remains a 'strong' regime, but it is lacking in certain aspects, for example, with regard to 'rules on interpretation, standard of review, [and] burden of proof'. Accordingly, the panels and the Appellate Body do not hesitate in looking outwards in search of rules and tools that can assist them in the application of substantive law.[119] Moreover, the Appellate Body has also relied on *external* precedent to justify its approach to *internal* precedent.[120] By so doing, it bestows what Joseph Weiler called 'external legitimacy' on a practice meant to ensure 'internal legitimacy' in the dispute settlement dimension.[121] This approach has allowed the DSB to strike a compromise between efficiency and legitimacy that has suited the WTO's centralized machinery.

Conversely, the more diffused nature of the investment regime, the comparative scarcity of 'legitimacy capital'[122] of investor-state dispute

---

[116] (2012) ICJ Reports 3.

[117] See, e.g. Lorand Bartels, 'Applicable Law in WTO Dispute Settlement Proceedings' (2001) 35 *Journal of World Trade* 499; Joost Pauwelyn, 'The Role of Public International Law in the WTO: How Far Can We Go?' (2001) 95 *American Journal of International Law* 535; Pauwelyn (n. 73) *passim*; Petros C Mavroidis, 'No Outsourcing of Law? WTO Law as Practiced by WTO Courts' (2008) 102 *AJIL* 421.

[118] *European Communities – Regime for The Importation, Sale and Distribution of Bananas*, WT/DS27/AB/R. See also Joanna Gomula, 'The Heritage of the PCIJ in WTO Dispute Settlement' in Christian J Tams and Malgosia Fitzmaurice, *Legacies of the Permanent Court of International Justice* (Martinus Nijhoff Publishers, 2013).

[119] Bruno Simma and Dirk Pulkowski, 'Of Planets and the Universe: Self-Contained Regimes in International Law' (2006) 17 *European Journal of International Law* 483, 510.

[120] *United States –Steel*, citing *Saipem*.

[121] Joseph HH Weiler, 'The Rule of Lawyers and the Ethos of Diplomats: Reflections on the Internal and External Legitimacy of WTO Dispute Settlement' (2001) 35 *Journal of World Trade* 191, 201.

[122] Yuval Shany, *Assessing the Effectiveness of International Courts* (Oxford University Press, 2014) p. 145.

settlement, and the ISDS system's quest for effectiveness have all militated in favour of a more proactive invocation of external authority. Tribunals, of course, know that this is a successful strategy and, as Pellet contends, 'judicial or arbitral bodies hardly resist the temptation when they see a possibility to extend their power – if not their legitimacy'.[123] While this reliance cannot always be downplayed as – to stick to Pellet's analysis – hiding behind a fig leaf, it is probably true that investment tribunals have often taken advantage of external decisions more shrewdly, if perhaps less rigorously and carefully.

6   Conclusion: Convergence and the Pitfalls of Analogical Reasoning

Writing about the common law, Justice Holmes observed that 'just as the clavicle in the cat only tells of the existence of some earlier creature to which a collarbone was useful, precedents survive in the law long after the use they once served is at an end and the reason for them has been forgotten. The result of following them must often be failure and confusion from the merely logical point of view.'[124] This remark seems apt to describe some of the problems arising from the practice of citing external legal authorities, where time or systemic distance might lead a tribunal to yield to the temptation of looking at the precedents of another judicial body, especially one that is effective and respected, with the looming risk of borrowing the wrong law or getting it wrong – or both.[125] In other words, the citation of external authorities is not devoid of consequences. Concerning investment arbitration in particular, the practice of following extra-systemic decisions has long been denounced as having the potential for dangerous abuses and failures.[126] Of course, the jurisprudence of specialized judicial bodies seems a more likely candidate for disruption than that of a more general court such as the ICJ – in this regard, it is easy to understand why many have called for improved methodology in the use of analogies,[127] or the appointment of arbitrators well-versed in specialized fields.[128] While it is true that the use of extra-systemic

---

[123] Pellet (n. 23) 239.
[124] Oliver Wendell Holmes, *The Common Law* (Courier Corporation, 2013) p. 34.
[125] Alvarez (n. 26).
[126] Kurtz (n. 94); Ortino (n. 94).
[127] Vadi, *Analogies in International Investment Law and Arbitration* (n. 26).
[128] Jürgen Kurtz, 'The Use and Abuse of WTO Law in Investor-State Arbitration: Competition and Its Discontents' (2009) 20 *European Journal of International Law*

decisions cannot always be blamed for confusion and controversy, it may nevertheless prompt mistrust.[129]

In conclusion, the question of whether the use of external precedent prompts interaction and convergence is complex, and this chapter reflects, with its largely empirical approach, this difficulty. Interaction exists, though its direction is quite unidirectional. And if convergence is to be found, it is in the larger picture: international dispute settlement bodies display awareness of the fact that they 'all function – or at least purport to function – within the same ocean of international law' and their use of external precedent reflects shared effectiveness concerns.[130]

749, 770. It might be observed that, while experience is certainly desirable, it has been argued that 'judges who know more about a particular field of law are less deferential toward precedent than equally able (and no more "re-strained") judges who know less about the same field', Richard A Posner, 'The Jurisprudence of Skepticism' (1988) 86 *Michigan Law Review* 827, 864.

[129] Robert Howse and Efraim Chalamish, 'The Use and Abuse of WTO Law in Investor-State Arbitration: A Reply to Jürgen Kurtz' (2009) 20 *European Journal of International Law* 1087, 1092 (discussing the difficulty of attributing the approaches by the *Continental* and *Methanex* tribunals to their interpretation of WTO only).

[130] James Crawford, *Chance, Order, Change: The Course of International Law, General Course on Public International Law* (Martinus Nijhoff Publishers/Brill Academic, 2014) p. 292.

6

Engagement between International Trade and Investment Adjudicators

MICHELLE Q ZANG

In the context of international adjudication, the term 'engagement' occupies a large middle ground on the continuum between resistance and convergence. It highlights the willingness of the participating adjudicator to consider external sources in the appropriate case and it denotes commitments to judicial deliberation. Nevertheless, the outcome of 'engagement' is open to either 'harmony', with the external source, or 'dissonance'. Deliberative engagement is based on the adjudicators' own initiative, as opposed to inter-judiciary communication based on an institutional framework, i.e. the preliminary reference mechanism of the Court of Justice of the European Union (CJEU) and the interaction between the national courts and the ECtHR. Opposite to dialogue, engagement usually takes the form of monologue, i.e. referencing, deliberating and comparing the practice and decisions of other courts or tribunals that are not necessarily aware of the ongoing proceedings. In most cases, the initiating adjudicator does not treat the decision from another jurisdiction as a binding source, but rather as a source of inspiration, evidence or authority; it focuses on the course of deliberation and comparison as regards the persuasiveness and applicability of the practice and the decision being invoked; it serves as a judicial screen filter and might possibly end up with disagreement, completely or partially.

The subject of this chapter is 'engagement' between the WTO adjudicators on the one hand, and the ISDS arbitral tribunals, on the other. The chapter will assess how the adjudicators have engaged with each other and the reasons for the engaging activities, as well as the implications of engagement. This subject has been well explored in the scholarship on a case-by-case or subject-by-subject basis;[1] furthermore, several recent studies[2] offer the empirical foundation for an overarching survey of this adjudicatory phenomenon. For this purpose, this chapter is arranged as follows. It will first offer a recount of the current practice, i.e. how the WTO jurisprudence is used in the ISDS proceedings. It will then explore the potential causes of the status quo, i.e. why the WTO jurisprudence is used by ISDS arbitrators in the current pattern. Afterwards, the analysis will look into the implications and consequences that result from engagement, i.e. what the use of WTO jurisprudence suggests and where it leads.

1 The Use of WTO Jurisprudence in ISDS Proceedings

To date, WTO jurisprudence has been used in ISDS proceedings mainly under three circumstances. The categorization used in this chapter is, to a certain extent, similar to the classification of 'objective settings' discussed by Marceau, Izaguerri and Lanovoy. In their investigation into the WTO's influence on other international dispute settlement mechanisms, they found that the WTO *acquis* is applied in four major objective settings, namely, establishing or confirming factual details, considering the applicability and use of procedural and process-related rules in a dispute, clarifying a principle or rule of treaty interpretation or a general principle of law, and aiding in the interpretation of a substantive norm or a legal test.[3] Although all the argued 'objective settings' have emerged in the WTO-ISDS context, categorizing the circumstances of adjudicatory engagement as it is shown below would better demonstrate the role and function of the WTO case law invoked, as well as the nuanced relationship between the trade and investment regimes.

---

[1] Joost Pauwelyn, 'Editorial Comment: Adding Sweeteners to Softwood Lumber: the WTO-NAFTA "Spaghetti Bowl" Is Cooking' (2006) 9 *Journal of International Economic Law* 1, 197; Jeffrey Dunoff, 'The Many Dimensions of Softwood Lumber' (2007) 45 *Alta. L. Rev* 319; Jürgen Kurtz, 'The Use and Abuse of WTO Law in Investor–State Arbitration: Competition and Its Discontents' (2009) 20 *European Journal of International Law* 3, 749; Jürgen Kurtz, 'Adjudging the Exceptional at International Investment Law: Security, Public Order and Financial Crisis' (2010) 59 *International & Comparative Law Quarterly* 2, 325; Nicholas DiMascio and Pauwelyn Joost, 'Nondiscrimination in Trade and Investment Treaties: Worlds Apart or Two Sides of the Same Coin?' (2008) 102 *American Journal of International Law* 1, 48; Allen Brooks and Tommaso Soave, 'Jurisdictional Overlap in WTO Dispute Settlement and Investment Arbitration' (2014) 30 *Arbitration International* 1, 1.

[2] Gabrielle Marceau, Izaguerri Arnau and Lanovoy Vladyslav, 'WTO's Influence on Other Dispute Settlement Mechanisms: A Lighthouse in the Storm of Fragmentation' (2013) 47 *J. World Trade* 3, 481.

[3] Ibid., 487.

The first circumstance is where WTO case law is invoked and referenced as an interpretative aid. On the one hand, the rulings of WTO adjudicators are used to elaborate the meaning of the substantive norm that is under dispute in the ISDS proceedings. On the other hand, the interpretative process does not necessarily lead to the endorsement of the invoked WTO jurisprudence. Rejection and discard are very often the case. Furthermore, on many occasions ISDS awards have revealed partial approval and agreement with the legal reasoning put forth in the WTO cases.

The ICSID award in *Continental* is the best known example of a full 'implantation' of WTO jurisprudence.[4] The tribunal in that case was faced with the task of determining the content of the concept of 'necessity' as stipulated in Article XI of the US – Argentina BIT, which provides that:

> This Treaty shall not preclude the application by either Party of measures necessary for the maintenance of public order, the fulfillment of its obligations with respect to the maintenance or restoration of international peace or security, or the Protection of its own essential security interests.

The tribunal was well aware of the prevailing approach among the ISDS tribunals on this issue, namely the recourse to customary international law and to the customary pleas of necessity under the draft ILC articles.[5] Nevertheless, it decided to 'refer to the GATT and WTO case law which has extensively dealt with the concept and requirements of necessity in the context of economic measures derogating to the obligations contained in GATT'.[6] For the tribunal, 'the text of Article XI [of the BIT] derives from the parallel model clause of the U.S. FCN treaties and these treaties in turn reflect the formulation of Article XX of GATT 1947'.[7]

Rather than the full endorsement above, ISDS tribunals in most cases have adopted a more complicated approach towards WTO jurisprudence. For example, during its 'likeness' assessment under national treatment, the tribunal in *SD Meyers* firstly concurred with the Appellate Body's ruling in *Japan – Alcoholic Beverages* that the concept

---

[4] See *Continental Casualty Company v. Argentine Republic*, ICSID Case No. ARB/03/9, 5 Sept 2008.
[5] Kurtz 2010 (n. 1), 327.
[6] Award, *Continental Casualty Company v. Argentine Republic*, ICSID Case No. ARB/03/9, 5 Sept 2008, para. 192.
[7] Ibid.

of 'likeness' is a relative one and should be assessed in light of the specific context. It was of the view that the meaning of 'like circumstances' under Article 1102 of the NAFTA has to be evaluated in the specific legal context.[8] Nevertheless, after this brief importation of the WTO case law, the tribunal immediately pointed out the contextual difference that distinguishes the GATT from NAFTA Chapter 11, that is, the former provides a set of general exceptions that are nevertheless missing in the latter.[9] This point of difference eventually resulted in the tribunal's move to ground a reading of national treatment as a discipline based on purposeful protectionism.[10]

The straight rejection of the WTO *acquis* is also not uncommon in ISDS proceedings. In *Occidental*, while being mindful of the likeness assessment under the GATT/WTO, the tribunal considered the views of the WTO adjudicators not specifically pertinent to the issues under dispute. For the tribunal, not only the purpose of national treatment at issue was the opposite of that under the GATT/WTO, but more importantly, the term 'in like situations' used in the BIT included all exporters that share such conditions, while the GATT/WTO 'like product' necessarily relates to only competitive and substitutable products.[11]

The second circumstance under which the WTO case law is often discussed in ISDS awards is when the arbitrators conceive WTO dispute settlement as one of the principal methods of international adjudication, quoting its practice and rulings in relation to the meaning of principles of law and certain procedural matters. In their application of the principle of in *dubio mitius*, both the tribunals in *Bureau Veritas, Inspection, Valuation, Assessment and Control, BIVAC B.V.*[12] and *SGS Société Générale*[13] made reference to the Appellate Body's statement on *dubio mitius* delivered in *EC Measures Concerning Meat and Meat Products (Hormones)*. In *Telefónica S.A. v. Argentina*, the tribunal referred to the

---

[8] Partial award, *S.D. Myers, Inc. v. Government of Canada*, NAFTA/UNCITRAL, paras. 244–246.

[9] Ibid.

[10] Kurtz 2009 (n. 1), 760; DiMascio and Pauwelyn (n. 1), 48.

[11] Final award, *Occidental Exploration and Production Company v. Ecuador*, UNCITRAL, 1 July 2004, paras. 174–176.

[12] Further objection to jurisdiction, *Bureau Veritas, Inspection, Valuation, Assessment and Control, BIVAC B.V. v. The Republic of Paraguay*, ICSID Case No. ARB/07/9, FN 379.

[13] Objection to jurisdiction, *SGS Société Générale de Surveillance S.A. v. The Republic of Paraguay*, ICSID Case No. ARB/07/29, FN 178.

Appellate Body report in *Japan – Alcoholic Beverages-II*, particularly the part elaborating the term 'subsequent practice' under Article 31.3(b) of the Vienna Convention.[14] The tribunal in *SD Myers* invoked the WTO concept of 'single undertaking' as elaborated by the Panel in *Korea – Definitive Safeguard Measure on Imports of Certain Dairy Products* and the Appellate Body in *Guatemala Cement*. In particular, the tribunal used the mentioned WTO reports to buttress its conclusion that NAFTA provisions should be read as complementary, unless there was a conflict in the sense that adherence to one provision would cause a violation of the other.[15]

On the procedural front, the WTO case law has offered significant guidelines for ISDS on a number of issues. In several cases, ISDS tribunals made recourse to the Appellate Body report on the question of burden of proof, which is famously settled in *United States – Measures Affecting Imports of Woven Wool Shirts and Blouses from India*.[16] In *Methanex*, the tribunal invoked the WTO practice on amicus curiae, which, according to the tribunal, should be made equally available at the pending proceedings.[17] Another instance under this category refers to the de facto 'precedent' in general international and international economic adjudication. (See also Chapter 5 in this volume by Niccolò Ridi). It was expressly raised by Thomas Wälde, who stated in his separate opinion to *International Thunderbird Gaming Corp. v. Mexico* that 'WTO, ICJ and in particular investment treaty jurisprudence shows the importance to tribunals of not "confronting" established case law by divergent opinion – except if it is possible to clearly distinguish and justify in-depth such divergence'.[18] In *Glamis Gold*, the tribunal was also of the view that 'a NAFTA tribunal, while recognizing that there is no precedential effect given to previous decisions, should communicate

---

[14] Objection to jurisdiction, *Telefónica S.A. v. The Argentine Republic*, ICSID Case No. ARB/03/20, FN 73.

[15] Partial award, *S.D. Myers, Inc. v. Government of Canada*, NAFTA/UNCITRAL, paras. 292–293.

[16] Final award, *International Thunderbird Gaming Corporation v. The United Mexican States*, UNCITRAL, para. 95, FN 2; Award, *Marvin Roy Feldman Karpa v. United Mexican States*, ICSID Case No. ARB(AF)/99/1, para.177.

[17] Amicus decision, *Methanex Corporation v. United States of America*, UNCITRAL, paras. 31 and 33.

[18] Separate Opinion, *International Thunderbird Gaming Corp. v. United Mexican States*, UNCITRAL, para. 129. Similar reasoning may be found in Award, *Duke Energy v. Ecuador*, paras. 116–117; Decision on Jurisdiction, *Saipem v. Bangladesh*, paras. 66–67; Decision on Jurisdiction, *Noble Energy v. Ecuador*, paras. 49–50.

its reasons for departing from major trends present in previous decisions, if it chooses to do so'.[19]

The last category in which adjudicatory engagement often took place is when ISDS tribunals had to deal with the measures that had already been settled by the WTO adjudicators or measures that are inextricably linked to existing WTO disputes. This is particularly the case where the same or closely related measures are subject simultaneously to disputes between not only exporting and importing states but also private investors and host states.

The best known examples include the softwood lumber saga between Canada and the United States and sweetener/sugar products between Mexico and the United States. In both cases, the ISDS tribunals made reference to both the facts found and legal reasoning made in WTO dispute settlement. In *Canfor*, where Canadian producers claimed that the USA's countervailing and anti-dumping measures against softwood lumber products were in breach of NAFTA Chapter 11, the tribunal was of the view that 'while the conduct of the United States before the WTO and the findings of WTO Panels and its Appellate Body have no binding effect upon this Tribunal, they constitute relevant factual evidence that the Tribunal can and should appropriately take into account'.[20] In *Archer Daniels*, a case concerning the Mexican tax applied to imports of high fructose corn syrup, the tribunal validated the WTO ruling in *Mexico – Tax Measures on Soft Drinks and Other Beverages* that the disputed tax was discriminatory due to the fact that it was imposed so as to afford protection to Mexican domestic production of cane sugar.[21] Thus, it is often practically impossible to simply ignore the factual and legal issues, arguments and rulings that occur across both systems.[22]

2 Why do ISDS Tribunals Choose to Use the WTO *Acquis*?

There are three main reasons that can explain why ISDS tribunals choose to 'engage' with WTO jurisprudence. First of all, WTO adjudicators have

---

[19] Final Award, *Glamis Gold, Ltd.* v. *The United States of America*, UNCITRAL, p. 5.
[20] Decision on preliminary question, *Canfor Corporation* v. *United States of America; Terminal Forest Products Ltd.* v. *United States of America*, UNCITRAL, para. 327.
[21] Award, *Archer Daniels Midland Company and Tate & Lyle Ingredients Americas, Inc.* v. *The United Mexican States*, ICSID Case No. ARB (AF)/04/5, paras. 190 and 212.
[22] Jürgen Kurtz, *The WTO and International Investment Law: Converging Systems* (Cambridge University Press, 2016), p. 14.

successfully established themselves as one of the major fora for international dispute resolution; the practice and rulings of the WTO Appellate Body and panels are thus regarded as a source of authority in international adjudication.[23] It is not only the case in relation to procedural matters, such as amicus submissions and burden of proof; the elaborations of WTO panels and the Appellate Body on legal concepts and general principles of law are also often quoted.[24] Particularly in the trade-investment context, the WTO Appellate Body is widely considered one of the most prestigious adjudicators specialized in economic matters.[25]

Second, as a result of economic reality, it is often the case that the same domestic measure can be challenged under both the trade and investment regimes. Nowadays, trade and investment are no longer substitutes, but support each other.[26] Traditionally, the establishment of a foreign subsidiary is regarded as a way for delivering goods or services to a foreign market; foreign investment was thus an alternative to trade. In this global era, however, investment is no longer regarded as a means of replacing trade but as a way of supplementing or promoting it. In the construction of global supply chains, foreign direct investment is a complement rather than substitute to cross-border trade in goods and services. Consequently, a domestic measure with restricting effects on certain products will usually affect both trade and investment.[27] When parallel or serial litigations happen, the adjudicators involved, as shown in the litigation saga of softwood lumber and sweetener/sugar, are inclined to look into the findings made at another forum, owing to the identical or inextricably linked measures and contexts under dispute.[28]

The third and most relevant factor for trade and investment adjudicatory engagement is the normative connection underlying the

---

[23] Marceau, Arnau and Lanovoy (n. 2), 487.
[24] Ibid.
[25] See José E Alvarez, *The Boundaries of Investment Arbitration: The Use of Trade and European Human Rights Law in Investor-State Disputes* (Jurist Publishing, 2018) Ch 3.
[26] Kenneth Vandevelde, 'A Brief History of International Investment Agreements' (2005) 12 UC Davis J. Int'l L. & Pol'y 1, 157; Sergio Puig, 'International Regime Complexity and Economic Law Enforcement' (2014) 17 *Journal of International Economic Law* 3, 491–516.
[27] Vandevelde (n. 26) 157; Puig (n. 26) 180–1.
[28] Decision on preliminary question, *Canfor Corporation v. United States of America; Terminal Forest Products Ltd. v. United States of America*, UNCITRAL, para. 327; Award, *Archer Daniels Midland Company and Tate & Lyle Ingredients Americas, Inc. v. The United Mexican States*, ICSID Case No. ARB (AF)/04/5, paras. 190 and 212.

two regimes. As shown in the earlier survey (Chapter 5 in this volume; see also Chapter 11 in this volume), the most common category of engagement between WTO dispute settlement and ISDS takes the form of interpretative aids: ISDS tribunals made reference to WTO case law to buttress their preferred understanding of the substantive rules. The fact that such reference leads not only to endorsement but also to the discard and partial acknowledgement by the arbitral tribunals of WTO jurisprudence discloses further the nuanced connection between the two branches of international economic law: on the one hand, trade and investment share the common regulatory aims of economic integration and equal competition; and, on the other hand, they nevertheless bear substantial regime diversion in treaty text, enforcement apparatus and policy priority.

The point of departure is that both trade and investment law are regulatory instruments of global economic governance; they share the regulatory aims of economic integration and equal competition. Objections against the commonality between trade and investment have been raised, arguing that the normative orientations of the two regimes are fundamentally different[29] and investment law, different from trade law, is about protection not liberalization, about individual rights not state-to-state exchanges of market opportunities.[30] This argument, however, bears an inherent bias, with a 'tunnel vision' exclusively focusing on the enforcement mechanism and dispute settlement, while overlooking the common fundamentals underlying the disparate rules and policies. It has mainly, if not solely, focused on the most disputed matters, or the type of disputes that prevail. While cases before trade courts and tribunals have generally focused on legal issues in relation to liberalization, most investment arbitrations are established for one single category of dispute, that is the losses claimed by the foreign investor against certain domestic regulatory activities of the host state. Distinguishing between the functions of the trade and investment regimes on the basis that one protects economic opportunities and the other protects property rights is misleading. In fact, the right of investors being protected is a right to equality in economic opportunity; and thus

---

[29] Mark Wu, 'The Scope and Limits of Trade's Influence in Shaping the Evolving International Investment Regime' in Zachary Douglas, Joost Pauwelyn and Jorge E Vinuales (eds.), *The Foundations of International Investment Law: Bringing Theory into Practice* (Oxford University Press, 2014), pp. 169–212.

[30] DiMascio and Pauwelyn (n. 1), 56.

non-discrimination in investment agreements similarly aims at preserving a level playing field for economic competition.[31]

Another point of weakness of the theory that separates trade and investment is that it considers protection as the sole purpose of investment law, which, as the regulatory instrument beyond nation states, entails instead all types of policy required for economic governance. Apart from protection, most BITs also bear the aims of investment liberalization and promotion,[32] and the emerging trend is to include policy objectives related to sustainable development, e.g. the improvement of living standards and the protection of health, safety and consumers.[33] Investment protection, as one major legal principle, is the normative setting in response to the very nature of investing activities. However, it stands in parallel with other equally important disciplinary requirements, e.g. non-discrimination, transparency and good administration. To claim it as the very purpose of investment law would neglect the multifaceted functions of the rule of law and substantively narrow down the spectrum of governance of the regime.

However, although sharing the common regulatory aims in economic integration and equal competition, the trade and investment regimes have witnessed significant differences in their system design and evolutionary trajectory. Such difference is plainly reflected in the treaty text that is tailored to the specific economic circumstance under each regime. For example, the national treatment provision of trade, as stipulated under Article III GATT, requires no-less-favourable treatment between domestic and foreign 'like products', while the parallel provision in BITs focuses on foreign and domestic investments and investors in 'like circumstances', rather than 'like investments' or 'like investors'. As a result, judicial criteria associated with the 'likeness' test normally varies from one regime to another. Furthermore, the trade and investment regimes also have established different enforcement apparatuses, i.e. dispute settlement mechanisms. As mentioned earlier, trade disputes mainly take the

---

[31] Donald McRae, 'The World Trade Organization and International Investment Law: Converging Systems—Can the Case for Convergence be Made?' (2014) 9 *Jerusalem Review of Legal Studies* 1, 15.

[32] US-Uruguay; Canada-Peru; Czech Republic-China; Thailand-Germany; UK-Vietnam. In the preamble of these BITs, the term 'protection' goes hand-in-hand with 'promotion': 'promotion and protection' of investments are considered as 'conducive to the stimulation of business activity/initiative'.

[33] US-Uruguay; Canada-Peru.

form of litigation between nation states, while investment arbitration mainly deals with claims submitted by foreign investors against the host state. The design of dispute settlement does not suggest fundamental systemic divergence or divergence in legal tradition;[34] instead, it simply endorses the arguably effective model for conflict resolution and norm enforcement in light of the nature of the disputes raised, as well as the specific historical and social backgrounds at the time of the dispute.

Last but not least, the policy priorities of the two regimes were also distinct during the different phases of their development. For trade, domestic barriers[35] against imports have been the most often raised issue for dispute settlement and treaty negotiation. In contrast, domestic barriers against foreign investment have never caused much tension in practice. Instead, the first group of modern BITs was created in response to a growing concern, during the mid-twentieth century, over the expropriation of foreign investments in developing countries.[36] Similar to the design of the enforcement apparatus, disparate policy priority simply represents the normative response, under different economic contexts, to the same ultimate aims of economic integration and equal competition, and thus cannot be considered a sign of divergence in regime orientation. In other words, disparate policy priority should not affect the recognition of the fundamental commonality throughout the entire realm of international economic law.

Therefore, the nuanced regime connection between trade and investment can be summarized as follows: they are twins, not identical but fraternal, from one single family; they do not have the same appearance and they have grown up alongside distinct growth tracks; however, they share the same family tree DNA and they are doomed to have a number of crossing points and overlaps during different phases of their lives.

---

[34] Wu (n. 29).
[35] The term 'domestic barrier' is used in the broad sense including any type of measures of the importing country that might negatively affect the circulation of foreign products into and within the domestic market. Typical examples include tariffs and customs charges, taxation and domestic measures, and technical and sanitary standards.
[36] The concern reached its zenith when developing countries as a group took the position in the United Nations that customary law did not require compensation for expropriation. Alan Sykes, 'Public versus Private Enforcement of International Economic Law: Standing and Remedy' (2015) 34 *The Journal of Legal Studies* 2, 642.

3 What Does the Engagement Reveal?

3.1 Adjudicatory Engagement: Signal of Regime Convergence or Divergence?

In scholarly discourse on the relationship between trade and investment, adjudicatory engagement has been used to argue both in favour and against convergence.[37] This chapter holds the position that the state of play of adjudicatory engagement alone is not an adequate parameter to mirror the relationship between the regimes within which the adjudicators are founded. At most, it serves as one of the parameters that might be simultaneously affected by many other elements. For example, Jürgen Kurtz, when arguing for systemic convergence between trade and investment, listed five major factors that are pushing them together.[38]

Convergence, as an ongoing process (see Chapter 1 in this volume), does not mean identity. Any analysis of the relationship between trade and investment would have to respect the systemic differences between them, either inherent or acquired. During the adjudication process, such differences might, as shown in the ISDS awards mentioned above, reasonably lead to potential endorsement or even rejection of the case law from the other regime. While unconditional implantation should not be expected as the usual outcome, rejection or partial acknowledgement should not be considered as the signal of a hostile approach against regime convergence. Instead, it simply discloses the adjudicators' awareness of the discrepancy, together with the similarity, between the two regimes as well as between the concepts and norms under dispute. In this sense, it is plausible that the ISDS arbitrators are reticent about drawing on trade-infused arguments and when they do so their reliance on WTO jurisprudence is cautious and nuanced.

However, it is not always plausible to judge the extent of convergence or divergence by counting the quantity or ratio of references made by the ISDS tribunals to WTO case law (see the previous discussion in Chapter 5). While regime relation involves the analysis of historical developments, normative similarity, political economy and regulatory purposes, engagement is only part of the exercise of norm application, which is further constrained by factors such as jurisdictional independence, the background and experience of the adjudicators and facts of the

---

[37] Kurtz 2016 (n. 22), p. 14.
[38] Ibid., pp. 10–19.

disputes. That is to say, the exercise of invoking the WTO *acquis* is the combined outcome of a number of factors that in most cases stand remotely from the inter-regime relationship.

All in all, the review of the status quo of 'engagement' can help form our understanding of the relationship between the regimes, but is unable to lead to any definite conclusions. What we can tell is – given the causes of adjudicatory engagement mentioned earlier – that ISDS tribunals will probably continue referencing the WTO *acquis* when confronted with certain issues.

3.2 Adjudicatory Engagement: A Signal of System Fragmentation or Legitimacy Enhancement?

The review of the engagement between trade and investment tribunals offers empirical evidence for the argument that the often suspected adjudicatory 'chaos' associated with the plurality and proliferation of international courts and tribunals is more perceived than real. In the case of international economic adjudication, the most often raised concerns lie in the coexisting and parallel dispute settlement mechanisms which are not only empowered with jurisdiction over the same domestic measures, but also very often encounter identical or highly similar legal questions. Therefore, some worry that multiple adjudicators might deliver diverging, inconsistent or even conflicting decisions over the same measure and/or issue.

For the disputes concerning the same domestic measures that are submitted for resolution to both trade and investment adjudicators, the survey of engagement shows that the adjudicators involved not only were aware of the parallel proceedings and/or existing reports but also took full account of them during their deliberations. The ISDS tribunals appeared comfortable endorsing the WTO adjudicators' findings concerning both the facts and relevant legal matters. In this sense, judicial actors increasingly view their function as including the need to serve as guardians of the fabric of international dispute settlement by ensuring its coherence through coordination.[39]

One of the most well-known examples of a legal issue encountered by both trade and investment adjudicators is the matter of non-discrimination

---

[39] Laurence de Chazournes Boisson, 'Plurality in the Fabric of International Courts and Tribunals: The Threads of a Managerial Approach' (2017) 28 *European Journal of International Law* 1, 32.

under the national treatment test. On this point, adjudicators have delivered a high number of opinions that are not necessarily coherent or complementary to each other.[40] However, such a disorganized state of play is not so problematic that it exposes the system to serious legitimacy risks. Arguably, where there has been divergence, there are often legitimate justifications for it, e.g. the textual and contextual differences of the law and facts applied to the case; or the divergence can simply remain unproblematic so long as the disputes from which it stems remain isolated and do not develop into trends.

In the trade-investment context, the most accessible justification is the regime difference in system design and evolutionary trajectory, as mentioned earlier, that to a large extent renders impossible direct importation of WTO jurisprudence into ISDS proceedings. On the other hand, even if concepts such as non-discrimination are applied differently in different legal orders, what is important is the fact that the concepts that are applied are common – for example, equal competition is recognized as one of the common regulatory aims shared between trade and investment – and are arguably the 'cohesive forces' that hold the two regimes together.[41]

The myth of fragmentation as a result of the proliferation of international adjudicators is also contested by a reality check. The frequent reference to the WTO *acquis* on procedural matters as well as the meaning of general principles of law suggests that international law offers sufficient common idioms or vocabulary on what might be called procedural or generic questions to allow positive conversation, interaction and mutual influence between different tribunals.[42] It is further argued that sophisticated legal interpretation allows for and indeed arguably requires greater openness to various kinds of outside and diverse influences or factors and the judges are comfortable bringing in 'external' normative

---

[40] Partial award, *S.D. Myers, Inc.* v. *Government of Canada*, NAFTA/UNCITRAL, paras. 244–246; Final Award, *Occidental Exploration and Production Company* v. *Ecuador* (UNCITRAL, 1 July 2004), 174–176; Award, *Archer Daniels Midland Company and Tate & Lyle Ingredients Americas, Inc.* v. *The United Mexican States*, ICSID Case No. ARB (AF)/04/5, paras. 190 and 212; Decision on Responsibility, *Corn Products International, Inc.* v. *United Mexican States*, ICSID Case No. ARB (AF)/04/1, paras. 121–122; Award, *Mesa Power* v. *Canada*, UNCITRAL, PCA Case No. 2012-17, para. 346.

[41] de Chazournes Boisson (n. 39) 34.

[42] Robert Howse and Ruti Teitel, 'Cross-Judging: Tribunalization in a Fragmented but Interconnected Global Order' (2008) 41 *New York University Journal of International Law and Policy* 1, 959; Chester Brown, *A Common Law of International Adjudication* (Oxford University Press, 2007).

material simply through a conception of its relevance to the adjudicative task before them.[43]

While the claimed adjudicatory chaos associated with the plurality and proliferation of international adjudicators did not really take place, some positive developments emerged through adjudicatory engagement. Despite the overlapping jurisdiction, there is actually very little chance for parallel or repeated litigations that involve the same disputing parties over the same disputed measure and subject to the same applicable law. What actually happened in trade and investment adjudication is not only that a wider range of interested parties, i.e. both nation states and individual investors, is granted access to dispute settlement, but also the legality of the disputed measure is subject to scrutiny under a wider set of norms. There is also an implicit and evolving recognition by the adjudicators that they belong to an epistemic community where a common idiom or vocabulary of international law prevails.[44] The most outstanding instances of such commonality include the rules of procedure and general principles of law.

Another positive development lies in the repeated adjudicatory exercise of elaborating several critical legal questions. Divergent outcomes of deliberation should be expected not only as the result of the different contexts applicable under each dispute; more importantly, it is also part of the natural outcome and inherent nature of ad hoc adjudication. However, diverging outcomes do not mitigate the value of repeated adjudicatory deliberations. Arguably, norms are generally strengthened through their encounters with judicial actors, and their content is made more determinate, not indeterminate.[45]

4 Conclusions

This chapter does not aim to assess the correctness and accuracy of the use of the WTO *acquis* by the ISDS tribunals. This topic has been well discussed elsewhere.[46] This chapter places the focus on the engaging activities per se as a specific category of adjudicatory exercise, exploring their pattern, causes, indication and consequences.

---

[43] Howse and Teitel (n. 42) 988–9.
[44] See Brown (n. 42).
[45] de Chazournes Boisson (n. 39) 35.
[46] Kurtz 2009 (n. 1), 749–71. See also Chapter 11 in this volume by José E Alvarez.

The use of WTO rules and rulings has been and will continue to be the practice of ISDS arbitral tribunals. To date, ISDS tribunals have invoked the WTO *acquis* for a number of issues, ranging from norm interpretation and legal understanding to evidential and factual verification. Nevertheless, the impact the invoked WTO *acquis* has upon ISDS proceedings varies. The case law does not only show full endorsement and straight rejection by the arbitral tribunals, it further discloses a number of nuanced uses of WTO law, i.e. partial approval of the facts found, and the legal reasoning made.

As for the question whether and if so, to what extent, the engaging activities between adjudicators suggest the trend of convergence or divergence between trade and investment regimes, this chapter holds the view that the state of play of the adjudicators' engaging activities is not an adequate parameter to mirror the relationship between the two regimes. At the maximum, it serves as one of the parameters that can help to form our understanding of the relationship between the two regimes, but it is unable to lead to any definite conclusions on convergence or divergence. Not only did the unwanted events of forum shopping, inconsistent decisions and systemic fragmentation not appear in practice, but adjudicatory engagement actually brings in several positive developments that further enhance the legitimacy and credibility of international economic adjudication. They include, for example, extended access to justice, a more comprehensive scope of the legality review, and the evolving recognition among adjudicators that they belong to an epistemic community as guardians of the international legal system.

PART III

Interpretive Powers and Adjudicative Behaviour

7

Inherent Powers of the WTO Appellate Body and ICSID Tribunals – A Tale of Cautious Convergence

RIDHI KABRA[*]

1 Introduction

The principle of 'inherent powers' is among the many tools used by international courts to converge their procedural laws.[1] However, the 'inherent powers' principle in international dispute settlement (IDS) is notoriously elusive. Several attempts have been made to comprehend the legal basis for the exercise of inherent powers in international law.[2] Some attribute the origins of the principle to the notion of 'implied powers'; others find its source in the doctrine of 'general principles of international law', while yet others argue that inherent powers emanate from a court's performance of the 'judicial function'. Although international courts refer to their inherent powers as a basis for judicial

---

[*] The author would like to thank J Christopher Thomas, Giorgio Sacerdoti, Markus Wagner, Niccolò Ridi and other participants at the Pluricourts conference 'Adjudicating International Trade and Investment Disputes: Between Interaction and Isolation' for their comments. The views expressed in this chapter do not necessarily reflect the views of Three Crowns or any of its clients.

[1] See for example: Chester Brown, *A Common Law of International Adjudication* (Oxford University Press, 2007).

[2] Paola Gaeta, 'Inherent Powers of International Tribunals' in Lal Chand Vohrah et al. (eds.), *Man's Inhumanity to Man: Essays on International Law in Honour of Antonio Cassese* (Kluwer, 2003); Chester Brown, 'The Inherent Powers of International Courts and Tribunals' (2005) 76 *British Yearbook of International Law* 195; Friedl Weiss, 'Inherent Powers of National and International Courts: the Practice of the US-Iran Claims Tribunal' in Christina Binder et al. (eds.), *International Investment Law for the 21st Century: Essays in Honour of Christoph Schreuer* (Oxford University Press, 2009); Andrew D Mitchell and David Heaton, 'The Inherent Jurisdiction of WTO Tribunals: The Select Application of Public International Law Required by the Judicial Function' (2010) 31 *Michigan J Intl L* 559.

action otherwise unsupported by their constitutive instruments, the amorphous nature of the concept makes it prone to unnecessarily broad or restrictive interpretations. Such interpretations do injustice to the doctrine's role in assisting courts with their adjudicative functions and in turn promote, in Chester Brown's words, a 'common law of international adjudication'.[3]

This is particularly the case for the World Trade Organization (WTO) Appellate Body and tribunals (ICSID tribunals) constituted under the Convention on the Settlement of Investment Disputes between States and Nationals of Other States (ICSID Convention). Both bodies are engaged in the function of resolving economic disputes. Yet, it is often assumed that while ICSID tribunals have broad inherent powers, the WTO Appellate Body's inherent powers are restricted.[4] What explains these assumptions? Have they resulted from divergences in the judicial functions of these bodies, or a more systemic misunderstanding of the ability of these bodies to exercise inherent powers? Is there a rational explanation for these assumptions?

This chapter answers the above questions by examining the manner in which the Appellate Body and ICSID tribunals perceive their authority to exercise inherent powers. While existing literature has engaged critically with the exercise of particular types of inherent powers by these bodies,[5] little systematic effort has been made to unravel the factors that affect the overall scope and limits of the inherent powers of the WTO Appellate Body and ICSID tribunals, particularly when seen in the context of their *own* nature and judicial functions and the broader universe of international judicial functions.

---

[3] Brown (n. 1).

[4] See for example: Martins Paparinskis, 'Inherent Powers of ICSID Tribunals: Broad and Rightly So' in Ian Laird and Todd Weiler (eds.), *Investment Treaty Arbitration and International Law* (JurisNet, 2012); Lorand Bartels, 'The Separation of Powers in the WTO: How to Avoid Judicial Activism' (2004) 53 *International & Comparative Law Quarterly* 861.

[5] See for example: Mitchell and Heaton (n. 2); Paparinskis (n. 4); Brown (n. 2); Friedl Weiss, 'Inherent Powers of National and International Courts' in Federico Ortino and Ernst-Ulrich Petersmann (eds.), *The WTO Dispute Settlement System 1995–2003*, vol. 18 (Kluwer, 2004); Charles N Brower and Stephan W Schill, 'Regulating Counsel Conduct before International Arbitral Tribunals' in Pieter HF Bekker, Rudolf Dolzer and Michael Waibel (eds.), *Making Transnational Law Work in the Global Economy: Liber Amicorum for Detlev Vagts* (Cambridge University Press, 2010).

To do so, this chapter studies the treatment by the WTO Appellate Body and ICSID tribunals of (i) objections to a dispute's admissibility; and (ii) amicus curiae submissions. I have chosen these illustrations because the way in which these issues have been dealt with by the Appellate Body and ICSID tribunals represent two opposing ends of the spectrum. On the one hand, these bodies have demonstrated convergence by readily employing inherent powers to admit amicus submissions, but on the other hand, divergent approaches have been adopted in relation to questions of admissibility. The Appellate Body has been hesitant to accept a general power to rule on questions of admissibility but has nevertheless undertaken admissibility-related analysis, while ICSID tribunals have attempted to seek statutory support for their power to rule on admissibility.

Using these examples, this chapter challenges absolutist assumptions about the inherent powers of the Appellate Body and ICSID tribunals,[6] and moves past the binary question of whether inherent powers can be exercised by the Appellate Body and ICSID tribunals. Instead, this chapter develops a nuanced understanding of the scope of the inherent powers of these bodies through a study of the similarities and differences in their respective judicial functions. Section 2 provides an overview of the origins of inherent powers and explores the correlation between 'inherent powers' and 'judicial function'. Section 3 is dedicated to the case studies. Section 4 attempts to rationalize the approaches of the Appellate Body and ICSID tribunals by studying the factors that contribute to the convergences and divergences in the exercise of inherent powers by these bodies. In doing so, the chapter argues that the Appellate Body and ICSID tribunals have a similar understanding of the principle of inherent powers, but their application of the principle differs because of the differences in their judicial functions. Alongside, by drawing on the divergences in the judicial framework of the tribunals, this chapter cautions against promoting convergence at the cost of carefully structured differences in the functioning of these bodies. Section 5 concludes the chapter.

---

[6] This chapter uses the example of ICSID tribunals as (a) the ICSID is the only institution specialized to hear investment disputes; and (b) such assertions have been made in relation to the authority of ICSID tribunals. This does not take away from the fact that the observations made in this chapter may also be applicable to investment tribunals operating under other rules.

2 Inherent Powers of International Courts: An Overview

Inherent powers have been defined as follows:

> The power ... to determine incidental legal issues which arise as a direct consequence of the procedures of which the Tribunal is seized by reason of the matter falling under its primary jurisdiction.[7]

Inherent powers have their origins in domestic common law courts.[8] These courts derive their inherent jurisdiction from their nature as a court of law; the scope of such jurisdiction is concomitant to the court's judicial functions.[9]

International courts are courts *d'attribution*,[10] established by international agreements between nations. Consequently, unlike domestic courts which enjoy compulsory jurisdiction *ipso facto*, the jurisdiction of international courts is limited and dependent on the consent of states. Despite the conventional and consensual nature of their jurisdiction, international courts are deemed to possess certain 'inherent powers' to determine procedural issues not covered by their constitutive instruments or rules of procedure.[11] The dictum of the International Court of Justice (ICJ) in the *Nuclear Tests Case* has clarified the origin and extent of inherent powers:

> [T]he Court possesses an inherent jurisdiction enabling it to take such action as may be required, on the one hand, to ensure that the exercise of its jurisdiction over the merits, if and when established, shall not be frustrated, and on the other, to provide for the orderly settlement of all matters in dispute, to ensure the observance of the 'inherent limitations on the exercise of the judicial function' of the Court, and to 'maintain its judicial character'. Such inherent jurisdiction ... derives from *the mere existence of the Court as a judicial organ* established by the consent of States, and is *conferred upon it* in order that its *basic judicial functions may be safeguarded.*[12]

---

[7] *In the matter of El Sayed*, Decision on Appeal of Pre-Trial Judge's Order Regarding Jurisdiction and Standing, Special Tribunal for Lebanon, Appeals Chamber, CH/AC/2010/2 (10 November 2010) para. 45. See also: *United States* v. *Hudson*, 11 US 32 (Mem) (1812).

[8] For a history of inherent powers in domestic courts, see: IH Jacobs, 'The Inherent Jurisdiction of the Court' (1970) 23(1) *Current Legal Problems* 23.

[9] *Metropolitan Bank* v. *Pooley* (1885) 10 App Cas 210, 220–1 (Lord Blackburn); *Connelly* v. *D.P.P.* [1964] AC 1254,1301 (Lord Morris); Jacobs (n. 8) 24, 33.

[10] Anthony Arnull, 'Does the Court have Inherent Jurisdiction?'(1990) 27 *CMLR* 683.

[11] Gaeta (n. 2) 353–4; Brown (n. 2) 195; Caroline Foster, *Science and the Precautionary Principle in International Courts* (Cambridge University Press, 2013) 249; Danesh Sarooshi, 'The Powers of International Criminal Tribunals' (1998) 2 *Max Planck YB UN L* 141, 150–4.

[12] *Nuclear Tests Case (Australia* v. *France)* [1974] ICJ Rep 253, para. 23 (emphasis added).

The ICJ's conclusion that inherent powers inhere in courts because of their identity as judicial bodies and exist to assist in the performance of the adjudicative function now finds widespread support in judicial decisions of, and scholarly opinion on, other international courts and also aligns with the approach of domestic courts.[13] Prior to this consensus, the early years of the principle's application by international courts saw reference to other sources. Inherent powers were said to derive either from 'general principles of law'[14] or could alternatively be implied from the constitutive instrument of the court (implied powers doctrine).[15]

For this study, it is not necessary to ascertain which legal basis for inherent powers is correct/best. International courts have rarely used the doctrines of general principles and implied powers to source their inherent powers. In any event, even if the source of inherent powers lies in the application of the general principles or implied powers doctrine, the scope of the power is eventually contingent upon the court's nature and functions. In the case of general principles, inherent powers have been applied by interpreting a court's constitutive instrument in accordance with any '*relevant* rule of international law'.[16] In the case of the implied powers doctrine, inherent powers have been applied by interpreting a court's constitutive instrument on the basis of the principle of effectiveness in treaty interpretation, which in turn rests on the requirement that treaties should be interpreted in good faith and in accordance with

---

[13] *Rio Grande Irrigation and Land Company (Great Britain v. USA)*, (1923) 6 RIAA 130; *Northern Cameroons (Cameroon v. United Kingdom)* (Preliminary Objections) [1963] ICJ Rep 1, 29; *Tadić Case* (Judgment) ICTY-94-1-A (15 July 1999), para. 322; *Hrvatska Elektroprivreda, dd v. Slovenia*, ICSID Case ARB/05/24, Tribunal's Ruling regarding the participation of David Mildon QC in further stages of the proceedings (6 May 2008) para. 33; *Mexico: Tax Measures on Soft Drinks and Other Beverages – Appellate Body Report* (6 March 2006) WT/DS308/AB/R, para. 45; Joost Pauwelyn and Luiz Eduardo Salles, 'Forum Shopping before International Tribunals: (Real) Concerns, (Im)Possible Solutions' (2009) 42(1) *Cornell J Intl L* 77, 99–100; Gerald Fitzmaurice, *The Law and Procedure of the International Court of Justice*, vol. II (Cambridge University Press, 1986) 533, 770–1.

[14] Shabtai Rosenne, *The Law and Practice of the International Court of Justice, 1920–1996*, vol. II (3rd ed.) (Springer Netherlands, 1997) 600–1; *Genie-Lacayo Case*, Order, Inter-American Court of Human Rights (13 September 1997).

[15] E Lauterpacht, '"Partial Judgments" and the Inherent Jurisdiction of the International Court of Justice' in Vaughan Lowe and Malgosia Fitzmaurice (eds.), *Fifty Years of the International Court of Justice, Essays in Honour of Sir Robert Jennings* (Cambridge University Press, 1996) 465–86.

[16] Vienna Convention on the Law of Treaties (adopted 23 May 1969, entered into force 27 January 1980) 1155 UNTS 331 (VCLT) art. 31(3)(c).

their object and purpose.[17] In both instances, it can be argued that it is a court's identity and judicial function that necessarily inform: (a) the 'relevance' of a general principle of law for the identification of the court's inherent jurisdiction;[18] and (b) the object and purpose of the court and consequently whether an inherent power can be implied from the court's constitutive instrument.

Having thus concluded that: (a) every institution engaged in the judicial resolution of disputes should enjoy certain inherent powers; and (b) the scope of a court's inherent powers is dependent on its nature and the judicial functions it performs, the next section undertakes a comparative study of the approach of the Appellate Body and ICSID tribunals towards the admissibility of a dispute and amicus curiae submissions.

3 The Exercise of Inherent Powers by the Appellate Body and ICSID Tribunals – A Comparative Case Study

Neither the Appellate Body nor ICSID tribunals have the express power to decide issues of admissibility. The same applies to acceptance of amicus submissions. Amicus submissions are not explicitly permitted before the Appellate Body. Even at the ICSID, the power to accept amicus submissions has only recently been codified.[19] This section thus looks at whether amicus submissions and objections to a dispute's admissibility have been entertained by these bodies, and if so on what basis.

3.1 The Power to Rule on the 'Admissibility' of Disputes

A necessary consequence of the consent-based foundations of IDS is that an international court, whether enjoying general or specific jurisdiction, has to establish its entitlement to do so.[20] These preliminary objections to an international court's power to adjudge the merits of a dispute are classified under two headings: (i) objections to jurisdiction; and (ii) objections to admissibility. The former concerns a court's power to

---

[17] VCLT, art. 31(1); Richard Gardiner, *Treaty Interpretation* (Oxford University Press, 2007) 168–70.

[18] For example, see: *Tadić Case* (Judgment on Allegations of Contempt) ICTY-94-1-A-R77 (31 January 2000) paras. 13–19.

[19] ICSID Rules of Procedure for Arbitration Proceedings (ICSID Arbitration Rules) (April 2006) r 37(2).

[20] James Crawford, *Brownlie's Principles of Public International Law* (8th ed., Oxford University Press, 2012) 693; *Corfu Channel case* (*United Kingdom v. Albania*) (Preliminary Objections) [1948] ICJ Rep 15,27.

adjudicate a dispute.[21] The latter 'take[s] the form of an assertion that, even if the Court has jurisdiction ... nonetheless there are reasons [other than the merits of the case] why the Court should not proceed to an examination of the merits'.[22]

That international courts have the inherent power to decide on their own jurisdiction is uncontested; its codification in the constitutive instruments of certain courts (such as Article 36(6) of the ICJ Statute) is a mere 'reflection' of its existence as an inherent power.[23] However, case law and literature have not been similarly unequivocal in identifying inherent powers as the source of rulings on admissibility. Only the ICJ has been categorical in holding that it can decline to hear a case on the merits, even if it has the jurisdiction to do so, if adjudication of the case would conflict with its judicial function.[24] By relying on its judicial function as the legal basis for engaging with the question of a dispute's admissibility, the ICJ had thus indicated that it has the inherent power to decide admissibility questions. However, other sources have also been identified. Shany, for example, suggests that the authority to decide on admissibility of claims can also arise from explicit conferral in constitutive instruments[25] or from general rules of international law.[26] However, a better explanation is that the power to rule on admissibility objections derives from a court's inherent powers, but its limits may be illustrated by provisions in a court's constitutive instrument and general rules of international law.

Compared to the ICJ, the jurisprudence on admissibility is not as developed in decisions of WTO panels/Appellate Body and ICSID tribunals. In WTO jurisprudence, *Mexico – Soft Drinks* continues to be the central ruling. The case arose out of a broader dispute between the USA and Mexico concerning the USA's regulation of its sugar market. Mexico

---

[21] Yuval Shany, *Questions of Jurisdiction and Admissibility before International Courts* (Cambridge University Press, 2015) 131.
[22] *Oil Platforms Case (Iran v. US)* (Merits) [1996] ICJ Rep 803, para. 29. See also: Fitzmaurice (n. 13) 438–9.
[23] *Legality of Use of Force (Serbia and Montenegro v. Belgium)* (Preliminary Objections) [2004] ICJ Rep 279, para. 34; *Mexico – Soft Drinks* (n. 13) para. 45; *Klöckner v. Cameroon* (1985) 114 ILR 243, 251–2.
[24] For example, see: *Northern Cameroons* (n. 13) 37. ICJ Rule 79 codifies this power – ICJ Rules of Court (ICJ Rules) (14 April 1978) r 79.
[25] Rome Statute of the International Criminal Court (adopted 17 July 1998, entered into force 1 July 2002) 2187 UNTS 90, art. 17; United Nations Convention on the Law of the Sea (adopted 10 December 1982, entered into force 16 November 1994) 1833 UNTS 3, art. 294.
[26] Shany (n. 21) 49 citing, inter alia, *Monetary Gold Removed from Rome in 1943 (Italy v. France, United Kingdom and USA)* (Preliminary Question) [1954] ICJ Rep 19, 32.

challenged these measures under the North American Free Trade Agreement (NAFTA) but could not obtain a ruling on the matter as the USA refused to cooperate in the establishment of a NAFTA panel. Consequently, Mexico imposed discriminatory taxes on US soft drink imports in retaliation, which became the subject of dispute before the WTO Dispute Settlement Body (DSB). Mexico argued that although the WTO panel had jurisdiction over the dispute, it should refrain from exercising it because the dispute was inseparable from the NAFTA claims.[27] To support its claim, Mexico argued that the panel had 'implied jurisdictional powers' to rule on the admissibility of the dispute because it was an adjudicative body.[28] Mexico's argument was rejected by the panel on two grounds: (i) the panel held that it had no discretion to decide whether or not to exercise jurisdiction and (ii) it found that Mexico had failed to identify a specific 'legal impediment' that could prevent its exercise of jurisdiction.[29]

Similar arguments were presented on appeal, although this time Mexico argued that the power to rule on admissibility was 'inherent to the "adjudicative function" of panels'.[30] But the Appellate Body upheld the panel's reasoning. It agreed with Mexico that WTO panels 'have certain powers that are inherent in their adjudicative function'.[31] However, it found that it had no power to decline adjudication of entire claims if jurisdiction was validly established.[32] It reasoned that to decline jurisdiction would be contrary to the use of the mandatory language 'shall address', 'should make an objective assessment' and 'shall have recourse to' in Articles 7, 11 and 23 of the WTO Understanding on Rules and Procedures Governing the Settlement of Disputes (DSU) respectively.[33] It further held that a decision 'to decline to exercise validly established jurisdiction would "diminish" the right of a complaining Member to "seek the redress of a violation of obligations"' under DSU Article 23 'and to bring a dispute' under DSU Article 3.3.[34]

The NAFTA has a fork-in-the-road clause that makes a choice of forum exclusive – once dispute settlement procedures have been initiated

---

[27] *Mexico: Tax Measures on Soft Drinks and Other Beverages – Panel Report* (7 October 2005) WT/DS308/R, paras. 4.102–4.106.
[28] Ibid., para. 4.102.
[29] Ibid., paras. 7.1, 7.5–7.9, 7.13.
[30] *Mexico – Soft Drinks* (AB Report) (n. 13) para. 11.
[31] Ibid., para. 45.
[32] Ibid., para. 46.
[33] Ibid., paras. 49, 51–52.
[34] Ibid., para. 53.

INHERENT POWERS OF WTO AB AND ICSID TRIBUNALS   175

under the NAFTA or the GATT, the forum first selected has exclusive jurisdiction.[35] Curiously, Mexico did not rely on this provision to make its case. Given the limited scope of Mexico's challenge, the Appellate Body left open-ended the question whether such a clause could constitute a 'legal impediment' preventing the exercise of its jurisdiction.[36]

Few other panels or the Appellate Body have used the language of admissibility even though they have undertaken an admissibility analysis in relation to, inter alia, choice of forum clauses,[37] existence of legal interest[38] and presence of necessary third parties.[39] A notable exception is *US – Upland Cotton (Article 21.5)*. The dispute concerned whether the USA had implemented the DSB's recommendations in *US – Upland Cotton*. The Appellate Body distinguished jurisdiction from admissibility, albeit without elucidation. It held that for the claim to be admissible, the complainant would have to 'establish the existence of adverse effects'.[40]

The approach of ICSID tribunals towards admissibility has been at best, confused.[41] Instead of deliberating on the normative basis for entertaining admissibility objections, some tribunals have found the distinction between jurisdiction and admissibility controversial.[42] They have declared that they do not have the power to decide on a dispute's admissibility since ICSID Convention Article 41(2) (and Rule 41(1) of the ICSID Arbitration Rules) only allows objections to the jurisdiction or 'competence' of a tribunal.[43] These tribunals have also assumed that once

---

[35] NAFTA (adopted 17 December 1992, entered into force 1 January 1994) (1993) 32 ILM 289, art. 2005.6.
[36] *Mexico – Soft Drinks* (AB Report) (n. 13) paras. 53–54.
[37] *United States: Tax Treatment for 'Foreign Sales Corporations'* – Panel Report (8 October 1999) WT/DS108/R, paras. 7.12–7.22.
[38] *European Communities: Regime for the Importation, Sale and Distribution of Bananas* – Appellate Body Report (9 September 1997) WT/DS27/AB/R, paras. 132–136.
[39] *Turkey: Restrictions on Imports of Textile and Clothing Products* – Panel Report (31 May 1999) WT/DS34/R, paras. 9.4–9.11. For a complete list, see: Graham Cook, *A Digest of WTO Jurisprudence on Public International Law Concepts and Principles* (Cambridge University Press, 2015) 2–19.
[40] *United States: Subsidies on Upland Cotton – Article 21.5* Appellate Body Report (2 June 2008) WT/DS267/SB/RW, para. 246. This reasoning is seemingly similar to the admissibility rule that a party must have a legal interest in the case.
[41] For an overview of the subject, see: David AR Williams, 'Jurisdiction and Admissibility' in Peter Muchlinski, Federico Ortino and Christoph Schreuer (eds.), *The Oxford Handbook of International Investment Law* (Oxford University Press, 2008) 919.
[42] *Pan American Energy LLC and BP Argentina Exploration Company v. Argentina*, ICSID Case ARB/03/13, Decision on Preliminary Objections (27 July 2006) para. 54.
[43] *CMS Gas Transmission Company v. Argentina*, ICSID Case ARB/01/8, Decision of the Tribunal on Objections to Jurisdiction (17 July 2003) para. 41; *Enron Corporation and*

a tribunal's jurisdiction is established, a dispute would be automatically admissible.[44] Others have adopted a more pragmatic approach, noting that the distinction between jurisdiction and admissibility is without practical consequences.[45] Yet others have used the terms interchangeably, or have treated admissibility objections as objections to the tribunal's jurisdiction.[46]

Tribunals that have exercised their power to rule on admissibility claims have again done so either without normative reasoning,[47] or when parties have agreed that admissibility challenges can be decided under the ICSID Convention.[48] These tribunals have classified claims including exhaustion of local remedies, abuse of process, timeliness, and forum selection as admissibility claims.[49]

However, two cases shed some light on the source of admissibility rulings in ICSID arbitrations. In *Rompetrol v. Romania*, the tribunal had to decide whether the claimant's claim was a disguised denial of justice claim, and as such inadmissible because the claimant had failed to exhaust local remedies.[50] Since the parties had crossed swords over the

---

Ponderosa Assets, LPv v. Argentina, ICSID Case ARB/01/3, Decision on Jurisdiction (14 January 2004) para. 33. See also: Ian Laird, 'A Difference without a Distinction? An Examination of the Concepts of Admissibility and Jurisdiction in *Salini v. Jordan* and *Methanexv. USA*' in Todd Weiler (ed.), *International Investment Law and Arbitration: Leading Cases from the ICSID, NAFTA, Bilateral Treaties and Customary International Law* (Cameron May, 2005) 222.

[44] *Enron* (n. 43) para. 52.

[45] *Bayindir Insaat Turizm Ticaret Ve Sanayi AS v. Pakistan*, ICSID Case ARB/03/29, Decision on Jurisdiction (14 November 2005) para. 87; *Consortium Groupement L.E.S.I.-DIPENTA v. Algeria*, ICSID Case ARB/03/08, Award (10 January 2005), at 12[2].

[46] *Salini Costruttori SpA and Italstrade SpA v. Jordan*, ICSID Case ARB/02/13, Decision on Jurisdiction (9 November 2004) para. 151; *LG&E Energy Corp and others v. Argentina*, ICSID Case ARB/02/1, Decision of the Arbitral Tribunal on Objections to Jurisdiction (30 April 2004) para. 68; *Camuzzi International SA v. Argentina*, ICSID Case ARB/03/2, Decision on Objections to Jurisdiction (11 May 2005) para. 98; *Burlington Resources Inc v. Ecuador*, ICSID Case ARB/08/5, Decision on Jurisdiction (2 June 2010) para. 340.

[47] *Saipem SpA v. Bangladesh*, ICSID Case ARB/05/07, Decision on Jurisdiction and Recommendation on Provisional Measures (21 March 2007) para. 77; *HOCHTIEF AG v. Argentina*, ICSID Case ARB/07/31, Decision on Jurisdiction (24 October 2011), para. 96; *Impregilo SpA v. Pakistan*, ICSID Case ARB/03/3, Decision on Jurisdiction (22 April 2005) paras. 222–223.

[48] *Ioan Micula and others v. Romania*, ICSID Case ARB/05/20, Decision on Jurisdiction and Admissibility (24 September 2008) para. 58.

[49] *Saipem* (n. 47) paras. 150–158; *SGS Société Générale de Surveillance SA v. Philippines*, ICSID Case ARB/02/6, Decision of the Tribunal on Objections to Jurisdiction (29 January 2004) paras. 288–290.

[50] *The Rompetrol Group NV v. Romania*, ICSID Case ARB/06/3, Decision on Respondent's Preliminary Objections on Jurisdiction and Admissibility (18 April 2008) para. 111.

tribunal's power to decide on admissibility objections, the tribunal took the opportunity to discuss the source of such a power. According to the tribunal, the authority to rule on admissibility-related objections emanated from the tribunal's authority to address issues of its competence under Rule 41(1) of the ICSID Arbitration Rules.[51] The tribunal stated:

> [I]n the absence of any indication of what the precise intention was behind the wording of Rule 41(1) – it seemed to the Tribunal only realistic to interpret the Rule with a degree of flexibility, one that would allow the respondent party some discretion over the formulation of reasoned objections, but on the basis that that party would bear the onus not merely of showing that its objection was well founded in substance, but also of demonstrating that, if the objection did not go to jurisdiction as such, it was nevertheless within the terms of the Convention and the Rules.

Adopting a comparative reasoning, the tribunal asserted (albeit mistakenly and contrary to the ICJ's decisions on the point)[52] that the ICJ similarly derives its power to rule on a dispute's admissibility from Rule 79 of the Rules of the Court (and not from its inherent powers).[53]

The second case, *Abaclat v. Argentina*, had to address whether a 'mass claim' constituted a hurdle to the tribunal's jurisdiction or affected the admissibility of the claims.[54] Citing *Rompetrol v. Romania*, the tribunal yet again held that the concept of jurisdiction under ICSID Convention Articles 25 and 41 also encompassed issues of admissibility.[55]

To sum up, in WTO jurisprudence, panels and the Appellate Body have either denied their inherent power to decide questions of admissibility or have engaged in admissibility analysis without clarifying their legal basis to do so. At the ICSID, on the other hand, the *Rompetrol* and *Abaclat* awards indicate that the legal basis for admissibility objections lies in the text of the ICSID Convention. However, as shown in Section 4, this apparent divergence in approaches does not, in any way, demonstrate that the WTO Appellate Body and ICSID tribunals have a fragmented understanding of the principle of inherent powers. To the contrary, it is the application of the principle that has varied because of limiting factors present in the structure of the bodies or in their constitutive instruments.

---

[51] Ibid., para. 112.
[52] See for example: *Northern Cameroons* (n. 13) 37.
[53] Ibid., para. 112.
[54] *Abaclat and others v. Argentina*, ICSID Case ARB/07/5, Decision on Jurisdiction and Admissibility (4 August 2011) para. 296.
[55] Ibid., para. 245.

3.2 The Power to Accept Amicus Curiae Submissions

Amicus curiae or 'friend of the court' describes persons who are not parties to the dispute but assist the court in its judicial duties by providing their special perspective or expertise on legal and/or factual aspects of the dispute.[56] Domestic courts accept amicus briefs in the exercise of their inherent powers.[57] In international law, there is no consistent practice on accepting amicus submissions – the approach varies from court to court. Some courts, such as human rights and international criminal courts, have sidestepped the issue of their inherent power to accept amicus submissions by providing explicit rules on the subject.[58] Other courts, such as the ICJ, have explicitly prevented amicus presentations in contentious proceedings.[59]

The most cogent articulation of the legal basis for amicus interventions before international courts is found in *Prosecutor* v. *Kallon*, a decision of the Appeals Chamber of the Special Court for Sierra Leone (SCSL). Although Rule 74 of the SCSL's Rules of Procedure granted the SCSL the power to accept amicus submissions, the Appeals Chamber in the case held: 'Appeal Courts, in particular, when confronted with new or complex points of law, have an inherent power to permit or invite submissions from an *amicus*.'[60] In WTO law and investment law, the first set of unsolicited amicus briefs received were rejected for lack of

---

[56] *Prosecutor* v. *Kallon*, Decision on Application by the Redress Trust, Lawyers Committee for Human Rights and the International Commission of Jurists for Leave to File Amicus Curiae Brief and Present Oral Submissions, Special Tribunal for Sierra Leone, Appeals Chamber, SCSL-03-07-AR72 (1 November 2003) para. 3; *Aguas Argentinas, SA, Suez, Sociedad General de Aguas de Barcelona, SA and Vivendi Universal, SA* v. *Argentina*, ICSID Case ARB/03/19, Order in Response to a Petition for Transparency and Participation as *Amicus Curiae* (19 May 2005) para. 8; Lance Bartholomeusz, 'The Amicus Curiae Before International Courts and Tribunals' (2005) 5 *Non-State Actors & Intl L* 209, 211.

[57] *Ex parte* Peterson, 253 US 300, 312–13 (1920); *In Re Utilities Power & Light Corporation*, 90 F.2d 798, 800 (7th Cir. 1937); US Tobacco Co v. Minister for Consumer Affairs (1988) 20 FCR 520, 534.

[58] 2001 Rules of Procedure of the Inter American Court of Human Rights, art. 62(3); Rules of Procedure and Evidence of the International Criminal Tribunal for the former Yugoslavia/ International Criminal Tribunal for Rwanda, rule 74. For a full discussion on the practice of international courts, see: Philippe J Sands and Ruth Mackenzie, 'The Practice of International Courts and Tribunals as Regards Amici Curiae' in *Max Planck Encyclopedia of Public International Law* (2008).

[59] ICJ Statute (adopted 26 June 1945, entered into force 24 October 1945) 33 UNTS 993, art. 34(2).

[60] *Kallon* (n. 56) para. 3.

authority to entertain them.[61] At the WTO, this changed with the ruling in the *US – Shrimp Turtle* case. The panel in that case rejected submissions from two environmental non-governmental organizations (NGOs) on the basis that panels only have the right to '*seek* information and technical advice' under DSU Article 13, but not the authority to accept unsolicited submissions.[62] The Appellate Body reversed the panel's report to allow the NGOs' submissions. It held that the thrust of Article 13 is to authorize panels to receive information about all relevant facts and legal principles; consequently the term 'seek' should not be interpreted restrictively.[63] More interestingly (and in line with the focus of this chapter on the Appellate Body), amicus submissions made to the Appellate Body were appended to the appellant state's submission. Without delving into a discussion on its *own* inherent authority to accept amicus briefs, the Appellate Body accepted the submissions on the basis that they formed an integral part of the participant state's submission.[64]

This changed when the Appellate Body was again presented with the opportunity to examine its own ability to entertain amicus submissions in *US – Lead and Bismuth II*. This time, the Appellate Body looked at DSU Article 17.9, which allows the Appellate Body to draw up working procedures. The Appellate Body also referred to Rule 16(1) of its working procedure (albeit in a footnote), by which it has the residual power to develop procedures for procedural issues that have not been addressed in the working procedures. The Appellate Body held that it had the legal authority to consider amicus submissions because Article 17.9 (and Rule 16(1)) confers upon it 'broad [inherent] authority to adopt procedural rules which do not conflict with any rules and procedures in the DSU or the covered agreements'.[65]

---

[61] *United States: Standards for Reformulated and Conventional Gasoline – Panel Report* (29 January 1996) WT/DS2/R; *European Communities: Measures Concerning Meat and Meat Products (Hormones) – Panel Report* (18 August 1997), WT/DS26/R; Yang Guohua et al., *WTO Dispute Settlement Understanding: A Detailed Interpretation* (Kluwer, 2005) 174. ICSID: *Aguas del Tunari, SA v. Bolivia*, ICSID Case ARB/02/3, Letter from the President to the Tribunal (29 January 2003) 1.

[62] *United States: Import Prohibition of Certain Shrimp and Shrimp Products – Panel Report* (15 May 1998) WT/DS58/R, para. 7.8.

[63] *United States: Import Prohibition of Certain Shrimp and Shrimp Products – Appellate Body Report* (12 October 1998) WT/DS58/AB/R, paras. 106–107.

[64] Ibid., para. 89.

[65] *United States: Imposition of Countervailing Duties on Certain Hot-Rolled Lead and Bismuth Carbon Steel Products Originating in the United Kingdom – Appellate Body Report* (10 May 2000) WT/DS138/AB/R, paras. 39, 42.

The Appellate Body's approach towards amicus presentations in *US – Lead and Bismuth II* has since been followed consistently. The Appellate Body has accepted amicus briefs from states that choose not to appear as third parties in a trade dispute,[66] and has developed ad hoc procedural rules to admit amicus briefs when it expects to receive several such briefs.[67]

Turning to ICSID tribunals, as discussed above, the first amicus submission was rejected because the tribunal considered that the request was beyond the authority of the tribunal, and subject to the consent of the parties.[68] However, in the next case to deal with amicus presentations, this opinion was reversed. An ICSID tribunal appointed to hear a dispute in *Suez and Vivendi* v. *Argentina* received requests from five NGOs claiming that the dispute raised matters of public interest. The tribunal first clarified that admission of amicus submissions is a procedural question since they assist the tribunal in exercising its function of settling the dispute at hand.[69] It decided that amicus submissions from suitable non-parties in appropriate cases can be entertained under an ICSID tribunal's inherent power to decide procedural questions (articulated in ICSID Convention Article 44).[70] The tribunal's view was motivated by the significant public interest element in the case, as the dispute concerned water distribution and sewage systems.[71]

The doors opened by *Suez and Vivendi* v. *Argentina*, and the increased calls for transparency in investment arbitration, collectively led to the codification of an ICSID tribunal's power to entertain amicus briefs. Pursuant to the 2006 amendments to the ICSID Arbitration Rules, Rule 37(2) now provides a legislative basis for tribunals to entertain amicus briefs. ICSID tribunals dealing with amicus briefs after the 2006 amendment have done so under the authority of Rule 37(2) without referring to their inherent powers.[72]

---

[66] *European Communities: Trade Description of Sardines – Appellate Body Report* (26 September 2002) WT/DS231/AB/R, paras. 161–167.
[67] *European Communities: Measures Affecting Asbestos and Asbestos-Containing Products – Appellate Body Report* (12 March 2001) WT/DS135/AB/R, paras. 51–52.
[68] *Aguas* (n. 61).
[69] *Vivendi* (n. 56) para. 11. See also: *Suez, Sociedad General de Aguas de Barcelona S.A., and InterAguas Servicios Integrales del Agua S.A.* v. *Argentina*, ICSID Case ARB/03/17, Order in Response to a Petition for Participation as Amicus Curiae (17 March 2006) para. 12.
[70] *Vivendi* (n. 56) para. 16; *InterAguas* (n. 69) para. 16.
[71] *Vivendi* (n. 56) para. 19.
[72] For example: *Philip Morris Brands Sàrl and others* v. *Uruguay*, ICSID Case ARB/10/7, Procedural Order 3 (17 February 2005) para. 21; *Electrabel SA* v. *Hungary*, ICSID Case

4 Inherent Powers – Rationalizing the Approach of the Appellate Body and ICSID Tribunals

At first blush, the attitudes of the Appellate Body and ICSID tribunals towards matters concerning their inherent jurisdiction appear confusing. When faced with objections to admissibility, the Appellate Body has shown great deference to the text of the DSU, to explicitly decline its inherent power to engage in admissibility analysis. ICSID tribunals, on the other hand, have not looked into the issue of their inherent jurisdiction. They appear to consider the power to rule on admissibility objections as part of their statutory jurisdiction. Contrastingly, both bodies have readily accepted that the power to entertain amicus briefs is an extension of their inherent power to decide questions of procedure. The Appellate Body, in particular, has agreed to entertain amicus briefs despite vehement opposition from a majority of the WTO Member States.[73] The WTO Member States have maintained that it is beyond the mandate of the DSB to entertain amicus submissions and to do so would add to or diminish the rights and obligations of Member States.[74]

Does this ostensible difference in the exercise of inherent powers indicate that the two bodies diverge in their understanding of the principle of inherent powers? Some appear to argue, for instance, that the WTO panels and Appellate Body have been slow to recognize the existence of these powers;[75] others claim that WTO panels and the Appellate Body do not enjoy the full panoply of inherent powers simply because they are quasi-judicial in nature.[76]

This section instead argues that the practices of the Appellate Body and ICSID tribunals are susceptible to a more nuanced understanding. International dispute settlement bodies share the same objective; they all operate to fulfil the 'international judicial function'. In pursuit of this

---

ARB/07/19, Procedural Order 4 (28 April 2009) para. 22; *Biwater Gauff (Tanzania) Ltd v. Tanzania*, ICSID Case ARB/05/22, Procedural Order 5 (2 February 2007) para. 46; *Bernhard von Pezold and others v. Zimbabwe*, ICSID Case ARB/10/25, Procedural Order 2 (26 June 2012) para. 48.

[73] Weiss (n. 5) 179; CL Lim, 'The *Amicus* Brief Issue at the WTO' (2005) 4(1) *ChineseJ Intl L* 85.

[74] For a complete list of objections, see: Brigitte Stern, 'The Intervention of Private Entities and States as "Friends of the Court" in WTO Dispute Settlement Proceedings' in Patrick J Macrory et al. (eds.), *The World Trade Organization: Legal, Economic and Political Analysis*, vol. I (Springer, 2005) 1447–51.

[75] Mitchell and Heaton (n. 2) 568.

[76] Lorand Bartels, 'The Separation of Powers in the WTO: How to Avoid Judicial Activism' (2004) 53 *ICLQ* 861, 885.

common objective, all courts attempt to implement a 'common law' on international judicial procedure,[77] often by using their inherent powers. Inherent powers, thus, inure to the benefit of all international courts – no matter their institutional design as a court, an arbitral tribunal or a quasi-judicial institution. However, as this section demonstrates, the international judicial function is tempered by (a) the individual structure and functions of each court; and (b) the presence of a conflicting provision in the constitutive instrument or rules of procedure. This, as the section then argues, explains the differences in the scope of the inherent powers of international courts, including the Appellate Body and ICSID tribunals.

4.1 Convergence and Divergence in the Functions of the Appellate Body and ICSID Tribunals

Enough has been written about the 'international judicial function' and its impact on the functioning of the diverse network of international courts and tribunals.[78] At its core, it includes elements such as independence, due process and binding determinations of disputes according to the law.[79] However, the international judicial function does not operate in a vacuum. Each court's implementation of the international judicial function is affected by its structural and institutional set-up, the specific functions it has been called upon to perform and the limitations in its constitutive instruments. Thus, as Georges Abi-Saab opined, the decision-making process of an international court is dependent on several considerations that operate as a set of three concentric circles. The outermost circle encompasses the interests of the international community at large. Within this circle lies the second circle – the circle of the international judicial function. Finally, the innermost circle represents the parameters and institutional balance of the particular international court. The collective content of these circles explains an international court's range of powers.

---

[77] Georges Abi-Saab, 'The Normalization of International Adjudication: Convergence and Divergencies' (2010) 43 *NYU J Intl L & Pol* 1, 8–9.

[78] Abi-Saab (n. 77) 7ff.; Hersh Lauterpacht, *The Function of Law in the International Community* (Oxford University Press, 1933); Armin von Bogdandy and Ingo Venzke, 'On the Functions of International Courts: An Appraisal in Light of Their Burgeoning Public Authority' (2013) 26(1) *Leiden J Intl L* 49.

[79] Abi-Saab (n. 77) 1.

In many ways, the Appellate Body's anatomy and the framework within which it operates is dissimilar to ICSID tribunals. Dispute settlement at the WTO is formally a quasi-judicial, intergovernmental process. Unlike as with truly judicial bodies, reports issued by the Appellate Body (and panels) are not binding unless they receive political approval from the DSB.[80] The shades of institutional dependency are reflected throughout the DSU. For instance, the Appellate Body can formulate its working procedures only after consulting the DSB's chairman and the Director-General, and communicating with Member States.[81] In contrast, ICSID tribunals are ad hoc arbitral tribunals, adjudicating disputes between foreign investors and states. The institutional support provided by the Centre is merely administrative in nature.

Yet, the functions of the two courts converge significantly, and also accord with the international judicial function. The primary responsibility of both bodies is one of settling economic disputes.[82] At the WTO, this 'private' function of settling disputes is supplemented,[83] and tempered, by other provisions in the DSU that make clear that the WTO dispute settlement system is intended to fulfil broader 'public' functions such as 'providing security and predictability to the multilateral trading system'; clarifying the existing provisions; and preserving the rights, obligations and interests of all Member States.[84] Unsurprisingly then, its quasi-judicial nature has not prevented the Appellate Body from functioning as a court.[85]

ICSID tribunals similarly serve the broader 'public' function of developing a harmonious and effective regime of investment law.[86] However,

---

[80] Understanding on Rules and Procedures Governing the Settlement of Disputes (adopted 15 April 1994, entered into force 1 January 1995) 1869 UNTS 401 (DSU) arts. 16, 17.14.
[81] DSU art. 17.9.
[82] DSU art. 3.7; *United States: Measures Affecting Imports of Woven Wool Shirts and Blouses from India – Appellate Body Report* (25 April 1997) WT/DS33/AB/R, at 19; Convention on the Settlement of Investment Disputes between States and Nationals of Other States (adopted 18 March 1965, entered into force 14 October 1966) 575 UNTS 159, art. 42(1); *AES Corp v. Argentina*, ICSID Case ARB/02/17, Decision on Jurisdiction (26 April 2005) para. 30.
[83] Dispute settlement is generally referred to as a 'private' function because it concerns only the (two or more) parties to the dispute.
[84] DSU arts. 3.2,10.1,19.2.
[85] Donald McRae, 'What Is the Future of WTO Dispute Settlement?' (2004) 7 *J Intl Econ L* 3, 8; Georges Abi-Saab, 'The Appellate Body and Treaty Interpretation' in Giorgio Sacerdoti et al. (eds.), *The WTO at Ten – The Contribution of the Dispute Settlement System* (Cambridge University Press, 2006) 455–6.
[86] *Saipem SpA v. Bangladesh*, ICSID Case ARB/05/7, Award (30 June 2009) para. 90; Michael Waibel, 'Coordinating Adjudication Processes' in Zachary Douglas et al. (eds.),

the ICSID's broader functions are moderated by the peculiar environment in which it operates. First, ICSID tribunals are mixed arbitral tribunals, operating in a paradigm of vertical investor-state relationships (and not interstate relationships). Secondly, the boundaries of an ICSID tribunal's powers are defined not just by the ICSID Convention, but also by a network of overlapping yet separate bilateral investment treaties. Finally, ICSID tribunals initially settled contractual disputes, but have progressively shifted towards treaty-based disputes. Consequently, remnants of the privatized nature of contractual dispute resolution continue to influence the decision-making process of ICSID tribunals.

4.2 Admissibility and the Judicial Function

Questions of admissibility form part of the broader universe of preliminary objections. The important role that they perform in protecting the international judicial function is well recognized by international courts other than the Appellate Body and ICSID tribunals. The ICJ has made it abundantly clear that it is not compelled to exercise validly established jurisdiction in every case; it can decline to hear a case if it perceives a threat to its judicial integrity.[87]

The question then is not whether international courts can rule on admissibility. To that, the answer is a yes. The better question to ask is: what grounds of admissibility can international courts entertain? Admittedly, as the only international court possessing general jurisdiction, the ICJ has few obstacles that chip away at its ability to give the broadest interpretation to questions of admissibility. The same cannot be said of courts with specific mandates. Such courts have to balance conflicting considerations in determining whether they have the discretion to hold a particular case inadmissible.

Although the DSU does not use the admissibility terminology, the concept is embodied in the treaty. For instance: a complainant's request for the establishment of a panel is defective if it fails to (a) identify the measure at issue; and (b) provide a brief summary of the legal basis of the complaint.[88] Beyond explicit treaty language, the Appellate Body has also

The Foundations of International Investment Law: Bringing Theory into Practice (Oxford University Press, 2014) 502.
[87] *Northern Cameroons* (n. 13) 29.
[88] DSU art. 6.2; *Korea: Definitive Safeguard Measure on Imports of Certain Dairy Products – Appellate Body Report* (14 December 1999) WT/DS98/AB/R, para. 120. For other treaty grounds of admissibility, see: Cook (n. 35) 1 (fn. 2).

considered general grounds of admissibility. For instance, in *EC – Bananas III*, the Appellate Body considered whether a Member State has a 'legal interest' in initiating a case. Regrettably, the Appellate Body's reasoning began from an incorrect premise. Initially, it held that the presence of a 'legal interest' is not a general requirement in international litigation, and that the requirement cannot be implied from the text of the DSU.[89] Eventually, however, its conclusion was rightfully based on the fact that under DSU Article 3.7, panels and the Appellate Body cannot deny admissibility for lack of 'legal interest' because the matter is self-regulated by Member States.[90] The Appellate Body's consideration of 'legal interest' as a ground of admissibility is a good example of how the exercise of the inherent power to rule on admissibility is limited by a clause in the court's constitutive instrument.

The Appellate Body's reasoning in *Mexico – Soft Drinks* can similarly be rationalized. In that case, the Appellate Body did not rule that it does not have the inherent power to decide admissibility objections. Instead, it held that the power has to be balanced in light of other provisions of the DSU which confer a right to dispute settlement on Member States and mandate that a DSB decision cannot diminish the rights of Member States.[91] This language, coupled with the general member-driven environment of the WTO, necessitates a restrictive construction of admissibility in WTO jurisprudence.[92] Perhaps this is the trade-off that the Appellate Body sought when it left open-ended the question whether certain 'legal impediments' could prevent its exercise of jurisdiction. A codified waiver of jurisdiction (e.g. through an exclusive jurisdiction clause),[93] or an instance of *res judicata*, could be examples of a 'legal impediment' that balance the Appellate Body's inherent power to rule on admissibility and its institutional dependency.

The approach of ICSID tribunals has been unnecessarily incoherent. ICSID tribunals have been thrown off guard by the use of the terms 'jurisdiction' and 'competence' in ICSID Convention Article 41(2) (and Rule 41(1) of the ICSID Arbitration Rules). Matters have been made

---

[89] *EC – Bananas III* (n. 38) paras. 132–133.
[90] *EC – Bananas III* (n. 38) para. 135.
[91] DSU art. 3.2.
[92] *US – FSC* (n. 37) para. 7.17.
[93] In *Mexico – Soft Drinks*, Mexico did not rely on the NAFTA's fork-in-the-road clause. WTO panels have previously hinted that an exclusive jurisdiction clause can be considered a 'legal impediment'. See: *Argentina: Definitive Anti-Dumping Duties on Poultry from Brazil – Panel Report* (19 May 2003) WT/DS241/R, para. 7.38; *US – FSC* (n. 37) para. 7.7.

worse by the manner in which disputing parties have made their presentations on preliminary objections.[94] As we have seen, admissibility rulings are made in furtherance of the international judicial function. Tribunals that present ICSID Convention Article 41(2) as a *clause contraire* barring admissibility determinations, and tribunals that base admissibility rulings on the Convention's Article 41(2), are both misguided. First, admissibility determinations by ICSID tribunals are not an exercise of statutory jurisdiction. Georges Abi-Saab's dissenting opinion in *Abaclat* makes it clear that admissibility in investment arbitration emanates from the adjudicative functions performed by investment tribunals.[95]

Secondly, unless specifically excluded in an investment treaty, an ICSID tribunal's inherent power to decide questions of admissibility cannot be curbed by restrictively interpreting the Convention's Article 41(2) as a *clause contraire*. This is because unlike the Appellate Body, ICSID tribunals are not quasi-judicial courts and the performance of their judicial function is not hindered by political considerations. Moreover, the correct classification of admissibility issues in the ICSID context is arguably of critical importance because it affects the reviewability of decisions. A tribunal's decision can only be contested before national courts or ICSID annulment committees with respect to its exercise of jurisdiction.

Perhaps a better exercise is to identify when a ruling of admissibility would breach the rights of disputing parties, as was done in *Rompetrol v. Romania*. The tribunal in that case declared that the respondent's objection to the dispute's admissibility was intertwined with the substance of the dispute and was best resolved after a hearing on the merits.[96]

In sum, this section has attempted to clarify that a crude dismissal of the powers of the Appellate Body and ICSID tribunals to consider admissibility objections is unjustified. Without attempting to define the precise boundaries of this power, this section has highlighted that a decision to exercise such powers is based on careful considerations of the interplay between the international judicial function and the parameters within which courts of specific jurisdiction operate.

---

[94] Laird (n. 43) 216.
[95] *Abaclat* (n. 54) Dissenting Opinion to Decision on Jurisdiction and Admissibility (4 August 2011) para. 17 viii.
[96] *Rompetrol* (n. 50) paras. 113–114. See also: *Duke Energy Electroquil Partners & Electroquil SA v. Ecuador*, ICSID Case ARB/04/19, Award (18 August 2008) para. 166.

4.3 Amicus Curiae and the Judicial Function

Amicus curiae contribute to the performance of the international judicial function by assisting in the proper administration of justice.[97] Such assistance is provided in two different ways.[98] For some courts, such as the Appellate Body, amicus presentations are useful because they assist the court in making an objective determination of the facts and law relevant to a case.[99] Other courts, such as ICSID tribunals, find that amicus presentations assist in understanding the broader implications of decisions on matters of public interest.[100]

As indicated above, the Appellate Body's acceptance of amicus presentations was met with some scorn from WTO Member States. Those who agree that international courts have the inherent power to accept amicus submissions have nevertheless criticized the Appellate Body's willingness to accept such submissions on the grounds that comparable intergovernmental courts such as the ICJ do not admit amicus briefs.[101] Bearing in mind that WTO panels (and consequently the Appellate Body) have the responsibility to make an objective assessment of a dispute,[102] the outright rejection of the power to entertain amicus briefs appears erroneous. First, the ICJ's refusal to admit amicus briefs stems from a restriction in its constitutive instrument – ICJ Statute Article 34(2) – which prevents the Court from entertaining amicus briefs from persons other than 'public international organizations'. The WTO DSU does not contain a similar restriction. Secondly, although the essence of a dispute before the DSB concerns breaches of a state's obligations under the WTO-covered agreements, the activities regulated by the covered agreements are by their very nature commercial and undertaken largely by private actors.[103] Thus, amicus curiae may have relevant information to share with the Appellate Body which could assist it in objectively reviewing the legal findings of a panel.

---

[97] Bartholomeusz (n. 56) 274.
[98] Jona Razaaque, 'Changing Role of Friends of the Court in the International Courts and Tribunals' (2001) 1 *Non-St Actors & Intl L* 169, 170.
[99] This is also the approach of international criminal tribunals.
[100] This is also the approach of human rights tribunals. Domestic courts similarly understand the role of amicus curiae as representing the public interest; see *United States v. Barnett*, 376 US 681, 738 (1964).
[101] Stern (n. 74) 1454.
[102] DSU art. 11.
[103] *United States: Sections 301-310 of the Trade Act of 1974 – Panel Report* (22 December 1999) WT/DS152/R, paras. 7.72–7.73.

The result is that at the WTO, what must be regulated is the extent of the acceptance of amicus briefs, not the power to accept such briefs itself. While considering an amicus submission under its inherent power, the Appellate Body must keep two points in mind. First, since appeals are limited to points of law, the Appellate Body should not entertain amicus briefs that seek to provide factual information not relevant for reviewing a panel's legal conclusions. Secondly, amicus briefs should be considered only for the purposes of determining the law, and not to accommodate public interest. The Appellate Body's acceptance of amicus submissions that further public interest considerations could result in a situation wherein the rights and interests of non-state entities are taken into account and could thereby create a conflict with DSU Article 3.2, which prohibits DSB rulings from diminishing the rights of Member States.

The value of a debate on the inherent powers of an ICSID tribunal to entertain amicus briefs has diminished after the power's codification in Rule 37(2) of the ICSID Arbitration Rules. Nevertheless, it is interesting to note that while ICSID tribunals have classified amicus admissions as a procedural matter since they assist in arriving at a correct decision, the tribunals have eventually accepted amicus interventions only in matters of public interest. The test to accept amicus submissions is a cumulative one: the amicus submission should assist the tribunal in the determination of relevant factual and/or legal issues;[104] and the amicus must have a significant interest in the proceedings.[105] As a consequence of equating 'significant interest' with public interest, amicus submissions are more likely to be accepted at the ICSID if the case involves broader issues concerning, for instance, the environment or public services. However, this (disproportionate) focus on public interest discounts the fact that there may be other cases in which tribunals can benefit from the information supplied by amicus curiae. Given the nature of investment arbitration, both investors and states have uneven access to evidence. This evidentiary gap can be filled by amicus submissions. It is hoped that future ICSID tribunals are mindful of this concern.

To sum up, this section has attempted to demonstrate that any structural and rules-based objections notwithstanding, the Appellate Body and ICSID tribunals have treated amicus submissions under their inherent powers. The actual exercise of the power has depended on the disputes that these bodies are entitled to handle. ICSID tribunals, for

---

[104] ICSID Arbitration Rules, r 37(2)(a).
[105] Ibid., r 37(2)(c).

instance, accept amicus submissions to take account of public interest considerations, that in turn, have an impact on their assessment of a state's breach of its investment obligations, while the Appellate Body's consideration of amicus submissions must be limited to a review of a panel's legal conclusions.

5 Conclusion

Absolutist statements on the inherent powers of international courts fail to appreciate that such powers are applied to varying degrees by all international courts. The reach of a particular inherent power depends on a range of factors – the origin and historical development of the system, the organization of the court's structure, the nature of the disputes heard, the limitations in the court's constitutive instrument and its application by comparable international courts.

This chapter has suggested that the twin approach of (a) citing the Appellate Body's institutional dependency for its inability to exercise the full panoply of inherent powers;[106] and (b) assuming that ICSID tribunals have broad inherent powers,[107] is erroneous. Using the examples of the admissibility of disputes and amicus curiae submissions, this chapter has outlined the interactions between the international judicial function and the nature and functions of the WTO Appellate Body and ICSID tribunals, and their impact on the manner in which these bodies exercise their inherent powers. It has shown that inherent powers are not differently understood and applied by the WTO Appellate Body and ICSID tribunals. Instead, if the application of inherent powers by these bodies is fragmented, that fragmentation is based on limitations arising from the judicial functions of these bodies and explicit limitations in their constitutive instruments. Going forward, thus, any attempts at promoting convergence in the adjudicative law of these bodies must be mindful of the carefully structured differences in the institutional set-up and functioning of these bodies.

---

[106] See for example: Bartels (n. 4) 885.
[107] Paparinskis (n. 4).

8

The Use of Object and Purpose by Trade and Investment Adjudicators: Convergence without Interaction

GRAHAM COOK

1 Introduction

'The Uncanny Case of the Jim Twins, Two Estranged Twins Who Led Identical Lives'[1] tells the incredible story of twin boys who were put up for adoption to different families in 1940. Their adoptive parents coincidentally named them both James, and both came to be named Jim for short. As schoolchildren, both had a proclivity for math and woodworking, but neither was very good at spelling. Both Jims married women named Linda, divorced, and went on to remarry women named Betty. Both Jims had a son, and each gave their boy the same name. Both Jims were heavy smokers, and each drove a Chevrolet. One of the Jims became a security guard, while the other Jim was a deputy sheriff. The Jims took vacations at the same Florida beach. Neither of the Jims knew any of these facts about his brother. They had no interaction with one another before meeting for the first time at the age of thirty-nine years old.

Article 31(1) of the Vienna Convention on the Law of Treaties (VCLT) provides that '[a] treaty shall be interpreted in good faith in accordance with the ordinary meaning to be given to the terms in their context in the light of its object and purpose'. In seeking to apply the general rule of interpretation, an adjudicator is necessarily confronted with a series of interpretative issues/choices relating to the 'object and purpose' element. Taken together, the following five questions can serve as a framework for comparing the practices of WTO and ISDS adjudicators in relation to 'object and purpose' as an element of treaty interpretation.

---

[1] C Littlechild, 28 May 2018, from www.ripleys.com/weird-news/jim-twins/ (last accessed 8 June 2018).

1. Are 'object and purpose' to be treated as two distinct concepts when used in the context of Article 31(1), or are they to be understood as a single, composite term?
2. Does the reference in the singular to 'its' object and purpose justify favouring liberal interpretations of treaty obligations furthering the main or predominant purpose of the treaty?
3. Can arguments based on object and purpose be used to justify a restrictive, rather than liberal, interpretation of treaty obligations?
4. Is an interpreter entitled to interpret provisions in the light of the object and purpose of individual provisions, or only the object and purpose of the treaty as a whole?
5. Must any consequentialist arguments be linked to the particular object and purpose of the treaty, or may an interpreter rely on consequentialist arguments that appeal to widely held notions of reasonableness and fairness?

There are several reasons why we might not expect that WTO and ISDS adjudicators would have developed a consistent interpretative practice in relation to all these specific issues during the formative years of WTO and investor-state dispute settlement (i.e. the mid-1990s to the present). First, none of these issues is directly or specifically addressed by the text of Article 31(1) VCLT. Thus, the absence of guidance in the text, beyond a general direction to interpret a treaty 'in the light of its object and purpose', creates the possibility of different adjudicators following different approaches within those broad parameters.

Second, there is simply too much WTO and ISDS case law to realistically expect that adjudicators working in one area would be able to directly research the prevailing practice in the other in relation to the kind of issues set out above. Indeed, there are few WTO practitioners who are able to keep up with the constantly accumulating body of WTO law. (In its first twenty years, the WTO dispute settlement system generated over 350 decisions totalling more than 60,000 pages).[2] The jurisprudence of ISDS tribunals also comprises tens of thousands of pages.

To be clear, adjudicators are capable of identifying the practice of other international courts and tribunals in relation to a wide range of issues. Chester Brown, who coined the phrase 'a common law of international adjudication', has explained instances of convergence as the product of cross-fertilization and interaction – in the sense of 'a discernible

---

[2] G Cook, *A Digest of WTO Jurisprudence on Public International Law Concepts and Principles* (Cambridge University Press, 2015), preface.

tendency for international courts to reach out and consider the practice of other international tribunals'.[3] Indeed, my colleague Gabrielle Marceau has methodically and systematically catalogued and analysed the extensive references to WTO precedents in ISDS jurisprudence.[4] As one would expect, other tribunals are typically able to find and cite to fairly easy-to-find WTO pronouncements on topics like treaty interpretation, burden of proof, amicus curiae briefs, the standard of review, the treatment of municipal law, the use of judicial economy, and so on. Likewise, while WTO panels and the Appellate Body have referred to the ISDS jurisprudence infrequently, there are also indications that they would be able to find and cite easy-to-find ISDS pronouncements on basic and fundamental issues related to topics like *stare decisis*.[5]

However, there is no reason to think that other international tribunals would study tens of thousands of pages of WTO jurisprudence to discern the emergent practice in relation to more granular technical issues like the five questions set out above. Nor is there any reason to believe that WTO adjudicators methodically read through ISDS awards.

Assuming for the sake of argument that some adjudicators might look to books or other secondary sources for guidance on practice relating to 'object and purpose', it seems that there was no common resource they could have looked to for answers. In this regard, the 1966 commentary of the International Law Commission accompanying the draft articles on interpretation provides little or no guidance on any of these issues.[6] There were very few books on treaty interpretation in the decades following the Vienna Convention. This is evidenced by the Appellate Body's proclivity in its first decade to cite most frequently the 1984 edition of Sir Ian Sinclair's book on the Vienna Convention, which included a chapter on interpretation, and to Yasseen's 1976

---

[3] C Brown, 'The Cross-Fertilization of Principles Relating to Procedure and Remedies in the Jurisprudence of International Courts and Tribunals' (2008) 30 *Loy. L.A. Int'l & Comp. L. Rev.* 219, at 243–4. See generally C Brown, *A Common Law of International Adjudication* (Oxford University Press, 2007).

[4] G Marceau, A Izaguerri and V Lanovoy, 'The WTO's Influence on Other Dispute Settlement Mechanisms: A Lighthouse in the Storm of Fragmentation' (2013) 47(3) *Journal of World Trade* 481–574. This article identifies 150 references as of 2013. An updated version shared by one of the authors (unpublished, on file) identifies that the number has increased to 190 references as of 2017.

[5] Appellate Body Report, *US – Stainless Steel (Mexico)*, footnote 313 (citing to *Saipem S.p.A v. The People's Republic of Bangladesh*, ICSID IIC 280 (2007), p. 20, para. 67).

[6] *Yearbook of the International Law Commission* (1966), Vol. II, pp. 217–23.

lecture, delivered in French, to The Hague Academy of International Law.[7]

Given this combination of circumstances, it is difficult to see how there could be much cross-fertilization in relation to the five issues listed above. Therefore, it is surprising to discover that, notwithstanding this circumstance, WTO and ISDS adjudicators have coincidentally developed a remarkably consistent interpretative practice in relation to all of these specific issues during the formative years of WTO and investor-state dispute settlement (i.e. the mid-1990s to the present). The remainder of this chapter surveys WTO and ISDS practice in relation to each of these five issues, based on my own review of the WTO and ISDS jurisprudence and occasionally relying on some prior surveys of WTO or ISDS jurisprudence. This survey is followed by a general conclusion that suggests a hypothesis to explain the interesting similarities that emerge from this comparison.

2   Are 'Object and Purpose' Two Distinct Concepts?

Article 31(1) VCLT refers to both the 'object' and 'purpose' of the treaty. These two elements could quite naturally be read as setting forth two distinct concepts that need to be considered. Indeed, as a matter of textual analysis, the Appellate Body has repeatedly emphasized that 'interpretation must give meaning and effect to all the terms of a treaty', and an interpreter is not free to adopt a reading that would result in reducing individual words or clauses to 'redundancy or inutility'.[8] In addition, this dual reference to 'object and purpose' was carefully chosen and deliberate, as reflected by the fact that it is consistently used throughout the Vienna Convention (see Articles 18, 19, 20(2), 41 and 58 VCLT).[9] In some domestic legal contexts, there is also a meaningful distinction between the concepts of 'object' and 'purpose'.[10]

On the other hand, an interpreter may read two associated terms together, as what is sometimes called a 'composite' term. As one panel

---

[7] I Sinclair, *The Vienna Convention on the Law of Treaties*, 2nd edition (Manchester University Press, 1984); M Yasseen, 'L'interprétation des Traités d'après la Convention de Vienne sur le Droit des Traités', in *Recueil des Cours de l'Académie de Droit International* (1976), Vol. III.
[8] See e.g. Appellate Body Report, *US – Gasoline*, p. 23.
[9] The words 'object *or* purpose' appear in Article 60 VCLT.
[10] I Buffard and K Zemanek, 'The "Object and Purpose" of a Treaty: An Enigma?' (1998) 3 *Austrian Review of International and European Law* 311, at 326.

has observed, 'where the terms are a single term, or ordinarily used together, then the treaty interpreter should refer to the ordinary meaning of that single term, or of each term in the particular context of each other'.[11] Furthermore, when two terms such as 'object' and 'purpose' have meanings that are not easily distinguishable from one another, the presumption against redundancy or inutility does not force an interpreter to give them different meanings so as to avoid redundancy or inutility at all costs.[12]

The foregoing suggests that there are two possible ways of reading the words 'object and purpose', and we might expect some divergence in the practice of trade and investment adjudicators from the mid-1990s to the present. As it happens, there is perfect convergence in practice in how WTO and ISDS adjudicators have approached this issue. In the WTO context, there is not a single instance in which a panel or the Appellate Body has made any pronouncement to the effect that the terms 'object' and 'purpose' have distinct meanings: these terms are instead employed as a composite term, and interchangeable with one another. In the ISDS context, it likewise appears that in virtually all cases, the notion of 'object and purpose' has been employed as a unitary concept rather than as two terms having two distinct meanings.[13] Furthermore, it appears that where ISDS adjudicators make reference only to the object or to the purpose, either tends to be used synonymously with the phrase 'object and purpose'.[14]

For the purposes of our mini-case study on methodological issues relating to the role of 'object and purpose' in treaty interpretation, this serves as a good first example of parallelism and convergence in practice.

3 Does the Reference to 'Its' Object and Purpose Justify Interpretations that Further the Main or Predominant Purpose of The Treaty?

Article 31(1) VCLT refers to the object and purpose of the treaty in the singular. It states that '[a] treaty shall be interpreted in good faith in

---

[11] Panel Report, *China – Intellectual Property Rights*, para. 7.558. In that case, the panel considered that the term 'on a commercial scale' was what one might call a 'composite' or 'single' term.

[12] Appellate Body Report, *EC – Hormones*, paras. 175–176.

[13] J Weeramantry, *Treaty Interpretation in Investment Arbitration* (Oxford University Press, 2012), pp. 68–9.

[14] Ibid.

accordance with the ordinary meaning to be given to the terms in their context in the light of *its* object and purpose' (emphasis added). As Ian Sinclair noted, '[M]ost treaties have no single, undiluted object and purpose but a variety of differing and possibly conflicting objects and purposes.'[15] Having said that, the use of the singular could still quite naturally be understood to mean that each treaty has its main or predominant 'object and purpose', and to indicate that a treaty interpreter must interpret obligations broadly to advance that main or predominant object and purpose.

On the other hand, the reference in the singular to 'its' object and purpose does not compel an interpreter to adopt a one-sided or reductionist conception of a treaty's object and purpose. To the contrary, where a treaty has a variety of competing objectives and purposes, it does not do violence to the text of Article 31(1) to proceed on the understanding that 'its' object and purpose is to establish a balance between those competing objectives and purposes.

As elaborated below, there are striking parallels in how GATT/WTO and ISDS adjudicators have approached this issue. Beginning with the GATT practice, there was a tendency towards the more one-sided approach above. In the context of presenting a critique of GATT panels, Rob Howse refers to the tendency of panels 'to assume a certain purpose prior to careful textual interpretation, thereby taking a shortcut to the establishment of treaty meaning that bypasses the exact text',[16] resulting in biased outcomes in favour of liberal interpretations of obligations and narrow interpretations of exceptions. Howse is right, insofar as a number of GATT panel reports contain statements to the effect that 'Article XX [GATT], as a provision for exceptions, should be interpreted narrowly in a way that preserves the basic objectives and principles of the General Agreement.'[17] This tendency was vividly reflected in the analysis of the panel in *US - Shrimp*, an early WTO case involving a trade restriction related to the conservation of exhaustible natural resources. In that case, the panel stated that '[w]hile the WTO Preamble confirms that environmental considerations are important for the interpretation of the WTO

---

[15] I Sinclair, *The Vienna Convention on the Law of Treaties*, 2nd edition (Manchester University Press, 1984), p. 130.

[16] R Howse, 'Adjudicative Legitimacy and Treaty Interpretation in International Trade Law: The Early Years of WTO Jurisprudence' in J Weiler (ed.), *The EU, the WTO, and the NAFTA: Towards a Common Law of International Trade?* (Oxford University Press, 2000), p. 54.

[17] GATT Panel Report, *US - Tuna (EEC)*, para. 5.38.

Agreement, the central focus of that agreement remains the promotion of economic development through trade; and the provisions of GATT are essentially turned towards trade liberalization of access to markets on a non-discriminatory basis'.[18] The Appellate Body, however, reversed multiple aspects of the panel's interpretation and analysis under Article XX of the GATT. The Appellate Body attached greater significance to the environmental and 'sustainable development' objectives in the preamble.

The Appellate Body continued the transition towards a more balanced approach in numerous other cases. Early on in its jurisprudence, it rejected the premise that exceptions should be interpreted narrowly, affirming instead that 'merely characterizing a treaty provision as an "exception" does not by itself justify a "stricter" or "narrower" interpretation of that provision than would be warranted ... by applying the normal rules of treaty interpretation'.[19] The Appellate Body also confirmed that while part of the object and purpose of the WTO agreement is the 'substantial reduction of tariffs and other barriers to trade', this could not justify a principle of interpretation showing 'bias towards the reduction of tariff commitments'.[20]

Today, the Appellate Body has repeatedly characterized the object and purpose of various WTO agreements in terms of 'balance'. For instance, it has articulated the object and purpose of the Agreement on Technical Barriers to Trade (TBT Agreement) as striking a 'balance ... between, on the one hand, the desire to avoid creating unnecessary obstacles to international trade and, on the other hand, the recognition of Members' right to regulate', and has said that this 'is not, in principle, different from the balance set out in the GATT 1994'.[21] Likewise, the Appellate Body has stated that the General Agreement on Trade in Services (GATS) also 'seeks to strike a balance' between a Member's obligations and its right to pursue national policy objectives.[22] The Appellate Body has defined the object and purpose of the Agreement on Subsidies and Countervailing Measures (SCM Agreement) as reflecting a 'delicate balance'[23] between Members that sought to impose more disciplines on the use of subsidies and those that sought to impose more disciplines on the application of countervailing measures. Accession

---

[18] Panel Report, *US - Shrimp*, para. 7.42.
[19] Appellate Body Report, *EC - Hormones*, para. 104.
[20] Appellate Body Report, *EC - Chicken Cuts*, para. 243.
[21] Appellate Body Report, *US - Clove Cigarettes*, para. 96.
[22] Appellate Body Report, *Argentina - Financial Services*, para. 6.114.
[23] Appellate Body Report, *US - Countervailing Duty Investigation on DRAMS*, para. 115.

protocols have likewise been described as a 'delicate balance of rights and obligations'.[24] The same kind of approach has been applied at the level of individual provisions in many cases.[25]

One finds a very similar evolution in the ISDS context. In *SGS v. Philippines*, the tribunal considered that it 'is legitimate to resolve uncertainties in [the investment agreement's] interpretation so as to favour the protection of covered investments'.[26] The *Enron v. Argentina* tribunal, assessing when and how a dedicated exception in the investment agreement should apply, considered that '[t]he object and purpose of the Treaty is, as a general proposition, to apply in situations of economic difficulty and hardship that require the protection of the internationally guaranteed rights of its beneficiaries'.[27] It then stated that '[t]o this extent, any interpretation, resulting in an escape route from the obligations defined cannot be easily reconciled with that object and purpose', and reasoned therefore that 'a restrictive interpretation of any such alternative is mandatory'.[28] Kurtz observed that the interpretative practices at play in this case 'echo the crude adjudicatory habits employed by GATT panels prior to the emergence of the WTO'.[29]

However, in the same way that the WTO Appellate Body appears to have adopted a more balanced approach in reaction to one-sided statements by some GATT/WTO panels, a number of ISDS tribunals have, without referencing WTO case law, similarly articulated the overall object and purpose of investment agreements as reflecting a balance between competing interests and values. A textbook example is the *Saluka v. Czech Republic* tribunal, which reviewed the various recitals of the preamble of the investment agreement at issue and concluded:

> This is a more subtle and balanced statement of the Treaty's aims than is sometimes appreciated. The protection of foreign investments is not the

---

[24] Panel Report, *China – Raw Materials*, para. 7.112.
[25] See e.g. Panel Report, *EU – Poultry (China)*, para. 7.218 (referring to 'the need to strike a delicate balance between the different objectives of Article XXVIII' of the GATT 1994); Panel Report, *India – Pharmaceuticals*, para. 7.31 (referring to the need to avoid upsetting 'the delicate balance of the transitional arrangements of Articles 65, 70.8 and 70.9 [of the TRIPS Agreement] that was negotiated during the Uruguay Round').
[26] *SGS v. Philippines*, ICSID Case No. ARB/02/6, Decision on Objection to Jurisdiction, 29 January 2004, para. 116.
[27] *Enron v. Argentina*, ICSID Case No. ARB/01/3, Award, 22 May 2007, para. 331.
[28] Ibid.
[29] J Kurtz, 'On the Evolution and Slow Convergence of International Trade and Investment Law' in G Sacerdoti, P Acconci, M Valenti and A De Luca (eds.), *General Interests of Host States in International Investment Law* (Cambridge University Press, 2014).

sole aim of the Treaty, but rather a necessary element alongside the overall aim of encouraging foreign investment and extending and intensifying the parties' economic relations. That in turn calls for a balanced approach to the interpretation of the Treaty's substantive provisions for the protection of investments.[30]

Along the same lines, the tribunal in *El Paso* v. *Argentina* considered that 'a balanced interpretation is needed, taking into account both State sovereignty and the State's responsibility to create an adapted and evolutionary framework for the development of economic activities, and the necessity to protect foreign investment and its continuing flow'.[31] In *Noble Ventures* v. *Romania*, the tribunal stated that 'it is not permissible, as is too often done regarding BITs, to interpret clauses exclusively in favour of investors'.[32]

The question raised above is whether the reference in the singular to 'its' object and purpose justifies the liberal interpretation of obligations that favours the main or predominant purpose of the treaty. The foregoing survey shows that there is a striking parallel in the evolution of GATT/WTO and ISDS practice in relation to this question. The Appellate Body came to embrace the view that the 'object and purpose' of the WTO agreements embodies a balance of competing objectives and values, thereby rejecting what many saw as a more simple, one-sided approach followed by some GATT/WTO panels of equating 'trade liberalization' as the single or predominant 'object and purpose' of the GATT/WTO agreements. In the context of ISDS, adjudicators also came to articulate more balanced conceptions of an investment agreement's 'object and purpose' in reaction to the more one-sided approach, attributed to some investment tribunals, of equating the object and purpose solely or predominantly with 'investment protection' in a way that risked systematically tilting the interpretative exercise towards pro-investor outcomes.

4 Can Arguments Based on 'Object and Purpose' be Used to Justify a Restrictive Interpretation of Treaty Obligations?

In the conventional rhetoric of treaty interpretation, purposive or teleological interpretation is often associated with interpretations that

---

[30] *Saluka* v. *Czech Republic*, UNCITRAL, Decision on Jurisdiction over the Czech Republic's Counterclaim, 17 March 2006, para. 300.
[31] *El Paso* v. *Argentina*, ICSID Case No. ARB/03/15, Decision on Jurisdiction, 27 April 2006, para. 70.
[32] *Noble Ventures* v. *Romania*, ICSID Case No. ARB/01/11, Award, 12 October 2005, para. 52.

result in relatively broad, liberal or expansive interpretations of obligations. That is the premise in the ILC commentary when it stated that '[s]ome give great weight to the object and purpose of the treaty and are in consequence more ready, especially in the case of general multilateral treaties, to admit teleological interpretations of the text which go beyond, or even diverge from, the original intentions of the parties as expressed in the text'.[33] This statement equates teleological interpretations with liberal interpretation. Likewise, Sinclair's discussion of object and purpose proceeds in similar terms, giving examples of jurisprudence from the European Court of Human Rights (ECtHR) jurisprudence in which the Court 'stretched the interpretation' of obligations 'by adopting the teleological approach'.[34]

In the practice of WTO adjudicators, however, it appears that arguments based on 'object and purpose' are just as often invoked to justify a narrow or restrictive interpretation of obligations and a broad interpretation of exceptions. The following paragraphs provide a couple of examples of the Appellate Body relying on language contained in the preamble to support a relatively broad interpretation of exceptions or a relatively restrictive interpretation of obligations. In *US – Shrimp*, the Appellate Body found that the general exception for measures relating to the conservation of 'exhaustible natural resources' in Article XX(g) of the GATT 1994 should be interpreted broadly, so as to include not only non-living resources (e.g. minerals), but also living natural resources (e.g. endangered sea turtles). The Appellate Body justified its interpretation by reference to the objective of 'sustainable development' contained in the preamble to the WTO Agreement.[35] In *EC – Hormones*, the Appellate Body found that the obligation in Article 3.1 of the SPS Agreement – to ensure that measures are 'based on' international standards – should be interpreted relatively restrictively, as not requiring that measures 'conform to' those international standards. The Appellate Body justified its interpretation by reference to the preamble's statement that Members were '*Desiring* to further the use of harmonized sanitary and phytosanitary measures between Members, on the basis of international standards, guidelines and recommendations'.[36] In the Appellate Body's view, this supported a relatively restrictive interpretation by implication, because it made clear 'that harmonization of SPS measures of Members on the basis

---

[33] *ILC Yearbook* (1966), Vol. II, p. 218.
[34] Sinclair, p. 131.
[35] Appellate Body Report, *US – Shrimp*, para. 131.
[36] SPS Agreement, preamble, fifth recital.

of international standards is projected in the Agreement, as a *goal*, yet to be realized *in the future*' (emphasis added)[37]

It appears that in the practice of ISDS adjudicators, arguments based on 'object and purpose' are also just as often invoked to justify a narrow or restrictive interpretation of obligations. In *Banro* v. *Congo*, for example, the tribunal dismissed the claim for lack of jurisdiction based on its understanding of the object and purpose of the ICSID Convention. The tribunal considered that 'since the ICSID Convention has as its purpose and aim to protect the host State from diplomatic intervention on the part of the national State of the investor and to "depoliticize" investment relations, it would go against this aim and purpose to expose the host State to, at the same time, both diplomatic pressure and an arbitration claim'.[38] In *Alps* v. *Slovak Republic*, the tribunal interpreted a scope and coverage provision in the underlying BIT providing that a legal entity must have 'real economic activities' in the territory of the host state in order to benefit from the protections in the treaty. The tribunal interpreted the language in a manner that excluded 'shell' companies from the scope of the BIT, and considered that such an interpretation was justified by the object and purpose of the BIT:

> The BIT preamble underlines that the purpose pursued by the two Contracting States was intensifying the economic cooperation to the mutual benefit of both States and fostering their economic prosperity. It is illogic to assume that the above goals could be achieved by giving treaty protection or by attracting into the host country 'shell' companies which are unable to establish the kind and level of activities that they conduct in their own State. No State is anxious to promise special guarantees, privileges and protections to investors which bring no benefit to its economy.[39]

In sum, there is an interesting convergence: notwithstanding the conventional rhetoric of treaty interpretation that associates purposive or teleological interpretation with the liberal or expansive interpretations of obligations, the legal reasoning of trade and investment adjudicators reveals a readiness to just as frequently invoke a treaty's object and purpose to justify a narrow or restrictive interpretation of obligations and a broad interpretation of exceptions.

---

[37] Appellate Body Report, *EC – Hormones*, para. 165.
[38] *Banro* v. *Congo*, ICSID Case No. ARB/98/7, Award, 1 September 2000, para. 19.
[39] *Alps* v. *Slovak Republic*, Award, 5 March 2011, para. 226.

5 The Object and Purpose of Individual Provisions, or Only that of the Treaty as a Whole?

Article 31(1) VCLT envisages an interpretation in the light of the object and purpose of the whole treaty, not the object and purpose of the individual provision under interpretation.

Notwithstanding the wording of Article 31(1), there are numerous instances of GATT/WTO panels and the Appellate Body engaging in reasoning by reference to the object and purpose of the individual provision under consideration. Taking some key GATT provisions by way of example, the Appellate Body has explained that the 'object and purpose' of Article I 'is to prohibit discrimination among like products originating in or destined for different countries'.[40] The Appellate Body has resolved various interpretative issues relating to the scope of the national treatment obligation in Article III by reasoning from the premise that '[t]he fundamental purpose of Article III of the GATT 1994 is to ensure equality of competitive conditions between imported and like domestic products'.[41] Citing to the drafting history of Article XX, the Appellate Body has stated that it is 'important to underscore that the purpose and object of the introductory clauses [i.e. chapeau] of Article XX is generally the prevention of "abuse of the exceptions"'.[42] All of these statements concern fundamental principles regarding the object and purpose of individual provisions, rather than statements contained in the preamble to the GATT or the WTO Agreement.

In *EC – Chicken Cuts*, the Appellate Body specifically addressed the relationship between the object and purpose of particular provisions and that of the treaty as a whole. The Appellate Body observed that the term 'its object and purpose' makes it clear that 'the starting point' for ascertaining object and purpose is the treaty 'in its entirety'.[43] However, the Appellate Body stated that it did not believe that Article 31(1) VCLT excludes taking into account the object and purpose of particular treaty terms, 'if doing so assists the interpreter in determining the treaty's object and purpose on the whole'.[44] In this regard, the Appellate Body stated:

---

[40] Appellate Body Report, *Canada – Autos*, para. 84.
[41] Appellate Body Report, *Canada – Periodicals*, p. 18 (citing various prior GATT panel reports).
[42] Appellate Body Report, *US – Gasoline*, p. 22.
[43] Appellate Body Report, *EC – Chicken Cuts*, para. 238.
[44] Ibid.

> We do not see why it would be necessary to divorce a treaty's object and purpose from the object and purpose of specific treaty provisions, or vice versa. To the extent that one can speak of the 'object and purpose of a treaty provision', it will be informed by, and will be in consonance with, the object and purpose of the entire treaty of which it is but a component.[45]

How does this compare with the practice of ISDS adjudicators? Once again, there is a remarkable convergence in the practice of WTO and ISDS adjudicators. In his survey of ISDS practice, Romesh Weeramantary notes that on a 'strict reading' of Article 31(1), 'the object and purpose must be that of the treaty, i.e. the use of "its" – from a grammatical perspective – is a reference to the treaty as a whole rather than the terms'. He observes that '[n]evertheless, many [tribunals] appear to emphasize the object and purpose not of the treaty as a whole but of a specific provision'.[46] Referring to the 2008 survey of ICSID awards by Ole K Fauchald, he notes that of the ninety-eight ICSID decisions examined, thirty-seven relied on the object and purpose of the treaty, and twenty-one relied on the object and purpose of a specific provision (or set of provisions).[47]

Thus, notwithstanding that Article 31(1) VCLT envisages an interpretation in the light of the object and purpose of the whole treaty, and not the individual provision under interpretation, the practice of WTO and ISDS adjudicators aligns again in that both regularly rely on the object and purpose of individual provisions.

6 Must any Consequentialist Arguments Be Linked to the Particular Object and Purpose of the Treaty?

When interpreting a treaty provision, an adjudicator is interested in knowing what the practical consequences of the alternative interpretations will be. An interpretation that leads to good consequences is apt to be justified as being consistent with the 'object and purpose' of the treaty under Article 31(1) VCLT. An interpretation that leads to bad consequences is apt to be rejected in terms of undermining, frustrating or defeating the 'object and purpose' of the treaty. Depending on how bad

---

[45] Ibid.
[46] JR Weeramantry, *Treaty Interpretation in Investment Arbitration* (Oxford University Press, 2012), p. 73.
[47] OK Fauchald, 'The Legal Reasoning of ICSID Tribunals– An Empirical Analysis' (2008) 19(2) *EJIL* 301, at pp. 322–3.

the consequences are, it may even be seen as constituting a 'result that is manifestly absurd or unreasonable' (Article 32(b) VCLT).

An important interpretative issue that arises in relation to consequentialist reasoning is whether any consequentialist arguments must be linked to the particular object and purpose of the treaty at issue, or whether an interpreter may freely rely on consequentialist arguments that appeal to widely held notions of reasonableness and fairness, as opposed to treaty-specific objects and purposes. The issue is important because the answer circumscribes (or not) the extent to which WTO and ISDS adjudicators could engage in consequentialist reasoning to resolve questions of treaty interpretation.

This question is not answered by the text of Article 31 or 32 VCLT, but it was touched upon by ILC members in the context of drafting the articles on interpretation. The original version of Article 32(b), prepared in 1964, provided for recourse to supplementary means of interpretation if the natural and ordinary meaning of a term led to an interpretation which was 'manifestly absurd or unreasonable in the context of the treaty as a whole'.[48] Sir Humphrey Waldock's commentary accompanying the first draft of the articles on interpretation explained that '[t]his exception to the clear meaning rule must, it is thought, be considered as strictly limited to cases where the natural and ordinary meaning gives a result which in the context is objectively and manifestly absurd or unreasonable; for otherwise, it might unduly weaken the rule'.[49]

The initial formulation was revised in a subsequent draft, which instead presented a formulation that referred to a result that was 'manifestly absurd or unreasonable in the light of the objects and purposes of the treaty'.[50] When this draft was discussed, several ILC members proposed that the qualifying words 'in the light of the objects and purposes of the treaty' be deleted, on the grounds that reference to the treaty's object and purpose was already covered by the precursor to VCLT Art. 31(1), and also on the grounds that absurdity-based arguments should not be limited to cases of absurdity 'in the light of the objects and purposes of the treaty'.[51] As one ILC member observed, 'the result obtained might be "absurd or unreasonable" in itself, quite apart from the teleological aspect

---

[48] *ILC Yearbook* (1964), Vol. II, at p. 52.
[49] Ibid. at p. 57.
[50] Ibid. at p. 199.
[51] *ILC Yearbook* (1966), Vol. I, Part I, 872nd meeting, at p. 200, para. 28; and at p. 202, para. 51.

of the matter'.[52] The Special Rapporteur at the time responded by reiterating that '[t]he phrase "in the light of the objects and purposes of the treaty" had been inserted as an objective criterion in order to discourage disingenuous recourse to the notion of an "absurd" interpretation'.[53]

The words 'in the light of the objects and purposes of the treaty' were ultimately deleted from the text that in the end became VCLT Article 32(b). However, the drafting history reveals a certain degree of uncertainty, among those tasked with codifying the rules of interpretation, as to the legitimate scope and basis for consequentialist arguments in the context of treaty interpretation. Furthermore, although the answer to this question has important implications for the kinds of consequentialist arguments that an interpreter may legitimately rely on, it has received scant attention in the literature on treaty interpretation.[54]

However, in the absence of clarity in the express terms of Article 31(1) VCLT and academic works, once again the practice of WTO and ISDS adjudicators reveals striking parallels. A review of consequentialist arguments by adjudicators shows that, in many instances, adjudicators link consequentialist arguments to the particular object and purpose of the treaty at issue. However, in many other instances, adjudicators freely develop consequentialist arguments that appeal to widely held notions of reasonableness and fairness, as opposed to treaty-specific objects and purposes. Furthermore, one finds some striking commonalities in the kinds of consequentialist arguments that are relied upon. In cases involving very different types of provisions, trade and investment adjudicators have engaged in almost identical forms of consequentialist reasoning.

The first example of a common consequentialist argument is found in both *Azinian v. Mexico*, the first award on the merits issued pursuant to NAFTA Chapter 11, and *US - Stainless Steel (Korea)*, a WTO panel report involving various claims arising in the anti-dumping context. In *Azinian*, the arbitral tribunal rejected the complainant's claim of expropriation, reasoning among other things that

> [t]he problem is that the Claimants' fundamental complaint is that they are the victims of a breach of the Concession Contract. NAFTA does not, however, allow investors to seek international arbitration for mere contractual breaches. Indeed, NAFTA cannot possibly be read to create such

---

[52] Ibid., Part I, 872nd meeting, at p. 202, para. 51.
[53] Ibid., Part I, 873rd meeting, at p. 206, para. 39.
[54] For a useful discussion in the context of statutory interpretation, see R Sullivan, *Sullivan and Driedger on the Construction of Statutes*, 4th edition (LexisNexis Canada, 2002), chapter 9 ('Consequential Analysis').

a regime, which would have elevated a multitude of ordinary transactions with public authorities into potential international disputes.[55]

Thus, the tribunal, in the context of examining a claim of expropriation, rejected an interpretation on the grounds that it would have transformed a multitude of disputes over simple contractual breaches under domestic law into violations of treaty obligations. About one year later, in *US – Stainless Steel (Korea)*, a WTO panel rejected a claim under Article X:3(a) of the GATT 1994 related to the requirement that laws be administered in a 'reasonable' manner. In the course of its analysis, the panel indicated that it sought to avoid the same consequence:

> [Article X:3(a)] was not in our view intended to function as a mechanism to test the consistency of a Member's particular decisions or rulings with the Member's own domestic law and practice; that is a function reserved for each Member's domestic judicial system, and a function WTO panels would be particularly ill-suited to perform. An incautious adoption of the approach advocated by Korea could however effectively convert every claim that an action is inconsistent with domestic law or practice into a claim under the WTO Agreement.[56]

The second example of a common type of consequentialist argument is found in *Azian v. Mexico* and *India – Solar Cells*, a WTO panel report issued fifteen years later. Continuing with its analysis of the expropriation claim, the tribunal in *Azinian* found that mere breach of a contract could not constitute an expropriation on the grounds that it might be labelled 'confiscatory'. On this point, the tribunal reasoned that

> [l]abelling is, however, no substitute for analysis. The words 'confiscatory', 'destroy contractual rights as an asset', or 'repudiation' may serve as a way to describe breaches which are to be treated as extraordinary, and therefore as acts of expropriation, but they certainly do not indicate on what basis the critical distinction between expropriation and an ordinary breach of contract is to be made. The egregiousness of any breach is in the eye of the beholder – and that is not satisfactory for present purposes.[57]

Thus, the *Azinian* tribunal, in the context of examining a claim of expropriation, rejected an interpretation on the grounds that it would have had the consequence of introducing a legal standard that was overly subjective. In *India – Solar Cells*, the panel rejected the respondent's interpretation of what it means for products to be in 'short supply' in

---

[55] *Azinian v. Mexico*, ICSID Case No. ARB(AF)/97/2, Award, 1 November 1999, para. 87.
[56] Panel Report, *US – Stainless Steel (Korea)*, para. 6.50.
[57] *Azinian v. Mexico*, ICSID Case No. ARB(AF)/97/2, Award, 1 November 1999, para. 90.

the context of Article XX(j) of the GATT 1994. In the context of its reasoning, the panel presented the following consequentialist argument:

> [W]e consider that there must be some objective point of reference to serve as the basis for an objective assessment of whether there is a 'deficiency' or 'amount lacking' in the 'quantity' of a product that is 'available'. We have concluded that the ordinary meaning of the terms 'products in general or local short supply' refers to a situation in which the quantity of available supply of a product does not meet demand in the relevant geographical area or market.. . . India's alternative interpretation of Article XX(j) does not present any objective point of reference to serve as the basis for an objective assessment of whether a product is in 'short supply' within the meaning of Article XX(j). India has not adequately explained what would constitute a 'lack' of domestic manufacturing capacity amounting to a 'short supply' under its interpretation of Article XX(j).[58]

This type of consequentialist argument may be made with or without reference to any particular object and purpose of the provision or treaty at issue. As an example of the same kind of consequentialist argument regarding legal subjectivity and uncertainty being made with reference to the particular object and purpose, one may note the Appellate Body's consequentialist reasoning in *US/Canada – Continued Suspension* in the context of an entirely different provision, when it stated as follows:

> However, without a proper identification of the time at which the continued suspension of concessions would be found to constitute a unilateral determination inconsistent with the DSU, WTO Members would be unsure as to when or for how long they could properly rely on a DSB authorization to suspend concessions. Such an outcome is contrary to the DSU's objective of providing security and predictability.[59]

A third example of a common type of consequentialist argument may be found in the award in *Ethyl v. Canada*, and in the Appellate Body report in the compliance proceeding in *US – Zeroing (Art. 21.5 – Japan)*. In both cases, the adjudicators took a relatively flexible approach to the interpretation of applicable procedural rules in the context of measures that only entered into force following the institution of proceedings and referred to the desirability of avoiding the consequence of imposing undue and pointless inconvenience on the complainant. In *Ethyl*, the respondent argued that the complainant had jumped the gun by

---

[58] Panel Report, *India – Solar Cells*, paras. 7.225–7.226.
[59] Appellate Body Report, *US/Canada – Continued Suspension*, para. 404.

initiating its claim prior to the coming into force of the legislation being challenged. The arbitral tribunal reasoned, with a general reference to the 'object and purpose of NAFTA', that

> the fact is that in any event six months and more have passed following ... the coming into force of the MMT Act. It is not doubted that today Claimant could resubmit the very claim advanced here (subject to any scope limitations). No disposition is evident on the part of Canada to repeal the MMT Act or amend it. Indeed, it could hardly be expected. Clearly a dismissal of the claim at this juncture would disserve, rather than serve, the object and purpose of NAFTA.[60]

In *US – Zeroing (Art. 21.5 – Japan)*, the Appellate Body was presented with a somewhat similar situation in which a measure was initiated before the commencement of the proceeding, and only 'completed' during that proceeding. The Appellate Body employed a consequentialist argument that was similar to that developed by the *Ethyl* tribunal. The Appellate Body reasoned that to exclude such a measure from a panel's terms of reference would lead to the consequence that the complainant would have to initiate a new panel proceeding in which it could resubmit the claim, which would be inconsistent with the objective of providing for the prompt settlement of disputes.[61] While the Appellate Body linked its reasoning to one of the declared objects and purposes of the DSU (i.e. the 'prompt settlement of situations'), its reasoning is essentially the same form of consequentialist argument employed by the tribunal in *Ethyl v. Canada*.

A fourth and final example of a common type of consequentialist argument may be found in the award in *City Oriente v. Ecuador* and in the Appellate Body report in *Canada – Aircraft*. The *City Oriente* tribunal is one of several ISDS tribunals to have held that it had the power to issue legally binding and final awards on requests for provisional measures. The tribunal reached this finding notwithstanding that Rule 39 of the ICSID Arbitration Rules uses the term 'to recommend' instead of 'to order' which appears in other rules. In *Canada – Aircraft*, the Appellate Body found that a party is legally bound to comply with a panel's request for information. The Appellate Body reached this finding notwithstanding that Article 13.1 of the DSU uses the words 'should respond promptly and fully' instead of 'shall' which appears in various other DSU provisions.

---

[60] *Ethyl v. Canada*, UNCITRAL, Award on Jurisdiction, 24 June 1998, p. 36.
[61] Appellate Body Report, *US – Zeroing (Art. 21.5 – Japan)*, para. 122.

In both cases, the adjudicators rejected the literal meaning of the words 'recommend' and 'should' in favour of an interpretation leading to a legally binding obligation, by reference to consequences that the opposing interpretation would have on the functioning and effectiveness of international dispute settlement proceedings. Following a semantic discussion of the terms 'to recommend' and 'to order', the tribunal in *City Oriente* v. *Ecuador* presented the following functional argument:

> [A] teleological interpretation of [Rule 39 and Article 47 of the ICSID Convention] leads to the conclusion that the provisional measures recommended are necessarily binding. The Tribunal may only order such measures if their adoption is necessary to preserve the rights of the parties and guarantee that the award will fufill its purpose of providing effective judicial protection. Such goals may only be reached if the measures are binding, and they share the exact same binding nature as the final arbitral award. Therefore, it is the Tribunal's conclusion that the word 'recommend' is equal in value to the word 'order'.[62]

In *Canada – Aircraft*, the Appellate Body referred to dictionary definitions of the word 'should' to sustain the view it may connote a 'duty' or 'obligation' rather than merely an 'exhortation'. The Appellate Body then found the existence of a 'legally binding' obligation based on a teleological interpretation of Article 13:

> If Members that were requested by a panel to provide information had no legal duty to 'respond' by providing such information, that panel's undoubted legal '*right* to seek' information under the first sentence of Article 13.1 would be rendered meaningless. A Member party to a dispute could, at will, thwart the panel's fact-finding powers and take control itself of the information-gathering process that Articles 12 and 13 of the DSU place in the hands of the panel.... To hold that a Member party to a dispute is not legally bound to comply with a panel's request for information relating to that dispute, is, in effect, to declare that Member legally free to preclude a panel from carrying out its mandate and responsibility under the DSU.[63]

In sum, there is a lack of clarity in Article 31(1) VCLT on whether consequentialist arguments must be linked to the particular object and purpose of the treaty. We see a readiness in both the ISDS and WTO contexts to rely on consequentialist arguments that appeal to widely held notions of reasonableness and fairness, rather than any treaty-specific

---

[62] *City Oriente* v. *Ecuador*, ICSID ARB/06/21, Provisional Measures, 19 November 2007, para. 52.
[63] Appellate Body Report, *Canada – Aircraft*, paras. 188–189.

object and purpose. Even where adjudicators do link consequentialist arguments to a treaty-specific object and purpose, we can find examples of essentially the same argument being employed by other adjudicators by reference to widely held notions of reasonableness and fairness. Furthermore, we see striking commonalities in the specific kinds of such consequentialist arguments that are developed coincidentally in different contexts, without any interaction or conscious convergence on the part of ISDS and WTO adjudicators.

7 Conclusion

There is a natural tendency in the literature to associate cross-fertilization and judicial interaction with convergence, and to associate isolation and fragmentation with divergence. In relation to certain kinds of issues, however, there appears to be the possibility of parallelism and convergence in practice without any express form of interaction and cross-fertilization, without any express reliance on prior precedent, and without any demonstrated mutual awareness of the practice of other international tribunals. This is the phenomenon of *convergence without interaction*.

As a case study, this chapter has shown that there is a remarkable degree of convergence in the legal reasoning of trade and investment adjudicators regarding the use of 'object and purpose' in treaty interpretation. As elaborated above, these parallels include the following:

1. Notwithstanding the very real potential for a different reading based on established canons of textual analysis, there is a pervasive understanding that the two elements in the phrase 'object and purpose' should be understood as interchangeable elements of a single, composite term.
2. Notwithstanding the singular reference to 'its' object and purpose in Article 31(1) VCLT, there has been parallel evolution in the GATT/WTO and ISDS contexts of balanced conceptions of the 'object and purpose' that rejected, respectively, more one-sided conceptions of 'trade liberalization' and 'investment protection' as predominant objectives.
3. Notwithstanding the conventional rhetoric of treaty interpretation that associates purposive or teleological interpretation with the liberal or expansive interpretations of obligations, there is a readiness to just as frequently invoke a treaty's object and purpose to justify a narrow

or restrictive interpretation of obligations and a broad interpretation of exceptions.
4. Notwithstanding that Article 31(1) VCLT envisages an interpretation in the light of the object and purpose of the whole treaty, and not (just) of the particular provision under interpretation, there is regular reliance on the object and purpose of individual provisions.
5. Notwithstanding the lack of clarity in Article 31(1) VCLT on whether consequentialist arguments must be linked to the particular object and purpose of the treaty, there is a readiness to rely on consequentialist arguments that appeal to widely held notions of reasonableness and fairness, and striking commonalities in the specific *kinds* of such consequentialist arguments.

This convergence in practice suggests that while some practices in international legal reasoning are the product of an adjudicator's specialized knowledge of prior precedent (such that convergence in respect of those practices is not possible without sufficient knowledge of the practices of other international tribunals), other practices in international legal reasoning are the product of practical reasoning and general analytical skills – for lack of a better term, 'legal common sense' (or 'nature' and not 'nurture'). When that is the case, we can expect to find parallels in practice across different areas of international law, even in circumstances where there are insurmountable barriers to cross-fertilization or interaction. This holds true even in circumstances where adjudicators purport to be interpreting and applying certain specialized rules of legal reasoning and treaty interpretation, such as the 'object and purpose' element of Article 31(1) VCLT.

9

Assessing Convergence between International Investment Law and International Trade Law through Interpretative Commissions/ Committees: A Case of Ambivalence?

YULIYA CHERNYKH[*]

The divergent and contradictory interpretations of similar treaty provisions are constantly blamed for being a major problem in investment treaty arbitration.[1] No legal concept has attracted so many emotionally charged epithets from parties and tribunals in awards than treaty interpretation. Characterizations range from negative adjectives such as 'far-reaching',[2] 'contrary',[3] and 'highly restrictive',[4] to descriptions

---

[*] The author would like to thank Andrea M. Steingruber, Daniel Behn and Szilárd Gáspár-Szilágyi for their comments on earlier drafts of the chapter. All treaties are referenced in the chapter as of 12 October 2017. As of 15 October 2019, the status of some of the treaties has changed. Some treaties were terminated, whereas others were signed or entered into force. For instance, the Australia-Mexico BIT (2005) was terminated on 30 December 2018; the Mexico-United Arab Emirates BIT (2016) entered into force on 25 January 2018; the EU-Singapore FTA was signed on 13 February 2019; the EU-Vietnam FTA was signed on 30 June 2019; the EU-Japan Economic Partnership Agreement was signed on 17 July 2018 and entered into force on 1 February 2019; Belgium and Luxembourg adopted a new model BIT in 2019. These changes do not affect the principle ideas put forward in the chapter.

[1] Overview of the areas of criticism in G. Kaufmann-Kohler and M. Potestà, 'Can the Mauritius Convention Serve as a Model for the Reform of Investor-State Arbitration in Connection with the Introduction of a Permanent Investment Tribunal or an Appeal Mechanism? Analysis and Roadmap' (2016) CIDS Research Paper 10–5, www.uncitral.org /pdf/english/CIDS_Research_Paper_Mauritius.pdf, accessed 12 October 2017.

[2] *SGS Société Générale de Surveillance S.A. v. Islamic Republic of Pakistan*, ICSID case No. ARB/01/13, Decision of the Tribunal on Objections to Jurisdiction, para. 163.

[3] *SGS Société Générale de Surveillance S.A. v. Republic of the Philippines*, ICSID case No. ARB/02/6, Decision of the Tribunal on Objections to Jurisdiction, para. 50.

[4] *SGS Société Générale de Surveillance S.A. v. Republic of the Philippines* (n. 4) para. 120.

which frequently emphasize positive aspects, such as 'balanced',[5] 'correct',[6] 'definitive',[7] 'effective',[8] 'generous',[9] 'good faith'[10] and 'proper'.[11] This list is by no means exhaustive and could be complemented by more neutral characterizations including terms such as 'broad',[12] 'historical',[13] 'literal',[14] 'textual'[15] and 'possible'.[16]

More recently, the legal characterization 'binding' has found its way directly into treaty wording. Model bilateral treaties (Model BITs), newly concluded bilateral investment treaties (BITs) and the investment chapters of Free Trade Agreements (FTAs) (all treaties hereinafter referred to collectively as international investment agreements – IIAs) increasingly include institutional arrangements in the form of joint commissions/committees made up of government representatives which have the power to adopt binding interpretations of the treaties in question. The interpretative functions shared by tribunals and commissions/committees have therefore been distributed in the latter's favour to foster IIA readings that are both predictable and coherent.[17]

---

[5] *Bureau Veritas, Inspection, Valuation, Assessment and Control, BIVAC B.V. v. The Republic of Paraguay*, ICSID case No. ARB/07/9, Decision of the Tribunal on Objections to Jurisdiction, para. 59.

[6] *Compañía de Aguas del Aconquija S.A. and Vivendi Universal S.A. v. Argentine Republic*, ICSID Case No. ARB/97/3, Decision on Annulment, para. 39.

[7] *SGS Société Générale de Surveillance S.A. v. Republic of the Philippines* (n. 4) para. 157.

[8] *SGS Société Générale de Surveillance S.A. v. Republic of the Philippines* (n. 4) para. 116.

[9] *Hupacasath First Nation v. Canada (Minister of Foreign Affairs)*, Challenge to Canada-China FIPA in Federal Court of Canada, Federal Court Decision, para. 56.

[10] *SGS Société Générale de Surveillance S.A. v. Republic of the Philippines* (n. 4) paras. 59, 77.

[11] Ibid. para. 126.

[12] *Bureau Veritas, Inspection, Valuation, Assessment and Control, BIVAC B.V. v. The Republic of Paraguay* (n. 10) paras. 139, 140.

[13] *Suez, Sociedad General de Aguas de Barcelona, S.A. and Vivendi Universal, S. A. v. Argentine Republic*, ICSID Case No. ARB/03/19 (formerly *Aguas Argentinas, S.A., Suez, Sociedad General de Aguas de Barcelona, S.A. and Vivendi Universal, S. A. v. Argentine Republic*), Decision on Liability, para. 177.

[14] *SGS Société Générale de Surveillance S.A v. the Republic of Paraguay*, ICSID Case No. ARB/07/29, Decision on Jurisdiction, para. 169.

[15] *SGS Société Générale de Surveillance S.A. v. Republic of the Philippines* (n. 4) paras. 50, 59, 90, 116, 120, 122, 123, 126, 157.

[16] *SGS Société Générale de Surveillance S.A v. the Republic of Paraguay* (n. 22) Decision on Annulment, para. 134.

[17] In 2011, joint interpretative commissions or committees as institutional bodies created by states within the framework of bilateral and multilateral treaties were named by UNCTAD as useful tools at the disposal of state actors. Much hope was placed on the binding character of such interpretations. See UNCTAD, 'Interpretation of IIAs: What States Can Do' (IIA Issues Note No. 3 2011), http://unctad.org/en/Docs/webdiaeia2011 d10_en.pdf, accessed 12 October 2017.

The result of introducing this institutional arrangement has not only been to weaken the depoliticized nature of disputes that is so important in international investment law, but also to increase the need for interstate dialogue inherent in international trade law. The spread of joint commissions/committees across investment law regimes may therefore be viewed as a sign that some form of convergence between investment law and international trade law is taking place. On a deeper level though, these interpretative commissions/committees have not been fully integrated into the dispute resolution mechanisms provided by IIAs. What is more, the state's dual role in both issuing a binding interpretation and acting as a respondent may clash with the fundamental principles of international adjudication.

This chapter aims to explore whether, and to what extent, the existence of joint interpretative commissions/committees is in fact a sign of convergence between international investment law and international trade law. The discussion begins with a description of the methodological approach and then goes on to define interpretative commissions/committees and their origins. Convergence is addressed through four dimensions (spatial, temporal, ideological and functional) and the impact of the interpretative commissions/committees on international investment law.

1 The Methodological Approach

Measuring convergences and divergences that occur among subfields of law is a difficult task, and there are no precise systems or formal tools for doing so. Given this absence of methodological rigour, there is a tendency for the degrees of similarity that are sufficient for drawing conclusions on convergence or divergence to vary from one publication to another, as further evidenced by the wish of the editors of this book not to confine its authors to predetermined concepts of 'convergence' or 'divergence' (see Chapter 1). What some authors categorize as convergence may not necessarily be so for others.[18] The concept is therefore somewhat flawed and requires clarification each time it is used.

The challenge of becoming involved in unmeasurable forms of analysis has not diminished the topic's appeal for academics. Views on converging and diverging trends are constantly put forward in studies on

---

[18] Mads Andenas and Eirik Bjorge confirm the plurality of views on convergence by stressing the desirability for more empirical investigation into convergence. See Mads Andenas and Eirik Bjorge (eds.), *A Farewell to Fragmentation* (Cambridge University Press, 2015) p. 3.

harmonization,[19] unification,[20] Europeanization,[21] internationalization,[22] and fragmentation-defragmentation,[23] to name but a few. These opinions stem from a perception of international law as a system within which certain trends can be identified.[24] However, instead of attempting to agree on criteria for identifying and measuring these trends, legal scholars *compare* certain changes and attribute them to the importance of reducing or aggravating differences between the objects under comparison. Despite the diversity of approaches and the variety of factors that are considered, legal studies of convergence-divergence share a methodological axis that is

[19] See, for instance, Larry Catá Backer, *Harmonizing Law in an Era of Globalization: Convergence, Divergence and Resistance* (Carolina Academic, Press, 2007); Silvia Fazio, *The Harmonization of International Commercial Law* (Kluwer Law International, 2007); Fernando Gomez-Pomar, 'The Harmonization of Contract Law through European Rules: A Law and Economics Perspective' (2008) 2, https://ssrn.com/abstract=1371515, accessed 14 December 2017; Stephen Weatherill and Stefan Vogenauer (eds.), *The Harmonisation of European Contract Law: Implications for European Private Laws, Business and Legal Practice* (Hart Publishing, 2006).

[20] See, for instance, Alkuin Kölliker, *Flexibility and European Unification: The Logic of Differentiated Integration* (Rowman & Littlefield, 2006); Sacha Prechal and Bertvan Roermund (eds.), *The Coherence of EU Law: The Search for Unity in Divergent Concepts* (Oxford University Press, 2008); Paul Stephan, 'The Futility of Unification and Harmonization in International Commercial Law' (1999) University of Virginia School of Law Legal Studies Working Paper No. 99-10, www.jus.unitn.it/DSG/ricerche/dottorati/allegati/ 1999_Stephan.pdf, accessed 14 December 2017.

[21] See, for instance, Francis Snyder (ed.), *The Europeanisation of Law: The Legal Effects of European Integration* (Hart Publishing, 2000); Thomas Watkin (ed.), *Europeanisation of Law* (British Institute of International and Comparative Law, 1998); Jan Wouters et al. (eds.), *The Europeanisation of International Law* (Springer, 2011); Christian Twigg-Flesner, *The Europeanisation of Contract Law: Current Controversies in Law* (Routledge-Cavendish, 2013).

[22] Marcelo Dias Varella, *Internationalization of Law: Globalization, International Law and Complexity* (Springer, 2014); Jan Klabbers and Mortimer Sellers (eds.), *The Internationalization of Law and Legal Education* (Springer, 2009); Jens Drolshammer and Michael Pfeifer (eds.), *The Internationalization of the Practice of Law* (Springer, 2001).

[23] Martti Koskenniemi (ed.), 'Fragmentation of International Law: Difficulties Arising from the Diversification and Expansion of International Law' (Report of the Study Group of the International Law Commission, Erik Castrén Institute Research Reports, 2007); Margaret Young (ed.), *Regime Interaction in International Law: Facing Fragmentation* (Cambridge University Press, 2015); Mads Andenas and Eirik Bjorge (n. 27); Andrzej Jakubowski and Karolina Wierczyńska (eds.), *Fragmentation vs the Constitutionalisation of International Law: A Practical Inquiry* (Routledge-Cavendish, 2016); Philippa Webb, *International Judicial Integration and Fragmentation* (Oxford University Press, 2016).

[24] Jean d'Aspremont, 'The International Court of Justice and the Irony of System-Design' (2017) 8 (2) *Journal of International Dispute Settlement* 366–87.

mainly grounded in the comparative method;[25] this chapter is no exception.

The starting point of this analysis lies in the understanding that interpretative commissions/committees originate from Free Trade Agreements (FTAs), some with investment chapters. The next step is to view their implications in the context of investment treaty arbitration. The comparison thus turns to the features of international trade law that are channelled into the international investment law regime together with interpretative commissions/committees. Integrating and disintegrating elements are judged against conventional interpretation in investment treaty arbitration exercised by arbitral tribunals. The chapter is therefore structured around the dimensions that facilitate an understanding of the spread, speed and depth of the phenomena under analysis: the spatial, temporal, ideological and functional dimensions. The spatial and temporal dimensions show the geographical spread of interpretative commissions/committees in IIAs over time. The UNCTAD's Investment Policy Hub has been used to identify the twenty-three IIAs in force, ten Model BITs, six signed IIAs and at least two draft IIAs at various stages of approval which include interpretative commissions/committees (from a total of 2,573). The ideological dimension shows which values are channelled into international investment law via interpretative commissions/committees. Finally, the functional dimension is useful in addressing whether the availability of interpretative commissions/committees actually brings about convergence in practice.

Although no claims are made regarding the four dimensions' universality for characterizing convergence and divergence, it is posited that they are particularly useful for assessing the appearance, spread and possible impact of interpretative commissions/committees in the field of international investment law, thus enabling conclusions to be reached on convergence or divergence between the two fields.

2 Definition of Interpretative Commissions/ Committees

Before addressing these dimensions, it is important to understand what interpretative commissions and committees are, followed by their origins.

---

[25] Other methods, including empirical methods, may of course also be relevant, but comparison (express or implicit) is the mainstream.

Despite the differences that have led to these bodies being categorized as either commissions[26] or committees,[27] both are essentially joint interstate arrangements consisting of state representatives entrusted with specific functions, including binding treaty interpretation. Appearing frequently in FTAs that cover trade and investment, commissions or committees are part of both fields. Just over half of the treaties analysed[28] specify that commissions/committees are to be made up of or chaired by high-level government representatives, defined as ministerial/cabinet level or, more broadly, senior level;[29] the remainder do not expressly restrict government representation on the basis of seniority.[30]

[26] Benin-Canada BIT (2013), BLEU (Belgium-Luxembourg Economic Union)-Estonia BIT (1996), BLEU (Belgium-Luxembourg Economic Union)-Madagascar BIT (2005), BLEU (Belgium-Luxembourg Economic Union)-Republic of Moldova(1996), BLEU (Belgium-Luxembourg Economic Union)-Montenegro BIT (2010), BLEU (Belgium-Luxembourg Economic Union)-Peru BIT (2005), BLEU (Belgium-Luxembourg Economic Union)-Bolivarian Republic of Venezuela BIT (1998), Canada-Honduras FTA (2013), Canada-Jordan BIT (2009), Canada-Republic of Korea FTA (2014), Canada-Peru BIT (2006), Colombia-Costa Rica FTA (2013), Colombia-Panama FTA (2013), Colombia-Peru BIT (2007), Czech Republic-Morocco BIT (2001), Greece-Morocco BIT (1994), Republic of Korea-New Zealand FTA (2015), Mexico-Panama FTA (2014), Morocco-Poland BIT (1994), New Zealand-Taiwan Province of China ECA (2013), Pacific Alliance Additional Protocol (2014), TPP (2016), Canada Model BIT (2004), Uganda Model BIT (2003), Burundi Model BIT (2002), Belgium-Luxemburg Model BIT (2002), Ghana Model BIT (2008), Israel Model BIT (2003), Burkina Faso Model BIT (2012).

[27] Australia-China FTA (2015), Australia-Republic of Korea FTA (2014), Canada-EU CETA (2016), Chile-Hong Kong China SAR BIT (2016), India-Malaysia FTA (2011), Republic of Korea-Vietnam FTA (2015), Draft of TTIP, Draft of EU-Singapore Free Trade Agreement, Draft of EU-Vietnam Free Trade Agreement, Norway Model BIT (2007), Norway Model BIT (2015).

[28] Twenty-eight treaties containing institutional arrangements in the form of interpretative commissions/committees are analysed. For more information, see the following section, which addresses the space and time dimensions of the spread of interpretative commissions/committees in IIAs.

[29] Australia-China FTA (2015), Australia-Republic of Korea FTA (2014), Canada-EU CETA (2016), Canada-Honduras FTA (2013), Canada-Jordan BIT (2009), Canada-Republic of Korea FTA (2014), Canada-Peru BIT (2006), Colombia-Costa Rica FTA (2013), Colombia-Panama FTA (2013), India-Malaysia FTA (2011), Republic of Korea-New Zealand FTA (2015), Republic of Korea-Vietnam FTA (2015), Mexico-Panama FTA (2014), Pacific Alliance Additional Protocol (2014), TPP (2016).

[30] Benin-Canada BIT (2013), BLEU (Belgium-Luxembourg Economic Union)-Estonia BIT (1996), BLEU (Belgium-Luxembourg Economic Union)-Madagascar BIT (2005), BLEU (Belgium-Luxembourg Economic Union)-Republic of Moldova (1996), BLEU (Belgium-Luxembourg Economic Union)-Montenegro BIT (2010), BLEU (Belgium-Luxembourg Economic Union)-Peru BIT (2005), BLEU (Belgium-Luxembourg Economic Union)-Bolivarian Republic of Venezuela BIT (1998), Chile-Hong Kong, China SAR BIT (2016), Czech Republic-Morocco BIT (2001), Greece-Morocco BIT (1994), Morocco-Poland BIT (1994), New Zealand-Taiwan Province of China ECA (2013).

Irrespective of their hierarchical positions, representatives are mainly government officials who act on the basis of delegated authority. They do not need to have any legal education (at least, there is no express requirement for legal training), which may be expected for duties that require treaty interpretation.

In addition to interpreting treaties, commissions/committees have a number of consultative, constitutive and other functions.[31] Where their interpretative functions are concerned, IIAs have somewhat varying provisions. Depending on the treaty, interpretations can be issued on the initiative of commissions/committees,[32] at the request of either of the contracting parties,[33] at the request of the tribunal if a respondent[34] or a 'disputing party'[35] asks for an interpretation, or as the result of various

---

[31] According to Article 48 of the Benin-Canada BIT (2013), the Joint Commission is also entitled to implement and apply the treaty, propose amendments to it, and consult on any measure that is adopted or proposed as well as any other question that would be likely to affect the treaty's operation. The Canada-Jordan BIT (2009) and the Canada-Peru BIT (2006) endow the Commission with the functions of resolving disputes, supervising the implementation of the treaties, considering any other matter that may affect the operation of the Agreement and adopting a Code of Conduct for Arbitrators. At the same time, several FTAs entrust joint committees with specific functions; for instance, the Australia-China FTA (2015) also gives the FTA Joint Committee authority to establish additional committees and ad hoc working groups, to seek the advice of non-governmental persons or groups on any matter and to explore measures for the further expansion of trade and investment between the parties. The TPP (2016) has the longest list of non-exclusive functions (fifteen functions, plus a sixteenth whose open wording is to 'take any other action as the Parties may agree').

[32] Australia-China FTA (2015), Colombia-Peru BIT (2007), Chile-Hong Kong, China SAR BIT (2016), Australia-Republic of Korea FTA (2014), Benin-Canada BIT (2013), Canada-EU CETA (2016), Canada-Honduras FTA (2013), Canada-Jordan BIT (2009), Canada-Republic of Korea FTA (2014), Canada-Peru BIT (2006), Republic of Korea-New Zealand FTA (2015), Republic of Korea-Vietnam FTA (2015), Mexico-Panama FTA (2014), Pacific Alliance Additional Protocol (2014), TPP (2016).

[33] BLEU (Belgium-Luxembourg Economic Union)-Estonia BIT (1996), BLEU (Belgium-Luxembourg Economic Union)-Republic of Moldova (1996), BLEU (Belgium-Luxembourg Economic Union)-Montenegro BIT (2010), BLEU (Belgium-Luxembourg Economic Union)-Peru BIT (2005), BLEU (Belgium-Luxembourg Economic Union)-Bolivarian Republic of Venezuela BIT (1998), Colombia-Costa Rica FTA (2013) (in the context of local administrative/judicial proceedings), Greece-Morocco BIT (1994), India-Malaysia FTA (2011), Mexico-Panama FTA (2014) (in the context of local administrative/judicial proceedings), Morocco-Poland BIT (1994).

[34] Australia-China FTA (2015), Australia-Republic of Korea FTA (2014), Colombia-Costa Rica FTA (2013), Republic of Korea-New Zealand FTA (2015), Mexico-Panama FTA (2014), Pacific Alliance Additional Protocol (2014), TPP (2016).

[35] Canada-Honduras FTA (2013), Canada-Jordan FTA (2009), Canada-Republic of Korea FTA (2014), Canada-Peru BIT (2006), Republic of Korea-Vietnam FTA (2015).

combinations of grounds.[36] Some treaties give commissions/committees the exclusive authority to issue interpretations, which expires within a certain time limit[37] in case no interpretation is issued,[38] although not all treaties contain the same or even similar provisions.[39] While some include provisions on the exclusive authority of the commissions/committees to interpret certain provisions or annexes,[40] others do not subject this authority to a specifically defined object of interpretation.[41] In

---

[36] The most frequent combinations of grounds triggering interpretation are either interpretations that are carried out on the commission's own initiative and at the tribunal's request if the respondent asks for one, or on the commission's initiative and at the tribunal's request if the 'disputing party' requests said interpretation. The Canada-EU CETA (2016) and the Republic of Korea-New Zealand FTA (2015) also provide for other committees to be able to recommend or advise joint committees on the adoption of a treaty interpretation, while the latter is also entitled to issue interpretations on its own initiative or at the tribunal's request.

[37] Bilateral treaties mostly provide for sixty days for the issuance of an interpretation, with the exception of the Australia-China FTA (2015), although as a multilateral treaty TPP sets a ninety-day limit.

[38] Australia-China FTA (2015), Australia-Republic of Korea FTA (2014), BLEU (Belgium-Luxembourg Economic Union)-Madagascar BIT (2005), BLEU (Belgium-Luxembourg Economic Union)-Estonia BIT (1996), BLEU (Belgium-Luxembourg Economic Union)-Bolivarian Republic of Venezuela BIT (1998), Canada-Honduras FTA (2013), Canada-Jordan BIT (2009), Canada-Republic of Korea FTA (2014), Canada-Peru BIT (2006), Colombia-Costa Rica FTA (2013), Colombia-Panama FTA (2013), Czech Republic-Morocco BIT (2001), Greece-Morocco BIT (1994), Republic of Korea-New Zealand FTA (2015), Republic of Korea-Vietnam FTA (2015), Mexico-Panama FTA (2014), Morocco-Poland BIT (1994), Pacific Alliance Additional Protocol (2014), TPP (2016), Colombia-Peru BIT (2007).

[39] Benin-Canada BIT (2013), BLEU (Belgium-Luxembourg Economic Union)-Republic of Moldova BIT (1996), BLEU (Belgium-Luxembourg Economic Union)-Montenegro BIT (2010), BLEU (Belgium-Luxembourg Economic Union)-Peru BIT (2005), Canada-EU CETA (2016), Chile-Hong Kong, China SAR BIT (2016), India-Malaysia FTA (2011), New Zealand-Taiwan Province of China ECA (2013).

[40] Australia-China FTA (2015), Australia-Republic of Korea FTA (2014), Canada-Honduras FTA (2013), Canada-Republic of Korea FTA (2014), Canada-Jordan BIT (2009), Canada-Peru BIT (2006), Colombia-Costa Rica FTA (2013), Colombia-Panama FTA (2013), Republic of Korea-New Zealand FTA (2015), Republic of Korea-Vietnam FTA (2015), Mexico-Panama FTA (2014), Pacific Alliance Additional Protocol (2014), TPP (2016).

[41] Benin-Canada BIT (2013), BLEU (Belgium-Luxembourg Economic Union)-Estonia BIT (1996), BLEU (Belgium-Luxembourg Economic Union)-Madagascar BIT (2005), BLEU (Belgium-Luxembourg Economic Union)-Republic of Moldova (1996), BLEU (Belgium-Luxembourg Economic Union)-Montenegro BIT (2010), BLEU (Belgium-Luxembourg Economic Union)-Peru BIT (2005), BLEU (Belgium-Luxembourg Economic Union)-Bolivarian Republic of Venezuela BIT (1998), Canada-EU CETA (2016), Chile-Hong Kong, China SAR BIT (2016), Colombia-Peru BIT (2007), Czech Republic-Morocco BIT (2001), Greece-Morocco BIT (1994), India-Malaysia FTA (2011), Morocco-Poland BIT (1994), New Zealand-Taiwan Province of China ECA (2013).

addition, some treaties also entrust commissions/committees with a mandate to settle interstate interpretation disputes.[42]

With regard to voting and interpretative methods, most IIAs provide for mutual agreement or consensus[43] and do not specify the interpretative methods that commissions/committees should use. IIAs may sometimes refer to the application of the customary rules of interpretation as reflected in the Vienna Convention on the Law of Treaties (VCLT) or may refer directly to the VCLT.[44] On other occasions, they might indicate a need to interpret treaties in compliance with interpretations adopted in the WTO system.[45] However, such methodological clarifications in fact relate to arbitration tribunals constituted under the respective treaties and not to treaty commissions/committees.

Historically, interpretative commissions/committees evolved from FTAs containing investment chapters; however, their origins are not self-evident and require clarification. The difficulty of tracing the origins of

---

[42] See, for instance, Australia-Republic of Korea FTA (2014), BLEU (Belgium-Luxembourg Economic Union)-Estonia BIT (1996), BLEU (Belgium-Luxembourg Economic Union)-Madagascar BIT (2005), BLEU (Belgium-Luxembourg Economic Union)-Republic of Moldova BIT (1996), BLEU (Belgium-Luxembourg Economic Union)-Montenegro BIT (2010), BLEU (Belgium-Luxembourg Economic Union)-Peru (2005), BLEU (Belgium-Luxembourg Economic Union)-Bolivarian Republic of Venezuela BIT (1998), Canada-EU CETA (2016), Canada-Republic of Korea FTA (2014), Canada-Peru BIT (2006), Colombia-Peru BIT (2007), Czech Republic-Morocco BIT (2001), Republic of Korea-New Zealand FTA (2015), Republic of Korea-Vietnam FTA (2015), Mexico-Panama FTA (2014), Morocco-Poland BIT (1994), New Zealand-Taiwan Province of China ECA (2013), Pacific Alliance Additional Protocol (2014).

[43] Consensus is the most natural means of decision-making for interpretative commissions/committees. However, the wording of the voting procedures differs: the Australia-China FTA (2015), the Republic of Korea-New Zealand FTA (2015), the Republic of Korea-Vietnam FTA (2015), the Canada-Republic of Korea FTA (2014), the New Zealand-Taiwan Province of China ECA (2013) and the Colombia-Costa Rica FTA (2013) stipulate that decisions are to be taken by 'mutual agreement', while the Australia-Republic of Korea FTA (2014) and Canada-EU CETA (2016) require 'mutual consent' and the TPP (2016), the Pacific Alliance Additional Protocol (2014), and the Mexico-Panama FTA (2014) refer to 'consensus'. Several treaties do not mention any such procedure but entrust the interpretative commissions/committees with the duty to establish procedural rules to govern the voting procedure, as is the case in the Canada-Jordan BIT (2009), the Canada-Peru BIT (2006) and the India-Malaysia FTA (2011). Given the bilateral character of most treaties containing institutional interpretative arrangements, consensus seems to be the only mechanism in place.

[44] Australia-China FTA (2015), Australia-Korea FTA (2014), Canada-EU CETA (2016), Canada-Korea FTA (2014), Korea-New Zealand FTA (2015), Korea-Vietnam FTA (2015), TPP (2016).

[45] Canada-EU CETA (2016), TPP (2016), Australia-China FTA (2015), New Zealand-Taiwan Province of China ECA (2013).

interpretative commissions/committees to international trade law (from FTAs and not BITs) is explained by certain similarities between the features of interpretative commissions/committees and available interpretative arrangements in the context of international investment law.

Indeed, states have a right to joint interpretation as a matter of international law, regardless of the subfield. According to Article 31(3) VCLT 'any subsequent agreement between the parties regarding the interpretation of the treaty' shall be taken into account together with the treaty's context. BITs concluded mostly after 2000 expressly refer to the option of joint interpretation without establishing any institutional arrangements for putting it into practice.[46] The option is nevertheless available to states, absent any specific reference to it in BITs. Joint interpretations involving two states have sometimes been undertaken in the context of investment treaty arbitration in the absence of any institutional arrangements, though the examples that are known emanate from the recent period of 2002 and 2016.[47] Furthermore, some BITs, the earliest of which was

[46] ASEAN-India Investment Agreement (2014), Australia-Mexico BIT (2005), Bahrain-Mexico BIT (2012), Belarus-Mexico BIT (2008), Burkina Faso-Canada BIT (2015), Cameroon-Canada BIT (2014), Canada-Côte d'Ivoire BIT (2014), Canada-Guinea BIT (2015), Canada-Hong Kong, China SAR BIT (2016),Canada-Kuwait BIT (2011), Canada-Mali BIT (2014), Canada-Mongolia BIT (2016), Canada-Nigeria BIT (2014), Canada-Senegal BIT (2014), Canada-Serbia BIT (2014), Canada-Slovakia BIT (2010), Canada-United Republic of Tanzania BIT (2013), Canada-Bolivarian Republic of Venezuela BIT (1996), Chile-Uruguay BIT (2010), China-Mexico BIT (2008), Cuba-Mexico BIT (2001), Iceland-Mexico BIT (2005), India-Mexico BIT (2007), Islamic Republic of Iran-Slovakia BIT (2016), Republic of Korea-Mexico BIT (2000), Republic of Korea-Turkey Investment Agreement (2015), Republic of Korea-Vietnam BIT (2003), Kuwait-Mexico BIT (2013), Mexico-Netherlands BIT (1998), Mexico-Portugal BIT (1999), Mexico-Singapore BIT (2009), Mexico-Slovakia BIT (2007), Mexico-Spain BIT (2006), Mexico-Switzerland BIT (1995), Mexico-Trinidad and Tobago BIT (2006), Mexico-United Arab Emirates BIT (2016), Mexico-United Kingdom BIT (2006), Rwanda-United States of America BIT (2008), United States of America-Uruguay BIT (2005), Mexico-Panama BIT (2005).

[47] In 2002, the Netherlands and the Czech Republic expressed a joint view on the interpretation of the BIT concluded between them in the context of *CME Czech Republic B. V. v. The Czech Republic*. The Partial Award triggered consultations which were conducted between representatives of the two states and were reflected in the Agreed Minutes signed by their respective governments. Another joint interpretation in the form of an exchange of letters between the Lao People's Democratic Republic and the People's Republic of China (PRC) has been made in the context of the PCA Case No. 2013-13 (UNCITRAL) *Sanum Investments Ltd. v. Laos*. In the letters, the Ministry of Foreign Affairs of the Lao People's Democratic Republic asked the PRC Embassy in Vientiane, Laos, to confirm that the BIT between Lao and China did not cover Macau. The PRC Embassy in Lao responded by confirming that the BIT was indeed not applicable to Macau; the letters served as a ground for the High Court of Singapore to set aside an award (*Government of the Lao People's Democratic Republic v. Sanum Investments Ltd*

concluded in 1994, contain certain institutional arrangements (in the form of commissions), which are entrusted with the mission of conciliating or settling interstate disputes on matters of interpretation.[48]

No information is available on any single interpretative dispute between states that was settled by such commissions. The listed examples of non-institutionalized joint committees and commissions tasked with settling interstate disputes concerning treaty interpretation, however, are not the topic of this chapter as they do not cover interstate institutions authorized to issue binding treaty interpretations when there is no dispute between states as to the content of their treaty commitments.

The very first interpretative commission – in the form of a treaty body – entrusted to issue binding treaty interpretations appeared not in a BIT, but in a FTA. In 1992, in the course of negotiations for the North American Free Trade Agreement (NAFTA) – one of the first multi-party FTAs – the Mexican delegation proposed introducing a provision allocating the function of interpreting the Annexes exclusively to a joint commission – the Free Trade Commission (referred to hereinafter as the

[2015] SGHC 15). On 29 September 2016 the Court of Appeals of Singapore disagreed with the decision of the High Court of Singapore and found that the PRC-Laos BIT did apply to Macau and that the tribunal had subject-matter jurisdiction over the claims brought by Sanum (*Sanum Investments Ltd* v. *Government of the Lao People's Democratic Republic* [2016] SGCA 57).

[48] Provisions empowering commissions to settle interstate disputes on interpretation are present in the following treaties: BLEU (Belgium-Luxembourg Economic Union)-Estonia BIT (1996), BLEU (Belgium-Luxembourg Economic Union)-Madagascar BIT (2005), BLEU (Belgium-Luxembourg Economic Union)-Republic of Moldova BIT (1996), BLEU (Belgium-Luxembourg Economic Union)-Montenegro BIT (2010), BLEU (Belgium-Luxembourg Economic Union)-Peru BIT (2005), BLEU (Belgium-Luxembourg Economic Union)-Bolivarian Republic of Venezuela BIT (1998), Czech Republic-Morocco BIT (2001), Greece-Morocco BIT (1994), Morocco-Poland BIT (1994). The arrangements were likely to have been inspired by interstate commissions that were routinely formed for interstate dispute resolution at the beginning of the last century, prior to the BIT epoch. The existence of the mixed interstate commissions as dispute resolution bodies served as evidence of arbitration's suitability for investment disputes and for the architects of investor-state dispute settlement. See Commentary to the Abs-Shawcross Draft Convention: H Abs and H Shawcross, 'The Proposed Convention to Protect Private Foreign Investment: A Round Table' (1960) 9 *J Pub L* 115, 123. Ivar Alvik described interstate commissions as 'an early 'precursor' to modern investment arbitration'. See Ivar Alvik, *Contracting with Sovereignty: State Contracts and International Arbitration* (Hart Publishing, 2011) p. 12. A valuable overview of the work of interstate commissions is available in an article on contractual claims in international law published more than a hundred years ago. See Edwin M Borchard, 'Contractual Claims in International Law' (1913) 13 (6) *Columbia Law Review* 457, 471–74.

FTC).[49] The proposal was accepted by the other contracting parties (the USA and Canada).[50] According to the provision, a request from a respondent in an investor-state arbitration triggers the FTC's exclusive interpretative function, following which it has sixty days to issue an interpretation. If the FTC fails to do so within this time period, the interpretative function reverts to the investment tribunal. Later in the negotiations, a provision was added to Article 1131 NAFTA concerning the governing law to reflect the binding nature of interpretations issued by the FTC and to extend the scope of interpretations beyond the Annexes to other NAFTA provisions. FTC unanimity was a necessary precondition for any interpretations issued.

Two years later, in 1994, the World Trade Organization introduced an institutional arrangement for issuing authoritative binding interpretations,[51] empowering the Ministerial Conference and, in its absence, the General Council, to issue binding treaty interpretations; interpretative commissions/committees are often compared with these WTO arrangements.[52]

Even though certain elements of non-institutionalized joint interpretations or institutional arrangements for resolving interstate disputes over interpretation can be found in international investment law, as mentioned, the origin of interpretative commissions/committees is not attributed to BITs. Because of their first appearance in FTAs (albeit with an investment chapter) and then in the WTO context, interpretative commissions/committees are largely perceived to be creatures of international trade law. Relatively recently, in the course of the – presently frozen – Transatlantic Trade and Investment Partnership (TTIP) negotiations, the European Commission explained that the provisions on

---

[49] Meg Kinnear, Andrea Bjorklund and John FG Hannaford, 'Article 1132 –Interpretation of Annexes' in Meg Kinnear et al., *Investment Disputes under NAFTA: An Annotated Guide to NAFTA Chapter 11* (Kluwer Law International, 2006) p. 1132-1.

[50] Ibid.

[51] Examples of institutional arrangements dealing with interpretation can be found both in other contexts and also in various other organizations that may delegate interpretative functions to extra-judicial structures in the form of a commission or a committee. The International Monetary Fund (IMF), for instance, entrusts an interpretative function to its Executive Board.

[52] See, for instance, Gabrielle Kaufmann-Kohler, 'Interpretative Powers of the NAFTA Free Trade Commission and the Rule of Law' in Emmanuel Gaillard and Frédéric Bachand (eds.), *Fifteen Years of NAFTA Chapter 11Arbitration* (Juris Publishing, 2011) pp. 175, 179; Jaemin Lee, 'Taming Investor– State Arbitration?' in Julien Chaisse and Tsai-Yu Lin (eds.), *International Economic Law and Governance: Essays in Honour of Mitsuo Matsushita* (Oxford University Press, 2016) p. 131.

committee interpretation had become 'standard'[53] in international trade law, giving the example of authoritative interpretations in Article IX:2 of the 1994 Marrakesh Agreement. The trend was confirmed by a recent survey of regional FTAs, which concluded that 60 per cent of regional FTAs provided for institutionalized interpretations by interpretative commissions/committees.[54]

This study is thus based on the understanding that commissions/committees (referred to here as interpretative commissions/committees to emphasize their interpretative function, among many others) consist of state government representatives and hold exclusive authority for issuing binding interpretations, thus limiting the interpretative space of investment tribunals. The epistemic implications that interpretative commissions/committees bring to international investment law are not affected by differences in their composition or the exercise of their interpretative functions. In fact, the underlying similarities – such as being made up of government representatives, decision-making based on consensus, and the lack of express regulations as to the methods of interpretation – reaffirm the political origin and nature of such commissions/committees.

3 The Spatial and Temporal Dimensions

The next step in this analysis is to determine how frequently interpretative commissions/committees have been included in IIAs in terms of the number of treaties, geographical scope and the intensity of their appearance over time.

According to UNCTAD's Investment Policy Hub, 125 of the 2,573 IIAs analysed[55] (4.9 per cent) are marked as expressly allowing for binding interpretations by the contracting parties or by interpretative commissions/committees. Only thirty-one treaties, or slightly over 1 per-cent,[56] contain institutional arrangements in the form of interpretative commissions/committees.

---

[53] Transatlantic Trade & Investment Partnership Advisory Group, 'Meeting Report' (23 June 2016), http://trade.ec.europa.eu/doclib/docs/2016/august/tradoc_154838.pdf, accessed 12 October 2017.
[54] Vasyl Chornyi et al., 'A Survey of Investment Provisions in Regional Trade Agreements' (2016) WTO Working Paper ERSD-2016-07, www.wto.org/english/res_e/reser_e/ersd201607_e.htm, accessed 12 October 2017.
[55] As of 12 October 2017, 2,573 IIAs have been analysed at the UNCTAD Investment Policy Hub; the overall number of IIAs as of that date is 3,257.
[56] Australia-China FTA (2015), Australia-Republic of Korea FTA (2014), Benin-Canada BIT (2013), BLEU (Belgium-Luxembourg Economic Union)-Estonia BIT (1996), BLEU

When compared to the total of 2,573 IIAs, 1 per cent of treaties with provisions on interpretative commissions/committees seems like a drop in the ocean. However, when factors such as geographical coverage, presence in Model BITs and the intensity of inclusion over time are considered, a clear trend for the spread of interpretative commissions/committees emerges, reinforced by academic and institutional scrutiny of the topic.[57]

There are ten Model BITs[58] and twenty-three IIAs in force, six IIAs signed and two IIAs at various stages of approval[59] that contain provisions on interpretative commissions/committees. While concluded

[57] (Belgium-Luxembourg Economic Union)-Republic of Moldova BIT (1996), BLEU (Belgium-Luxembourg Economic Union)-Montenegro BIT (2010), BLEU (Belgium-Luxembourg Economic Union)-Peru BIT (2005), BLEU (Belgium-Luxembourg Economic Union)-Bolivarian Republic of Venezuela BIT (1998), BLEU (Belgium-Luxembourg Economic Union)-Madagascar BIT (2005), Canada-EU CETA (2016), Canada-Honduras FTA (2013), Canada-Jordan BIT (2009), Canada-Republic of Korea FTA (2014), Canada-Peru BIT (2006), Chile-Hong Kong, China SAR BIT (2016), Colombia-Costa Rica FTA (2013), Colombia-Panama FTA (2013), Colombia-Peru BIT (2007), Czech Republic-Morocco BIT (2001), EU-Singapore FTA (2014), Greece-Morocco BIT (1994), India-Malaysia FTA (2011), Republic of Korea-New Zealand FTA (2015), Republic of Korea-Vietnam FTA (2015), Mexico-Panama FTA (2014), Morocco-Poland BIT (1994), New Zealand-Taiwan Province of China ECA (2013), Pacific Alliance Additional Protocol (2014), TPP (2016), TTIP, EU-Vietnam FTA. The number of treaties containing institutional arrangements for interpretation in the form of interpretative commissions/committees is slightly less than a quarter (only 22.4 per cent) of those 125 treaties that choose to expressly recognize the right of the states to joint interpretation.

[57] See, for instance, Lee (n. 62) 10; Chornyi et al. (n. 64) 46; UNCTAD (n. 26) 11; Szilárd Gáspár-Szilágyi, 'Binding Committee Interpretations in the EU's New FTIAs' (2017) 2 *European Investment Law and Arbitration Review* 90.

[58] Overall seventy-one Model BITs affirm joint interpretation, but only ten contain an institutional arrangement: Burundi Model BIT (2002), Belgium-Luxemburg Model BIT (2002), Israel Model BIT (2003), Uganda Model BIT (2003), Canada Model BIT (2004), Norway Model BIT (2007), Ghana Model BIT (2008), Burkina Faso Model BIT (2012), Norway Model BIT (2015), International Agreement on Investment (1998).

[59] According to the UNCTAD Investment Policy Hub, twenty-three IIAs in force are Australia-China FTA (2015), Australia-Republic of Korea FTA (2014), Benin-Canada BIT (2013), BLEU (Belgium-Luxembourg Economic Union)-Estonia BIT (1996), BLEU (Belgium-Luxembourg Economic Union)Madagascar BIT (2005), BLEU (Belgium-Luxembourg Economic Union) Republic of Moldova BIT (1996), BLEU (Belgium-Luxembourg Economic Union)-Peru BIT (2005), BLEU (Belgium-Luxembourg Economic Union)-Bolivarian Republic of Venezuela BIT (1998), Canada-Honduras FTA (2013), Canada-Jordan BIT (2009), Canada-Republic of Korea FTA (2014), Canada-Peru BIT (2006), Colombia-Costa Rica FTA (2013), Colombia-Peru BIT (2007), Greece-Morocco BIT (1994), India-Malaysia FTA (2011), Republic of Korea-Vietnam FTA (2015), Mexico-Panama FTA (2014), Morocco-Poland BIT (1994), New Zealand-Taiwan Province of China ECA (2013), Pacific Alliance Additional Protocol (2014); six signed IIAs are BLEU (Belgium-Luxembourg Economic Union)-Montenegro BIT (2010), Canada-EU CETA (2016), Chile-Hong, China SAR BIT (2016), Colombia-Panama FTA

treaties and those under negotiation give a firm number of treaties that include interpretative commissions/committees, the presence of Model BITs that provide for interpretative committees broadens the perspective, as they are traditionally seen as representing state investment policy and fuelling immediate changes. Figure 9.1 shows a geographical span covering sixty-two states.[60]

Regarding the temporal dimension, there was an increase in the inclusion of interpretative committees as of 2013,[61] which coincided with greater criticism of international investment arbitration and a call for states to take a more active role in treaty interpretation (Figure 9.2).

As can be seen above, the question of whether the spatial and temporal spread of interpretative commissions/committees is sufficient for any conclusions on convergence to be reached depends very much on which evaluative judgment and which factors are taken into account. Overall, the fact that such a small percentage of treaties include provisions on interpretative commissions/committees may raise doubts as to whether the spread merits attention in the context of convergence-divergence analysis. Nonetheless, it is clear that increased criticism of the investment treaty dispute settlement mechanism has influenced the inclusion of interpretative commissions/committees in treaties, as they are largely viewed as part of the proposed solution for reinforcing the legitimacy of investment treaty arbitration. The fact that there is a visible trend, albeit with a somewhat modest spread at present, may be used as evidence in favour of convergence.

Having said that, even if the spread of interpretative commissions/ committees was far less visible than it is now, a single treaty could still be

---

(2013), TPP (2016) and EU-Singapore FTA (2014); two draft IIAs are Draft of EU-Vietnam Free Trade Agreement and Draft of TTIP.

[60] Australia, Austria, Belgium, Benin, Brunei Darussalam, Bulgaria, Burkina Faso, Burundi, Canada, Chile, China, Colombia, Costa Rica, Croatia, Cyprus, Czech Republic, Denmark, Estonia, Finland, France, Germany, Ghana, Greece, Honduras, Hong Kong, Hungary, India, Ireland, Israel, Italy, Japan, Jordan, Latvia, Lithuania, Luxembourg, Madagascar, Malaysia, Malta, Mexico, Moldova, Montenegro, Morocco, Netherlands, New Zealand, Norway, Panama, Peru, Poland, Portugal, Republic of Korea, Romania, Singapore, Slovakia, Slovenia, Spain, Sweden, Taiwan, Uganda, United Kingdom, United States of America, Venezuela, Vietnam.

[61] In 2013, five treaties were concluded that provided for interpretative commissions/ committees: the Benin-Canada BIT (2013), the Canada-Honduras FTA (2013), the Colombia-Costa Rica FTA (2013), the Colombia-Panama FTA (2013), the New Zealand-Taiwan Province of China ECA (2013). The slight decline in inclusion in the last three years when compared with a rise in 2013 may be explained by a smaller number of treaties concluded recently.

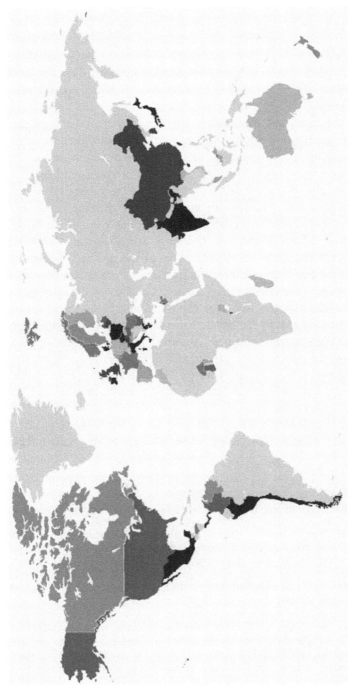

Figure 9.1 Countries with concluded treaties, treaties under negotiation and model treaties that contain a reference to interpretative commissions/committees

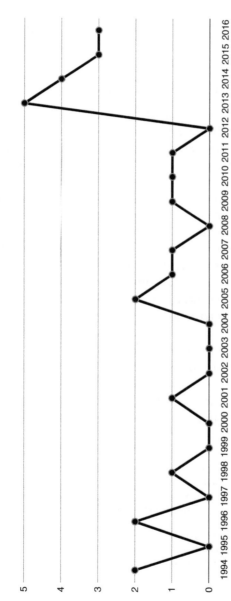

Figure 9.2 Inclusion of interpretative commissions/committees in IIAs over time

analysed from the perspective of international trade law's epistemic influence on international investment law, and thus be deemed a sign of convergence. This is to say that as long as there is a minimum amount of similarity, the spread or insignificant frequency of occurrence is not an impediment for analysing convergence as a matter of principle. This finding brings us back to the issue of imprecision, or the evaluative nature of a concept of convergence and the usefulness/relevance of other criteria, which is addressed below.

4 The Ideological Dimension

Any attempt to analyse the commissions/committees in the field of international investment law by means of an ideological dimension needs to be based on an understanding of the different ideological bases inherent in modern international investment and international trade law. Both these subfields developed from the regulation of the treatment of aliens in international law. Customary international law and the general principles of international law addressed this as a common area and did not divide it into trade and investment. Similarly, bilateral friendship, commerce and navigation treaties (FCNs), which influenced the early drafts of multilateral and bilateral treaties where the protection of private investment was concerned, brought both international trade and investment under one umbrella.[62] After the Second World War, international investment law and international trade law expanded, with a clearer ideological agenda. Efficiently protecting foreign investments by means that went beyond the diplomatic realm became the most important objective for the former, whereas the liberalization of trade via interstate dialogue was the latter's foremost concern.[63] Their agendas evolved into ideological axes for the emerging subfields, and framed their dispute resolution mechanisms and epistemic communities.

---

[62] The United States treaties of friendship, commerce and navigation, concluded with seventeen countries, including Colombia, Ethiopia, Germany, Iran, Italy, Japan, the Netherlands and Uruguay, were expressly mentioned as influencing the structure of the first draft of the multi-party convention on the protection of foreign investment. See H Abs and H Shawcross (n. 58) 115, 119–21.

[63] A thorough account of the common roots and diverging evolution of international investment law and international trade law is provided by DiMascio and Pawelyn in Nicholas DiMascio and Joost Pawelyn, 'Nondiscrimination in Trade and Investment Treaties: Worlds Apart or Two Sides of the Same Coin? (2008) 102 (1) *The American Journal of International Law* 48, 51–53.

The driving forces for the architects of international investment law were disengagement from politics and possible interstate confrontation.[64] They believed that depoliticization could be achieved thanks to efficient dispute resolution mechanisms that enabled private investors to arbitrate directly with states (ISDS). In 1961, Lord Shawcross, one of the authors of the first drafts of the multi-party convention on the protection of foreign investment (the Abs-Shawcross Draft Convention) emphasized that that the system's value lay 'in tending to keep this kind of disputes out of the arena of international politics and prestige'.[65] More than half a century later, in addressing the future of investment arbitration, Christoph Schreuer pointed to depoliticization as a continuously valued feature of international investment law, not only for investors but also for states, as 'by consenting to investment arbitration the host state usually protects itself against other forms of foreign or international litigation and political pressure'.[66] Efforts to depoliticize international investment law resulted in the emergence of asymmetric ISDS, anchored in the principles of international arbitration. This system grew thanks to the establishment of thousands of BITs[67] and trade agreements with investment chapters (see Chapter 2), most of which recognized ISDS,[68] and

---

[64] International investment law has emerged as an initiative driven by states through numerous BITs. Concurrently, some causes/triggers were provided by advocates of the specialized treaties on investment protection, who participated in the first drafts of the multi-party conventions – the Abs-Shawcross Draft Convention 1959 and the OECD Draft Convention on Protection of Foreign Property 1968. For more on the history of the two drafts, see Yuliya Chernykh, 'The Gust of Wind: The Unknown Role of Sir Elihu Lauterpacht in the Drafting of the Abs-Shawcross Draft Convention' in Rainer Hofmann, Stephan W Schill and Christian J Tams (eds.), *International Investment Law and History* (Edward Elgar Publishing, 2017).

[65] Hartley Shawcross, 'The Problems of Foreign Investment in International Law' (1961) 102 *Collected Courses of The Hague Academy of International Law* 339, 362. The article was subsequently relied upon as authoritative in the commentary on the OECD Draft Convention on the Protection of Foreign Property 1968 – Annex A Current Development. OECD Draft Convention of the Protection of Foreign Property Adopted by the OECD Council on 12 October 1967. Text with Notes and Comments (1967–1968) 2 *Int'l L*, 331, 336.

[66] Christoph Schreuer, 'The Future of Investment Arbitration' in Mahnoush H Arsanjani et al. (eds.), *Looking to the Future: Essays on International Law in Honor of W. Michael Reisman* (Martinus Nijhoff Publishers, 2010) p. 803.

[67] According to the UNCTAD Investment Policy Hub, 3,257 IIAs have been concluded as of 12 October 2017 (http://investmentpolicyhub.unctad.org/IIA, accessed 12 October 2017).

[68] According to the UNCTAD Investment Policy Hub, 2,442 IIAs out of 2,573 mapped IIAs contain ISDS (http://investmentpolicyhub.unctad.org/IIA/mappedContent#iiaInnerMenu, accessed 12 October 2017).

hundreds of awards[69] were issued in disputes initiated by foreign investors against states. It substantially diminished diplomatic protection, as well as reducing states' exposure to interstate confrontation.

In turn, the expansion of international trade law fostered interstate dialogue and consensus on questions of trade liberalization. Political consultation was and still is at the very heart of the system,[70] which developed from the General Agreement on Tariffs and Trade (GATT) in 1947 and culminated in the creation of the World Trade Organization (WTO) in 1995. Unsurprisingly, dispute resolution mechanisms took on symmetrical forms – the Dispute Settlement Body (DSB) and the Appellate Body (AB) were empowered to settle interstate disputes, and over 500 disputes have been submitted for resolution to the WTO system since 1995.[71] In addition to the multilateral WTO system, regional trade treaties also flourished, reflecting the relative ease of reaching agreements at bilateral and limited multilateral levels within a smaller geographical area[72] in comparison with the WTO's 164 members.[73]

These features, which stemmed from different ideological axes, informed interpretation in both subfields.[74] In international investment, when private investors and states fail to agree on treaty interpretation, each party puts forward its own point of view and the issue is settled by

[69] According to the UNCTAD Investment Policy Hub, 528 investment treaty cases were concluded with either the issuance of awards or the discontinuance of proceedings without awards (http://investmentpolicyhub.unctad.org/ISDS, accessed 12 October 2017).

[70] Claus-Dieter Ehlermann and Lothar Ehring provide a comprehensive examination of the role of consensus and the practice of voting in decision-making in the WTO in 'Decision-Making in the World Trade Organization: Is the Consensus Practice of the World Trade Organization Adequate for Making, Revising and Implementing Rules on International Trade?' (2005) 8 (1) *Journal of International Economic Law*, 51–75.

[71] As of 13 October 2017, 532 disputes have been submitted for resolution within the WTO system (www.wto.org/english/tratop_e/dispu_e/dispu_status_e.htm, accessed 13 October 2017).

[72] An increasing number of regional trade agreements can be seen on the map on the WTO website, www.wto.org/english/tratop_e/region_e/region_e.htm#facts, accessed 13 October 2017.

[73] According to the WTO's official website as of 29 July 2017, www.wto.org/english/thewto_e/whatis_e/tif_e/org6_e.htm, accessed 12 October 2017.

[74] On fragmentation in interpretation, see Michael Waibel, 'Uniformity versus Specialization (2): A Uniform Regime of Treaty Interpretation?' in Christian J Tams, Antonios Tzanakopoulos and Andreas Zimmermann (eds.), *Research Handbook on the Law of Treaties* (Edgar Elgar, 2014) pp.75–412. On views emphasizing unity of interpretative method, see Eirik Bjorge, 'Convergence of Methods of Treaty Interpretation' in Mads Andenas and Eirik Bjorge (eds.), *A Farewell to Fragmentation* (Cambridge University Press, 2015) 498–535.

a tribunal, and the treaty interpretation provisions in the Vienna Convention encourage these argumentative practices.[75] As a rule, there is no institutional arrangement that could intervene in the arbitrators' de facto monopoly over interpretation.[76] In turn, interpretation in international trade law has become more institutionalized. The WTO divides interpretative space between the adjudicatory (the DSB and the Appellate Body) and legislative bodies (the Ministerial Conference and the General Council), with the DSB and the AB exercising judicial interpretation that is limited to specific cases and the Ministerial Conference and the General Council having the power to issue authoritative interpretations that are binding for all WTO members. Complex coordination between participating entities comes into play in authoritative interpretation,[77] and the WTO provides for extra-safeguards in addition to the interpretative tools provided by the VCLT. Adjudicatory bodies that interpret treaties are only authorized to issue interpretations that do not reduce the parties' rights and obligations (Article 3.2 DSU), whereas the Ministerial Conference and the General Council may not undermine amendment provisions while interpreting treaty provisions (Article IX:2 WTO Agreement).

---

[75] Christian Djeffal, *Static and Evolutive Treaty Interpretation. A Functional Reconstruction* (Cambridge University Press, 2016) pp. 97–106. On a larger trend in the emergence of explicit sources of international law as a reaction to the devastation after the Second World War, see Charles T Kotuby, Jr. and Luke A Sobota, *General Principles of Law and International Due Process: Principles and Norms Applicable in Transnational Disputes* (Oxford University Press, 2017) p. 4.

[76] States still have *de jure* power of interpretation under the VCLT that can be exercised through joint statements or subsequent practice, etc. As illustrated above (n. 57) this non-institutionalized power is rarely exercised. Some authors suggest that depending on treaty wording, interpretative commissions/committees might serve in the exclusion of recourse to informal agreements on interpretation between states. See Anthea Roberts, 'Power and Persuasion in Investment Treaty Interpretation: The Dual Role of States' (2010) 104 (2) *Am. J. Int'l L.* 179, 216.

[77] For instance, to issue an authoritative interpretation of the General Agreement on Tariff and Trade (GATT) and the General Agreement on Trade in Services (GATS) or Agreement on Trade-Related Aspects of Intellectual Property (TRIPS), the Ministerial Conference and the General Council have to exercise authority on the basis of recommendations from the respective councils. See General Council, Rules of Procedure for Meetings of the Council for Trade in Goods, WT/L/79, 7 August 1995. In practice, the influence of AB interpretations goes beyond the limits of a particular case, and one of the reasons behind this is the complexity of political dialogue in multilateral systems and their practical inability to issue authoritative interpretations which are addressed in a functional dimension. The presence of a political component as a matter of principle is emphasized here.

In other words, interpretation in international investment law reflects its non-centralized, ad hoc nature, and its interpretative mandate is limited by the contours of a particular case.[78] Interpretation in international trade law has become an institutionalized system with powers divided among various structures, including a system for appeal, and with additional express restrictions on interpretation. As a result of these distinctions, interpretation in investment arbitration has been fiercely criticized over coherency issues[79] (no system was designed to ensure coherence and centralization from the beginning), whereas, despite some criticism of passivity on the part of political organs, or their incapability to issue authoritative interpretations,[80] interpretation within the WTO system has had a relatively positive reception.[81]

If analysed from an ideological perspective, the inclusion of interpretative commissions/committees in the international investment law context therefore represents an attempt to limit the arbitrators' interpretative monopoly by increasing the role of states. Arbitrators are faced with the need to comply with binding interpretations issued by state representatives participating in interpretative commissions/committees. Furthermore, many treaties expressly redistribute interpretative space between arbitral tribunals and interpretative commissions/committees, giving interpretative commissions/committees exclusive interpretative powers with respect to certain parts of treaties (chiefly, exceptions and restrictions that have been introduced). The option of a tribunal to interpret these provisions only arises if the interpretative commissions/committees fail to issue an interpretation

---

[78] The situation describes a typical case when no institutional arrangement for interpretation has been inserted.

[79] See, for instance, Tomoko Ishikawa's analysis addressing trends in expansive subject-matter jurisdiction in international investment arbitration and calling for a more active state role in interpretation that would respond to developments and ensure coherency. Tomoko Ishikawa, 'Keeping Interpretation in Investment Treaty Arbitration "on Track": The Role of State Parties' in Jean E Kalicki and Anna Joubin-Bret (eds.), *Reshaping the Investor-State Dispute Settlement System: Journeys for the 21st Century* (Brill/Nijhoff, 2015) 115–49.

[80] Isabelle Van Damme, *Treaty Interpretation by the WTO Appellate Body* (Oxford University Press, 2009) 26–30.

[81] See, for instance, Isabelle Van Damme, 'Treaty Interpretation by the WTO Appellate Body' (2010) 21(3) *European Journal of International Law* 605, 648. More generally, on the success of the WTO dispute settlement system see, for instance, W Davey, 'The WTO Dispute Settlement System: Dealing with Success' in Julien Chaisse and Tsai-Yu Lin (eds.), *International Economic Law and Governance: Essays in Honour of Mitsuo Matsushita* (Oxford University Press, 2016) pp. 11–25.

within sixty or ninety days, depending on the treaty. When viewed through the lens of delegated interpretative authority, the result represents the limitation of the tribunals' implicit and partial interpretative functions by the express and exclusive interpretative authority of the interpretative commissions/committees.

To understand the ideological implications, the fact that any natural extension of the powers of an interstate commission or committee is a form of politicization needs to be borne in mind. States delegate government representatives to participate in the work of commissions/committees, and their work is fully dependent on agreement, or in most cases, consensus between members. Unlike arbitrators, interpretative commissions/committees are not obliged to give reasons for their decisions,[82] but generally set the rules for their work themselves.[83]

A convergence from international trade law towards international investment law can thus be identified in the expansion of the epistemic community[84] of interstate commissions/committees consisting of political representatives. This community's role is maximized so that it can advocate a somewhat distinct normative view of international investment law and align both subfields. This represents a clear ideological shift: a political element has been introduced into the non-politicized dispute resolution mechanism.

It is interesting to note that the composition of investment treaty tribunals has been increasingly criticized by both practitioners and academics,[85] mainly because of the combined roles of the major players – arbitrators who are also acting in parallel as counsels in investment treaty

---

[82] No reference to VCLT and few or no reasons were generally given in the first and only interpretation exercised by the FTC in NAFTA on 31 July 2001.

[83] The following treaties specify that commissions/committees are entitled to decide on the internal rules of their work: Australia-Republic of Korea FTA (2014), Canada-EU CETA (2016), Canada-Honduras FTA (2013), Canada-Jordan BIT (2009), Canada-Republic of Korea FTA (2014), Canada-Peru BIT (2006), Colombia-Costa Rica FTA (2013), Colombia-Panama FTA (2013), Colombia-Peru BIT (2007), India-Malaysia FTA (2011), Republic of Korea-New Zealand FTA (2015), Republic of Korea-Vietnam FTA (2015), Mexico-Panama FTA (2014), Pacific Alliance Additional Protocol (2014), TPP (2016).

[84] The mere concept of epistemic communities originates from politics and international relations, which have penetrated analyses of interpretation in international law. On the role of epistemic communities in international law, see Michael Waibel, 'Interpretative Communities in International Law' in Andrea Bianchi, Daniel Peat and Matthew Windsor (eds.), *Interpretation in International Law* (Oxford University Press, 2015) pp. 147–65.

[85] Malcolm Langford et al., 'The Revolving Door in International Investment Arbitration' (2017) 20 (2) *Journal of International Economic Law* 301–32; Malcolm Langford et al.,

cases. On the other hand, critics have failed to address the system's political dimensions; ISDS has been praised for reducing political confrontation between states.[86] With the introduction of interpretative commissions/committees, critics have turned to the politicization of international investment disputes, characterizing it as the 'taming'[87] of international investment arbitration by means of an extra-arbitral body composed of governmental officials from the contracting state.[88] This 'taming' is yet another metaphor for the convergence observed between the two fields, and which emphasizes the deep ideological implications.

5 The Functional Dimension

Functionalism is by no means a novel way of analysing legal developments and is afforded a central methodological place in comparative law.[89] The method emphasizes utility, the importance of looking not at rules or dogmas but at their effect on factual examples of specific cases or events. This is a particularly valuable approach for investigating convergence between the two fields, not merely at the level of the rules and institutions that have been introduced, but also in practice. As the rare attempts made to theorize on the basis of the concepts of convergence and divergence expressly acknowledge the importance of functionalism's role,[90] this section examines interpretative practices within the two fields in light of interpretative institutional set-ups, and more particularly, by

---

'ESIL Reflection: The Ethics and Empirics of Double Hatting' (2017) 6 (7) Turn to Empiricism Series, https://esil-sedi.eu/post_name-118/, accessed 12 October 2017.

[86] See Christoph Schreuer (n. 76) and August Reinisch, 'The Future of Investment Arbitration' in Christina Binder et al. (eds.), *International Investment Law for the 21st Century: Essays in Honour of Christoph Schreuer* (Oxford University Press, 2009) pp. 894, 900.

[87] Lee (n. 62) 131–52.

[88] A similar criticism of politicization can be seen in recent discussions about the attempts to create an investment court. See, for instance, Eduardo Zuleta, 'The Challenges of Creating a Standing International Investment Court' in Jean E Kalicki and Anna Joubin-Bret (eds.), *Reshaping the Investor-State Dispute Settlement System: Journeys for the 21st Century* (Brill/Nijhoff, 2015) pp. 403–23.

[89] For comprehensive observations on functional method(s) in comparative law, including criticism, see Ralf Michaels, 'The Functional Method of Comparative Law' in Mathias Reimann and Reinhard Zimmermann (eds.), *The Oxford Handbook of Comparative Law* (Oxford University Press, 2009) pp. 340–80.

[90] See, for instance, Filomena Chirico and Pierre Larouche, who emphasize the value of functionalism in their analysis of convergence that 'involves looking beyond "the rules and principles" layer of legal concepts and reasoning to also incorporate "the lower layer" of practical outcomes', in 'Convergence and Divergence, in Law and Economics and

looking at how interpretative commissions/committees function in the international investment law context. Rather than being a classical functional *method*, this study instead represents a functional *inquiry* that facilitates a dynamic assessment of interpretative commissions/committees as evidence of convergence and divergence between the two fields.

If, ideologically, interpretative commissions/committees serve as a converging bridge between international investment law and international trade law, a functional dimension produces contradictory observations. Signs of both convergence and divergence can be identified in the way in which treaty interpretation in international investment law and international trade law is practised when there are institutional arrangements for authoritative interpretation. Two aspects require emphasis here. Firstly, it is important to ascertain whether institutional arrangements – pertaining to authoritative interpretations in the WTO and in FTAs – affect interpretative routines: in other words, whether the availability of an institutional arrangement for a binding interpretation is significant as a matter of practice. Secondly, in cases in which an authoritative interpretation has been issued, it is also important to assess whether it has been accepted 'smoothly', i.e. without clashing with principles inherent to the field of international investment law.

Where the first focal point is concerned, it should be noted that the mere availability of institutional arrangements for authoritative interpretation has not developed into a working system of checks and balances. As mentioned in the footnote,[91] the sheer number of WTO members would make the adoption of such interpretations almost impossible, especially when consensus is needed. Therefore, interpretation in international trade law mainly appears and evolves through adjudicative bodies. The Ministerial Conference and the General Council, the bodies responsible for authentic authoritative interpretations within the WTO, have not entirely succeeded in discharging their

Comparative Law' in Pierre Larouche and Péter Cserne (eds.), *National Legal Systems and Globalization* (Asser Press, 2013) p. 19.

[91] A political incapacity to implement sufficient voting regarding interpretation as the major reason for a lack of authoritative interpretations has been addressed, for instance, in Claus-Dieter Ehlermann and Lothar Ehring, 'The Authoritative Interpretation Under Article IX:2 of the Agreement Establishing the World Trade Organization: Current Law, Practice and Possible Improvements' (2005) 8 (4) *Journal of International Economic Law* 803–24. On reasons for dominance of the judicial as opposed to authentic interpretation, see Van Damme (n. 90) 610–16.

interpretative mandate.[92] Instead, the Appellate Body, as part of the WTO dispute resolution mechanism, has gained prominence in issuing interpretations with 'de facto finality'.[93] Interpretative commissions/committees in regional FTAs are also largely inactive.[94] This development is not foreign to international investment arbitration. Even though arbitrators' interpretations are limited by the circumstances of individual cases, they might possess a high persuasive value comparable to a certain degree with interpretations adopted by the Appellate Body, and require reflection and assessment in subsequent cases as a matter of practice.[95] Thus, adjudicative interpretation as a dominant interpretative mode brings the two fields closer together, and this complicates attempts to pin down evidence of convergence in fields that share this similarity.[96]

The current dominance of adjudicative interpretation raises certain questions regarding future developments, more specifically as to whether authoritative interpretation will remain unexercised as a matter of practice in international trade law, and whether this practice will be inherited by the interpretative commissions/committees recently introduced into FTAs. It could be argued that given the dynamics and complexities associated with decision-making in the past, it is unlikely that bodies geared towards authoritative interpretation, whether the WTO system or the FTAs, will become active.[97]

---

[92] So far the two requests for authoritative interpretation have not succeeded. General Council, 'Request for an Authoritative Interpretation Pursuant to Article IX:2 of the Marrakesh Agreement Establishing the World Trade Organization, Communication from the European Communities' (WT/GC/W/133 1999); General Council, 'Request for an Authoritative Interpretation Pursuant to Article IX:2 of the Marrakesh Agreement Establishing the World Trade Organization, Communication from the European Communities' (WT/GC/W/143 1999). Examples that could potentially lead to authoritative interpretation are analysed in Claus-Dieter Ehlermann and Lothar Ehring (n. 101).

[93] Robert Howse, 'The Most Dangerous Branch? WTO Appellate Body Jurisprudence on the Nature and Limits of the Judicial Power' in Thomas Cottier and P. Mavrodis (eds.), The Role of the Judge in International Trade Regulation – Experience and Lessons for the WTO, Vol.4 (University of Michigan Press, 2003) pp. 11, 15.

[94] The FTC Interpretative Note of 31 July 2001 is addressed below.

[95] There are numerous publications on the subject. By way of illustration, see Tomoko Ishikawa (n. 89).

[96] Deeper distinctions can be found between the fields, including a greater coherence and persuasiveness of adopted interpretations in the WTO system than in the field of international investment law, which are not considered in this paper, as the focus lies with the introduction of institutional set-ups empowered to deliver authoritative interpretations in the field of international investment law.

[97] However, some authors admit that 'for the reasons that are difficult to predict', authoritative interpretation within the WTO can become active (Claus-Dieter Ehlermann and Lothar Ehring (n. 101) 824).

However, it is necessary to differentiate between the WTO, whose complex decision-making system requires consensus for issued interpretations in practice, and FTAs with a limited number of contracting parties (bilateral, regional) for which reaching agreement might be easier. In the absence of reform, there seems to be nothing to affect the WTO system's present status.[98] At the same time, in the context of the limited number of parties involved, reaching consensus on interpretation might be less problematic in bilateral and regional trade agreements. Furthermore, given the appearance of new treaty provisions, which are more sophisticated and complex, and frequently with numerous exceptions,[99] it would not be unreasonable to expect interpretative commissions/committees to become more active in the future. The expectation that interpretative commissions/committees will be kept reasonably busy, if it becomes a reality, will impact on convergence between international trade and international investment law as a matter of practice.

The second focal point is situations in which authoritative interpretations, if and when they are issued, clash with the fundamentals of international investment law, and more particularly with investment treaty arbitration. In other words, the focus is on the possibility of convergence meeting resistance at a functional level. Since interpretative commissions/committees appeared twenty-four years ago, only one example has provoked discussion within the respective pending proceedings and within the academic community:[100] the NAFTA FTC interpretation (the Interpretative Note) issued on 31 July 2001. The Interpretative Note

[98] Cosette Creamer and Zuzanna Godzimirska suggest an increased input from WTO members (in the form of statements during WTO Dispute Settlement Body meetings) prior to adopting dispute settlement rulings as a functional substitute for authoritative interpretation. See Cosette Creamer and Zuzanna Godzimirska, 'Deliberative Engagement within the World Trade Organization: A Functional Substitute for Authoritative Interpretation' (2016) 48 (2) *New York University Journal of International Law & Politics* 413–62.

[99] Asif Qureshi argued in favour of having a theory of exceptions and a theory of interpretation of exceptions. See Asif Qureshi, 'Interpreting Exceptions in the WTO Agreements' in Asif Qureshi, *Interpreting WTO Agreements: Problems and Perspectives* (Cambridge University Press, 2015) pp. 132–79.

[100] As an illustration of some of the critical notes, see Charles Brower, 'Why the FTC Notes of Interpretation Constitute a Partial Amendment of NAFTA Article 1105'(2006) 46 *Va. J. Int'l L.* 347–53; Jack Coe, 'The State of Investor-State Arbitration-Some Reflections on Professor Brower's Plea for Sensible Principles' (2005) 20 (5) *American University International Law Review*, 929–56; Charles Brower and Lee Steven, 'Who Then Should Judge? Developing the International Rule of Law under NAFTA Chapter 11 (2001) 2 (1) *Chicago Journal of International Law*, http://chicagounbound.uchicago.edu/cjil/vol2/iss1/12, accessed 12 October 2017; Todd Weiler, 'NAFTA Chapter 11 Jurisprudence:

referred to confidentiality and public access to documents in NAFTA Chapter 11 arbitrations and a minimum treatment standard under Article 1105 NAFTA. The latter was deemed to be controversial in several pending arbitrations at the time.[101] The interpretation issued by the FTC connected fair and equal treatment and full protection and security to the minimum standard of protection as defined by customary international law. The relevant part of the interpretation of the minimum standard was quite brief:

1. Article 1105(1) prescribes the customary international law minimum standard of aliens as the minimum standard of treatment to be afforded to investments of investors of another party.
2. The concepts of 'fair and equitable treatment' and 'full protection and security' do not require treatment in addition to or beyond that which is required by the customary international law minimum standard of treatment of aliens.
3. A determination that there has been a breach of another provision of the NAFTA, or of a separate international agreement, does not establish that there has been a breach of Article 1105(1).

Canada was a respondent in a number of pending proceedings at the time and pleaded that this interpretation meant that the most restrictive interpretation of fair and equal treatment should be favoured, as recognized by customary international law.

The arbitral tribunals dealing with disputes under Chapter 11 understood the Interpretative Note somewhat differently. Though they all abided by the interpretation's binding nature (as did subsequent tribunals), their analysis showed a certain difficulty in accepting the Interpretative Note as a genuine interpretation, informed by the state's dual role as both respondent and interpreter. The main difficulty was

---

Coming Along Nicely' (2003) 9 *Southwestern Journal of Law and Trade in the Americas* 254; Gabrielle Kaufmann-Kohler (n. 62).

[101] *Pope & Talbot Inc. v. Government of Canada*, UNCITRAL (1976), Award in Respect of Damages, 31 May 2002, para. 47; *Mondev International Ltd. v. United States of America*, ICSID Case No. ARB (AF)/99/2, Award, 11 October 2002, para. 122; *ADF Group Inc. v. United States of America*, ICSID Case No. ARB (AF)/00/1, Award, 9 January 2003, para. 177; *Waste Management, Inc. v. United Mexican States*, ICSID Case No. ARB(AF)/98/2, Award, 30 April 2004, paras. 89–99; *Methanex Corporation v. United States of America*, UNCITRAL (1976), Final Award of the Tribunal on Jurisdiction and Merits, 9 August 2005, para. 20; *United Parcel Service of America Inc. v. Government of Canada*, ICSID Case No. UNCT/02/1, Award on Jurisdiction, 22 November 2002, para. 97. For a summary of cases, see also Kinnear, Bjorklund and Hannaford (n. 59).

whether an interpretation constituted an amendment, and whether the interpretation was self-serving/self-judging.

Another important question relates to the allocation of interpretative authority between the tribunal and the state; more precisely, the tribunal's inherent authority to interpret the treaty provisions. In *Pope & Talbot* the tribunal made it clear that it was not simply empowered to consider the question, but also had a duty to do so, and not merely to accept the FTC's interpretation. Although the tribunal indicated that if required to decide whether the NAFTA Interpretative Note was an amendment, it would find that it was,[102] it failed to draw any workable conclusion from this, stressing instead that the partial award[103] would still comply with the NAFTA Interpretative Note. The tribunal ultimately preferred to proceed on the assumption that the Note was a genuine interpretation and to explore the evolutionary character of customary international law.

In *Merrill & Ring*, the tribunal somewhat hesitantly decided that the interpretation looked 'in some respect to be closer to an amendment of the treaty, than a strict interpretation',[104] a rather vague conclusion that did not lead to a firm decision in respect to the Note. The tribunal continued to act on the premise that it was dealing with a binding interpretation. In a similar way to *Pope & Talbot* and several other tribunals,[105] this opened the door for the tribunal's subsequent interpretations rather than closing it. The tribunal accepted that fair and equal treatment equated to the minimum standard under customary international law, and at the same time emphasized that given its evolutionary nature, the content of customary international law had to be determined by the tribunal.

In response to the complexities surrounding the NAFTA Interpretative Note, Gabrielle Kaufmann-Kohler suggested that new interpretations had to be analysed through the prism of promulgation and clarity, prospectively and non-retroactively, in the light of congruence and fundamental rights (what may be called 'the Kaufmann-Kohler test').[106] The first element, promulgation and clarity, aims to avoid interpreting interpretations. The second element, prospectivity and non-retrospectivity, aims to avoid disguised treaty amendments. The third

---

[102] *Pope & Talbot Inc.* (n. 111).
[103] The tribunal issued the partial award before the NAFTA Interpretative Note appeared.
[104] *Merrill & Ring Forestry L.P.* (n. 112).
[105] *ADF Group Inc.* (n. 111).
[106] Kaufmann-Kohler (n. 62) 175–94.

element, congruence and fundamental rights, is devised to ensure that interpretation does not breach fundamental procedural rights, a situation that may arise when an interpretation issued in the course of a pending arbitration influences the arbitration's outcome in favour of a respondent who in fact contributed to the interpretation's content as a member of the interpretative commission/committee. While the first element seems to be inherent to the concept of interpretation, given that the purpose of interpretation is to clarify and not to complicate, the second and third elements are somewhat more controversial, as seen from the jurisprudence surrounding the NAFTA FTC Interpretative Note, academic discourse and treaty practice.

The major obstacle for the smooth integration of authoritative interpretations within the framework of international investment arbitration appears to be the states' dual role as both respondents and treaty interpreters in pending disputes. Several propositions have emerged in response to this, some of which have been reflected in recently concluded IIAs. These responses attempted to limit, but not completely exclude, occasions when an interpretation can be issued in the course of pending proceedings so as to limit undue intervention in the pending arbitration. If Mads Andenas and Eirik Bjorge's perspective on convergence is taken as a *response* to divergence,[107] the propositions aiming to ensure convergence – to the extent they are implemented in new IIAs – are themselves signs of convergence.

The 2015 Norwegian Model BIT[108] ('the Norwegian model') may be an example of an attempt to integrate interpretative commissions/committees' interpretations into the international investment law context (though no treaty has yet been concluded on this basis). The Norwegian model limits the treaty committee's interpretative function in relation to pending disputes, as follows: 'The Joint Committee should refrain from adopting an interpretation of provisions already submitted to a Tribunal in a dispute between a Party and Investor of the other Party.' Academic writing has described the lack of similar restrictions on

[107] In clarifying what convergence is, Andenas and Bjorge state: 'Much of what we see as convergence may also be seen as ways of dealing with fragmentation, and does not have to be based on, for instance, general principles or hierarchies of norms and institutions.' Andenas and Bjorge (n. 27) 4.

[108] The 2015 Norwegian Model BIT is available at www.regjeringen.no/contentassets/ e47326b61f424d4c9c3d470896492623/draft-model-agreement-english.pdf, accessed 12 October 2017. The previous draft of the 2007 Norwegian Model BIT contained similar limitations. See http://investmentpolicyhub.unctad.org/Download/TreatyFile/2873, accessed 12 October 2017.

intervening in pending disputes as a 'serious drawback'.[109] Although they contain no express limitations on the power to issue interpretations in relation to pending provisions, a number of FTAs allow the relevant interpretative commissions/committees to determine the date after which an interpretation is binding.[110] This option may be exercised to avoid a retrospective effect;[111] to limit undue interventions, some treaties further subject opportunities for the exercising of interpretative power to 'serious concern'.[112]

Thus, on a functional or operational level, there is little to distinguish one field from another. If interpretative commissions/committees are idle, these similarities will not make it easy to identify convergence, and if any conclusions are to be reached on the issue, the objects compared have to be different/distinguishable. If interpretative commissions/committees are to function,[113] they may experience some difficulties regarding the smooth acceptance of interpretations in the context of pending investment treaty cases, due to the state's dual role as both respondent and interpreter. Certain provisions may assist in achieving more coherent and harmonious acceptance, and thus a smoother convergence of interpretative commissions/committees.

6 Conclusion

This chapter has attempted to assess the potential convergence between international investment law and international trade law through the

---

[109] Christoph Schreuer, 'Diversity and Harmonization of Treaty Interpretation in Investment Arbitration' (2006) 2 *TDM*, www.transnational-dispute-management.com /article.asp?key=755, accessed 12 October 2017.
[110] Canada-EU CETA, EU-Singapore FTA, EU-Vietnam FTA, TTIP.
[111] For a detailed account of critical observations pertaining to the self-judging and retrospective character of binding interpretations in the context of new EU IIAs, see Gáspár-Szilágyi (n. 67).
[112] For instance, Canada-EU CETA, EU-Singapore FTA, EU-Vietnam FTA and TTIP.
[113] On a separate note, and to continue an observation on the fertilization between the two fields which goes beyond structural interpretative arrangements, the increasing references to interpretations adopted by the Appellate Body in investment treaty arbitration awards cannot be ignored. However, adjudicative bodies within the WTO rarely refer to interpretations adopted by investment tribunals, unlike international investment arbitration cases that refer sometimes to interpretation within the WTO. Furthermore, a growing number of treaties both specify rules for interpretation and expressly refer to the need to observe interpretations issued within the WTO system (for instance, Australia-China FTA 2015, Canada-EU CETA 2016, New Zealand-Taiwan Province of China ECA 2013, EU-Japan Economic Partnership Agreement, EU-Indonesia FTA, EU-Singapore FTA, EU-Vietnam FTA and TTIP).

bodies introduced to issue authoritative interpretations – interpretative commissions/committees. The analysis is premised on the understanding that the analytical paradigm embracing convergence-divergence trends is largely based on comparison. The major challenge and appeal of this analytical exercise consists of finding similarities and distinctions between compared objects/fields and attributing a certain significance to them. While no claims are made for their universality, the four dimensions discussed are useful in structuring an argument on convergence. The spatial dimension informs an understanding of the geography of countries for which provisions on interpretive commissions/committees are routinely included in treaties, while the temporal dimension clarifies the intensity of the appearance of interpretative commissions/committees. However, the most important are the ideological and functional dimensions shaping investigations into the intended and factual implications of interpretative commissions/committees in the field of international investment law.

In terms of geographical inclusion, interpretative commissions/committees appear in approximately 1 per cent of the investment treaties analysed. States have agreed on interpretative commissions/committees relatively more frequently in the last four years than previously (2013–2017). This is clearly not an overarching trend, but is noticeable, nonetheless.[114] The ideological dimension demonstrates a deeper convergence than can be seen from the space and time perspectives, namely the introduction of a new epistemic community into the field of international investment law. The interpretative function's reallocation between international investment tribunals and interpretative commissions/committees has in fact brought about increased politicization of a field that was originally developed specifically to diminish states' political influence, if not to prevent it altogether. The functional dimension shows lasting similarities and differences between the two fields. Both international investment law and international trade law are mainly dependent on adjudicative (judiciary) interpretation, and they are not dramatically distinct from one another when viewed from this functional perspective. However, deeper analysis shows complexity in reconciling states' dual role as both respondents and interpreters in pending proceedings, and this is where convergence meets resistance.

---

[114] Further development can be enhanced because the UNCITRAL Working Group III: Investor-State Dispute Settlement Reform plans to deal with treaty interpretation by the state parties at its next session in 2020. A/CN.9/WG.III/XXXVIII/CRP.1/Add.1, para. 13.

As well as presenting findings on the ideological convergence between international trade and international investment law, as a result of the introduction of interpretative commissions/committees, this chapter aims to open a perspective on convergence's flaws as a concept. Its imprecision reflects and emphasizes the concept's function in identifying rather than measuring changes and responses within the legal system.

10

Regime Responsiveness in International Economic Disputes

MALCOLM LANGFORD, COSETTE D CREAMER
AND DANIEL BEHN

1 Introduction

State backlash has marked strongly dispute settlement mechanisms in both the international trade and investment treaty regimes. For the former, the transition from the General Agreement on Tariffs and Trade (GATT) dispute panels to the World Trade Organization's (WTO) Dispute Settlement Mechanism (DSM) represented a notable instance of the turn towards international courts within world politics.[1] Yet, the decisions of the WTO Appellate Body and dispute panels (which comprise the DSM) soon engendered critique from both states and other stakeholders, against the backdrop of stalled negotiations over new trade rules. Greenwald encapsulated this disquiet when he wrote in 2003 that 'WTO dispute settlement has been far more an exercise in policy-making, and far less an exercise in even-handed interpretation of carefully negotiated language of WTO agreements'.[2]

The development of the modern investment treaty regime represents an equally remarkable extension of international law. Built on a network of more than 3,000 bilateral and multilateral treaties,[3] foreign investors are typically granted foreign investment protection rights in these

---

[1] J Jackson, 'The WTO "Constitution" and Proposed Reforms: Seven "Mantras" Revisited' (2001) 4 *Journal of International Economic Law* 67.

[2] J Greenwald, 'WTO Dispute Settlement: An Exercise in Trade Law Legislation?' (2003) 6 *Journal of International Economic Law* 113.

[3] UNCTAD provides an extensive database on IIAs, http://investmentpolicyhub.unctad.org /IIA, accessed 1 June 2019. Other types of treaties include regional free trade agreements (FTAs) and a handful of plurilateral investment treaties. Later examples include: Energy Charter Treaty (ECT), North American Free Trade Agreement (NAFTA), Association of South-East Asian Nations Comprehensive Investment Agreement, Central American-Dominican Republic Free Trade Agreement (DR-CAFTA), as well as recently concluded or

agreements that are in turn – and perhaps most importantly – enforceable through an investor-state dispute settlement mechanism (ISDS). [4] While each international investment treaty (IIA) is a stand-alone agreement, they are not identical; and if taken together there is considerable diversity across the agreements.[5] Mirroring trade, early litigation and initial awards quickly produced a backlash from states and an ongoing legitimacy crisis.[6] This phenomenon is not about the expansiveness of the substantive rights granted to foreign investors under IIAs, but rather the combination of such rights with a robust ISDS mechanism. Critiques of the regime include claims that ISDS is pro-investor, or anti-developing state; that the jurisprudence is incoherent, riddled with contested interpretations; and that the levels of monetary compensation are too high.[7]

To be sure, many claim that these critiques are misguided and that there is little evidence of 'judicial empowerment' or adjudicatory activism within both regimes. Others are more nuanced and point to the potential for self-correction. Indeed, various studies demonstrate that international courts and tribunals purposefully conform their rulings to the expressed preferences of member states, especially politically or economically influential ones, and do not always engage in expansive judicial law-making or assertions of authority.[8] In this vein, the legitimacy crises

---

late-round negotiated treaties: Trans-Pacific Partnership Agreement and the Regional Comprehensive Partnership Agreement.

[4] B Simmons, 'Bargaining over BITS, Arbitrating Awards: The Regime for Protection and Promotion of International Investment' (2014) 66 *World Politics* 12, 42.

[5] IIAs typically include: prohibitions against expropriation without adequate compensation, full protection and security, fair and equitable treatment (FET), most-favoured nation (MFN) treatment and national treatment.

[6] See, e.g. P Eberhardt and C Olivet, 'Profiting from Injustice: How Law Firms, Arbitrators, and Financiers are Fueling an Investment Arbitration, *Corporate Europe Observatory*, November 2012; M Langford, D Behn and OK Fauchald, 'Backlash and State Strategies in International Investment Law' in Thomas Gammeltoft-Hansen and Tanja Aalberts (eds.) *The Changing Practices of International Law: Sovereignty, Law and Politics in a Globalising World* (Cambridge University Press, 2018) ch. 4.

[7] See, e.g. G Van Harten, 'Arbitrator Behaviour in Asymmetrical Adjudication: An Empirical Study of Investment Treaty Arbitration' (2012) 50 *Osgoode Hall Law Journal* 211, 251; Z Douglas, 'The MFN Clause in Investment Arbitration: Treaty Interpretation off the Rails' (2011) 2 *Journal of International Dispute Settlement* 97; G Kahale 'Is Investor-State Arbitration Broken?' 7 *TDM* (2012), www.transnational-dispute-management.com, accessed 1 June 2019; 'The Arbitration Game: Governments are Souring on Treaties to Protect Foreign Investors', *Economist*, 11 October 2014.

[8] G Garrett, D Kelemen and H Schulz, 'The European Court of Justice, National Governments, and Legal Integration in the European Union' (1998) 52(1) *International Organization* 149; L Helfer and K Alter, 'Legitimacy and Lawmaking: A Tale of Three International Courts' (2013) 14(2) *Theoretical Inquiries in Law* 479; O Larsson and

are merely a – *crise de croissance* – 'growing pains'[9] – and as the systems mature, they will evolve (or have already done so) into more legitimate, consistent and effective forms of international adjudication. However, only a nascent and mostly doctrinal literature has examined the degree of adjudicatory responsiveness in international economic law.[10]

In light of the debate surrounding these legitimacy crises, we ask whether there is (or has been) a reflexive and evolutionary self-correction in each regime. Do adjudicators in international economic law seek to build their normative *and* sociological legitimacy[11] by displaying sensitivity to state signals in their resolution of substantive and procedural questions? Or are they largely indifferent to the storm outside?

This question of responsiveness is relevant for three reasons. The first is theoretical. A central division in the characterization of international courts and tribunals is the extent to which adjudicators act as 'trustees' or 'agents'.[12] Are they trustees that decide according to their own professional judgments; or are they agents, susceptible to the critique and influence of their principals, namely, states?[13] The second reason is policy based. Various reform processes are underway, such as the current

---

D Naurin, 'Judicial Independence and Political Uncertainty: How the Risk of Override Affects the Court of Justice of the EU' (2016) 70(2) *International Organisation* 377; Ø Stiansen and E Voeten, 'Backlash and Judicial Restraint: Evidence From the European Court of Human Rights' *SSRN Working Paper*, 17 August 2018.

[9] A Bjorklund, 'Report of the Rapporteur Second Columbia International Investment Conference: What's Next in International Investment Law and Policy?' in J Alvarez et al. (eds.) *The Evolving International Investment Regime: Expectations, Realities, Options* (Cambridge University Press, 2011) 219.

[10] D Schneidermann, 'Legitimacy and Reflexity in International Investment Arbitration: A New Self-Restraint' (2011) 2 *Journal of International Dispute Settlement* 471. The empirical exception is: M Busch and K Pelc, 'The Politics of Judicial Economy at the World Trade Organization' (2010) 64(2) *International Organization* 257.

[11] By normative legitimacy, we mean the extent to which an institution with the right to rule has moral grounds for doing so; and by sociological legitimacy, we mean the extent to which the ruled accept or believe in that exercise of power.

[12] See, e.g. K Alter, 'Agents or Trustees? International Courts in their Political Context' (2008) 14(1) *European Journal of International Relations* 33. Delegation is a fairly open framework such that principal-agent approaches are more a 'highly flexible family of models, rather than an overarching set of assumptions and results'. S Gailmard, 'Accountability and Principal-Agent Models' in M Bovens, T Schillemans and R Goodin (eds.), *Oxford Handbook of Public Accountability* (Oxford University Press, 2014). In this respect, see the response of M Pollack, 'Principal-Agent Analysis and International Delegation: Red Herrings, Theoretical Clarifications, and Empirical Disputes' (2007) *Bruges Political Research Papers*, No. 2 to claims that the fiduciary model of beneficiary-trustee is an alternative to the principal-agent model.

[13] Alter, ibid.

negotiations in UNCITRAL Working Group III on the reform of investor-state dispute settlement (ISDS). Yet, if courts and arbitral panels are responsive, the need for more drastic changes may be obviated. Likewise, if some institutional designs (especially a centralized model of adjudication) make dispute settlement more responsive, then that may be a preferable model. This belief explains in part the European Union's drive for a multilateral investment court in UNCITRAL Working Group III.[14] The third is comparative and is central to the core question of this book. An examination of the respective trade and investment regimes provides evidence of whether the systems are converging (or not) with respect to adjudicative posture. Is investor-state arbitration moving closer to what some claim (until recently) is the more responsive regime of the WTO?

We begin the chapter by theorizing how, why and when adjudicators in the two regimes might be sensitive to state signals (Section 2). We then review the evidence in the WTO DSM (Section 3) and ISDS (Section 4) before offering reflections on whether there is convergence between the two regimes and what this implies for debates on adjudicator behaviour and policy reform.

2 Theorizing Adjudicative Responsiveness

International courts and arbitral bodies undoubtedly possess some legal techniques to manage their legitimacy and respond to the concerns of states.[15] Such techniques include the ability to tighten jurisdictional criteria, exhibit greater deference to respondent states on the merits, reduce the number of claims upon which a claimant state or investor wins, minimize the extent of the remedy, shift legal costs, or a combination of all of these. In the context of investor-state arbitration, the formal space to deploy these techniques may be greater than in the WTO given that the latter operates

---

[14] *Multilateral investment court: Council gives mandate to the Commission to open negotiations*, 20 March 2018, www.consilium.europa.eu/en/press/press-releases/2018/03/20/multilateral-investment-court-council-gives-mandate-to-the-commission-to-open-negotiations, last accessed 1 June 2019.

[15] See, e.g. M Madsen, 'The Legitimization Strategies of International Courts: The Case of the European Court of Human Rights' in M Bobek (ed.), *Selecting Europe's Judges* (Oxford University Press, 2015); JHH Weiler, 'Journey to an Unknown Destination: A Retrospective and Prospective of the European Court of Justice in the Arena of Political Integration' (1993) 31(4) *Journal of Common Market Studies* 417; S Dothan, 'Why Granting States a Margin of Appreciation Supports the Formation of a Genuine European Consensus' *iCourts Working Paper Series No. 22* (2015). This section draws in part on Malcolm Langford and Daniel Behn, 'Managing Backlash: The Evolving Investment Arbitrator?' (2018) 29(2) European Journal of International Law 551.

under a centralized Appellate Body, while investor-state arbitration is a decentralized system with ad hoc, one-off arbitral tribunals operating with few formal mechanisms for control, none of which are centralized.

But why would international adjudicators turn to such techniques? Why would they sacrifice legal positivism to manage, consciously or unconsciously, the legitimacy of their respective regimes when resolving disputes? A useful way of distinguishing two competing sets of arguments is to employ the analytical framework of delegation theory. The extent to which adjudicators are reflexive arguably comes down to the extent to which they act as 'trustees' or 'agents'.[16]

2.1 Trustee Null Hypothesis

Some scholars argue that international adjudicators are best characterized as 'trustees'. They adjudicate through delegated authority and according to their own professional judgments on behalf of states and other beneficiaries,[17] and are relatively insulated from the signals of states as they 'serve publics with diverse and often conflicting preferences'.[18] This view would expect an external legitimacy crisis to exert little influence on adjudicative decision-making.

On its face, investor-state arbitration might lie at the trustee end of the delegation continuum. Besides partial party-appointment (which even then requires wing arbitrators to be formally independent and impartial), many of the typical characteristics of an agency relationship are not present as arbitrators wield significant discretionary powers with minimal accountability. Arbitral jurisdiction is made compulsory in most IIAs; arbitral appointments in a particular case are largely beyond successful challenge; awards can only be annulled on very narrow technical and procedural grounds;[19] it is difficult for states to amend treaty provisions in order to avoid any precedential effects that an award may have on future cases with a similarly placed investor;[20] and

[16] See (n. 12).
[17] Alter (n. 12).
[18] Y Lupu, 'International Judicial Legitimacy: Lessons from National Courts' (2013) 14(2) *Theoretical Inquiries in Law* 437, 438. Some scholars claim that the problem even extends to domestic courts. National judges will only have 'vague notions', for example, about parliamentary preferences and the risk of legislative override. See J Segal, 'Separation-of-Powers Games in the Positive Theory of Congress and Courts' (1997) 91 *The American Political Science Review* 1, 31.
[19] There are very limited grounds for appeal – either through annulment procedures (under the ICSID Convention) or domestic court set-aside proceedings (non-ICSID cases).
[20] K Gordon and J Pohl, 'Investment Treaties over Time: Treaty Practice and Interpretation in a Changing World' *OECD Working Papers on International Investment* (OECD Publishing, 2015).

there is no formal channel by which states can express their discontent with arbitral awards rendered against them. Moreover, arbitrators are usually selected on the basis of their 'personal and professional reputation'.[21]

If the trustee model captures the space in which investor-state arbitrators operate, we would therefore expect the underlying values of the regime and/or arbitrators to largely guide decision-making. As Karen Alter put it, the result will be a 'rhetorical politics' in which the appointing actors will appeal to the trustee's 'mandate' and 'philosophies'.[22] This might be legal positivism. Arbitrators, according to their professional judgment, seek to apply IIA provisions in good faith to the specific facts of the case. Indeed, the fact that arbitrators regularly find for respondent states as much as claimant-investors may suggest even-handedness.[23] Accordingly, any change in arbitral behaviour could only be explained by a change in the regime's substantive rules or the average set of factual circumstances. Yet, it is hard to say that there has been a shift in either.[24]

Paradoxically perhaps, an attitudinalist perspective of adjudicative behaviour also suggests trustee-like behaviour. Arbitrators make decisions according to their sincere ideological attitudes and values (their 'personal judgment')[25] because they are relatively unconstrained by other actors, including states.[26] Some claim that investment treaty arbitrators are on average more partial to investors, representing an elitist and largely

---

[21] Y Dezalay and B Garth, *Dealing in Virtue: International Commercial Arbitration and the Construction of a Transnational Legal Order* (University of Chicago Press, 1998).

[22] Alter (n. 12).

[23] See D Behn, 'Legitimacy, Evolution, and Growth in Investment Treaty Arbitration: Empirically Evaluating the State-of-the-Art' (2015) 46(2) *Georgetown Journal of International Law* 363; SD Franck, 'Conflating Politics and Development: Examining Investment Treaty Outcomes' (2014) 55 *Virginia Journal of International Law* 1.

[24] Some recent and revised IIAs include general but vague clauses concerning the right to regulate or greater exceptions for domestic environmental and labour policies, but their significance is not yet clear. See T Broude et al., 'Who Cares About Regulatory Space in BITs? A Comparative International Approach' in A Roberts et al. (eds.), *Comparative International Law* (Cambridge University Press, 2017); W Alschner and K Hui, 'Missing in Action: General Public Policy Exceptions in Investment Treaties', L Sachs, J Coleman and L Johnson (eds.), *Yearbook on International Investment Law and Policy* (Oxford University Press, 2018). An empirical study based on computational text analysis suggests that renegotiations of IIAs tend to result in less room for state regulatory powers and more investor-protective ISDS provisions. W Alschner, 'The Impact of Investment Arbitration on Investment Treaty Design: Myth versus Reality' (2017) 42(1) *Yale Journal of International Law* 1.

[25] See generally J Segal and H Spaeth, *The Supreme Court and the Attitudinal Model* (Cambridge University Press, 1993).

[26] Ibid., 28.

Western-based epistemic community with a commitment to promoting and protecting foreign investment. Arbitrators from Western Europe and North America make up a total of 70 per cent of all appointees to investment treaty arbitrations.[27] Even though such differences can matter, and even if it makes good sense to assume that they would, there is no clear correlation to be found between investor success and the nationality of the adjudicators in investor-state arbitration. However, Posner and Figueredo's well-known study on the International Court of Justice (ICJ) found that permanent judges were significantly more likely to vote for a disputing state that shares a similar level of economic development and democracy with their home state.[28] In the context of investor-state arbitration, there has been a slight uptick in the appointment of arbitrators hailing from lesser developed states in recent years but no corresponding significant effect on outcomes.[29] It is likely that many of these arbitrators tend to come from a similar 'epistemic community' and South America in particular,[30] and may need to adhere to the 'rules of the club' in order to gain appointments. However, the opposite may also be accurate: becoming an investor-state arbitrator and being welcomed into the club may turn not on one's nationality but rather on how closely an arbitrator's values, perspectives and ideological outlook conform to the views of those arbitrators already operating inside the club.

Turning to the WTO, given compulsory jurisdiction and that Appellate Body adjudicators act as authoritative and ultimate interpreters of WTO law, many assert that the WTO DSM operates virtually free from direct state control.[31] Commentators largely agree that states

---

[27] PITAD through 1 August 2017. M Langford, D Behn and R Lie, 'The Revolving Door in International Investment Arbitration' (2017) 20(2) *Journal of International Economic Law* 301.

[28] E Posner and M de Figueiredo, 'Is the International Court of Justice Biased?' 34 *Legal Studies* (2005) 599. Together, these correlations explained a remarkable 60 per cent to 70 per cent of variance among individual judicial votes.

[29] M Langford, D Behn and M Usynin, 'Does Nationality Matter? Arbitrator Background and Arbitral Outcomes' in D Behn, OK Fauchald and M Langford (eds.), *The Legitimacy of Investment Arbitration: Empirical Perspectives* (Cambridge University Press, forthcoming 2020).

[30] Langford, Behn and Lie (n. 26).

[31] K Alter, 'Agents or Trustees? International Courts in their Political Context' (2008) 14(1) *European Journal of International Relations* 33; D Cass, 'The "Constitutionalization" of International Trade Law: Judicial Norm-Generation as the Engine of Constitutional Development in International Trade' (2001) 12(1) *European Journal of International Law* 39; AC Sweet, 'The New GATT: Dispute Resolution and the Judicialization of the Trade Regime' in ML Volcansek (ed.), *Law above Nations: Supranational Courts and the Legalization of Politics* (University of Florida Press, 1997); AC Sweet and TL Brunell,

find it difficult if not impossible to engage in formal legislative responses to rulings of the organization's quasi-adjudicative bodies.[32] As with the international investment regime, then, few of the typical characteristics of an agency relationship are found within the WTO regime. While ad hoc panellists may be appointed by the disputing parties, the vast majority have been selected by the WTO Director General.[33] Given, however, that many panellists have served as government delegates to the WTO, we might expect panellists to act less like trustees than members of the Appellate Body, who enjoy a longer tenure on the bench. Indeed, trade scholars generally concur that the jurisprudence of the WTO Appellate Body has exhibited legalistic traits more akin to either a legal positivist or attitudinalist perspective of adjudicative behaviour in comparison to the WTO trade dispute panels.[34]

2.2 Agent Responsiveness Hypothesis

An alternative to these expectations of stable adjudicator behaviour is the view that international courts and tribunals follow the mood shifts of states as agents rather than trustees. This claim is relatively under-theorized within the literature, even though many recognize that states frequently employ such horizontal pressure. In our view, the principal prism through which to understand and model such behaviour is *rational choice*. Adjudicators: (1) may hold diverse preferences that extend beyond political ideology or good lawyering; (2) 'take into account the preferences and likely actions of other relevant actors, including their colleagues, elected officials, and the public'; and (3) operate in a 'complex institutional environment' that structures this interaction.[35]

Indeed, evidence from various domestic jurisdictions suggests that judges are strategically sensitive to signals from the executive and

---

'Trustee Courts and the Judicialization of International Regimes: The Politics of Majoritarian Activism' (2013) 1(1) *Journal of Law and Courts*, 61, 62.

[32] CD Ehlermann and L Ehring, 'The Authoritative Interpretation Under Article IX:2 of the Agreement Establishing the World Trade Organization: Current Law, Practice and Possible Improvements' (2005) 8 *Journal of International Economic Law* 803.

[33] CD Creamer, *Judicial Responsiveness in the World Trade Organization* (unpublished manuscript).

[34] R Howse, 'The World Trade Organization 20 Years On: Global Governance by Judiciary' (2016) 27 *European Journal of International Law* 9.

[35] L Epstein and J Knight, 'Reconsidering Judicial Preferences' (2013) 16 *Annual Review of Political Science* 11, 11. On diverse goals, see in particular L Baum, *Judges and Their Audiences: A Perspective on Judicial Behavior* (Princeton University Press, 2008).

legislature,[36] although the scholarship is divided on the extent of this shift.[37] As to public opinion, there is consensus that it has an *indirect* influence on judgments through judicial appointments but is divided over whether it exerts a *direct* influence on judges.[38] At the international level, empirical and doctrinal scholarship suggests that the Court of Justice of the EU (CJEU)[39] is sensitive to the balance and composition of member state opinion within institutional constraints.

For investor-state arbitrators, a strategic account would imply that a behavioural correction in response to legitimacy critiques could forestall certain material and reputational 'costs'. In practice, arbitrators may lack trusteeship freedoms and are reduced to agents engaged in 'contractual politics' with their principals. There might be two grounds for thinking so. First, arbitrators could be concerned collectively as a group about any backlash by principals (states) because it could eventually lead to regime collapse in extreme circumstances. However, it will almost assuredly increase the risk of non-compliance by respondent states, encourage greater exits from the regime, reduce the rate of new treaties being entered into, or result in weaker future and/or revised IIAs. Such state behaviour would inhibit the ability of arbitrators to impose their own political preferences (comparable to the concern with 'overrides' in the judicial context)[40] and thus maintain the general reputational standing of arbitrators working in the system. Second, investor-state

---

[36] See, e.g. JC Rodriguez-Rada, 'Strategic Deference in the Colombian Constitutional Court, 1992–2006' in G Helmke and J Rios-Figueroa (eds.), *Courts in Latin America* (Cambridge University Press, 2011) pp. 81–98; Epstein and Knight, ibid; D Kapiszewski, 'Tactical Balancing: High Court Decision Making on Politically Crucial Cases' (2011) 45 *Law and Society Review* 471.

[37] Compare, e.g. M Bergara, B Richman and P Spiller, 'Modeling Supreme Court Strategic Decision Making: The Congressional Constraint' (2003) 28(2) *Legislative Studies Quarterly* 247 with Segal (n. 24).

[38] R Flemming and D Wood, 'The Public and the Supreme Court: Individual Justice Responsiveness to American Policy Moods' (1997) 41 *American Journal of Political Science* (1997) 468, 480. See also B Friedman, *The Will of the People: How Public Opinion has Influenced the Supreme Court and Shaped the Meaning of the Constitution* (Farrar, Straus and Giroux, 2009); L Epstein and A Martin, 'Does Public Opinion Influence the Supreme Court? Possibly Yes (But We're Not Sure Why)' (2010) 13 *University of Pennsylvania Journal of Constitutional Law* 263, 270; I Unah et al., 'U.S. Supreme Court Justices and Public Mood' (2015) 30 *Journal of Law and Politics* 293.

[39] O Larsson and D Naurin, 'Judicial Independence and Political Uncertainty: How the Risk of Override Affects the Court of Justice of the EU' (2016) 70(2) *International Organisation* 377; M Pollack, *The Engines of European Integration: Delegation, Agency, and Agenda Setting in the EU* (Oxford University Press, 2003).

[40] Larsson and Naurin (n. 38).

arbitrators may be concerned about their own individual reputations and how they relate to their material chances of future appointment.[41] If they experience reversal through annulment procedures,[42] set-asides in domestic courts or criticism by their colleagues or scholars, they may shift course. Arbitrators interested in the role of chair or respondent-appointed arbitrators may be particularly sensitive, given the common role of states in these appointments.

Could arbitrators be so strategic and consequentialist? Well, arbitrators themselves have acknowledged the phenomenon. In a recent survey, 262 international arbitrators, which included a subset of 67 with experience in investor-state arbitration,[43] were asked whether they considered future reappointment when deciding cases.[44] A remarkable 42 per cent agreed or were ambivalent. Given the sensitive nature of the question, it is arguable that this figure is understated.[45]

These strategic predictions may be enhanced by sociological forces.[46] The theory of discursive institutionalism proposes that discourse (such as that surrounding the legitimacy crisis) is not simply a static, internal and slow-moving phenomenon but is also independent, dynamic and liminal. Shifts to stakeholder discourse may shape the 'background ideational abilities' of judicial agents.[47] Or as Cardozo put it, 'the great tides and currents which engulf the rest of men do not turn aside in their course and pass the judges by'.[48] Arbitrators may shift their background preferences as they become acquainted with or engaged in the legitimacy debate. The crisis may also affect their 'foreground discursive abilities' and the space in which they 'communicate critically about those institutions, to change (or maintain) them'.[49] Arbitrators may simply adapt to a different palette of

---

[41] Studies of domestic judges that are subject to reappointment processes reveal higher levels of strategic behaviour among this group. See I Lifshitz and SA Lindquist, 'The Judicial Behavior of State Supreme Court Judges' (2011) *APSA 2011 Annual Meeting Paper*.

[42] A Van Aaken, 'Control Mechanisms in International Investment Law' in Z Douglas et al. (eds.), *The Foundations of International Investment Law: Bringing Theory into Practice* (Oxford University Press, 2014) 409.

[43] S Franck et al., 'International Arbitration: Demographics, Precision and Justice' (2015) *ICCA Congress Series No. 18, Legitimacy: Myths, Realities, Challenges*, 33.

[44] Ibid., 91.

[45] Ibid.

[46] On this empirical conundrum, see A Gilles, 'Reputational Concerns and the Emergence of Oil Sector Transparency as an International Norm' (2010) 54 *International Studies Quarterly* 103.

[47] V Schmidt, 'Discursive Institutionalism: The Explanatory Power of Ideas and Discourse' (2008) 11 *Annual Review of Political Science* 303, 304.

[48] B Cardozo, *The Nature of the Judicial Process* (Yale University Press, 1921) 168.

[49] Schmidt (n. 46) 304.

legitimate reasons that can be foregrounded in their decision-making. Thus, a change in arbitrator behaviour may not only be strategic. It may also be a process of rapid adjustment to a new social norm that affects arbitrator preferences and speech acts.

How might we expect WTO adjudicators to respond to a legitimacy crisis or other changes in stakeholder discourse? From a strategic point of view, professional role orientations and self-interest may motivate WTO adjudicators to promote political support for the dispute settlement system and increase its legitimacy, as these factors critically influence their own personal salary potential, professional prestige and occupational ambition.[50] As strategic actors, then, WTO adjudicators may well adjust their behaviour to pre-empt further pushback or backlash. If sociological forces increase this sensitivity, then trade adjudicators should pay close attention to discursive shifts in WTO member government views. Given the difficulty of employing unilateral sanctioning within the WTO, we would expect them to have an interest in cultivating it among the wider membership, and not solely in relation to the largest economies or most 'powerful' states within the regime.

Notably, the extent to which agent or trustee motivations drive adjudicator behaviour likely varies across the two levels of WTO adjudication – the dispute panels and the Appellate Body. Appointed individuals serve as panellists on a part-time basis, in addition to their usual job.[51] As with investor-state arbitrators, WTO panellists have shorter time horizons than elected adjudicators, as they are appointed ad hoc for a given dispute and only have this 'one shot' to achieve their individual goals or motivations for agreeing to serve on a panel. Due to these shorter time horizons, we might expect panellists to be *more* sensitive to legitimacy crises or fluctuations in political support than members of the Appellate Body, who enjoy relatively longer tenures (renewable once) and thus act more as trustees of the trade rule of law.

Two connected rationalist reasons suggest that strategic motivations may shape panellist behaviour. First, for reasons of professional self-interest, a number of panellists are likely motivated by reappointment. A little over half appointed since 1995 have sat on more than one panel,

---

[50] F Schauer, 'Lecture: Incentives, Reputation, and the Inglorious Determinants of Judicial Behavior' (2000) 68 *University of Cincinnati Law Review* 615.

[51] To date, the majority of appointed panellists were current or previous government delegates to the WTO. Some were capital-based trade officials, with a few having served previously as WTO Secretariat officials or Appellate Body members. Even fewer have come from private practice or academia. See Creamer (n. 32).

with a few sitting on as many as ten or eleven separate panels. Repeat panellists are likely more integrated in the organizational life of the WTO, and some even go on to become Secretariat officials or Appellate Body members. For this reason, they seek to maintain a respected professional reputation and strive to issue reports that will not provoke widespread political backlash and sanctioning.[52] Second, even if a panellist is not motivated by reappointment, she both (a) possesses imperfect information on how the panel report will impact her long-term professional ambitions; and (b) must reach a collective agreement on the report's findings with two other panellists, who may themselves be motivated by reappointment.[53]

In sum, for both the investment and trade regimes, we might expect states to exert influence on investor-state and WTO adjudicators and can make the following hypothesis:

Hypothesis 1 – State Signals: *Adjudicators will respond strongly to the signals of states.*

However, and more narrowly, we might expect that investor-state and WTO adjudicators are particularly responsive to the views of certain audiences, namely large, powerful or particularly influential states.[54] Displaying such sensitivity may be strategic for reputational and survival reasons. In the case of investor-state arbitration, it may also enhance the prospect of more arbitrations entering into the pipeline (particularly due to the large capital exports of these states' foreign investors). Thus, we could state:

Hypothesis 2 – Influential State Signals: *Adjudicators will respond even more strongly to the signals of large, powerful or particularly influential states.*

Still, it is not clear that strategic incentives and discursive influences apply equally to all adjudicators. Repeat investor-state arbitrators

---

[52] Repeat panellists have an interest in cultivating support among the *wider membership* – and not always or necessarily with particular governments – because the majority of panellist appointments are made by the WTO Director General, and not by the disputing parties.

[53] The organizational norm of consensus decision-making also operates within the DSM, and there is considerable pressure for panel reports to reflect consensus among the three panellists, although individual panellists may – but very rarely do –anonymously include a separate or dissenting view.

[54] By large and powerful, we specifically include influential state actors participating actively in the regime: the United States, the EU (including its Member States), and China. We note that Larsson and Naurin (n. 38) found that influential states had a greater influence on the CJEU, although they theorized that this occurred through greater voting weights in potential overrides of judgments in the Council of Ministers.

(especially repeat tribunal chairs) are likely to be more sensitive to systemic threats and opportunities in comparison to one-shot arbitrators. They might constitute 'the guardians of the regime', engaged in wider discussions over investment treaty law practice, development and legitimacy. Within the WTO regime, panellists integrated into the organizational life of the WTO likely are more sensitive to vacillations in political support for the dispute settlement system and more wary about judicial overreaching into sovereign authority. Those who are concurrently WTO representatives must regularly interact with the individuals representing the complainant or respondent, within meetings of committees and other political bodies. In addition, WTO delegates likely are more attuned to the need to provide home state governments with some sort of political cover to implement adverse judgments. Tellingly, no WTO panel has been composed with all three panellists lacking any prior experience within or interaction with the WTO.[55] We thus propose as follows:

Hypothesis 3 – Prominent Adjudicators: *Repeat investor-state tribunal chairs and integrated WTO panellists will respond to signals from states and/or other stakeholders.*

2.3 Decentralized versus Centralized Adjudication

So far we have pointed to largely similar trustee and agent factors in both investor-state and WTO adjudication, with only a nod to potential differences. However, there are some important structural differences concerning the degree of centralization, which may significantly affect the degree of responsiveness.

First, investor-state arbitration faces major coordination problems compared to the trade system.[56] While the fifty or so oft-repeat investment arbitrators may provide some semblance of an epistemic and/or strategic community, these arbitrators only account for appointments in roughly half of the cases to date. They are thus quite limited in their ability to communicate and act in a collective fashion. The polycentric and ad hoc nature of investor-state arbitration may prevent arbitrators from acting in a systemic

---

[55] Between 1995 and 2013, only seven panels (less than 5 per cent) were composed with the majority of panellists having no prior experience within the WTO, while 62.5 per cent of panels were composed entirely of individuals with some prior experience within or interaction with the WTO.

[56] On this point, see also Michelle Zang, Chapter 6 and Graham Cook, Chapter 8.

manner, even if they wish to do so. Unlike a centralized court, an individual arbitral tribunal may feel it can make little contribution to signalling a systemic shift – it is one of many. The incentive to take extra *inter partes* action is thus minimal.[57] Moreover, arbitrators may be doctrinally constrained in considering general concerns: one line of investor-state arbitral jurisprudence suggests that individual arbitrators should not systemically reflect and act as they are constituted as specialist adjudicative bodies.[58]

Second, on the side of trade, the institutional structure of the WTO helps adjudicators and WTO officials in the Secretariat overcome potential coordination problems and act in a more systemic manner. Of note, regular meetings of the DSB facilitate collection and assimilation of discursive shifts and criticism among member state governments. Secretariat officials effectively provide a low-cost way of transmitting these rhetorical signals to WTO adjudicators, who are thereby able to pay attention to fluctuations in their political support among the wider membership and deliberate among themselves about whether they should behave in a responsive manner. Secretariat officials are incentivized to push adjudicators to do so because they have relatively longer time horizons than individual panellists. Moreover, these officials seem to hold strongly internalized role perceptions, in that they subscribe to the WTO's self-identification as a member-driven organization and view the Secretariat's role as serving the interests and needs of the member states. In the context of the dispute settlement system, this entails fulfilling its stated purpose: facilitating the settlement of disputes by drafting rulings in a way that will secure compliance.

The upshot is that even indifferent or lazy adjudicators can hedge their bets and engage in low-cost risk-averse decisional behaviour. They do not need to conduct extensive and time-consuming research to obtain information on government views because these preferences are pre-assimilated by the WTO Secretariat, who are tasked with assisting the dispute panels and the Appellate Body. Moreover, there is a differential in the jurisdictional powers granted in the constitutive documents that may further exacerbate reflexivity. WTO adjudicators have more curtailed powers than investment arbitrators. The former should never 'add to or

---

[57] On this challenge at the domestic level in civil law courts, see K Young and J Lemaitre, 'The Comparative Fortunes of the Right to Health: Two Tales of Justiciability in Colombia and South Africa' (2013) 26 *Harvard Human Rights Journal* 179.

[58] M Reisman, 'Case Specific Mandates versus Systemic Implications: How Should Investment Tribunals Decide? The Freshfields Arbitration Lecture' (2013) 29 *Arbitration International* 131.

diminish' the rights of the contracting parties, increasing the potential sensitivity of WTO adjudicators to state preferences.

Thus, we can articulate a final hypothesis concerning the respective reflexivity of the two regimes:

Hypothesis 4 – Structural Differences: *WTO adjudicators will respond more strongly than investor-state arbitrators to the signals of states.*

3 WTO Dispute Settlement Mechanism

3.1 Responsiveness of the Trade Regime

The WTO relies on a decentralized form of enforcement, with governments challenging other members' laws and policies as being in violation of WTO rules. Although governments are the ones who formally 'adopt' dispute rulings under the reverse-consensus rule, the primary responsibility for clarifying WTO rules and interpreting the scope of international trade authority rests with panels and the Appellate Body (together comprising the DSM). Governments are bound by these decisions and face retaliatory concessions if they do not comply with their rulings, with the result that most governments eventually do make costly changes to domestic laws and regulations to bring them into compliance.

Still, the institutional relationship between member governments and the WTO's adjudicative bodies reflects a pervasive tension between judicial independence and government control. Countries have hesitated to lash back at every instance of ostensible judicial law-making, but they do often engage in public expressions of dissatisfaction with the DSM's exercise of authority (and more recently blocking the appointment of AB members). That is, in terms of *who* communicates 'signals' of crisis to trade adjudicators, member states represent the primary stakeholders for the trade regime and thus are the most likely constituents to influence adjudicator behaviour. In terms of *what* sort of signals are communicated to adjudicators, governments regularly – either individually or collectively – criticize or praise legal interpretations and judicial practices through public statements made in meetings of the political body tasked with overseeing the dispute settlement system (the Dispute Settlement Body (DSB)). Not only do governments use these communicative acts on a regular basis, they do so with the explicit intention of signalling to the WTO's adjudicative bodies their (dis)satisfaction with those bodies' exercise of authority.[59] In fact, these rhetorical signals constitute the primary – and for many members the exclusive – means by which governments seek to shape the development of WTO jurisprudence.

Importantly, the majority of these statements do not represent cheap talk by states. Government officials engage in considerable research, analysis and drafting of the content of these statements. They place on the formal, public record of a political body their government's 'official' view on a given issue. Because these views may impact a country's bargaining position or diplomatic relationships within other political fora, governments carefully and intentionally decide when and what views to express. While a few statements may simply represent a losing party complaining about or a winning party approving of a ruling, many governments without a direct stake in a case often express views on the broader, systemic implications of the WTO's exercise of judicial authority. These procedural and systemic concerns now threaten the system's legitimacy and perhaps even its institutional survival.[60] Similar to the investment regime, while there are other actors that may also signal dissatisfaction with the trade regime, this section focuses on the relationship between trade rulings and government expressions of dissatisfaction.

As discussed above, there are strong reasons to expect trade adjudicators to respond to increases in collective dissatisfaction with the system. And until recently, the organization's adjudicative bodies have responded to spikes in collective criticism by seeking to build up their political support among member governments in distinct ways.[61] The WTO's Secretariat – both the Legal Affairs and Rules Divisions that assist panels and the separate Appellate Body Secretariat – has been absolutely central to monitoring systemic concerns and helping to identify practices to cultivate that political capital. These lawyers pay attention to government statements within the DSB and flag issues of concern for the adjudicators. Thus, we will examine whether this leads the WTO adjudicative bodies to slightly adjust rulings to account for these collective concerns or to signal their recognition of the issue through the language they use within decisions. Indeed, it can be argued that the growing legitimacy of the dispute settlement system during its first two decades

---

[59] CD Creamer and Z Godzimirska, '(De)Legitimation at the WTO Dispute Settlement Mechanism' (2016) 49 *Vanderbilt Journal of Transnational Law* 275.
[60] CD Creamer, 'From the WTO's Crown Jewel to its Crown of Thorns' (2019) 113 *AJIL Unbound* 51.
[61] Ibid; AS Sweet and TL Brunell, 'Trustee Courts and the Judicialization of International Regimes: The Politics of Majoritarian Activism' (2013) 1 *Journal of Law and Courts* 61, 63–4.

largely stemmed from such sensitivity and subtle responsiveness to changing government preferences.[62]

In sum, we have strong reasons to expect that a primary goal of panellists and Appellate Body members is to increase political support for and the institutional legitimacy of the DSM. If this is the case, we should see these bodies responding to spikes in collective criticism by signalling greater judicial restraint. The following section outlines an empirical strategy to evaluate this expectation.

3.2 Empirical Strategy: Data and Results

In order to capture signals of concern or dissatisfaction communicated by WTO member governments to trade adjudicators, we rely on automated and manual content analysis of statements made within the DSB. A coding scheme was developed and applied to all statements made in DSB meetings since the WTO's inception (12,168 statements in total), sorting these statements into four categories: statements expressing a supportive or critical view on the DSM ('Supportive' and 'Critical'); those that relate to the DSM, but do not express an evaluation of its exercise of authority ('Neutral'); and those that do not relate directly to the DSM ('Other'). Following manual coding of a training set of statements and validation tests, methods of automated content analysis were employed to estimate the percentage of all statements falling within each of these four categories.[63]

A subset of these statements is particularly central to signalling legitimacy concerns within the WTO regime: statements made prior to report (the trade 'ruling') adoption. These report statements typically comment on legal interpretations or procedural decisions, and are thus more likely to reflect governments' views on the DSM's legitimacy than other types of statements. This chapter focuses on supportive and critical report statements, as those most directly capture political support for the DSM as expressed by its core constituents – member governments – in a public forum within which we would expect governments to signal their views on the WTO's exercise of judicial authority. Drawing on the automated and manual classification of report statements discussed above, Figure 10.1 displays changes in the sentiment of report views of the collective WTO membership over time.

---

[62] J Pauwelyn, 'The WTO 20 Years On: "Global Governance by Judiciary" or, Rather, Member-driven Settlement of (Some) Trade Disputes between (Some) WTO Members?' (2016) 27 *European Journal of International Law* 1119, 1120.

[63] For a description of these data and methods, see Creamer and Godzimirska (n. 58).

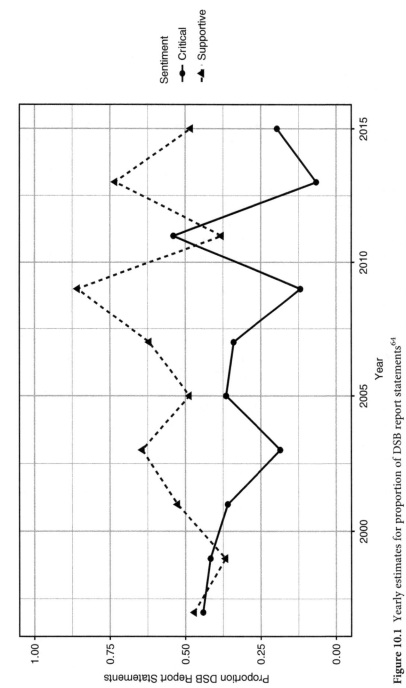

Figure 10.1 Yearly estimates for proportion of DSB report statements[64]

[64] Categorized by DSB statement sentiment (Critical and Supportive). Total report statements classified (includes compliance proceeding reports) = 1,161.

Since the first reports were adopted in 1996, member state governments have consistently – with the exceptions of 1999, 2002 and 2011 – voiced more support than criticism. The exceptions to this pattern are largely driven by third parties and non-parties to a dispute, as disputing parties have consistently been more supportive than critical within their report statements. This in and of itself is telling, as we might have expected the 'losing' party to always criticize adverse decisions and the 'winning' party to similarly express support for findings on which it prevailed. But that is not what we observe. Instead, parties – including many 'losing' parties – on average express diffuse support for the DSM's judicial authority in spite of or in addition to expressing disappointment with adverse findings related to their specific trade interests.

How might trade adjudicators respond to spikes in criticism? Each case that comes before the WTO's adjudicative bodies raises a number of distinct issues and claims that must be resolved. A single dispute ruling often finds some aspects of a trade measure in breach of WTO rules while simultaneously upholding other aspects of that trade measure. In fact, only 10 of the 188 panel reports issued between 1995 and 2013 found *no* violation of WTO rules across all claims raised (5.3 per cent).[65] Binary measures of dispute outcomes thus provide very little variation and moreover do not adequately capture the underlying extent to which panels and the AB signal to governments judicial restraint within a given ruling. Instead, a measure is developed under the assumption that panels and the Appellate Body are able to signal responsiveness when they make fewer breach (violation) findings within each dispute. Doing so allows panels and Appellate Body members to afford governments greater political cover to implement adverse rulings – by validating more elements of trade regulations within those rulings.

To construct this measure of adjudicative responsiveness, each dispute panel report issued between 1995 and 2014 was first assigned a score that represents the proportion of discrete findings made by the panel for which it upheld an element of the trade policy challenged. This score is a continuous variable that ranges from zero to one. Reports receiving a score of one found no instances of breach, signalling complete validation of the trade policy under review, while those receiving a score of zero

---

[65] Some studies of WTO disputes code case outcomes along three values: win, loss and 'mixed'. See, e.g. ML Busch and E Reinhardt, 'Three's a Crowd: Third Parties and WTO Dispute Settlement' (2006) 58 *World Politics* 446. Nearly 58 per cent of the panel reports issued between 1995 and 2013 are mixed, but there is considerable variance in the mixed category in terms of the number and type of violation findings.

contain only breach findings across claims, signalling complete invalidation. To construct a measure of judicial responsiveness for disputes that have been (partly) appealed, the score also takes into account the Appellate Body's decision to uphold or reverse the panel finding. A report's total responsiveness score thus represents the ultimate ruling on the dispute – by how much or how little a defendant government 'lost' the case.

Dispute panellists initially provided very little validation of government's trade policy choices, but then began to signal increasingly greater judicial restraint over the first six years of the DSM's operation. Following this initial sharp increase, however, average panel responsiveness has fluctuated around the 0.5 mark, though with relatively constant variance over those years. With the exception of the early years of the WTO, the Appellate Body rarely shifts considerably the proportion of panel findings in favour of the respondent. At least until 2015, the average total restraint afforded respondent governments does not differ significantly from that afforded by the panel alone.

Are WTO dispute panels responsive to diffuse political pressures? Do they tend to exercise greater restraint or to signal greater accommodation of trade policy choices when the DSM's political capital declines? And does the Appellate Body tend to shift significantly the degree of judicial restraint signalled within panel reports? To evaluate the *State Signals* hypothesis (Hypothesis 1), we can turn to research on the relationship between the judicial *Responsiveness Score* described above and signals of support for and criticism of the DSM's exercise of authority.[66] We proxy these government signals with half-year estimates of the proportion of DSB statements made by members that were critical or supportive, as described previously. The focus is first on panel reports, as these set the stage for the issues that the AB can subsequently decide and because total judicial responsiveness scores have not differed significantly from those for panel reports alone. If panels are responsive to collective political pressures, as the State Signals hypothesis suggests, we would expect a positive association between the proportion of critical statements and judicial responsiveness. Conversely, panels will likely exercise less restraint as political support for the DSM increases.

We further account for a range of alternative determinants of judicial restraint or responsiveness. To capture party characteristics and thus

---

[66] For the full study, see CD Creamer, *Judicial Responsiveness in the World Trade Organization* (unpublished manuscript).

Hypothesis 2, we control for disputes in which either the United States or the European Union were the respondent (*US/EU Respondent*). We additionally capture the power of the complainant state, by including its logged GDP per capita (*Complainant GDP*). While these two measures do not directly test the *Influential State Signals* hypothesis, they do provide some insight into the extent to which the DSM might defer to powerful countries.

The degree of restraint exhibited by panels may also vary with the type of trade policy or measure(s) challenged within a dispute. To account for the variable nature of review across types of measures, we include a factor variable (*Measure Type*) with three categories: legislation; executive/administrative regulation; and executive/administrative investigation(s). To control for politically sensitive disputes, we include a binary variable (*Politically Sensitive Agreements*) for reports that made findings under the Agreement on the Application of Sanitary and Phytosanitary Measures (SPS), the Agreement on Agriculture (AoA), or the Agreement on Textiles and Clothing (ATC). In addition, we control for disputes that involve trade remedies (claims falling under the Anti-Dumping Agreement (ADA), the Safeguards Agreement (SA), or the Subsidies and Countervailing Measures Agreement (SCM)) (*Trade Remedies*). We account for panellists' experiences with, and integration into, the life of the WTO (Hypothesis 3—*Prominent Adjudicators*) by including two binary variables for panels with a majority of *Repeat Panellists* and a majority of *WTO Delegates*. Finally, we include a cubic year trend variable to control for time trends.

Figure 10.2 reports the estimated relationship between the DSMs' political capital – both critical and supportive statements – and judicial responsiveness employing an ordinary least squares regression with robust standard errors. Criticism of the DSM is positively correlated with a report's judicial responsiveness score, supporting the State Signals hypothesis and this chapter's primary expectation. Panels do indeed appear to signal greater restraint when members have been relatively more critical. The influence of criticism is also substantively significant. Even when controlling for the level of political support, a 10 per cent increase in criticism increases the average panel responsiveness score by 17 per cent.

Similarly, in line with this chapter's argument, support for the DSM is negatively correlated with panel responsiveness, although not significantly. The substantive relationship is also less than that of criticism, with a 10 per cent increase in support associated with around a 9 per cent

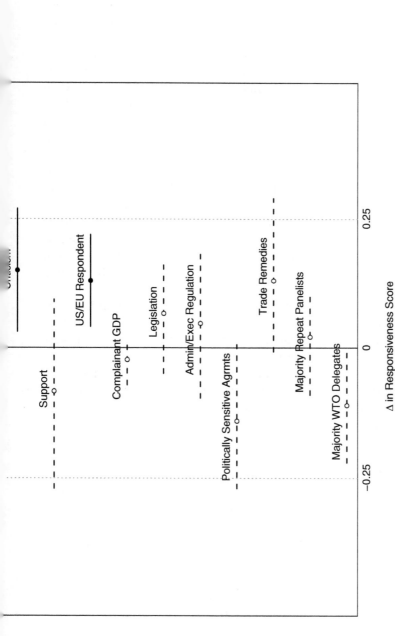

Figure 10.2 Estimated effects on WTO adjudicative responsiveness[67]

[67] The circles are estimates of the expected change in panel responsiveness as the indicated variable changes from 0 to 1 (for binary variables) or from their 25th to 75th percentile values (for continuous variables), and all other variables are held constant at their means. The lines are 95 per cent confidence intervals. The circles and lines are solid when there is at least 95 per cent confidence of a positive or negative effect on judicial responsiveness. Otherwise, circles are open and lines are dotted. Estimates obtained from simulated bootstrap parameters of ordinary least squares regression. N=182.

decrease in average responsiveness, even when accounting for the relative degree of member dissatisfaction with the DSM. These findings provide support for the argument that panels are not only paying attention to members' collective views on the WTO's adjudicative bodies, but also tend to rule more in favour of the defendant when challenges to their institutional legitimacy increase.

As for responsiveness to influential states, the wealth of the complainant state does not seem to make a difference for decisional outcomes. However, panels signal much greater judicial restraint when either the USA or the EU is the defending party, even when controlling for spikes in collective criticism within the WTO. This provides partial support for the Influential State Signals hypothesis (Hypothesis 2), although further research is needed to assess the extent to which the DSM responds to *direct* signals by these states. Finally, no support is found for the Prominent Adjudicators hypothesis (Hypothesis 3). While not reaching conventional levels of significance, more integrated panels (those with a majority of WTO delegates) are actually slightly less responsive than those with fewer WTO delegates. This should be interpreted with caution, however, given the fact that the Secretariat plays a large role in shaping panel judgments, which must be decided by consensus.

In sum, we find that WTO panels, under certain conditions, are responsive to fluctuations in the level of political support enjoyed by the DSM. The political capital of the DSM is not necessarily or always determined by the extent to which it has engaged in expansionist or activist judicial law-making, as courts can 'spark controversy due to the domestic political consequences of their rulings, whether or not those rulings are expansionist'.[68] Yet, the way panels respond to these diffuse political pressures is by signalling greater reflexivity by providing government authorities with slightly more domestic political cover for adverse decisions.

Appellate Body members are similarly concerned with establishing and maintaining the authority and credibility of the DSM. Even though they also take seriously their role as 'insulated' and independent adjudicators, the Appellate Body has signalled a similar degree of judicial restraint as that provided within panel reports. Until recently, the WTO's adjudicative bodies tended to exercise greater judicial restraint –

---

[68] LR Helfer and KJ Alter, 'Legitimacy and Lawmaking: A Tale of Three International Courts' (2013) 14 *Theoretical Inquiries in Law* 479, 502.

thereby signalling to the membership that they are sensitive to concerns about domestic policy autonomy and regulatory space – when the DSM's institutional legitimacy declined. Put differently, when governments began to voice – through statements made within the DSB – greater criticism and dissatisfaction with how dispute panels and the Appellate Body were exercising their authority, these bodies responded by providing government agencies with slightly more domestic accommodation for adverse decisions.

4 Investor-State Dispute Settlement

4.1 Legitimacy Crisis Periods

In order to understand and measure the potential reaction of investor-state arbitrators to the legitimacy crisis in ISDS, we need to chart the trajectory of the crisis. We are particularly interested in *who* communicates 'signals' of crisis, *what* sort of signals might be communicated to arbitrators, and *when*. As to *who*, states are of particular interest: they constitute the primary principals in the international investment treaty regime and may be thus particularly influential in affecting arbitrator behaviour, intentionally or otherwise.[69] As to *what*, state signals might include: *exit* actions such as the denouncement of the ICSID Convention[70] and the termination of IIAs; *voice* actions such as the adoption of more sovereignty-sensitive model IIAs; or *mixed* actions such as moratoriums on the signing of new IIAs, demands for renegotiations of IIAs or increasingly aggressive litigation tactics in defending ISDS claims.

Initially, investor-state arbitration was an obscure, largely unknown, and infrequently practiced specialization that attracted little attention. While the first modern BIT was signed in 1959,[71] it was not until 1968 that the first BIT providing for ISDS was signed,[72] and it took a further nineteen years until the first treaty-based arbitration was submitted.[73] After the first award in 1990,[74] there was only a slight trickle of cases

---

[69] Langford, Behn and Fauchald (n. 6). This section draws on Langford and Behn (n 15).
[70] *Convention on the Settlement of Investment Disputes Between States and Nationals of Other States* (ICSID Convention), 18 March 1965, 5 ILM 532.
[71] Pakistan-Germany BIT (1959).
[72] Indonesia-Netherlands BIT (1968).
[73] The first case under the ICSID Convention was filed in 1972 but this was a claim for a contractual breach: *Holiday Inn and Others v. Morocco*, ICSID Case No. ARB/72/1, settled.
[74] *Asian Agricultural Products v. Sri Lanka*, ICSID Case No. ARB/87/3, Award (27 June 1990).

throughout the 1990s, which we can describe as *pre-crisis*, and the field was largely overshadowed by contract-based investment and commercial arbitrations.

It was not until the early 2000s that the first high-profile investor-state arbitration cases occurred and a crisis began to build. These cases were raised under NAFTA against developed states, the most prominent being the *Loewen* case. Although dismissed on jurisdiction, the *Loewen* case revealed that the justice system of the United States had embarrassing shortcomings that might be challenged under international law, and that arbitrators might face significant political pressure when tasked with resolving these types of disputes.[75] Together with other NAFTA cases against the USA, Canada and Mexico, this early investor litigation highlighted a perceived threat to sovereignty and the regulatory autonomy of states. Significantly, this catalysed the production of a corrective interpretive note by the NAFTA Free Trade Commission in 2001 (with a more minimalist approach to the FET standard; see Chapter 9 by Yuliya Chernykh)[76] and the drafting of a new and influential US model BIT in 2004 (that was more deferential to state interests).[77]

Beyond NAFTA, several other cases in the early 2000s raised significant and specific concerns regarding the relationship between IIA standards and environmental or human rights-based policy measures.[78] These included the *Aguas del Tunari* case against Bolivia, which grew out of the infamous 'water wars of Cochabamba', resulting in the first-ever submission of an amicus curiae brief in an investor-state arbitration case;[79] some controversial examples of inconsistent

---

[75] *Loewen Group and Raymond Loewen* v. *United States*, ICSID Case No. ARB(AF)/98/3, Award (26 June 2003). See also A DePalma, 'NAFTA's Powerful Little Secret; Obscure Tribunals Settle Disputes, But Go Too Far, Critics Say', *New York Times* (11 March 2001).

[76] *Notes of Interpretation of Certain Chapter 11 Provisions*, NAFTA Free Trade Commission (20 July 2001); see G Kaufmann-Kohler, 'Interpretive Powers of the Free Trade Commission and the Rule of Law' in F Bachand (ed.), *Fifteen Years of NAFTA Chapter 11 Arbitration* (Juris, 2011) 175, 181–5.

[77] See Treaty Between the Government of the United States of America and the Government of [Country] Concerning the Encouragement and Reciprocal Protection of Investment, US Department of State (2004), and particularly the qualifications of the expropriation standard. See J Alvarez, 'The Return of the State' (2011) 20 *Minnesota Journal of International Law* 223, 235.

[78] See OK Fauchald, 'International Investment Law and Environmental Protection' in OK Fauchald and D Hunter (eds.), *Yearbook of International Environmental Law*, Vol. 17 (Oxford University Press, 2006) 3, 11–25.

[79] *Aguas del Tunari* v. *Bolivia*, ICSID Case No. ARB/02/3, settled.

case law;[80] and the *Lauder* and *CME* cases – in which two tribunals issued two different awards on essentially the same subject matter.[81]

In 2004 and 2005, the phrase 'legitimacy crisis' emerged in the academic scholarship for the first time, and the crisis discourse extended clearly beyond its NAFTA origins. The numerous investor-state arbitration awards rendered as a result of the Argentinian economic crisis of 2001–2002 were important in this regard,[82] as were the large number of cases filed against Venezuela, Bolivia and Ecuador following the passage of various nationalization laws; and the *Foresti* case against South Africa.[83] The result was not only expressions of displeasure but high-profile announcements of exit strategies. Bolivia (2007), Venezuela (2009) and Ecuador (2012) denounced the ICSID Convention; Ecuador and Bolivia terminated many of their BITs; and South Africa placed a moratorium on the signing of new IIAs pending an extensive policy review.[84] By the end of the first decade of the new millennium, the legitimacy crisis discourse and the practice of investor-state arbitration began to reach maturity.[85]

In the last six to seven years, the narrative of crisis became entrenched among a broader set of stakeholders but countervailing narratives also emerged sporadically. On the one hand, the Phillip Morris tobacco regulation cases against Australia[86] and Uruguay,[87] the energy utility Vattenfall cases against Germany,[88] and Chevron's 18 billion US dollar (USD) denial of justice case against Ecuador fuelled the critique[89] and triggered new partial exit strategies by

---

[80] SGS v. Pakistan, ICSID Case No. ARB/01/13, Award (6 August 2003); SGS v. Philippines, ICSID Case No. ARB/02/6, Award (29 January 2004).
[81] Lauder v. Czech Republic, UNCITRAL, Award (3 September 2001); CME v. Czech Republic, UNCITRAL, Final Award (14 March 2003).
[82] See, e.g. J Alvarez and K Khamsi, 'The Argentine Crisis and Foreign Investors. A Glimpse into the Heart of the Investment Regime' in K Sauvant (ed.), *Yearbook on International Investment Law and Policy 2008–2009* (Oxford University Press, 2009) 379.
[83] Piero Foresti and Others v. South Africa, ICSID Case No. ARB(AF)/07/01, discontinued.
[84] *Bilateral Investment Treaty Policy Framework Review*, Republic of South Africa, Department of Trade and Industry (June 2009).
[85] As the title of this book from the period indicates: M Waibel et al. (eds.), *The Backlash Against Investment Arbitration: Perceptions and Reality* (Kluwer, 2010).
[86] Philip Morris Asia v. Australia, PCA Case No. 2012-12, Jurisdiction Award (27 December 2015).
[87] Philip Morris Brands v. Uruguay, ICSID Case No. ARB/10/7, Award (8 July 2016).
[88] Vattenfall and Others v. Germany (Vattenfall I), ICSID Case No. ARB/09/6, settled; Vattenfall and Others v. Germany (Vattenfall II), ICSID Case No. ARB/12/12, pending.
[89] Chevron Corp and Texaco Petroleum Corp v. Ecuador (Chevron II), PCA Case No. 2009-23, pending.

a few states, including Australia[90] and the Czech Republic.[91] The discourse on the illegitimacy of investor-state arbitration moved into the public sphere for the first time in this period, while the popularity of ISDS as a preferable means of resolving foreign investment disputes only grew. During this period, the annual number of new cases registered rose and stabilized at around eighty.[92] Subject to investor-state arbitrations themselves or merely observing the growing criticism about the system, states made more attempts at exiting the regime by terminating and/or renegotiating some of their IIAs. Examples of states falling into this category include Romania, Indonesia, India and Poland.[93]

On the other hand, in the same period there was also a push by certain states to produce new agreements, indicating contradictory shifts in sovereign state policy that reflected a possible countervailing mood or tendency. Negotiations on new regional mega-agreements including ISDS provisions burst into life: the USA and the other NAFTA states formally joined (and largely took over) the negotiations for the Trans-Pacific Partnership (TPP). Moreover, negotiations for the Regional Comprehensive Economic Partnership (RCEP) among almost all South and East Asian states were launched and efforts to develop a Transatlantic Trade and Investment Partnership (TTIP) between the EU and the USA made progress.[94] In terms of bilateral treaties, the EU emerged as an IIA negotiator with third states following the entry into force of the Lisbon Treaty[95] and has sought to negotiate and sign new FTAs (including with Brazil, Peru, Colombia, Canada, India, Indonesia, Japan, Singapore and Vietnam). Brazil started signing new IIAs

[90] *Gillard Government Trade Policy Statement: Trading Our Way to More Jobs and Prosperity*, Australian Government, Department of Foreign Affairs and Trade (November 2011). This policy was reversed in 2013. See Chapter 2 by Szilárd Gáspár-Szilágyi and Maxim Usynin.
[91] K Gordon and J Pohl, 'Investment Treaties over Time: Treaty Practice and Interpretation in a Changing World' *OECD Working Papers on International Investment* (2015).
[92] See D Behn and OK Fauchald, 'Governments under Cross-Fire: Renewable Energy and International Economic Tribunals' (2015) 12(2) *Manchester Journal of International Economic Law* 117; PITAD (PluriCourts Investment Treaty Arbitration Database).
[93] See overview in Langford, Behn and Fauchald (n. 6); T Jones, 'Poland Threatens to Cancel BITs', *Global Arbitration Review* (26 February 2016).
[94] Mention of the TTIP was included in the United States president's state of the union address on the next day, and an announcement of new talks by the European Commission president came the day after that.
[95] The *Lisbon Treaty* conferred competence to the EU in the area of foreign direct investment for the first time: *Treaty of Lisbon Amending the Treaty on European Union and the Treaty Establishing the European Community*, 13 December 2007, 2007/C 306/01. See Chapter 2 by Szilárd Gáspár-Szilágyi and Maxim Usynin.

(although the new agreements have no options for investor-state arbitration) after famously refusing to ratify any of its previously signed agreements from the 1990s,[96] and Australia reversed its anti-ISDS policy and signed the TPP in February 2016.

To be sure, this mood change should not be overemphasized as more recent trends indicate that any renewed acceptance of the regime was short lived. In January 2017, Donald Trump entered office and immediately called for an end to US involvement in the TPP and the TTIP. He also led an effort to renegotiate the NAFTA. The result is a yet to be fully ratified treaty called the United States–Mexico–Canada Agreement (USMCA), which keeps ISDS provisions only between Mexico and the USA. The TPP agreement also re-emerged as the Comprehensive and Progressive Agreement for Trans-Pacific Partnership (CPTPP) and maintains ISDS options, but with numerous limiting provisions.

Additionally, this most recent period places the EU as a central player in the debate on the legitimacy of investor-state arbitration and what the future of the regime should look like. While accepting the utility of economic integration treaties, including those with provisions on investment protection, the EU is not entering into new agreements with traditional ISDS provisions. Instead the EU has envisioned an investment court system (ICS) to resolve investment-related disputes; and it is not only seeking to change its own treaties but has also advocated the pursuit of a multilateral investment court through its involvement in the recently launched UNCITRAL Working Group III on ISDS reform. Other recent developments do not bode well for the future of traditional ISDS. For example, in 2018 after nearly a decade-long fight, the Court of Justice of the European Union (CJEU) handed down its much awaited *Achmea* decision. The CJEU held that investor-state arbitration provisions in BITs concluded between EU Member States are incompatible with the EU legal order. Around the same time, Ecuador became the first state to completely exit the international investment regime by terminating every agreement that could result in an ISDS case against it. Furthermore, the Dutch government issued a new Model BIT that rolls back many of the investment protections that have previously labelled Dutch BITs as the 'gold standard'. And finally, state parties negotiating the Regional Comprehensive Partnership (RCEP) announced that there would be no

---

[96] P. Martini, 'Brazil's New Investment Treaties: Outside Looking ... Out?' *Kluwer Arbitration Blog* (15 June 2015).

ISDS in the agreement – a direct reversal of the negotiating positions at an earlier stage.

4.2 Empirical Strategy: Data and Results

How can we determine if investor-state arbitrators adjust their behaviour in response to the legitimacy crisis without asking arbitrators to disclose their approaches?

The first approach is doctrinal. Recent jurisprudential scholarship in investor-state arbitration suggests a potential reflex on a number of critical areas, whether it is an investor-state arbitration case involving an environmental component[97] or how investor-state arbitral tribunals analyse particular IIA standards such as the criteria for a breach of the (indirect) expropriation standard,[98] the FET standard,[99] the FPS standard,[100] MFN provisions[101] or the jurisdictional requirements relating to the definition of a 'foreign investor'.[102] The advantage of such a doctrinal approach is that it provides a fine-grained perspective on the legal mechanics of change and permits a focus on those areas which have attracted the most criticism. However, the disadvantage of a doctrinal lens is that it may simply track a symbolic rather than a material shift: arbitrators may simply craft and tweak their foregrounded discourse without visiting any real consequences upon actual decision-making.

Tracking the ongoing interaction between doctrine and factual and political contexts therefore also requires a broader aggregative perspective. An alternative approach is therefore quantitative. Our approach is thus outcome based and analyses patterns in arbitral tribunal decision-

---

[97] J Viñuales, 'Foreign Investment and the Environment in International Law: The Current State of Play' in K Miles (ed.), *Research Handbook on Environment and Investment Law* (Edward Elgar, 2018), ch. 2; D Behn and M Langford, 'Trumping the Environment? An Empirical Perspective on the Legitimacy of Investment Treaty Arbitration' (2017) 18 (1) *Journal of World Investment & Trade* 14–61.
[98] C Henckels, 'Indirect Expropriation and the Right to Regulate: Revisiting Proportionality Analysis and the Standard of Review in Investor-State Arbitration' (2012) 15(1) *Journal of International Economic Law* 223.
[99] R Dolzer, 'Fair and Equitable Treatment: Today's Contours' (2014) 12 *Santa Clara Journal of International Law* 7.
[100] S Alexandrov, 'The Evolution of the Full Protection and Security Standard' in M Kinnear et al. (eds.), *Building International Investment Law: The First 50 Years of ICSID* (Kluwer, 2015) 319.
[101] J Maupin, 'MFN-Based Jurisdiction in Investor-State Arbitration: Is There Any Hope for a Consistent Approach?' (2011) 14(1) *Journal of International Economic Law* 157.
[102] Van Harten (n. 10) 251.

making over time. Its prime advantage is its focus on the concrete nature of decisions and remedies, which cannot be obscured by written reasoning or oral speech.

Using a range of output variables, we firstly ask whether there is change in outcomes of investor-state arbitration cases across different periods of time. The measured outcomes are win/loss ratios for finally resolved cases, jurisdictional decisions, and liability/merits decisions, together with compensation ratios.

The data is obtained from a new and first-of-its-kind database (PITAD) that codes all investor-state arbitration cases since their inception.[103] As of 1 August 2017, the dataset included 389 finally resolved cases, based on a treaty, where the claimant-investor wins on the merits or loses on jurisdiction or the merits. These cases also include 748 discrete decisions, 453 on jurisdiction decisions[104] and 291 on liability/merits.[105] Both types of cases are useful in analysing responsiveness. 'Finally resolved' cases may capture diachronic strategic planning across a case, whereby arbitrators may allow a claimant-investor to win at the jurisdiction stage but not the liability/merits stage. 'Discrete decisions' may better capture synchronic signals from actors at a particular point in time.

The PITAD database also makes a distinction between full wins and partial wins. Figure 10.3 shows the *Any Win* success ratios across time for the claimant-investor at the jurisdiction stage and the liability/merits stage of the investor-state arbitration dispute. It also tracks the Any Win success ratios for finally resolved cases. Eyeballing the trends, it is relatively clear that claimant-investors did well in the first decade of litigation. In the period from 1990 to 2001, investors rarely lost at the jurisdiction stage (94 per cent success rate in thirty-two decisions) and they won in approximately 72 per cent of finally resolved cases (twenty-five cases) and 78 per cent of liability/merits awards (twenty-three decisions). From 2002, an observable drop in claimant-investor success occurs in finally resolved cases and liability/merits awards. The trend

[103] PluriCourts Investment Treaty Arbitration Database, www.jus.uio.no/pluricourts/english/topics/investment/research-projects/database.html, accessed 26 June 2019.
[104] The jurisdiction decisions include bifurcated and non-bifurcated cases. For a non-bifurcated case, a decision where the claimant-investor ultimately loses on the merits will be coded as two decisions: one jurisdiction decision counted as a win for the claimant-investor and one merits decision counted as a loss.
[105] These liability/merits decisions do not count quantum awards. In other words, a liability award in favour of a claimant-investor is counted in the same way as a merits award where damages are included.

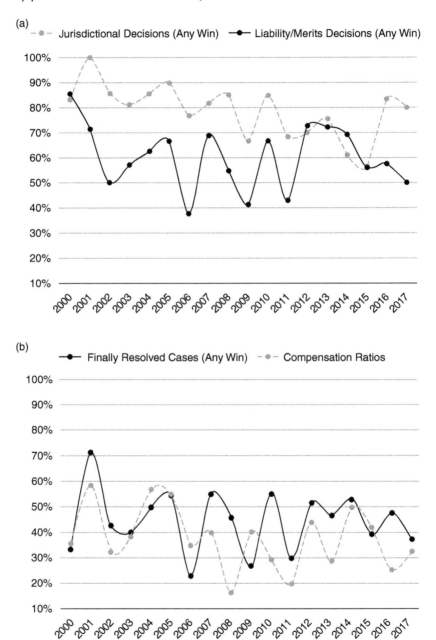

Figure 10.3 Claimant-investor success ratios (by year)

downwards appears to begin in 2002 and bottoms out a few years later. For the period of 2002 through 1 August 2017, success rates in finally resolved cases drop to 44 per cent for claimant-investors – not unlike the 50/50 ratio for trade decisions discussed in Section 3.

For liability/merits awards, the trends are slightly different. The success rates drop to 59 per cent for this period (2002 through 1 August 2017) overall, but there is a drift upwards in claimant-investor liability/merits awards successes from 2012, followed by a downward correction from about 2015. Jurisdictional decisions reveal a partially inverse pattern. There is a shift downwards to an average of 82 per cent success for investors in the period from 2002 to 2010, but a further drop downwards to about 69 per cent from 2011 onwards. These divergent patterns in recent years help explain why the success ratio for claimant-investors in finally resolved cases remains fairly steady at about 44 per cent throughout the period of 2002 through 1 August 2017 as jurisdiction and merits trends cancel each other out.

In addition, we created a compensation ratio in cases in which the claimant-investor won on the merits and was awarded compensation. The ratio is the amount awarded divided by the amount claimed. However, it could only be calculated for a subset of 148 cases (out of 178 cases where the investor won on the merits), since information on both the amount of compensation claimed and awarded was not always known. The ratio has a large amount of annual variation but a surprising amount of stability over time. Between 1990 and 2004, the ratio was 44 per cent; and fell to 36 per cent for the period 2005 onwards.

In seeking to test responsiveness expectations, we have operationalized the first hypothesis (State Signals) into different models. Each model tests the effects of a mood indicator with a lag of one year.

First, the State Signals hypothesis is operationalized by two separate indicators. The *State Mood I* indicator for treaty exits records a unilateral withdrawal by one state party to an IIA, including the ICSID Convention. As Figure 10.4 shows, this phenomenon begins in 2007 and peaks in 2008 (with nineteen treaty exits) and has remained at a steady annual average of about six treaty exits. An alternative version of this indicator weights the three ICSID Convention withdrawals by Latin American states by a factor of ten on the basis that they received tremendous media and academic coverage.

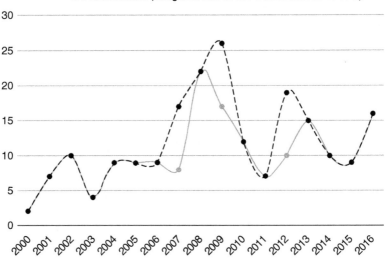

Figure 10.4 State Mood I – Number of unilateral treaty exits (by year)

The *State Mood II* indicator operationalizes a positive state signal and records the number of new treaties (IIAs) signed by year. This indicator is weighted for remaining available treaties that could be signed. As Figure 10.5 shows, the number trends steadily downwards throughout the 2000s.

In order to avoid potentially misleading bivariate results for the correlation between these three indicators and investor-state arbitration outcomes, we include a set of controls for each model. The basic attributes are summarized in Table 10.2 alongside the independent variables. First, we include a dummy variable for treaty-based arbitration, specifically *NAFTA-based Cases* and *ICSID-administered Cases*.[106] Second, we apply an *Extractive Industry Cases* dummy measuring whether the investment leading to a claim is in the extractive industries economic sector. These cases often involve varying degrees of nationalization with the dispute centering on levels of compensation not liability (and thus claimant-investors will be

---

[106] We include this dummy because NAFTA-based arbitrations matured earlier, while ICSID-administered arbitrations are based on a specific treaty (the ICSID Convention) with some specific structural features. ICSID-administered cases constitute 59 per cent (523 of 878 ITA cases) of all known treaty-based arbitrations registered through 1 August 2017.

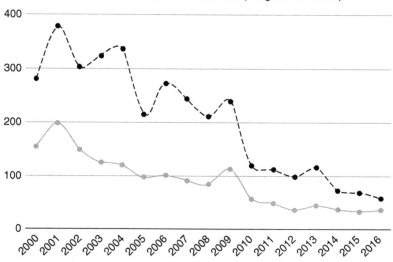

Figure 10.5 State Mood II – Number of new treaties signed (by year)

more likely to win). Third, we add a measure of *Law Firm Advantage* to control for the effect of the quality (or at least the expense) of legal counsel as measured by whether claimant-investors and respondent states retained counsel from a Global 100 law firm.[107] Fourth, we include a dummy variable for *State Learning* to control for the effect of previous exposure to investor-state arbitration.[108] Fifth, to control for situations where specific events or circumstances create an artificially large caseload against a respondent state in a short space of time, we use a *Case Cluster* dummy.[109] Sixth, we include

---

[107] See *American Lawyer*, www.law.com/americanlawyer/sites/americanlawyer/2017/09/25/the-2017-global-100/, accessed 1 June 2019. The dummy takes the value of (1) if only the claimant-investor counsel is from a Global 100 law firm; (-1) if only the respondent state retains a Global 100 law firm; or (0) if both the claimant-investor and the respondent state both have the same type of law firm representing them.

[108] We assume the marginal effect of state learning to diminish over time, and code how many cases any given respondent state has had filed against it at the time of case registration up until the tenth case.

[109] This measure takes the value of (1) if a respondent state has had five or more cases registered against it in a given year, and (0) otherwise. The case clusters in the full set of cases registered are: Argentina (2002, 2003, 2004), Czech Republic (2005), Ukraine (2008), Egypt (2011) and Venezuela (2011, 2012).

a *GDP Per Capita (Logged)* for respondent states as a control, particularly since states with lower GDP per capita are more likely to lose.[110] Finally, we have included a cubic year trend variable in all models.

However, this explanatory model has limits. It does not capture all potential reasons for claimant-investor success rates. First, states may adopt strategies that directly affect the underlying legal framework (i.e. the IIAs themselves) in which investor-state arbitrators operate. We doubt, however, that the legal framework governing foreign investment is particularly important as almost all of the decisions under analysis in this chapter are based on IIAs that were drafted before the emergence of the legitimacy crisis. Moreover, even where there is an arbitration based on a newer generation IIA, expected outcomes are not always generated.[111] Second, the relationship between claimant-investor success and future litigation may be partly endogenous. The growing awareness of the open legal opportunity structure[112] of investor-state arbitration may have prompted foreign investors to bring more dubious cases. However, the likelihood of claimant-investor success dropped quite early – well before the possibility of a wave of dubious cases entering the system. In the case of jurisdiction decisions, this endogeneity argument may have more explanatory power given the more recent decrease in claimant-investor success at this stage of the proceedings. Yet, even this might be explained by reflexivity – with arbitrators tightening jurisdictional criteria as a response to the legitimacy crisis. In any case, separating out these effects is a clear task for a future research agenda.

Table 10.1 below sets out the logit regression results. The controls in Model 1 are largely as expected. Law Firm Advantage and Extractive Industry Case controls are positively correlated with claimant-investor success while respondent state development status (as measured by GDP Per Capita (Logged)) is negatively correlated. The remaining control variables are not statistically significant and carry the expected sign with the exception of State Learning; respondent states do not appear to gain an advantage from facing repeat litigation.

---

[110] See D Behn, T Berge and M Langford, 'Poor States or Poor Governance? Explaining Outcomes in Investment Treaty Arbitration' (2018) 38(3) *Northwestern Journal of International & Business Law* 333.
[111] See Behn and Langford (n. 97); Alschner and Hui (n. 23).
[112] C Hilson, 'New Social Movements: The Role of Legal Opportunity' (2002) 9 *Journal of European Public Policy* 238.

Table 10.1 *Logit regression results for state mood*

	Controls	Treaty Exits	New Treaties	All
	Model 0	Model 1	Model 2	Model 3
Independent Variables				
State Mood I (Treaty Exits)		−0.03		−0.03
State Mood II (New Treaties)			0.01	0.01*
Controls				
NAFTA-based Case	−0.44	−0.50	−0.48	−0.53
ICSID-administered Case	−0.14	−0.15	−0.16	−0.17
Extractive Industry Case	0.58**	0.60**	0.58**	0.59**
Law Firm Advantage	0.38*	0.34*	0.35*	0.31
State Learning	0.06	0.07*	0.06*	0.07*
Case Cluster	0.70	0.63	0.70*	0.62
GDP Per Capita (Logged)	−0.33**	−0.34**	−0.33***	−0.35***
Cubic Year Trend	−0.00004**	−0.00004**	0.00008	−0.00005
Chi^2	33.80	39.40	36.13	40.03
Observations (Number of Cases)	388	388	388	388

* $p<.10$; ** $p<.05$; *** $p<.01$

Turning to the State Mood I indicator, the coefficient is negative as expected. An increase in unilateral IIA exits corresponds with a decrease in claimant-investor success. While this indicator is not significant in Model 1 and the full Model 3, it is so for the subset of liability/merits decisions.[113] The State Mood II indicator is positive, also as expected, but only significant in Model 4. A rise in the number of IIAs signed correlates with investor success.

We now look at the magnitude of the measured shift. In other words, how much work do these factors (which have been significant in some or many models) potentially do in explaining variation in outcomes? This can be graphically observed in Figure 10.6. It shows the predicted probabilities for five-unit differences in the treaty exits (State Mood I) indicator. Holding all other variables constant at their means, the

---

[113] See extra tables at www.jus.uio.no/pluricourts/english/topics/investment/research-projects/database.html, accessed 1 June 2019.

Table 10.2 *Summary statistics – fully resolved investor-state arbitration cases*

	Mean	Std. Dev.	Min	Max	Obs.
Outcome Variable					
Any Win	0.45	0.50	0	1	389
Independent Variables					
State Mood I (Treaty Exits)	13.01	6.01	2	26	389
State Mood II (New Treaties)	74.89	43.80	33	198	389
Controls					
NAFTA-based Case	0.09	0.29	0	1	389
ICSID-administered Case	0.62	0.48	0	1	389
Extractive Industry Case	0.17	0.38	0	1	389
Law Firm Advantage	−0.10	0.56	−1	1	389
State Learning	5.84	4.09	1	10	389
Case Cluster	0.11	0.31	0	1	389
GDP per Capita (Logged)	8.71	1.09	5.37	11.01	388

probability of a claimant-investor win is 56 per cent when the treaty exit indicator is at zero. Yet, it falls to 38 per cent when the number of annual IIA exits rises to twenty-five (which occurred in 2009). These differences are noticeable but not enormous.

In the case of the new treaties (State Mood II) indicator, the differences across the indicator's range are even more dramatic. Holding all other variables constant, claimant-investors achieved 80 per cent success rates in lagged years where there were close to 200 IIAs that were signed annually. But this drops to 30 per cent in lagged years where the number of annual IIAs signed bottoms out at thirty per year (see Figure 10.7). However, it is important to note that the confidence intervals at the ends of ranges for both State Mood indicators are large.

Overall, the tests on these yearly indicators suggest a weak or modest relationship between stakeholder mood and arbitral outcomes. The significance of the correlations is sensitive to changes in the model and sample period. Variables such as development and case-type (e.g. the extractives sector) explain significantly more of the variance in outcomes.

The next stakeholder hypothesis, Influential State Signals, is measured differently. We break up outcomes according to five three-year crisis

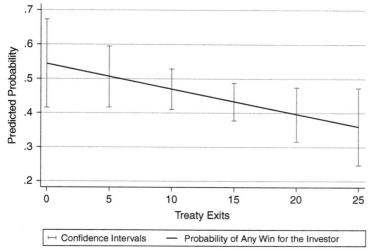

Figure 10.6 Predicted outcomes for State Mood I (treaty exits)

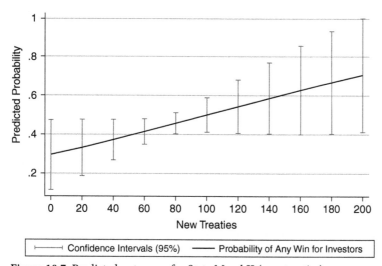

Figure 10.7 Predicted outcomes for State Mood II (new treaties)

periods that follow 2001 and correspond to our analysis in Section 4.1. This disaggregation allows us to examine possible structural breaks after interventions by a small number of large influential states (primarily the USA but also the EU) that we believe may have disproportionate signalling power. It is a crude approach but may better reflect the nature of legal adjudication with periodic rather than frequent paradigm shifts – i.e. 'doctrinal time'.[114] The key structural breaks relating to influential states are the pro-state signals sent by the NAFTA state parties after the issuance of the FTC Interpretive Note in 2001 and the release of the new US model BIT in 2004; and the pro-investor signals sent by the ramping up of negotiations[115] by the USA, the EU and China for large-scale bilateral and plurilateral trade and investment treaties (that include ISDS), particularly after February 2013.

Controlling for the same factors as above, Figure 10.8 shows the predicted probabilities in each period for claimant-investor success. It is notable that the probability of success does fall after the first break (after 2001) and the second break (after 2004) but the decrease in claimant-investor success is only statistically significant after the second break.[116] Turning to the last structural break (from 2013 to 2017), the probability of success rises and is not different (no statistical significance) from the period from 1990 to 2001. While the p-scores hover just over the 10 per cent level, the large confidence interval for 2014 to 1 August 2017 reveals the fact that many claimant-investors are enjoying success that is almost comparable to the first phase of investment arbitration. While the measure is crude, the recent pattern may suggest that the enthusiasm of influential states for investment treaties in that period may have exercised a renewed subtle influence on investor-state arbitrators. As discussed above, this enthusiasm partly tapered off in 2018 and 2019 but these years fall outside the sample.

Finally, we look at the Prominent Adjudicators hypothesis, which codes for the presence of an investor-state arbitration tribunal chair who has rendered five or more decisions (as a tribunal chair). Using an interaction term, we test whether the presence of a prominent tribunal president decreased the chances of claimant-investor success in the different periods after 2001 relative to other investor-state arbitration cases. Interestingly, the results are almost identical to those for trade. Investor-state arbitrations with a prominent tribunal chair were slightly more likely to award claimant-investors any success from 2005 onwards –

---

[114] P Rueda, 'Legal Language and Social Change during Colombia's Economic Crisis' in J Couso, A Huneeus and R Sieder (eds.), *Cultures of Legality: Judicialization and Political Activism in Latin America* (Cambridge University Press, 2010) 25–50.

[115] A number of these large bilateral and plurilateral negotiations were officially launched prior to 2012, but we use 2012 as the year when these negotiations ramped up significantly.

[116] See (n. 114).

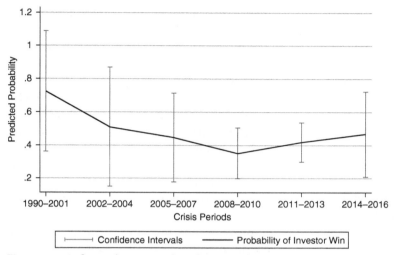

Figure 10.8 Influential state signals and structural breaks

the reverse of what was expected. However, the differences are not statistically significant.

5 Concluding Analysis

Since the mid-2000s, the international investment regime has been subject to a legitimacy crisis. And earlier, the international trade regime faced its own legitimacy crisis, particularly in the realm of dispute settlement. While both regimes have their ardent supporters, the mood of various stakeholders – from a diverse group of states, scholars and global social movements – has tilted towards viewing each regime as biased and/or flawed. We have not tried to solve this normative debate in this chapter but instead have focused on effects. We have asked whether trade adjudicators and investor-state arbitrators are reflexively evolving and have helped the system adapt to more legitimate and effective forms of international adjudication (by becoming more deferential to respondent states).

The chapter set out various rational choice and discursive-based reasons for thinking that trade adjudicators and investor-state arbitrators would be sensitive and adaptive. We countered these reasons with a competing set of legalistic (and attitudinal) reasons that may inhibit adjudicators from acting in such a fashion. Drawing from two new sets of data and research, we demonstrated that the WTO's adjudicative bodies tended to exercise greater judicial restraint when their institutional legitimacy declined. When governments voice greater criticism and dissatisfaction with how dispute panels and the AB are exercising their authority, these bodies respond by providing government agencies with slightly more domestic accommodation for adverse decisions. Turning to investment, we then demonstrated that there has been a significant drop in claimant-investor success across time and found suggestive evidence that investor-state arbitrators have moderately shifted their behaviour on some types of outcomes. Moreover, in both fields, we found modest evidence that powerful states (especially the USA and the EU) exert influence while more integrated and/or repeat adjudicators tend not to diverge from other adjudicators.

Overall, our main finding on reflexivity in the investment regime is that states matter. However, the empirical evidence suggests that the effect is much greater in the trade regime. Notably these results resonate with general doctrinal developments. Scholars point to strong corrections in trade jurisprudence and outcomes but investment jurisprudence tends to be characterized by fragmentation. Responsive doctrines emerge in some cases but approaches are not consistent.[117] These differences suggest that institutional design also matters. The investment arbitration regime may be less responsive to state signals because it lacks a centralized communication mechanism like the WTO. Signals ripple out diffusely in the sea of cases.

---

[117] See W Alschner, 'Correctness of Investment Awards: Why Wrong Decisions Don't Die', Special Issue of *The Law and Practice of International Courts and Tribunals* (forthcoming, 2020).

11

Epilogue: 'Convergence' Is a Many-Splendored Thing

JOSÉ E ALVAREZ

The distinguished editors of this collection of essays as well as the individual essay writers, circumspect scholars all, do not wear their normative agendas on their sleeves. For the most part, they do not express an explicit normative commitment that the trade and investment regimes *ought* to converge either structurally (so that, for example, both trade and investment disputes are resolved by the same dispute settlement methods or venues) or substantively (so that the same legal rules lead to the same results in the respective forums). The inquiries pursued in this book – based on comparing the two regimes' dispute system design, their respective use of precedent and their respective interpreters' interpretations of the law – are empirical, not normative. The editors and chapter authors do a careful job of limiting their conclusions to observations of facts on the ground. They do not espouse pre-determined articles of faith but are aware that other scholars have taken a normative stance on the binary expressed in this book's title.

Many international law scholars would prefer, all else being equal, to find evidence of structural or substance convergence. There are, as the editors of this book suggest, many underlying reasons: common interpretative techniques would allow the investment regime to respond to its legitimacy challenges in the (erstwhile) effective ways pursued by the WTO since the protests at Seattle; resort to common precedents would demonstrate both regimes' 'responsiveness' to desires for more coherent, consistent, stable, predictable and hierarchically respectful law; and uniform responses seem desirable at least with respect to parallel disputes filed in both trade and investment regimes. As the editors suggest, findings of convergence would also reshape our understanding of legal doctrine, orient the trajectory of IIA reform and rebuff criticisms of international law in general or of international economic law in particular.

There are other reasons to expect that scholars asked whether the adjudication of trade and investment disputes leads to convergence would answer with an emphatic 'yes'. There are abundant rival casebooks on the respective trade and investment regimes and a collection of essays that merely describes their disparate case law would be superfluous. And there are less banal reasons to expect confident 'convergence' findings. Consider the editors' initial framing of the question within the 'general debate on the fragmentation of international law.'[1] As is suggested by the work product of the International Law Commission, most international lawyers are disciples of multilateralism who hope that the disparate dispute settlement systems of ISDS and the WTO may, in this era of institutional challenge-cum-reform, creep towards one another, thereby becoming tools of legal defragmentation.[2] Opting for harmonious rules across the two most significant regimes of international economic law is an act of professional self-preservation. If the internationalization of distinct subject matter and the proliferation of international dispute settlers were to lead to wholly disparate legal regimes existing in separate silos, what would be the fate of those whose expertise is inter-national (and therefore inter-regime) law? Today, the angst that once greeted the 'proliferation' of international courts and tribunals has given way in many quarters to the belief (hope?) that these dispute settlers, however diverse, share common sociologically engrained traits – such as a shared affinity for jurisprudential precedents that head in the same direction.[3] For those committed to international law's progress narrative, it may simply be easier to believe that

---

[1] Szilárd Gáspár-Szilágyi, Daniel Behn and Malcolm Langford, Chapter 1.
[2] See International Law Commission, 'Fragmentation of International Law: Difficulties Arising from the Diversification and Expansion of International Law', Report, A/CN.4/L.682 (13 Apr. 2006).
[3] Compare Benedict Kingsbury, 'Is the Proliferation of International Courts and Tribunals a Systemic Problem?' (1999) 31 *NYU J. Int'l L. & Pol.* 679 to Joost Pauwelyn and Manfred Elsig, 'The Politics of Treaty Interpretation: Variations and Explanations across International Tribunals' in Jeffrey L Dunoff and Mark A Pollack (eds.), *Interdisciplinary Perspectives on International Law and International Relations* (Cambridge University Press, 2013) 445, 456 (discussing the ICJ, the WTO's Appellate Body, ISDS, the ECtHR and the IACHR as examples of international adjudicators that are systemic followers of precedent). See also Ingo Venzke, 'Making General Exceptions: The Spell of Precedents in Developing Article XX GATT into Standards for Domestic Regulatory Policy' (2011) 12 *German L. J.* 1111.

'the historical arc of proliferating courts and tribunals bends toward harmonization'.[4]

This book avoids the twin pitfalls of describing (yet again) the different trade and investment regimes or of becoming a vehicle for expressions of faith over experience. Despite the book's title, neither its editors nor its chapter authors see 'convergence *or* divergence' as a binary amenable to a single 'progressive' choice. As the editors refreshingly acknowledge in their introduction, '[n]ot all convergence may be healthy'.[5] From the start, the editors outline the competing reasons that might produce either outcome and, crucially, refuse to offer a definition of 'convergence' because of its 'complexity'.[6] Chapter authors take complexity as their byword, even at the risk of alienating readers looking for reassuring evidence of any of the positive-sounding synonyms for convergence, such as 'harmonization', 'unification', 'Europeanization', 'internationalization' or 'defragmentation'.[7]

Szilárd Gáspár-Szilágyi and Maxim Usynin's contribution finds nuance, and not a predictable recipe for trade/investment law convergence, in the increasing turn to what they call preferential trade agreements (PTAs) containing both trade and investment chapters. They find that the contents of these PTAs vary – including with respect to the extent they contain even basic NT and MFN obligations – as do their underlying rationales. Finding that these agreements also do not deviate from the traditional demarcation of dispute settlement to distinct chapters and epistemic communities, the two authors are sceptical that these treaties are effective vehicles of standardized trade/investment law at least beyond the regional level where these PTAs are found.

Hannes Lenk's chapter casts doubt on the proposition that the latest shiny object intended to produce at least investment law harmonization (if not more) – the EU's Investment Court System (ICS) – will become a stepping-stone towards trade/investment law convergence. He doubts whether the EU's establishment of multiple courts will lead even to a single multilateral investment court. Although the ICS seems to be

---

[4] Compare Dr. Martin Luther King, Jr., 'Remaining Awake Through a Great Revolution', Speech at the National Cathedral, 31 Mar. 1968 ('We shall prevail because the arc of the universe is long but it bends towards justice.').
[5] Gáspár-Szilágyi, Behn and Langford, Chapter 1.
[6] Ibid.
[7] Ibid. (enumerating various synonyms for 'convergence'). One might add 'Americanization' to the editors' list.

modelled on the WTO's Dispute Settlement System, Lenk goes beyond superficial structural similarities to identify the differences at the granular level among the envisioned investment courts contained in the CETA, the EU-Vietnam and the EU-Singapore agreements. He concludes that the EU's model court is unlikely to be a more effective vehicle for producing coherent, predictable law than is existing ad hoc cross-citation among ISDS arbitrators.[8]

Murilo Lubambo's examination of the rise (and fall) of entry rights in international investment agreements (IIAs) tells an equally complicated story. Lubambo agrees that some contemporary IIAs cut back on the enforcement of a set of substantive rights that distinguishes IIAs from the post-entry rights of traders under the GATT Agreements. He finds evidence that many recent IIAs make it harder for investors to successfully demand a right to invest. Whether this development – which applies after all only to some IIAs and not to others – is really a story of 'convergence' across the trade and investment regimes he leaves to readers to decide.

Niccolò Ridi's chapter targets the myth that trade and investment adjudicators' growing reliance on 'precedent' will lead to harmonious trade/investment law. In his account, WTO and ISDS arbitrators rely on external sources of authority for different things, for different reasons and to different extent. Whereas WTO adjudicators cite case law precedent for propositions of general international law and not trade law as such, ISDS arbitrators, who have greater motivations (namely, reputation, self-empowerment and legitimacy) to cite the views of others, rely on such sources more generally, including with respect to the meaning of some of the underlying investment obligations. Echoing the bottom line of other chapters, Ridi concludes that 'the question of whether the use of external precedent prompts interaction and convergence is complex'.[9]

Michelle Q Zang resists the binary of convergence/dissonance altogether. She chooses to describe the relationship between the two regimes – including the evidence of cross-citation between their adjudicators – in terms of 'engagement', a term defined as occupying 'a large middle ground on the continuum between resistance and convergence'.[10]

Ridhi Kabra, addressing how the WTO Appellate Body and ICSID tribunals have used their respective 'inherent powers', is equally cautious

---

[8] Hannes Lenk, Chapter 3.
[9] Niccolò Ridi, Chapter 5.
[10] Michelle Zang, Chapter 6.

in declaring a clear winner in favour of convergence. Her chapter accepts that both sets of adjudicators resort to the concept of inherent powers but points out that they do not apply these powers to the same ends. Kabra argues that while both sets of adjudicators have used their inherent powers to admit amicus briefs, they have differed on whether such powers permit them to rule on questions of admissibility. For her the broader lesson is that how inherent powers are used depends on the distinct institutional features of the particular adjudicative mechanism – its origins, its structure, its disputes, its limits. She concludes that 'any attempts at promoting convergence in the adjudicative law of these bodies must be mindful of the carefully structured differences in the institutional set-up and functioning of these bodies'.[11]

Yuliya Chernykh's chapter casts doubt on the proposition that the trade and investment regimes are converging to the extent that both are increasingly deploying political mechanisms for interpretation/enforcement alongside 'de-political' dispute settlement. She discusses the rise of commissions/committees authorized to issue authoritative interpretations of IIAs by their state parties and accepts that comparable limits on delegated adjudicatory authority has been a feature of the WTO regime, at least since its Ministerial Conference and, in its absence, the General Council has been authorized to issue binding interpretations. Chernykh describes the turn to committee interpretations in the investment regime as an effort to 'tame' its arbitrators and thereby re-politicize investment disputes. But Chernykh points out that few such interpretations have been issued despite the number of IIAs containing such provisions – perhaps because of their problematic nature in a regime designed precisely to avoid a return to state involvement in the resolution of investor-state disputes. Her chapter also identifies the differences between the functions of party-issued interpretations in the WTO – involving over 150 parties – and their role in IIAs that may encompass as few as two state parties. Like Kabra, she contends that institutional structure matters and that the functions of such interpretations may be starkly different in the two regimes. Chernykh seems at the very least agnostic about the possibility that a mechanism for interstate interpretations can serve as a comparable 'check and balance' conducive to convergence. Like other authors here, she ends on a cautionary note: 'this chapter aims to open a perspective on convergence's flaws as a concept'.[12]

---

[11] Ridhi Kabra, Chapter 7.
[12] Yuliya Chernykh, Chapter 9.

Caution amidst regime complexity also seems to characterize the conclusions reached by Malcolm Langford, Cosette D Creamer and Daniel Behn. In their chapter, these authors approach the convergence/dissonance question indirectly. They ask whether the regimes' adjudicators respond to sovereign backlash and/or specific critiques of their rulings as would state 'agents' or ignore them as would 'trustees' for the rule of law. The chapter argues that there is evidence that both sets of adjudicators are responsive to signals from states and other stakeholders and that those who judge trade and investment disputes are not the legal positivists operating in an apolitical vacuum that some idealists would like to believe exist. At the same time, theirs is no more a simple convergence story than any of the other chapters. The authors suggest that the centralized WTO DSU – and the opportunity that it accords WTO members and secretariat officials to transmit rhetorical signals to the WTO's adjudicators – makes the trade regime all the more likely to be 'responsive' to changing government preferences or at least makes that responsiveness easier to assess than the comparable phenomenon among ad hoc investment arbitrators. Further, as the authors acknowledge, the capacity to measure the extent to which ISDS arbitrators are more like 'agents' than 'trustees' is made more difficult by the number of ways sovereign backlash may be given effect – including termination of IIAs or the conclusion of more sovereign-sensitive IIAs – and the complexity of isolating the (non-endogenous) factors that might explain changing levels of claimant-investor success over time. In the end, the careful empiricists who authored this chapter acknowledge, as do the other chapter authors, that the structural differences between the two regimes make it difficult to say that both are equally susceptible to what they call 'reciprocity' or that adjudicator responsiveness in both regimes will lead to comparable substantive rules or outcomes. While Langford, Creamer and Behn conclude that there are 'strong reasons to expect that a primary goal of panellists and Appellate Body members is to increase political support for and the institutional legitimacy of the DSM',[13] they express no similar confidence about the 'primary goal' of ISDS arbitrators. Of course, to the extent these authors are right that both regimes respond to political concerns, it is a separate question whether the politics of trade in goods and capital flows will pull in the same directions and to the same ends.

[13] Malcolm Langford, Cosette Creamer and Daniel Behn, Chapter 10.

Notably, they find that the magnitude of responsiveness for WTO adjudicators is greater than that of investment arbitrators.

The only chapter in the book that finds clear evidence of substantive convergence across the two regimes is Graham Cook's essay on how trade and investment arbitrators have interpreted the standard rule of interpretation (contained in Article 31(1) of the Vienna Convention on the Law of Treaties) that a treaty should be interpreted in light of its 'object and purpose'. Cook demonstrates how trade and investment adjudicators have given the same answers to five key questions about the meaning of the notoriously ambiguous term, 'object and purpose'. This chapter will reassure those looking for evidence that international law contains some 'secondary rules' essential to HLA Hart's legal system and not merely motley bric-a-brac rules. It provides an example where both sets of arbitrators equally charged with adhering to the customary rules of treaty interpretation codified in the VCLT have turned to the 'common law of international adjudication' for harmonious answers. Cook argues that the consistent intra-regime interpretations of 'object and purpose' are remarkable instances of parallelism 'without any express reliance on prior precedent, and without any demonstrated mutual awareness of the practice of other international tribunals'.[14] For this reason, he calls this 'convergence without interaction'.[15]

But even Cook's example does not necessarily bode converging substantive law for the two regimes. Interpreting object and purpose in the five ways that Cook describes is most consistent with the view that traditional VCLT rules of treaty interpretation are malleable guideposts well suited to advance the discretionary power of international adjudicators – as well as suitable rules in a world of increasingly diverse treaties and proliferating venues for their interpretation. While Cook may be correct that the adjudicators in the two regimes share the view that object and purpose permits article-by-article interpretations as well as varying consequentialist arguments, *as applied* this view is likely to lead to *divergent* interpretations of the relevant trade and investment treaties precisely because it gives adjudicators more discretion in what they consider relevant. On closer inspection, Cook's ostensible example of 'convergence' is as complex in its potential implications as are the topics addressed by the book's other authors.

---

[14] Graham Cook, Chapter 8.
[15] Ibid.

1 The Difficulties of Measuring 'Convergence'

Originally, the editors invited this author to contribute a chapter to this volume considering the use of WTO case law in investment arbitration. Over time, my proposed chapter became instead part of a book comparing the use of trade and European human rights law in investor-state arbitration.[16] My attempt to measure the degree of convergence between the two regimes by considering the number of times that investor-state arbitrators cite to WTO authority in their rulings followed a path set by others. Gabrielle Marceau, Arnau Izaguerri and Vladyslav Lanovoy had previously identified 36 investor-state rulings containing such references as part of a larger study that found 150 such references in total through 1 February 2013, across an impressive range of international adjudicative forums.[17] As part of my book on 'boundary crossings', I supplemented that earlier work by turning to the impressive database of publicly available arbitral investor-state rulings maintained by PluriCourts.[18] Within the 395 ISDS rulings in that database dating from 1990 through 28 June 2017, I found 58 (14.68 per cent) containing one or more references to WTO law.[19] To that list of fifty-eight, I added an additional eight rulings identified in the earlier Marceau-Izaguerri-Lanovoy Study (consisting mostly of interim rulings in cases that had been already included in the initial list of fifty-eight). I culled through the cumulative list of sixty-five

---

[16] José E Alvarez, *The Boundaries of Investment Arbitration* (Juris, 2018) (henceforth *Boundaries*).

[17] Gabrielle Marceau, Arnau Izaguerri and Vladyslav Lanovoy, 'The WTO's Influence on Other Dispute Settlement Mechanisms: A Lighthouse in the Storm of Fragmentation' (2013) 47 *Journal of World Trade* 481, 482 n.6 (henceforth Marceau-Izaguerri-Lanovoy Study). The Marceau-Izaguerri-Lanovoy Study identified citations in ISDS rulings to what those authors called the 'WTO acquis' – that is, references to both the rules in the covered agreements as well as its jurisprudence (Panel reports and Appellate Body rulings).

[18] PluriCourts Investment Treaty Arbitration Database (PITAD). See Daniel Behn et al., PITAD Investment Law and Arbitration Database: Version 1.0, Pluricourts Centre of Excellence, University of Oslo (31 Jan. 2019).

[19] At my request, Daniel Behn and his colleagues at PluriCourts ran a search in the PITAD for 'WTO', 'World Trade Organization', 'Appellate Body Report', 'Panel Report', and 'International Trade'. As of 28 June 2017 when the search was conducted, that database contained 395 publicly available rulings from the larger total of 571 then in existence (or 69.18 per cent of known rulings). The search for trade terms among the 395 yielded an original list of 58 ISDS rulings with at least one reference to the search terms from 1990 through 28 June 2017. That list of fifty-eight rulings is set forth in Appendix II, Alvarez, *Boundaries* (n. 16) p. 303.

investor-state rulings that referred at least once to WTO law and eliminated those that cited trade rulings merely *en passant*. I then examined the remaining thirty-five ISDS rulings – identified as Table II in my book – to see what these cases tell us about the extent of trade/investment law convergence.[20]

At the most general level my analysis of these rulings throws cold water on the proposition that these two regimes, which some see as wrongly separated at birth,[21] are converging around substantive common principles, standards or rules. The reasons for my scepticism can be briefly summarized. First, if significant trade-investment law convergence exists, it is not occurring through explicit reliance on WTO law by ISDS arbitrators. The small pool of ISDS rulings with more than a passing reference to trade law suggests that the relatively few WTO references occurring (at least through the nearly twenty-seven-year period examined by my study) involve an exceedingly narrow slice of the over 3,000 International Investment Agreements (IIAs) in existence. Of the thirty-five investment rulings that I found with a more than passing reference to WTO law, seventeen emerged from claims made under the NAFTA's Chapter 11 and another five showed up in rulings issued against Argentina in the wake of its economic crisis in 2001 under the US-Argentina BIT.[22] Two IIAs, in short, accounted for over half of these rulings.

Second, the references to WTO law that I found were narrow not only with respect to the numbers of IIAs involved; they were narrow with respect to the kinds of issues on which trade law was deemed relevant. Twelve of the references dealt with the meaning of national treatment (NT) and related questions (such as the relevance of the absence of something comparable to GATT Article XX when interpreting NT clauses).[23] This is not surprising since, as the attention paid to this in the scholarly literature suggests, the NT guarantee offered to traders and investors seems to be the most likely candidate for genuine 'trade-infused' investment law. At the same time, despite considerable attention to and debate about the prospects for cross-fertilization between the

---

[20] Alvarez, *Boundaries* (n. 16) Table II identifying 'Significant GATT/WTO References in ISDS Rulings', p. 311.
[21] See Tomer Broude, 'Investment and Trade: The "Lotte and Lisa" of International Economic Law?' (2011) International Law Forum Research Paper 10–11, https://papers.ssrn.com/sol3/papers.cfm?abstract_id=1957686, accessed 23 Aug. 2017.
[22] Alvarez, *Boundaries* (n. 16) p. 128.
[23] Ibid., p. 133.

trade and investment regimes with respect to the interpretation of MFN, ISDS arbitrators do not appear to rely on WTO when it comes to interpreting MFN provisions in IIAs.[24] The other rights typically included in IIAs – FET, unimpeded transfers of capital, the international minimum standard of treatment and umbrella clauses, which are unique to IIAs and with no clear counterparts in the GATT-covered agreements – rarely elicit trade law references. The exceptions were a few cases where investor-state arbitrators refer to WTO law when addressing the level of deference owed to states under, for example, FET.[25] Given the distinct remedies deployed in WTO dispute settlement – which are directed at states *inter se* and prospective – it is also not surprising that references to WTO jurisprudence do not appear when ISDS arbitrators address remedies, namely, the extent of or calculation of damages owed to investors.[26]

After references to national treatment, the next most numerous WTO citations in ISDS rulings in my study emerged from efforts to compare the exceptions in the GATT (Articles XX or XXI) to 'measures not precluded' clauses found in some IIAs. Most of these claims involved claims filed against Argentina.[27] The other WTO references made in ISDS rulings identified in my table involve: (1) one-off contentions arising from special factual circumstances (e.g. a trio of rulings arising from Mexico's 'counterclaim' defence to measures that it imposed on high fructose corn syrup);[28] (2) references to the customary rules of treaty interpretation (usually in the VCLT);[29] (3) certain alleged 'terms of art' common to both trade and investment regimes (e.g. the meaning of 'services', 'taxation', 'performance requirements', 'relating to' or 'government procurement'); (4) alleged 'general principles' of international law (such as the principles of proportionality, estoppel and good faith); or (5) assertions of ostensibly common rules of international

---

[24] Ibid., p. 125. Indeed, in one case an investor-state tribunal rejected an attempt to use the MFN provision in the GATT to trigger jurisdiction under a BIT (discussing *Menzies Middle EAR AND Africa S.A. et Aviation Handling Services International Ltd. v. Egypt*).

[25] Ibid., pp. 134 and 180–2 (discussing *Total v. Argentina*).

[26] But see Alvarez, *Boundaries* (n. 16) p. 166 (discussing the exceptional reference to WTO law in the discussion of remedies in *Cargill v. Mexico*).

[27] Ibid., pp. 173–84 (discussing *CMS v. Argentina, Enron Corporation v. Argentina, Sempra Energy v. Argentina, Continental Casualty v. Argentina, El Paso Energy v. Argentina* and *Total v. Argentina*).

[28] Ibid., pp. 157–66 (discussing *Archer Daniels Midland Co. v. Mexico, Corn Products v. Mexico* and *Cargill Inc. v. Mexico*).

[29] See also Graham Cook, Chapter 8.

procedure (such as the principle that the party that makes an affirmative claim has the burden of proof).[30]

What do the ISDS rulings that explicitly draw on WTO law tell us about the prospect for substantive convergence of those provisions? The rulings dealing with the meaning of national treatment (almost entirely claims arising under the NAFTA's investment chapter (Chapter 11)) do not suggest that the older, well-established GATT/WTO jurisprudence on national treatment is being imported into the interpretation of investment law.[31] At the end of the day, despite multiple visitations of NT and discussions of the meaning of 'in like circumstances' as compared to 'like products', including with respect to a single treaty (the NAFTA) with a single NT text, I could only say with any confidence that *in some cases* the fact that two investors produce like products may or may not be relevant to determining whether they are 'in like circumstances'.[32] The rulings that I found tell us that sometimes, but not always, the state's regulatory concerns reflected in GATT Article XX are relevant to whether two investors are 'in like circumstances'. These are slim 'convergence' pickings despite over twenty years of attempts to use 'well-established' WTO jurisprudence. On the issue that is most likely to overlap with investment disputes – namely, whether a state's measures are a pretext to engage in protectionism – I found more evidence of substantive disagreement between trade and investment tribunals than agreement.

The rulings in my study also did not suggest that both sets of dispute settlers were coming to a common view on how to 'balance' the rights of traders of goods and investors vis-à-vis the regulatory needs of states. I found that ISDS arbitrators were generally reticent about relying on trade law-infused interpretations of the terms in IIAs and even when they did so, their reliance on WTO jurisprudence was cautious and nuanced. My study concluded that both advocates of greater 'convergence' between the trade and investment regimes and critics of the 'misuse' of

---

[30] Alvarez, *Boundaries* (n. 16) p. 135 and Table II.
[31] Ibid., p. 131. Despite claims that non-discrimination means the same thing in both regimes and reflect a common goal shared by both, namely, to resist protectionism, my study confirms the view that the meaning of NT in the trade and investment worlds are often distinguished. See also Nicholas DiMascio and Joost Pauwelyn, 'Nondiscrimination in Trade and Investment Treaties: Worlds Apart or Two Sides of the Same Coin?' (2008) 102 *AJIL* 48, 80.
[32] Alvarez, *Boundaries* (n. 16) pp. 195–6 (noting, for example, the listing in *Merrill & Ring* of the different ways that 'in like circumstances' had been interpreted by previous ISDS tribunals).

trade law in ISDS would be disappointed by these rulings. Relative to the number of investment claims and publicly available rulings, I found WTO law to be cited by ISDS arbitrators rarely and to be 'misused' even less.[33] Indeed, my comparison of the use of European Court of Human Rights (ECtHR) references in ISDS rulings suggested that European human rights law was at least as likely to be cited by ISDS arbitrators as was the law of the WTO.[34]

These conclusions are not inconsistent with those reached by prior studies of the same phenomenon conducted by Marceau, Izaguerri and Lanovoy. While that study found 150 references to trade law in the course of rulings under Free Trade Agreements, a great number of these WTO references occurred in the course of adjudicating the trade chapters of regional trade agreements, such as the NAFTA's trade chapters.[35] That regional adjudicators under the NAFTA's Chapter 19, for example, turn to WTO jurisprudence may provide some comfort to those that may be worried that such regional agreements will come to fragment trade law itself, but it says little about the broader WTO/investment convergence that is the subject of this book. Moreover, that earlier study also revealed that some thirty-six citations to WTO law in the course of ISDS involved references to general propositions, including general principles of treaty interpretation or general principles of law, or were used to interpret what Marceau and her colleagues called 'procedural' rules needed to resolve any dispute (including general rules of evidence and inherent powers arising from the judicial function).[36]

References to WTO jurisprudence to support the use of the customary rules of treaty interpretation, to indicate that a party that affirms a fact bears the general initial burden of proof, or to support the view that an international tribunal has the power to fill lacunae in its rules of procedure are all possible indicators that ISDS arbitrators respect the views of WTO panellists and its Appellate Body.[37] These citations may comfort

---

[33] This is certainly true to the extent misuse is shown by annulments. To date, no ISDS ruling has been annulled on the basis that it (wrongly) applied GATT/WTO law.

[34] My study, based on PITAD data over the comparable period, revealed virtually the same total number of ECHR/ECtHR citations (sixty-five rulings involving references to European human rights law). See Alvarez, *Boundaries* (n. 16), Appendix I, p. 269. See also ibid., Table I identifying 'Significant European Human Rights References ISDS Rulings', p. 275.

[35] Marceau-Izaguerri-Lanovoy Study (n. 17) Table 1, 483.

[36] Ibid., Table 1 and § 3.2 and § 3.3.

[37] See, e.g. Gregory Shaffer, Manfred Elsig and Sergio Puig, 'The Extensive (But Fragile) Authority of the WTO Appellate Body' (2016) 79 *Law and Contemporary Problems* 237,

'CONVERGENCE' IS A MANY-SPLENDORED THING 297

trade insiders familiar with the WTO's struggle to overcome its origins in power-oriented diplomacy; it suggests that at least in investment law circles, the WTO's DSU is seen as a legitimate tool for apolitical adjudication.[38] Some may find it heartening that both WTO and investor-state adjudicators rely on self-empowering rules (such as the principle of 'inherent powers' – see Chapter 7) that help to distinguish themselves from mere mediators and that associate them with judges empowered by compétence de la compétence. But, as noted above with respect to Cook's chapter, an ISDS ruling that relies on WTO law for general principles that are equally found in the jurisprudence of the ICJ or other international courts does not say much about whether the substantive law *of the WTO and investment* is itself converging.

It is important, however, to acknowledge the limitations of citation studies of this kind. Zang is not wrong to contend that such work, including my own, has limited value. As her chapter in this book suggests, there are distinct forms of 'engagement' that render explicit citation checks an inadequate 'parameter to mirror the relationship between the regimes'.[39] The two regimes may engage in other ways, apart from what happens at the final public stage of formal dispute settlement. The investment and trade regimes may be 'converging' through the work of a number of the WTO's committees,[40] through the abundant and non-transparent settlements reached even before a WTO panel under the DSU is convened, or, as Chernykh considers, through interpretations reached by interstate commissions or committees. Examining explicit citations made in public ISDS rulings also tells us nothing about whether the law governing the two regimes is converging without explicit cross-regime citation (as Cook suggests, happens with respect to the meaning of object and purpose). This can occur, for example, where an ISDS tribunal relies on the argument (frequently made in the course of WTO

262–3 (arguing that citations to the Appellate Body by other international courts is an indicator of what they call that body's 'extensive' authority).

[38] Ibid., pp. 267–72 (discussing the WTO's continuing struggles with politicization and compliance). See also Andrew D Mitchell and David Heaton, 'The Inherent Jurisdiction of WTO Tribunals: The Select Application of Public International Law Required by the Judicial Function' (2010) 131 *Mich. J. Intl L.* 559 (identifying and distinguishing rules applied by WTO adjudicators that are 'inherent' to the judicial function versus those that can be 'implied' from particular rules in the covered agreements, including the Dispute Settlement Understanding).

[39] Michelle Zang, Chapter 7.

[40] See, e.g. Andrew Lang and Joanne Scott, 'The Hidden World of WTO Governance' (2009) 20 *EJIL* 575.

disputes) that national treatment requires looking for comparators that produce 'directly substitutable' or 'competing products' in the marketplace – but does so without citing to WTO authority.[41]

Of course, citation studies are further limited by the database used.[42] Studies like mine also should not be seen as providing authoritative guidance on whether the WTO reference was initially made by the tribunal, one of the litigants or a third party amicus.[43] My own selective reading of some of the underlying briefs indicates that litigants and/or interveners referred to WTO law more often than the texts of arbitral rulings suggest. It is clear that ISDS arbitrators sometimes ignored trade law references made before them. What my table of thirty-five rulings most accurately captured is the extent to which ISDS arbitrators rely or cite to WTO law and the topics on which they do so. For all of these and many more reasons, citation analyses may overstate or understate the extent that trade law matters to the interpretation of IIAs.[44]

At a more granular level, my study of 'trade-infused investment law' yields the same conclusion reached by virtually all those involved in this book. Like most of them, I conclude that 'convergence' is a many-splendored thing, not an outcome reflective of a binary choice. My boundary-crossing book takes my table of thirty-five rulings as the starting point for a case-by-case description of how WTO law was used or rejected and why. In most of these instances, readers will probably come to different conclusions about whether the particular ruling reflects an example of 'convergence' or 'dissonance'. Consider the many instances in which WTO law is cited by ISDS arbitrators by way of

---

[41] This is also a limitation that applies to the Marceau-Izaguerri-Lanovoy Study. See also Cook, Chapter 8.

[42] Alvarez, *Boundaries* (n. 16) p. 3 (indicating that the designers of the PITAD estimated that, at the time my study was conducted, their database contained only 69.18 per cent of all known investor-state rulings; the PITAD only contained rulings from discontinued or settled cases to the extent these had been rendered after a jurisdictional ruling).

[43] While my table of thirty-five cases indicated which party referred to WTO law, this was based solely on what the arbitrators suggested in their rulings. In the absence of a comprehensive examination of all the pleadings (not all of which were public), these are not authoritative determinations.

[44] For a more detailed enumeration of hazards of citation analyses, see Alvarez, *Boundaries* (n. 16) pp. 48–9 and 131–3. Such studies may, for example, draw attention to WTO references that may appear in a single brief passage in an award of considerable length where there is little evidence that these had any impact on the final outcome. They may include references where WTO law is distinguished and even where an ISDS tribunal seems to assign some weight to trade law, it usually does so without any suggestion that WTO law is being 'applied' in terms of choice of law. See Alvarez, *Boundaries* (n. 16) pp. 214–16 (describing the usual reference to WTO law as essentially an analogy).

contrast – to suggest why investment law or the meaning of an IIA is *different* from a provision in the GATT-covered agreements (e.g. by way of showing why 'in similar circumstances' is different from 'like products' for purposes of a NT violation). One could argue that the convergence project goes off the rails most spectacularly on the multiple occasions where WTO provisions are explicitly distinguished from applicable investment law – as was the case with the NAFTA tribunal in *Methanex*.[45] While that tribunal in principle accepts that WTO law might provide interpretative guidance, it rejects that guidance on the meaning of 'relating to', refuses the invitation to read the NAFTA as permitting an 'envoi' to WTO law, objects to Methanex's idea that it should consider 'like products' as a stand-in for 'in like circumstances', and declines the claimant's invitation to use GATT Article XX and its burdens of proof to address the core contention that the USA had no good reason to prefer ethanol to methanol as a gas additive.[46] Whether *Methanex's* rulings on these matters are right or wrong, the fact remains that *Methanex's* refusal to identify 'in like circumstances' with 'like products' is reflected in other rulings in my study, such as *Merrill & Ring* and *Occidental*.[47]

These rulings are not examples of what most scholars or policymakers mean when they say trade law is 'affecting' the meaning of ISDS jurisprudence. And yet, at a more abstract level, the mere fact that ISDS arbitrators or litigants see WTO law as a relevant comparator – as all did in the *Methanex* case – supports Zang's concept of 'engagement'. Even when WTO case law is determined to be ultimately inapposite, ISDS arbitrators' reference to it indicates that it is a 'source of inspiration, evidence or authority'.[48] If 'convergence' includes such cases or if one considers the term to include ISDS references to general principles or procedural rules also used by WTO adjudicators (as does the Marceau-Izaguerri-Lanovoy Study), citation studies provide evidence of 'convergence'. At the other extreme, if 'convergence' means instances in which the substantive law of the WTO is incorporated lock, stock and barrel

---

[45] Alvarez, *Boundaries* (n. 16) pp. 143–50. As my case study demonstrates, while the *Methanex* tribunal does not completely reject the relevance of WTO jurisprudence (and, for example, uses it to justify its decision to admit amicus briefs), it generally refuses Methanex's efforts to incorporate WTO NT jurisprudence.

[46] See Alvarez, *Boundaries* (n. 16) pp. 143–50.

[47] Ibid., pp. 167–71 (discussing *Merrill & Ring v. Canada* and *Occidental Petroleum v. Ecuador*).

[48] Zang, Chapter 6.

into the interpretation of a substantial provision of an IIA, my work suggests that *that* is exceedingly rare. In my study I identify only "five rulings" (of the thirty-five rulings in my table) as clear examples of 'trade-infused' arbitral interpretations of substantive investment law.[49] Most of the other cases in my table are plausible examples of either convergence or dissonance depending on one's point of view and what future ISDS tribunals will do with these 'precedents'.[50]

2 Russia v. Ukraine: A Case Study of the Complexity of 'Convergence'

As noted above, WTO references have frequently appeared in ISDS rulings dealing with the interpretation of 'measures not precluded' (MNP) clauses in IIAs. ISDS arbitrators have repeatedly rejected Argentina's arguments that the provision in the US-Argentina BIT permitting a state to take 'measures necessary for the maintenance of public order, the fulfilment of its obligation with respect to the maintenance of restoration of international peace or security, or the protection of its own essential security interests' should be seen as 'self-judging' as is the exception in GATT Article XXI.[51] Taking their lead from rulings made by the International Court of Justice and the absence of relevant WTO case law on point, ISDS tribunals have distinguished the subjective language of Article XXI ('which it considers') from the 'objective' determination demanded by the MNP clause in the US-Argentina BIT

---

[49] Alvarez, *Boundaries* (n. 16) p. 186.
[50] Consider, for example, Methanex's use of WTO jurisprudence on inherent powers to support the admission of amicus briefs (an example of convergence discussed by Kabra in Chapter 7). While this holding arguably promotes 'defragmentation' among the procedural rules governing international adjudicative bodies, it may not ultimately produce convergence of the substantive rules governing trade and investment. Much depends on the amicus briefs accepted pursuant to the tribunals' newly found power and whether the respective adjudicators are persuaded by them. On the other hand, this 'procedural' ruling responds to common critiques of both regimes. While it may be disputed whether that ruling yields more convergence than dissonance, it is, in my view, a clear example of Zang's 'engagement' or what I call (more neutrally) 'trade-infused' investment law.
[51] Article XXI GATT provides in relevant part that '[n]othing in this Agreement shall be construed ... (b) to prevent any contracting party from taking any action which it considers necessary for the protection of its essential security interests (i) relating to fissionable materials ... ; (ii) relating to the traffic in arms, ammunition and implements of war ... ; (iii) taken in time of war or other emergency in international relations; or (c) ... any action in pursuance of its obligations under the United Nations Charter for the maintenance of international peace and security'. For descriptions of some of these cases, see Alvarez, *Boundaries* (n. 16) pp. 173–84.

(permitting states to take 'measures necessary').[52] While ISDS tribunals have differed on virtually every interpretative issue that has arisen with respect to MNP clauses in the Argentina cases, they have uniformly found that where an MPN clause like the one in the US-Argentina BIT appears that clause's 'objective' language enables the tribunal to determine for itself whether a state's claim that its actions were 'necessary' to defend its 'essential security' was established.[53] Since they were able to distinguish the language of the GATT's Article XXI from the typical MPN clause, ISDS tribunals never had to resolve whether the 'essential security' exception in the GATT was indeed 'self-judging' or instead was subject, as Argentina sometimes argued in the alternative, to some review to determine whether the exception was invoked in 'good faith'.

On 5 April 2019, for the first time, a WTO panel issued an interpretation of GATT Article XXI. In *Russia-Measures Concerning Traffic in Transit*, Ukraine complained about the WTO consistency of various rail and road restrictions imposed by Russia.[54] Russia argued that the panel had no jurisdiction to evaluate measures which it considered to be 'taken in time of war or other emergency in international relations' within the terms of GATT Article XXI(b)(iii).[55] Russia argued that serious security issues were intended to be 'kept out of the WTO, an organization which is not designed or equipped to handle such matters' and that involving the WTO in such political questions would 'upset the very delicate balance of obligations under the WTO Agreements and endanger the multilateral trading system'.[56] Accordingly, Russia did not present evidence to rebut Ukraine's specific claims but argued simply that

---

[52] For the distinct arguments made about the relevance of GATT Article XXI to the interpretation of the MPN clause in the US-Argentina BIT in the course of a number of ISDS rulings, see Alvarez, *Boundaries* (n. 16) pp. 174–5.

[53] See, e.g. José E Alvarez, *The Public International Law Regime Governing Foreign Investment* (ALI-Pocket, 2011), pp. 266–82 (noting that while all the tribunals rejected the contention that this exception was 'self-judging', the tribunals otherwise differed on the degree of deference to the states' determination that the requisite 'emergency' existed and whether the states' actions were indeed a 'necessary' response to that emergency). These distinctions turned, in part, on subsidiary determinations on whether the BIT's MNP clause was or was not distinct from the 'necessity' defence under customary international law (as codified in Article 25 of the Articles of State Responsibility) and whether a successful invocation of the MNP clause has no effect on liability, merely suspends liability while the emergency continues, or permanently excuses the state from any liability. Ibid., pp. 282–4.

[54] *Russia – Measures Concerning Traffic in Transit, Report of the Panel (Russia-Ukraine)*, WTO/DS512/R (5 Apr. 2019).

[55] Ibid., para. 7.4.

[56] Ibid., para. 7.22.

those claims were 'outside the Panel's terms of reference' simply because of Russia's invocation of Article XXI (b)(iii).[57]

In response to Russia's claims that the panel could not interfere with the 'internal and external affairs of a sovereign state' by doubting or evaluating a member's subjective assessment,[58] Ukraine argued that finding Article XXI to license such a unilateral determination by a state would violate WTO members' basic commitment to WTO dispute settlement.[59] Although Russia's views were endorsed by interveners such as the United States,[60] the panel affirmed that it possessed the 'inherent power' to decide its substantive jurisdiction and that the matter *was not* therefore 'self-judging'.[61]

Recalling that the traditional rules of treaty interpretation require 'good faith' applications of a treaty's text,[62] the panel decided that the subparagraphs of Article XXI (b) (i-iii) and (c) anticipate and require objective assessment and were not conditioned by the 'which it considers' language in the chapeau to Article XXI.[63] It found that the Article XXI subclause invoked by Russia, (iii), imposes a timeliness requirement, namely, that any measures be found as a matter of objective fact to be taken 'in time of' emergencies in international relations.[64] It also found that such emergencies required, given the like situations envisioned in Article XXI (b) (i-ii) and (c), grave situations comparable to armed conflicts or acute international crises requiring urgent action and not the existence of mere political or economic differences between members.[65] It therefore rejected the contention that Article XXI (b)(iii) was an 'incantation that shields a challenged measure from all scrutiny'.[66] By contrast to what many had assumed for decades, the WTO panel found that this exception was not 'self-judging' in the manner asserted by Russia[67] or 'non-justiciable' as argued by the United States.[68]

[57] Ibid., para. 7.23.
[58] Ibid., para. 7.29.
[59] Ibid., para. 7.31.
[60] Ibid., para. 7.51 (arguing that a WTO member has the authority 'to determine for itself those matters that it considers necessary' as an 'inherent right'); ibid., para. 7.52 (the dispute is 'non-justiciable' for lack of legal criteria).
[61] Ibid., para. 7.53.
[62] Ibid., para. 7.59.
[63] Ibid., para. 7.82.
[64] Ibid., paras. 7.70, 7.77.
[65] Ibid., paras. 7.71–75; 7.81.
[66] Ibid., para. 7.100.
[67] Ibid., para. 7.102.
[68] Ibid., para. 7.103.

The *Russia-Ukraine* panel then proceeded to evaluate Russia's measures in light of the requirements of Article XXI. It concluded that these measures were justified because they were indeed taken during a time of 'heightened tension or crisis' involving a publicly known emergency, affirmed by the UN itself, involving Ukraine, and that affected the security of Russia's border.[69] In response to Ukraine's argument that Russia had failed to identify the essential security interests that were threatened or the connection between Russia's actions and those interests, the panel found that while 'essential security interests' were indeed narrower than 'security interests', they referred to matters 'relating to the quintessential functions of the state, namely, the protection of its territory and its population from external threats, and the maintenance of law and public order internally'.[70] The panel concluded that Article XXI needed to be applied in 'good faith' not only to a state's definition of the essential security interests ostensibly at stake, but also to the connection between those interests and any challenged measures.[71] It also found that the requirement of good faith would not license a state's invocation of its essential security as a means to 'circumvent' its WTO obligations by, for example, simply relabelling its trade concerns as 'essential security'.[72] It indicated that the burden put on a state to articulate the threat to its essential security varies depending on the severity of the emergency that it faced; a state would face a higher burden of proof the further removed the 'emergency in international relations' required by (b) (iii) was from the situations of armed conflict at the heart of essential security threats.[73]

Applying these good faith tests to the facts at hand, the panel found Russia's articulation of its essential security interests 'minimally satisfactory' since the emergency in this case was 'very close to the "hard core" of war or armed conflict'; there was nothing to suggest Russia's measures were a means to circumvent its WTO obligations; its measures were 'not implausible as measures protective' of Russia's essential security; and Russia's measures were not so remote from or unrelated to the existing emergency between the two states.[74] For these reasons, the panel found that Russia had indeed met the requirements for invoking Article XXI.

---

[69] Ibid., paras. 7.119–7.122; 7.125.
[70] Ibid., para. 7.130.
[71] Ibid., para. 7.138.
[72] Ibid., paras. 7.132–7.133.
[73] Ibid., para. 7.135.
[74] Ibid., paras. 7.136–7.145.

The *Russia-Ukraine* panel ruling, which will probably not be appealed, is likely to be seen as a potent example of trade-investment law 'convergence' for a number of understandable reasons. That ruling establishes, first, that despite suggestions to the contrary by the International Court of Justice and scholars, as well as a number of ISDS tribunals, the exceptions for measures taken for 'essential security' in some BITs and the GATT are not worlds apart where only the first is subject to impartial objective evaluation and the second is a wholly self-judging excuse tantamount to the 'get out of jail free' card in Monopoly. The *Russia-Ukraine* panel is likely to open the door to impartial adjudicative scrutiny of 'emergency' action in the trade regime – as has been the case for some time under IIAs.

Second, once the *Russia-Ukraine* panel engaged in its 'good faith' review of the Russian defence, it made a number of substantive findings that parallel some of those articulated by those ISDS tribunals that had to rule on Argentina's invocation of the essential security exception in BITs. The relatively narrow interpretation in *Russia-Ukraine* of what constitutes an 'essential security' threat or an 'emergency in international relations' for purposes of the chapeau in Article XXI and Article XXI (b)(iii), is, for example, consistent with the narrow interpretation of what constitute such essential security threats in the original ISDS panel in *Enron v. Argentina*.[75] On the other hand, the ultimate deference accorded to Russia's invocation of its essential security by the WTO panel echoes the deference given to Argentina in ISDS rulings such as *LG & E v. Argentina*.[76]

Third, the *Russia-Ukraine* ruling provides examples of the cross-utilization of common legal principles – good faith, inherent power, compétence de la compétence, proportionality balancing – without resort to explicit cross-citation of external authority.[77] The *Russia-Ukraine*'s panel findings that it has the 'inherent power' to determine its own jurisdiction echoes the rulings cited in Kabra's chapter. Its

---

[75] *Enron Corp. v. Argentina*, Award, ICSID Case No. ARB/01/2 (22 May 2007), para. 306 (an 'essential interest' needs to 'compromise the very existence of the State and its independence'). Note that this is consistent with the customary defence of necessity as stated in the Articles of State Responsibility (requiring the state to show that its action was 'the only way to safeguard an essential interest against a grave and imminent peril'). Articles on State Responsibility, Article 25 (1)(a).

[76] See *LG & E Energy Corp. v. Argentina*, Decision on Liability, ICSID Case No. ARB/02/1 (3 Oct. 2006), paras. 251–256.

[77] Compare Chapter 7 by Kabra (on inherent powers) and Chapter 8 by Cook (on the VCLT's object and purpose).

conclusion that measures that 'circumvent' the delineation of reciprocal trade obligations in the WTO would not be excused by Article XXI would also appear to be in accord with Cook's view that trade and investment tribunals share a harmonious view of the meaning of the traditional rules of treaty interpretation (namely, the need to interpret a treaty in 'good faith' consistent with both text and object and purpose).[78] That panel's discovery of a sliding scale with respect to the burden of proof imposed on a state that seeks to invoke the affirmative Article XXI defence may suggest an implicit turn to the principle of proportionality balancing that some see as applying in both regimes.[79]

Finally, the *Russia-Ukraine* ruling would appear to advance converging trade/investment law at least to the extent the texts of some contemporary IIAs are incorporating an exception identical to the text of GATT Article XXI. That ruling will presumably predict, for example, how the international investment court envisioned for the CETA would be expected to interpret the Article 28.6 'national security' exception contained in that treaty since that exception replicates the language of GATT Article XXI.[80]

But the *Russia-Ukraine* ruling is not a simple tool of 'convergence'. On closer inspection, that decision's implications are as nuanced as any of the other ostensible examples of 'convergence' discussed in this book. To begin with the most obvious point: that ruling on how the essential security exception in the GATT ought to be interpreted – even if assumed to be controlling for purposes of the WTO – can hardly be the final word on how a state's plea of 'essential security' will be treated in investor-state arbitrations. The texts of MPN clauses in IIAs only rarely track the language of GATT Article XXI and differ considerably even among

---

[78] Compare Chapter 8 by Cook to *Russia-Ukraine* (n. 54), para. 7.79 (relying on prior Appellate Body findings that the object and purpose of the WTO Agreement is to promote the security and predictability of reciprocal and mutually advantageous arrangements and arguing that this would be undermined if Article XXI subjected WTO obligations to the unilateral will of members).

[79] See, e.g. Alec Stone Sweet, 'Investor-State Arbitration: Proportionality's New Frontier' (2010) 4 *Law & Ethics of Human Rights* 47.

[80] Article 28.6 of the CETA provides that '[n]othing in this Agreement shall be construed ... (b) to prevent a Party from taking an action that it considers necessary to protect its essential security interests: (i) connected to the production of or traffic in arms, ammunition and implements of war ... ; (ii) taken in time of war or other emergency in international relations; or (iii) relating to fissionable and fusionable materials or the materials from which they are derived; or (c) prevent a Party from taking any action in order to carry out its international obligations for the purpose of maintaining international peace and security'.

IIAs. The majority of existing BITs do not contain any such exception; MPN clauses like the heavily litigated one in the US-Argentina BIT are found in only some IIAs.[81] In such cases, the customary defence of necessity, not the meaning of GATT Article XXI, is likely to become relevant. Further, even the United States, which pioneered the use of MPN clauses, has not been consistent with respect to what measures such clauses preclude or what the invocation of 'essential security' protects. In only some US investment treaties since the US-Argentina BIT does the underlying MPN clause include 'the maintenance of public order', for example.[82] In more recent years, the United States has displaced the objective language of the US-Argentina MPN clause with the 'which it considers' term used in GATT Article XXI but without incorporating all the elements of Article XXI (b) (i-iii) and (c).[83] As the *Russia-Ukraine* panel's focus on those distinct elements of Article XXI suggests, these differences in treaty language may be relevant to interpretations of the meaning of 'essential security' or to the level of deference owed a state when it is exercising (as a reference to 'public order' might suggest) its 'police power' to 'maintain' the peace as opposed to responding to an acute crisis tantamount to armed conflict.

Whether or not due to differences in treaty text, ISDS rulings on the defence of 'essential security' – even if contained in an MPN clause or under the customary defence of necessity – are not consistent. While some of those rulings suggest (as does the WTO panel) that essential security or an international emergency requires an external threat to the very existence of a state comparable to an armed attack, other ISDS awards find that these terms apply to any serious economic, political or social threat faced by a state.[84] Some of these disagreements reflect unresolved views among international courts and tribunals on when treaty terms should be read in light of their contemporary as opposed to their historical meaning.[85] ISDS tribunals have also disagreed on the

---

[81] See José E Alvarez and Kathryn Khamsi, 'The Argentine Crisis and Foreign Investors: A Glimpse into the Heart of the Investment Regime' (2008–09) *Yearbk on Int'l Inv. L. & Pol'y* 379.

[82] Ibid., p. 423.

[83] See, e.g. US Model BIT 2012, Article 18 (2) 'Nothing in this Treaty shall be construed ... to preclude a Party from applying measures that it considers necessary for the fulfillment of its obligations with respect to the maintenance or restoration of international peace or security, or the protection of its own essential security interests.'

[84] See, e.g. *LG & E* v. *Argentina* (n. 76) para. 237.

[85] See, e.g. Marko Milanovic, 'The ICJ and Evolutionary Treaty Interpretation', EJIL: Talk! (14 July 2009) (problematizing the ICJ's decision in *Costa Rica* v. *Nicaragua* to give

level of deference owed to a state's invocation of essential security for understandable reasons: after all, no rules on the level of deference owed to states exist as a general matter. Few ISDS tribunals have suggested, as did the WTO panel, that the burden of proof imposed on a respondent state claiming an essential security threat varies with the kind of 'emergency' it faces and fewer still appear to believe that a generally applicable 'margin of appreciation' principle resolves the issue. It is hard to believe that the *Russia-Ukraine* panel ruling will settle such interpretative debates.

As many Argentina cases on point demonstrate, inconsistent outcomes with respect to any number of interpretative issues arise when an 'essential security' defence is invoked, even when ISDS tribunals are interpreting the same MPN clause in a single treaty.[86] The difficulties of harmonized interpretations only increase when even slight textual variations are introduced into the relevant exception.

Consider, for example, the crucial finding in *Russia-Ukraine* that the essential security exception is not 'self-judging'. One might assume that since the United States, in its recent Model BITs and concluded IIAs, has adopted the 'which it considers' language used in GATT Article XXI in connection with its treaties' more recent exceptions on essential security, the *Russia-Ukraine* decision is a powerful precedent for how such clauses will henceforth be interpreted. We might assume that, from now on, at least with respect to treaties containing the 'which it considers' language, invocation of such exceptions will no longer be subject to unilateral dismissal for lack of jurisdiction or admissibility. But consider the plight of interpreters of the Peru-US Trade Promotion Agreement. While that treaty includes the 'which it considers' language in its MNP clause relating to essential security, it also includes the following footnote: '[f]or greater certainty, if a Party invokes [the MPN clause] in an arbitral proceeding . . . the tribunal or panel hearing the matter shall find that the exception applies'.[87] Arbitrators who apply this footnote will be required to ignore the *Russia-Ukraine* precedent and adhere to a party's unilateral determination that a dispute cannot be objectively reviewed. Further, that footnote's 'for greater certainty' caveat suggests that this was always the understanding attached to the 'which it considers' language in the

---

a contemporaneous meaning to the word 'commerce' in an 1858 treaty because the parties meant the term to have a generic meaning).

[86] For an outline of those differences, see Alvarez, *The Public International Law Regime* (n. 53) Table 2, p. 268.

[87] US-Peru Trade Promotion Agreement (signed 12 Apr. 2006), Article 22.2 and note 2.

context of IIAs. ISDS arbitrators who take that caveat seriously may be tempted to ignore the *Russia-Ukraine* precedent even with respect to IIAs that lack the Peru-US Agreement's explicit footnote. At the very least that footnote, unusual as it may be, will inspire litigants to reconsider the WTO panel's exclusive reliance on the ITO's negotiating history. In the context of ISDS disputes, the 'for greater certainty' caveat is likely to elicit a search through the negotiating history of IIAs in general, the specific BIT or IIA at issue, or, at the very least, the history of the United States' use of 'which it considers' language in the investment context.

As this suggests, those who are trying to determine whether the *Russia-Ukraine* panel decision will have normative legs outside of trade should consider the way that panel reached its conclusions. To the extent that the WTO panel relied on WTO-specific authorities for its views, converging interpretations of the meaning of essential security exceptions across the trade and investment divides are not necessarily advanced. As noted, that WTO panel relied, in substantial part, on the negotiating history of the ITO, including the views of the key drafters of what ultimately became Article XXI, namely, the United States.[88] The panel also justified its turn to GATT's history on the basis of its own prior case law, and not on the basis of the traditional rules of treaty interpretation.[89] It also relied on historical practice specific to the trade regime – namely, that a significant majority of occasions on which Article XX(b)(iii) has been invoked concerned situations of armed conflict and acute crisis – for its interpretation of what that exception means.[90] These WTO-specific sources of authority are not presumptively applicable to the interpretation of individual IIAs. Moreover, as suggested above, to the extent the *Russia-Ukraine* panel inspires ISDS adjudicators to become historians with respect to interpreting terms in MPN or other 'essential security' clauses, this is not likely to produce harmonious interpretations across the two regimes. As is clear with respect to some ISDS rulings that have also resorted to the negotiating history of the underlying BITs before them, this is likely to produce interpretations that may reveal more about the

---

[88] See *Russia-Ukraine* (n. 54) section 7.5.3.1.2. This includes reliance on the views of the United States over time as expressed before trade bodies on what constitutes an 'emergency in international relations'. See, e.g. *Russia-Ukraine* (n. 54) note 152.

[89] *Russia-Ukraine* (n. 54) para. 7.83 and note 157. It is worth noting that this turn to history may have been inspired, at least in part, by the need to rebut the interpretation offered by the United States in the course of the Russia-Ukraine dispute. Indicating that the United States apparently took a very different view of the meaning of Article XI in the past was certainly an effective way of undermining the USA's contemporary view.

[90] *Russia-Ukraine* (n. 54) para. 7.81.

respective bilateral relationship of two BIT parties than they do about, for example, general sentiments at the time the ITO was drafted.

The *Russia-Ukraine* panel also turned at other points to WTO-specific law for its findings. To explain the meaning of Article XXI(b)(i) and (ii), it understandably cited the comparable use of the term 'relating to' in Article XX.[91] In explaining that it is for Russia to determine the 'necessity' of its measures, the tribunal suggested that this necessarily follows from the 'which it considers' language in Article XXI – which it compares to the 'margin of appreciation' found applicable in *EC-Bananas III* under the 'if that party considers' language in Articles 22.3(b) and 22.3(c) of the DSU.[92] These internal WTO reference points are not, of course, necessarily applicable or relevant to ISDS tribunals faced with comparable inquiries. ISDS tribunals faced with the need to interpret the word 'necessary' in MPM clauses have turned to completely different sources of authority, such as the necessity defence under Article 25 of the Articles of State Responsibility.

Despite its prominence in ISDS rulings dealing with essential security defences by respondent states, the customary defence of necessity does not make an appearance in the *Russia-Ukraine* panel ruling. As is well known, the CIL necessity defence contains its own requisites for its successful invocation. States that claim that they were compelled by necessity to breach a treaty need to, among other things, prove that their challenged action was the 'only way' to respond to the underlying emergency, and that they did not substantially contribute to the underlying emergency.[93] ISDS tribunals have divided on whether an MNP clause is a distinct defence from that of the customary necessity exception, supplements the CIL defence, or needs to be read in light of the CIL defence.[94] Most ISDS scholars have suggested that the vast majority of IIAs – which contain no relevant exception such as an MPN clause – nonetheless permit states to invoke the CIL defence as a relevant (and arguably fundamental) rule of international law that applies to the interpretation of investment agreements under Article 31(3)(c) of the VCLT.[95] If past is prologue, it would

[91] Ibid., para. 7.69.
[92] Ibid., paras. 7.146–147.
[93] See James Crawford, *The International Law Commission's Articles on State Responsibility* (Cambridge University Press, 2002), Article 25 and Commentary, pp. 178–86.
[94] See, e.g. Alvarez, *The Public International Law Regime* (n. 53) pp. 268–72.
[95] See, e.g. Alvarez, *The Public International Law Regime* (n. 53) pp. 272–3. This reflects the common (but not universal) assumption that even though IIAs enumerate rights of private investors they are nonetheless interstate treaties subject to the Articles of State Responsibility, including Article 25 on the defence of necessity.

not be unusual for an ISDS tribunal to demand to know whether, in a case comparable to that of *Russia-Ukraine*, the challenged measures were the 'only way' to respond to the international emergency between the two countries and whether the respondent state 'substantially contributed' to the underlying emergency or crisis.

The WTO panel did not demand that Russia answer such questions. Indeed, that panel goes out of its way to find that 'it is not relevant' to the determination of whether the situation between Russia and Ukraine constitutes an emergency in international relations 'which actor or actors bear international responsibility for the existence of this situation'.[96] For international lawyers – aware that the same UN General Assembly that recognized the international emergency between Russia and the Ukraine (cited by the tribunal) also concluded that Russia, by invading Crimea, violated international law and in all probability substantially contributed to the underlying emergency[97] – this seems to be an extraordinary abdication of responsibility. Even if the customary defence of necessity is not considered relevant applicable law, the suggestion by the WTO panel that it is not 'relevant' whether Russia violated international law or contributed to the underlying crisis ignores the concept of abuse of rights or the general principle of law that a state should not profit from its own wrong.

The WTO panel refuses to make the invocation of Article XXI contingent on whether Russia was in the wrong to begin with; it seems to be saying that Russia can invoke a war as an excuse even if it started the war.[98] Its application of 'good faith' goes only skin deep insofar as it is limited to whether a requisite crisis or emergency exists (regardless of how it came about) and to whether the offending measures were taken 'during' that crisis. For defenders of the WTO's decision, this is a 'legitimacy-preserving' or 'authority-enhancing' move that was rendered necessary by the structural constraints imposed on WTO dispute settlers.[99] In refusing to entertain such inquiries, the WTO panel was

---

[96] *Russia-Ukraine* (n. 54) para. 7.121.
[97] See G.A. Resolution 68/262 (27 Mar. 2014) (proclaiming the 'territorial integrity' of Ukraine despite the Russian occupation of Crimea).
[98] See, e.g. Ben Heath, 'Guest Post: Trade, Security, and Stewardship Part II: Making Legal Space to Adjudicate Security Matters', International Economic Law and Policy Blog (9 May 2019). Arguably the WTO panel was not suggesting that a state could deliberately manufacture an emergency to avail itself of the Article XXI exception since that would appear to be a wrongful 'circumvention' of WTO law.
[99] Ibid. See also DSU, Article 3 (3) directing dispute settlers to 'clarify' existing WTO obligations and not 'add or diminish the rights and obligations provided in the covered agreements'.

arguably responding to the oft-stated complaint that the GATT/WTO has no role to play when a trade dispute merely reflects a broader geopolitical dispute or the claim that such disputes should be dismissed because they raise 'political questions'.[100] In accord with the limits imposed on them under the DSU, the panel opted for preserving the boundary between trade law and other violations of international law by ignoring the latter.[101] As the WTO panel indicated, its role was not to 'assign responsibility' for the underlying emergency.[102]

But what was 'legitimacy-preserving' and 'authority-enhancing' for WTO adjudicators, would not be for other international courts and tribunals. International judges charged with interpreting international law (and not only trade law), such as the ICJ, have not hesitated to examine far more closely the good faith of a state's proclamation of a national emergency just as investor-state arbitrators have not hesitated before to ask whether Argentina in fact contributed to the economic emergency at issue in a number of ISDS cases. This reflects a broader distinction between ISDS arbitrators and WTO adjudicators: the former are far more likely to consider other international legal rules (including the law of human rights) in the course of adjudicating investment disputes.[103] ISDS tribunals, while charged with enforcing investment law, are not limited to the application of investment treaty law – at least not in the way WTO adjudicators are limited to applying the GATT-covered agreements.

And what about the claim that to the extent an IIA contains an exception identical to GATT Article XXI, the ruling in *Russia-Ukraine* will be an irresistible precedent leading to converging results? Will ISDS adjudicators in comparable cases, brought under CETA or the Comprehensive Economic and Trade Agreement (both of which have, as noted, exceptions identical to the GATT's Article XXI) also find it irrelevant whether a state that invokes an emergency caused it? This is unlikely. Faithfulness to 'precedent' points in opposite directions here. An ISDS panel or an international investment court that chooses to

---

[100] Heath, 'Guest Post' (n. 98).
[101] Ibid.
[102] *Russia-Ukraine* (n. 54) para. 7.5. This was also, of course, Russia's posture in arguing that such political matters were intended to be kept out of the WTO. Ibid., para. 7.22.
[103] This is in part because of the broad choice of law clauses in IIAs themselves as well as in the relevant arbitration rules but it is also built into the substantive provisions of IIAs, which offer investors the backdrop benefits of 'international law' or which incorporate customary international law as part of concepts like fair and equitable treatment. See, e.g. José E Alvarez, 'A BIT on Custom' (2009) 42 *NYU J. Int'l L. & Pol.* 17.

distinguish this aspect of the *Russia-Ukraine* case would be following a prominent line of cases where investor-state arbitrators have pursued inquiries into abuse of rights (and not only in the context of essential security defences claimed by Argentina) – precisely to preserve the legitimacy of investor-state arbitration.[104]

Converging outcomes should not be presumed just because treaty provisions originally found in the GATT Agreements are incorporated into IIAs. As a number of the authors in this valuable collection tell us, this is because the *structure* of dispute settlement, and not merely the texts that are being interpreted, matters. What a tribunal is established to do – that is, what it is *for* – may tell us much about whether it is likely to 'converge'.

---

[104] See, e.g. Emmanuel Gaillard, 'Abuse of Process in International Arbitration' (2017) 1 *ICSID Rev.* 271.

INDEX

Abaclat v. Argentina, 177
Abi-Saab, George, 102, 182, 183, 186
ad hoc arbitration, 101, 109
adjudicator, 8, 9, 14, 16, 17, 45, 46, 47, 65, 76, 81, 112, 124, 144, 145, 149, 151, 152, 154, 155, 159, 160, 161, 162, 163, 190, 191, 192, 194, 198, 199, 202, 204, 206, 208, 209, 210, 246, 247, 248, 250, 251, 254, 255, 257, 258, 259, 260, 262, 266, 283, 288, 289, 290, 296, 297, 299, 300, 311
  international, xiii, 13, 14, 124, 125, 128, 145, 161, 162, 248, 286, 291
  investment, 14, 16, 51, 155, 160, 194, 200, 204, 209, 288, 291
  selection, 29, 72, 73, 82, 83, 84, 86, 89, 90, 147, 250, 258
adjudicatory
  bodies, 16, 145, 235, 241, 251, 257, 258, 259, 262, 266, 284, 300
  chaos, 162
  function, 86, 90, 168, 171, 174, 186
admissibility objections, 15, 172, 173, 175, 177, 181, 185, 186
agent, 246, 248, 251, 252, 253, 254, 256, 290
Agreement on Agriculture (AoA), WTO, 264
Agreement on the Application of Sanitary and Phytosanitary Measures (SPS), WTO, 199, 264
Agreement on Trade-Related Aspects of Intellectual Property (TRIPS), WTO, 95, 231
Agreement on Trade-Related Investment Measures, 67, 95

Aguas del Tunari, 80, 81, 179, 268
Alle, Todd, 7, 22, 23, 35, 39, 44
alternative to investor-state arbitration, 94
amicus, 15, 153, 155, 169, 172, 178, 179, 180, 181, 187, 188, 189, 192
  brief, 178, 179, 180, 181, 187, 188
  presentations, 178, 180, 187
  submission, 180, 188
amicus curiae, 15, 153, 155, 169, 172, 178, 179, 180, 181, 187, 188, 189, 192, 268, 289, 298, 299, 300
Andenas, Mads, 4, 10, 127, 145, 213, 214, 230, 240
Appeals Chamber of the Special Court for Sierra Leone, 178
appeals mechanism, 4, 11, 65, 67, 69, 70, 74, 76, 83, 86, 87
Appellate Body, WTO, vii, viii, xiv, 4, 8, 11, 14, 15, 62, 65, 75, 76, 77, 78, 79, 80, 83, 84, 85, 87, 88, 89, 90, 112, 113, 114, 115, 117, 124, 129, 130, 133, 139, 141, 145, 146, 151, 152, 153, 154, 155, 167, 168, 169, 171, 172, 173, 174, 175, 177, 179, 180, 181, 182, 183, 184, 185, 186, 187, 188, 189, 192, 193, 194, 196, 197, 198, 199, 200, 201, 206, 207, 208, 230, 231, 232, 236, 241, 244, 248, 250, 254, 255, 257, 258, 259, 260, 262, 263, 266, 286, 288, 290, 292, 296, 305
applicable law, 74, 81, 98, 104, 113, 146, 162, 310
arbitrator, xii, 41, 62, 73, 144, 253, 254, 267
Articles on State Responsibility, 304, 309

backlash, 7, 17, 90, 244, 245, 252, 254, 255, 290
Barcelona Traction, 133
behaviour, adjudicative, 8, 14, 15, 17, 247, 249, 251, 254, 258
bilateral investment treaty, 26, 29, 30, 33, 34, 35, 52, 53, 62, 63, 68, 80, 81, 94, 99, 102, 104, 106, 107, 110, 151, 152, 200, 216, 217, 218, 219, 220, 221, 223, 224, 225, 240, 267, 294, 300, 301, 306, 308, 309, 311
binding treaty interpretations, 16, 48, 49, 212, 213, 221, 222, 223, 232, 235, 239, 241, 289

Canada, 2, 4, 13, 16, 22, 26, 27, 30, 31, 39, 48, 53, 55, 61, 64, 67, 68, 69, 70, 88, 93, 99, 102, 103, 104, 111, 139, 142, 143, 152, 153, 154, 157, 201, 204, 206, 207, 208, 212, 216, 217, 218, 219, 220, 222, 223, 224, 225, 238, 268, 270
Canada-Korea Free Trade Agreement, 68, 104, 219
centrality, system, 126
CETA, 2, 64, 69, 71, 72, 73, 74, 75, 77, 79, 80, 81, 82, 84, 85, 86, 87, 89, 90, 97, 98, 102, 104, 114, 216, 217, 218, 219, 224, 233, 241
China, 4, 5, 27, 29, 30, 31, 33, 34, 36, 39, 41, 42, 53, 56, 57, 61, 68, 87, 92, 93, 102, 104, 107, 114, 115, 116, 130, 140, 141, 157, 181, 194, 197, 212, 216, 217, 218, 219, 220, 223, 224, 225, 241, 255, 282
China-Audiovisuals, 116
China-Electronic Payments, 116
choice of forum, 174, 175
citation network, 130, 134, 139
citation patterns, 128, 146
City Oriente v. Ecuador, 207, 208
claim, declaratory, 107, 109
coherence, 11, 49, 67, 70, 86, 160, 232, 236
committee
  joint, 217, 218, 221
  trade, 72, 73, 84, 85, 89, 90
committee, treaty, 12, 16, 43, 45, 48, 49, 50, 53, 72, 85, 186, 212, 213, 215, 216, 217, 218, 219, 222, 223, 224, 225, 226, 227, 228, 231, 232, 233, 234, 235, 236, 237, 240, 241, 242, 243, 256, 289, 297
  interpretative, 25, 225
Common Commercial Policy, EU, 28
Common Market for Eastern and Southern Africa (COMESA), 28, 29, 36, 59
compensation, 39, 76, 77, 99, 101, 111, 158, 245, 273, 275, 276
Comprehensive Economic and Trade Agreement (CETA) 2, 2, 13, 22, 27, 44, 47, 48, 55, 64, 65, 69, 71, 72, 73, 74, 75, 77, 79, 80, 81, 82, 84, 85, 86, 87, 89, 90, 97, 98, 102, 104, 114, 216, 217, 218, 219, 224, 233, 241, 288, 305, 311
consequentialist argument, 16, 191, 203, 204, 205, 206, 207, 208, 210, 253, 291
Continental v. Argentina, 143
Convention on the Settlement of Investment Disputes between States and Nationals of Other States (ICSID Convention), viii, 4, 12, 15, 22, 34, 39, 40, 41, 44, 49, 51, 61, 63, 68, 69, 70, 73, 74, 80, 81, 83, 85, 86, 88, 89, 90, 93, 99, 101, 102, 103, 105, 111, 125, 130, 133, 139, 141, 142, 143, 144, 151, 152, 153, 154, 155, 167, 168, 169, 171, 172, 173, 175, 176, 177, 178, 179, 180, 181, 182, 183, 184, 185, 186, 187, 188, 189, 192, 197, 198, 200, 202, 205, 207, 208, 211, 212, 238, 248, 267, 268, 269, 272, 275, 276, 279, 280, 288, 304, 312
convergence, 2, 4, 5, 8, 9, 10, 11, 14, 15, 16, 17, 24, 25, 31, 41, 42, 43, 44, 45, 46, 47, 48, 49, 50, 52, 53, 75, 83, 87, 89, 91, 94, 96, 105, 114, 148, 149, 159, 163, 169, 189, 191, 194, 197, 200, 202, 209, 210, 213, 214, 215, 225, 228, 233, 234, 235, 236, 237, 240, 241, 242, 243, 247, 285, 286, 287, 288, 289, 290, 291, 292, 293, 295, 296, 298, 299, 300, 304, 305

INDEX

absolute, 9
adjudicatory, 94, 112, 117, 118
epistemic, 53
functional, 17, 43, 48, 91, 126, 208, 213, 215, 231, 234, 235, 237, 241, 242
ideological, 17, 30, 48, 213, 215, 228, 230, 232, 233, 234, 242, 243, 249
intersectional, 2
network, 13
normative, 155
parallel, 2, 65, 80, 114, 126, 151, 155, 157, 160, 162, 198, 209, 233, 285, 304
spatial, 2, 16, 25, 48, 213, 215, 225, 242
substantive, 2, 291, 295
temporal, 25, 215, 225, 242
without interaction, 209, 291
Court of Justice of the European Union, CJEU, 5, 36, 65, 71, 145, 149, 246, 252, 255
cross-citation, 9, 13, 288, 304
cross-fertilization, 16, 47, 86, 191, 193, 209, 210, 293
cross-judging, 14

decentralization, 17, 258
decision-making, 47, 125, 182, 184, 219, 223, 230, 236, 237, 248, 249, 254, 255, 272, 273
Deep and Comprehensive Trade Agreements (DCFTA), 27, 28, 36
delegation, 22, 217, 221, 233, 248, 289
design, 4, 8, 9, 13, 22, 31, 33, 36, 43, 45, 65, 66, 73, 74, 75, 83, 87, 89, 90, 102, 157, 158, 161, 182, 284
  dispute system, 285
  treaty, 11
developing countries, 46, 62, 67, 158
Diallo, 105, 146
diplomatic protection, 105, 107, 108, 109, 110, 112, 230
dispute
  investor-state, xii, 2, 4, 5, 7, 8, 11, 12, 13, 17, 21, 22, 23, 24, 25, 26, 27, 30, 31, 32, 33, 34, 35, 36, 39, 41, 44, 45, 47, 53, 61, 62, 63, 64, 65, 66, 67, 69, 70, 72, 73, 75, 77, 78, 80, 90, 93, 94, 97, 102, 117, 118, 146, 149, 150, 151, 152, 153, 154, 156, 159, 160, 161, 162, 163, 190, 191, 192, 193, 194, 195, 197, 198, 200, 202, 203, 204, 207, 208, 209, 221, 229, 230, 234, 247, 248, 249, 250, 253, 255, 256, 267, 268, 269, 270, 271, 272, 273, 276, 278, 282, 286, 288, 289, 290, 292, 293, 294, 295, 296, 297, 298, 299, 300, 301, 304, 306, 307, 308, 309, 311
  state-state, 13, 22, 35, 44, 47, 52, 78, 93, 94, 105, 106, 107, 108, 111, 112, 116, 117, 118, 156
  trade, xii, 7, 22, 24, 25, 43, 47, 65, 70, 75, 76, 77, 78, 79, 81, 83, 85, 87, 88, 89, 90, 113, 115, 128, 129, 130, 145, 146, 152, 154, 156, 157, 180, 183, 191, 232, 236, 244, 251, 262, 263, 294, 298, 302, 310
Dispute Settlement Body (DSB), WTO, 13, 43, 47, 52, 82, 83, 93, 115, 116, 117, 129, 141, 145, 146, 174, 175, 181, 183, 185, 187, 188, 206, 230, 231, 237, 257, 258, 259, 260, 261, 263, 267
dispute settlement mechanism, xii, 1, 2, 5, 7, 8, 9, 11, 12, 13, 14, 17, 18, 22, 24, 25, 31, 41, 42, 43, 44, 45, 46, 47, 49, 50, 52, 53, 64, 65, 66, 67, 69, 70, 76, 78, 79, 81, 82, 86, 88, 89, 90, 93, 97, 101, 102, 105, 108, 111, 112, 113, 118, 130, 142, 146, 156, 157, 158, 160, 162, 174, 183, 185, 191, 193, 207, 225, 237, 244, 247, 254, 256, 257, 258, 259, 283, 285, 286, 287, 289, 297, 312
Dispute Settlement Training Module, 129
Dispute Settlement Understanding (DSU), WTO, 4, 75, 76, 77, 78, 79, 80, 81, 82, 83, 85, 87, 88, 89, 95, 112, 113, 116, 117, 118, 130, 140, 146, 174, 179, 181, 183, 184, 185, 187, 188, 206, 207, 208, 231, 290, 297, 309, 310, 311

divergence, 8, 9, 10, 11, 13, 75, 86, 89, 90, 117, 153, 158, 159, 161, 163, 177, 194, 209, 213, 214, 215, 225, 234, 235, 240, 242, 287
   objectives, 89
   political influence, 90
   procedural, 90
domestic
   barrier, 158
   court, 74, 170, 171, 248, 253
   dispute settlement, 41
   law, 74, 87, 143, 205, 258
Dominican Republic-Central American Free Trade Agreement, DR-CAFTA, 5, 39, 48, 55, 68, 69, 244

Easton, David, 132
EC-Bananas, 117, 309
Economic Community of West African States, ECOWAS, 27, 28, 36, 39, 55, 59
economic integration, 11, 24, 156, 157, 158
ELSI, 108, 133
Elsig, Manfred, 7, 22, 45, 286, 296
empiricism, xii, 4, 17, 25, 52, 62, 127, 148, 150, 160, 213, 215, 246, 249, 252, 253, 260, 284, 285
enforcement, 13, 74, 94, 97, 105, 112, 114, 118, 155, 156, 157, 158, 258, 288, 289
engagement, judicial, 14, 150, 154, 159, 160, 162, 163
Enron v. *Argentina*, 197, 304
entry rights, 4, 13, 94, 95, 96, 97, 98, 99, 105, 106, 107, 110, 111, 112, 113, 115, 117, 118, 288
epistemic community, 17, 162, 163, 233, 242, 250
establishment, of investment, 13, 105, 109, 111
ethical standards, 73, 84
Ethyl v. *Canada*, 206, 207
European Court of Human Rights, ECtHR, 125, 133, 137, 139, 141, 143, 145, 149, 199, 246, 247, 286, 296

European Union, EU, vii, xiii, 2, 5, 10, 12, 13, 21, 22, 26, 27, 28, 30, 31, 36, 39, 43, 46, 47, 48, 49, 53, 55, 58, 59, 61, 62, 64, 65, 66, 69, 70, 71, 72, 73, 74, 75, 76, 78, 79, 81, 83, 84, 85, 86, 88, 89, 90, 95, 96, 97, 98, 100, 111, 117, 195, 197, 214, 216, 217, 218, 219, 224, 233, 241, 245, 247, 252, 255, 264, 266, 270, 281, 284, 287
   Commission, 26, 36, 46, 49
   Investment Court, ICS, vii, 12, 47, 62, 64, 65, 66, 70, 74, 75, 76, 78, 81, 83, 84, 100, 287
   Parliament, 46
   Singapore FTA, 5, 36, 39, 48, 64, 65, 71, 72, 73, 74, 84, 86, 88, 98, 216, 224, 225, 241, 288
   Vietnam FTA, 2, 48, 64, 65, 71, 72, 75, 84, 86, 88, 89, 99, 216, 224, 225, 241, 288
Europeanization, 10, 214, 287
exclusive
   interpretative powers, 232
   jurisdiction, 112, 175, 185
exit, 63, 267, 269, 271, 280
external
   precedent, 14, 125, 126, 127, 133, 142, 144, 146, 148, 288
   source, 14, 149, 288

Factory at Chorzów, 133, 135
fair and equitable treatment, FET, 26, 31, 38, 39, 245, 268, 272, 294
fork-in-the-road clause, FITR clause, 124, 174, 185
fragmentation, 1, 7, 15, 68, 70, 86, 123, 161, 163, 189, 209, 214, 230, 240, 284, 286
free trade agreement, FTA, xv, 2, 5, 26, 27, 28, 33, 34, 36, 39, 41, 42, 48, 58, 59, 64, 68, 96, 216, 217, 218, 219, 221, 223, 224, 225, 233, 241, 244
Free Trade Commission, 48, 49, 221, 222, 233, 236, 237, 239, 240, 268, 282
full protection and security, FPS, 26, 31, 38, 39, 50, 238, 245, 272
functionalism, 146, 234

INDEX 317

General Agreement on Tariffs and
Trade, GATT, 1, 8, 66, 67, 76, 82,
141, 151, 152, 157, 175, 195, 196,
197, 198, 199, 201, 205, 206, 209,
230, 231, 244, 250, 286, 288, 293,
294, 295, 296, 299, 300, 301, 304,
305, 307, 308, 311, 312
   Article XX, 76, 115, 141, 151, 195,
197, 199, 201, 206, 286, 293, 295,
299, 300, 301, 302, 303, 304, 305,
306, 307, 308, 309, 310, 311
   Article XXI, 76, 115, 141, 151, 195,
197, 199, 201, 206, 286, 293, 295,
299, 300, 301, 302, 303, 304, 305,
306, 307, 308, 309, 310, 311
General Agreement for Trade in
Services, GATS, 13, 30, 95, 96, 111,
113, 114, 115, 116, 117, 196,
231, 294
General Council, WTO, 222, 231, 235,
236, 289
general principles, of law, 140, 155, 161,
162, 167, 171, 228, 240, 294, 296,
297, 299
Gillard Government, Australia, 34, 270
Glamis Gold, 153, 154
Goodhart, Arthur, 122, 125

home state, 52, 106, 107, 109, 112, 113,
117, 118, 250, 256
host state, 77, 90, 94, 97, 99, 101, 102,
104, 107, 154, 156, 158, 200, 229
hub, network analysis, 139, 244

implied powers, 167, 171
India-Solar Cells, 205, 206
inherent jurisdiction, 170, 171, 172, 181
inherent powers, 15, 141, 167, 168, 169,
170, 171, 172, 173, 177, 178, 180,
181, 182, 185, 186, 187, 188, 189,
288, 296, 297, 300, 302, 304
institutional balance, 182
institutional memory, 86
institutionalism, discursive, 253
intergovernmental, 183, 187
International Centre for the Settlement
of Investment Disputes, ICSID,
viii, 4, 12, 15, 22, 34, 39, 40, 41, 44,
49, 51, 61, 63, 68, 69, 70, 73, 74, 80,
81, 83, 85, 86, 88, 89, 90, 93, 99,
101, 102, 103, 105, 111, 125, 130,
133, 139, 141, 142, 143, 144, 151,
152, 153, 154, 155, 167, 168, 169,
171, 172, 173, 175, 176, 177, 178,
179, 180, 181, 182, 183, 184, 185,
186, 187, 188, 189, 192, 197, 198,
200, 202, 205, 207, 208, 211, 212,
238, 248, 267, 268, 269, 272, 275,
276, 279, 280, 288, 304, 312
   Additional Facility Rules, 39, 68
   Administrative Council, 68
   Appeals Panel, 68
   Arbitration Rules, 39, 172, 175, 177,
180, 185, 188, 207
   Convention, 63, 74, 101, 168, 175,
176, 177, 180, 184, 185, 200, 208,
248, 267, 269, 275, 276
   Regulations and Rules, 68
   Secretariat, 68, 69, 86
   Tribunals, viii, 15, 167, 168, 172, 181,
182, 202
International Court of Justice, ICJ, 5,
105, 106, 108, 121, 122, 124, 125,
126, 127, 129, 130, 133, 134, 140,
141, 142, 145, 146, 147, 153, 170,
171, 172, 173, 177, 178, 184, 187,
214, 250, 286, 297, 300, 304,
306, 311
   Statute, 121, 122, 126, 173, 178,
187
international dispute settlement, xiii,
16, 73, 76, 122, 124, 148, 150, 155,
160, 167, 208
international economic law, xiv, 2, 5,
14, 126, 156, 158, 246, 286
international investment agreement(s),
3, 7, 25, 34, 35, 62, 95, 101, 106,
108, 110, 114, 117, 155, 212, 229,
244, 245, 249, 268, 270, 272, 275,
278, 279, 280, 285, 288, 299, 300,
308, 311
international investment law, xi, xiii, 4,
7, 8, 16, 47, 63, 66, 73, 80, 117, 118,
126, 132, 213, 215, 220, 222, 223,
228, 229, 232, 233, 235, 236, 237,
240, 241, 242, 243

INDEX

International Law Commission, ILC, 10, 108, 151, 192, 199, 203, 214, 286, 309
   1966 commentary, 192
international responsibility, 113, 310
International Thunderbird Gaming Corp. v. Mexico, 144, 153
international trade law, 4, 5, 7, 10, 16, 18, 47, 50, 73, 82, 87, 126, 156, 213, 215, 220, 222, 228, 230, 231, 232, 233, 235, 236, 241, 242, 288, 293, 295, 296, 298, 299, 311
interpretation, xii, 8, 11, 15, 16, 49, 50, 52, 53, 63, 74, 80, 81, 85, 106, 107, 110, 111, 115, 128, 142, 144, 146, 148, 150, 161, 163, 172, 184, 190, 191, 192, 193, 195, 196, 197, 198, 199, 200, 201, 202, 203, 204, 205, 206, 208, 209, 210, 215, 217, 218, 219, 220, 221, 222, 223, 224, 230, 231, 232, 233, 235, 236, 237, 238, 239, 240, 241, 242, 244, 289, 291, 294, 295, 298, 300, 301, 304, 308, 309
   broad, 199, 200, 210
   expansive, 199, 200, 209
   narrow, 195, 304
   restrictive, 168, 197, 199, 200, 210, 238
   strict, 239
   teleological, 199, 208
interpretative, 4, 10, 11, 12, 15, 16, 25, 48, 49, 50, 52, 81, 86, 106, 151, 156, 190, 191, 193, 197, 198, 201, 203, 212, 213, 215, 216, 217, 219, 221, 222, 223, 224, 225, 226, 227, 230, 231, 232, 233, 234, 235, 236, 237, 239, 240, 241, 242, 243, 268, 285, 299, 301, 307
   aid, 151, 156
   committee, 242
inter-regime, 114, 160, 286
investment, xi, xii, 1, 2, 4, 5, 7, 8, 9, 10, 11, 12, 13, 14, 15, 16, 17, 21, 23, 24, 25, 26, 27, 28, 29, 30, 31, 33, 34, 35, 36, 39, 41, 42, 43, 44, 45, 46, 47, 48, 50, 51, 52, 53, 61, 62, 63, 64, 65, 66, 67, 69, 70, 74, 75, 77, 78, 80, 81, 83, 86, 90, 93, 94, 95, 96, 97, 98, 99, 100, 101, 102, 103, 104, 105, 107, 108, 110, 111, 112, 113, 114, 115, 116, 117, 118, 124, 126, 128, 130, 132, 133, 134, 135, 136, 137, 138, 139, 141, 142, 145, 146, 147, 150, 153, 155, 156, 157, 158, 159, 160, 161, 162, 163, 169, 178, 180, 183, 186, 188, 189, 194, 197, 198, 200, 204, 209, 211, 212, 213, 215, 216, 217, 219, 220, 221, 222, 223, 225, 228, 229, 230, 232, 233, 234, 235, 236, 237, 240, 241, 242, 244, 247, 250, 251, 255, 256, 257, 259, 267, 268, 270, 271, 273, 276, 278, 279, 282, 283, 284, 285, 286, 287, 288, 289, 290, 291, 292, 293, 294, 295, 296, 297, 298, 300, 304, 305, 306, 308, 309, 311
   chapter(s), 5, 12, 22, 24, 25, 27, 31, 33, 34, 35, 36, 41, 42, 43, 44, 45, 46, 48, 50, 51, 52, 53, 96, 212, 215, 219, 222, 229, 287, 295
   dispute settlement, xii, 2, 4, 5, 7, 8, 11, 12, 13, 17, 21, 22, 23, 24, 25, 26, 27, 30, 31, 32, 33, 34, 35, 36, 39, 41, 44, 45, 47, 53, 61, 62, 63, 64, 65, 66, 67, 69, 70, 72, 73, 75, 77, 79, 90, 93, 94, 97, 102, 117, 118, 147, 149, 150, 151, 152, 153, 154, 156, 159, 160, 161, 162, 163, 190, 191, 192, 193, 194, 195, 197, 198, 200, 202, 203, 204, 207, 208, 209, 221, 229, 230, 234, 247, 248, 249, 250, 253, 255, 256, 267, 268, 269, 270, 271, 272, 273, 276, 278, 282, 286, 288, 290, 292, 293, 294, 295, 296, 297, 298, 299, 300, 301, 304, 306, 307, 308, 309, 311
   protection, 2, 12, 21, 23, 24, 25, 27, 30, 31, 33, 34, 35, 36, 39, 42, 48, 50, 51, 52, 53, 61, 63, 64, 66, 77, 198, 209, 229
   treaty, 3, 25, 26, 29, 30, 33, 34, 35, 45, 52, 53, 62, 63, 66, 67, 68, 69, 70, 78, 80, 81, 86, 95, 99, 101, 102, 104, 106, 107, 108, 110, 111, 114, 117, 151, 152, 153, 186, 200, 211, 212,

INDEX

215, 216, 217, 218, 219, 220, 221, 223, 224, 225, 229, 230, 233, 237, 240, 241, 244, 249, 250, 256, 267, 268, 270, 272, 275, 278, 279, 280, 285, 294, 299, 300, 301, 306, 308, 309, 311
Investment Court, 2, 12, 65, 66, 70, 71, 83, 234, 247, 288
   EU, vii, 62, 64, 66, 75, 76, 78, 81, 83
   International, 70, 305, 311
   Multilateral, 2, 11, 12, 79, 247, 287
   System, 12, 64, 65, 66, 70, 72, 73, 74, 75, 77, 78, 79, 81, 82, 83, 84, 85, 86, 87, 88, 89, 90, 287
investor-state, 4, 5, 7, 8, 11, 12, 13, 17, 21, 22, 35, 44, 47, 62, 63, 65, 68, 70, 72, 75, 76, 77, 78, 80, 84, 90, 93, 94, 97, 99, 101, 102, 107, 109, 117, 118, 146, 221, 247, 248, 249, 252, 253, 254, 255, 256, 258, 267, 268, 269, 270, 272, 273, 276, 278, 282, 283, 289, 292, 294, 297, 298, 311, 312
   arbitration, 4, 5, 7, 8, 11, 12, 13, 17, 22, 35, 44, 47, 62, 63, 65, 70, 72, 90, 93, 94, 97, 102, 117, 118, 247, 248, 250, 253, 255, 256, 267, 268, 269, 270, 272, 273, 276, 278, 282, 292, 312
   backlash against, 7
   treaty arbitration, 45, 62, 80, 81, 211, 215, 220, 225, 237, 241, 250
Iran-US Claims Tribunal, 133, 135, 136
ISDS, 11, 12, 17, 23, 24, 25, 31, 34, 36, 39, 41, 44, 45, 47, 63, 64, 65, 66, 67, 69, 70, 73, 75, 79, 90, 149, 150, 151, 152, 153, 154, 156, 159, 160, 161, 162, 163, 190, 191, 192, 193, 194, 195, 197, 198, 200, 202, 203, 204, 207, 208, 209, 234, 245, 247, 249, 267, 270, 286, 288, 290, 292, 293, 294, 295, 296, 297, 298, 299, 300, 301, 304, 306, 307, 308, 309, 311
   adjudicators, 190, 191, 193, 194, 195, 200, 202, 203, 204, 308, 311
   awards, 151, 152, 159, 192, 306

   reform, 5, 7, 42, 63, 65, 66, 68, 69, 75, 79, 87, 89, 90, 237, 246, 247, 285, 286
   tribunals, 53, 94, 97, 149, 151, 153, 154, 156, 159, 160, 162, 163, 183, 184, 191, 197, 207, 215, 232, 238, 272, 295, 300, 304, 306, 307, 309, 311

joint committee, 212, 213, 217, 218, 221
judicial empowerment, 245
judicial function, 15, 16, 167, 168, 169, 170, 172, 173, 181, 182, 183, 184, 186, 187, 189, 296, 297
judicialization, 1, 123
jurisprudence, 11, 13, 43, 122, 130, 131, 133, 135, 139, 140, 141, 142, 145, 147, 150, 153, 173, 191, 192, 193, 196, 199, 240, 245, 251, 257, 284, 292, 295, 297, 299
   WTO, 150, 151, 154, 156, 159, 161, 173, 177, 185, 192, 259, 294, 295, 296, 299, 300

Kaufmann-Kohler, Gabrielle, 49, 68, 69, 132, 211, 222, 238, 239, 268
Kurtz, Jürgen, 2, 7, 34, 94, 96, 112, 114, 143, 147, 148, 150, 151, 152, 154, 159, 162, 197

LaGrand, 142
Lauterpacht, Hersch, 122, 123, 140, 171, 182, 229
lawmaking, judicial, 245, 258
legal subjectivity, 206
legitimacy, 4, 5, 11, 15, 62, 70, 84, 123, 145, 146, 161, 163, 225, 245, 246, 247, 248, 252, 253, 254, 256, 259, 260, 266, 267, 269, 270, 272, 278, 283, 284, 285, 288, 290, 310, 311, 312
   crisis, 4, 62, 123, 245, 248, 253, 254, 267, 269, 272, 278, 283
   normative, 246
   sociological, 246
legitimate regulation, 96
Legum, Barton, 125
LG & E v. Argentina, 304, 306

INDEX

liberalization of trade, 12, 27, 51, 53, 196, 198, 209, 228, 230
like circumstance, 152, 157, 295, 299
like investment, 53, 157
like investors, 157
like products, 157, 201, 295, 299
London Court of International Arbitration, LCIA, 139

manifestly unreasonable, 203
Marceau, Gabrielle, 114, 150, 192, 292, 296, 298, 299
market access, 4, 96, 97, 98, 110, 113, 115, 118
Marrakesh Agreement, 95, 112, 223, 236
Mavroidis, Petros, 21, 95, 111, 129, 146
McDougall, Robert, 23, 45, 47
Merrill & Ring, 239, 295, 299
Methanex, 148, 153, 176, 238, 299, 300
Mexico, 16, 44, 48, 51, 56, 58, 64, 65, 76, 78, 93, 111, 130, 140, 141, 153, 154, 171, 173, 174, 175, 185, 192, 204, 205, 216, 217, 218, 219, 220, 224, 225, 233, 268, 294
Mexico–Soft Drinks, 140, 154, 171, 173, 174, 175, 185
Ministerial Conference, 222, 231, 235, 289
minority opinions, 134, 139, 145
MNP, 300, 301, 307, 309
model BIT, 95, 99, 268, 271
  US, 99, 282
most-favoured-nation treatment, MFN, 26, 31, 37, 39, 50, 61, 81, 95, 100, 107, 116, 245, 272, 287, 294
Multilateral Agreement on Investment, 66, 67
Multilateral Investment Court, 2, 11
multilateral trading system, 76, 83, 183, 301
multilateralization, 12, 69, 79

national treatment, 8, 26, 31, 39, 50, 96, 97, 98, 100, 103, 104, 107, 110, 111, 113, 115, 143, 151, 152, 157, 161, 201, 245, 293, 294, 295, 298

neoliberal, 12
network analysis, 14, 128, 135
Noble Ventures v. Romania, 198
non-compliance, 90, 252
non-discrimination, 66, 157, 160, 161, 295
non-economic objectives, concerns, 12, 51, 126
North American Free Trade Agreement, NAFTA, 5, 16, 21, 24, 25, 26, 27, 28, 29, 33, 49, 51, 52, 54, 55, 67, 93, 96, 99, 103, 111, 150, 152, 153, 154, 174, 175, 176, 185, 195, 204, 207, 221, 222, 233, 237, 238, 239, 244, 268, 269, 270, 276, 279, 280, 282, 293, 295, 296, 299
  Article 1102, 103, 152
  Chapter 11, 26, 33, 49, 93, 152, 154, 222, 237, 268
Nuclear Tests Case, 170

object and purpose, treaty, 16, 51, 80, 81, 142, 172, 190, 191, 192, 193, 194, 195, 196, 197, 198, 199, 200, 201, 202, 203, 204, 206, 207, 208, 209, 210, 291, 297, 304, 305
objections to admissibility/jurisdiction, 15, 169, 172, 175, 181
objective criterion, 204
obstacles to international trade, 196
operational principles, 65, 76, 78, 79, 81
Opinion 2/15, CJEU, 5, 36, 47, 64

parallel proceedings, 80, 160
party autonomy, 72
Pauwelyn, Joost, 5, 7, 47, 112, 124, 125, 130, 140, 146, 150, 152, 156, 158, 171, 260, 286, 295
Permanent Court of Arbitration, PCA, 4, 27, 103, 105, 130, 135, 139, 142, 143, 220, 269
Permanent Court of International Justice, PCIJ, 122, 130, 133, 134, 135, 140, 145, 146
permanent tribunal, 89
persuasiveness, 149, 236
Philip Morris, 269

PluriCourts Investment Treaty Arbitration Database, PITAD, 23, 45, 250, 273, 292, 296, 298
Pope & Talbot, 142, 143, 238, 239
positivism, legal, 248, 249
Potestà, Michele, 69, 109, 211
preamble, 157, 196, 197, 199, 200, 201
precedent, 14, 16, 121, 122, 123, 124, 125, 126, 127, 128, 129, 132, 133, 144, 146, 148, 153, 209, 210, 285, 286, 288, 291, 307, 311
  external, 14, 125, 126, 127, 133, 142, 144, 146, 148, 288
Preferential Trade Agreement, PTA, 7, 21, 22, 23, 111
  African, 23, 29, 35
  Australian, 34, 39
  Canadian, 33, 35, 41
  Chinese, 33, 41
  EU, 26, 28
  Indian, 33
  MERCOSUR, 35
  South African, 33, 53
principal, 246
prohibition of expropriation, 38

rational choice, 17, 251, 283
Regional Economic Integration Organization, REIO, 30, 39
regulation of foreign investment, 66
regulatory conduct, 77
remedies, 2, 63, 65, 76, 78, 108, 113, 116, 143, 176, 264, 273, 294
res judicata, 124, 185
responsiveness, 17, 246, 256, 260, 262, 263, 264, 265, 266, 273, 285, 290
  adjudicative, 2, 4, 7, 8, 12, 14, 15, 16, 17, 76, 78, 86, 90, 94, 101, 105, 112, 117, 118, 145, 150, 154, 159, 160, 162, 168, 171, 174, 186, 189, 197, 231, 235, 236, 241, 242, 245, 247, 248, 249, 251, 257, 258, 259, 262, 266, 284, 289, 292, 300, 304
  judicial, 263, 264, 265
  score, 263, 264
review, factual, 88
Rompetrol v. *Romania*, 176, 177, 186

Russia-Measures Concerning Traffic in Transit, 301, 303, 304, 305, 307, 308, 309, 310, 311

Saluka v. *Czech Republic*, 130, 197, 198
SCC, 101
Schill, Stephan, 31, 46, 50, 51, 52, 86, 123, 132, 133, 145, 168, 229
Schreuer, Christoph, 50, 63, 66, 80, 95, 167, 229, 234, 241
SCM Agreement, 196
SD Meyers, 151
services, 2, 13, 29, 30, 48, 92, 96, 102, 113, 115, 155, 188, 294
Shawcross, Lord, 221, 228, 229
Simma, Bruno, 133, 145, 146
Singapore, 5, 27, 33, 34, 36, 39, 55, 56, 57, 65, 68, 71, 72, 73, 75, 85, 220, 225, 270
  Exception, 39
South African Development Community, 27, 28, 36, 55, 59
South African Development Community, SADC, 28
SPS Agreement, WTO, 199
standard, 16, 62, 82, 88, 96, 101, 103, 110, 141, 146, 192, 205, 238, 239, 264, 291, 294
  ethical, 73, 84
  professional, 89
standard of review, 88, 146, 192
stare decisis, 121, 192
state-state arbitration, 35, 52, 93, 105, 111, 117
Stockholm Chamber of Commerce, SCC, 101
substantive rules, 94, 123, 156, 249, 290, 300

teleological interpretation, 199, 208
trade, xii, 1, 2, 4, 5, 7, 8, 9, 10, 11, 12, 13, 14, 15, 16, 17, 21, 22, 24, 25, 26, 27, 28, 29, 31, 33, 34, 35, 36, 41, 42, 43, 44, 45, 46, 47, 48, 50, 51, 52, 53, 63, 64, 65, 67, 70, 72, 73, 75, 82, 84, 85, 89, 90, 96, 97, 105, 107, 108, 111, 112, 114, 117, 118, 150, 155, 156,

157, 158, 159, 160, 161, 162, 163, 180, 187, 194, 195, 197, 198, 200, 204, 209, 213, 216, 217, 223, 228, 229, 230, 231, 235, 237, 242, 243, 244, 247, 251, 254, 255, 256, 258, 259, 260, 262, 263, 264, 275, 282, 283, 284, 285, 286, 287, 288, 289, 290, 291, 292, 293, 294, 295, 296, 297, 298, 299, 300, 303, 304, 305, 308, 311
   agreement, 2, 7, 11, 21, 26, 27, 28, 31, 33, 34, 35, 36, 65, 68, 107, 108, 111, 229, 230, 237, 287, 296
   dispute settlement, 7, 23, 24, 25, 43
   liberalization, 12, 27, 51, 53, 196, 198, 209, 230
Transatlantic Trade and Investment Partnership, TTIP, 2, 22, 26, 29, 47, 64, 65, 66, 69, 70, 71, 74, 75, 77, 83, 84, 85, 97, 100, 216, 222, 224, 225, 241, 270
Transpacific Partnership, TPP, 2, 22, 26, 55, 57, 99, 216, 217, 218, 219, 224, 225, 233, 270
treaty, 1, 8, 11, 12, 16, 26, 27, 29, 33, 42, 43, 44, 45, 48, 49, 50, 51, 53, 62, 63, 68, 69, 70, 78, 80, 81, 94, 97, 98, 99, 100, 101, 105, 106, 107, 108, 109, 110, 111, 114, 118, 132, 140, 142, 150, 156, 157, 158, 171, 184, 190, 191, 192, 193, 194, 195, 196, 198, 200, 201, 202, 203, 204, 205, 206, 208, 209, 210, 211, 212, 215, 216, 217, 218, 219, 220, 221, 222, 225, 230, 231, 233, 235, 237, 239, 240, 248, 267, 273, 275, 276, 279, 291, 294, 295, 296, 302, 305, 306, 307, 308, 309, 312
   context, 50, 53, 108
   interpretation, 16, 50, 80, 81, 94, 140, 142, 150, 171, 190, 192, 194, 196, 198, 200, 203, 204, 209, 210, 211, 216, 218, 220, 221, 222, 225, 230, 235, 291, 294, 296, 302, 305, 308
   object and purpose, 16, 51, 80, 81, 142, 172, 190, 191, 192, 193, 194, 195, 196, 197, 198, 199, 200, 201, 202, 203, 204, 206, 207, 208, 209, 210, 291, 297, 304, 305

TRIPS, 95, 231
trustee, 246, 248, 249, 254, 256
Tulip Real Estate, 141, 142, 143

UN General Assembly, 310
United Nations Commission on International Trade Law, UNCITRAL, 4, 12, 17, 39, 41, 63, 67, 69, 73, 74, 90, 99, 101, 103, 106, 139, 142, 143, 144, 152, 153, 154, 155, 198, 207, 220, 238, 247, 269
   Arbitration Rules, 39, 74, 106
   Working Group III, 4, 17, 63, 69, 247
United Nations Conference on Trade and Development, UNCTAD, 3, 22, 25, 29, 62, 70, 95, 98, 102, 212, 215, 223, 224, 229, 230, 244
   International Investment Agreements Navigator, 25
   Investment Policy Hub, 215, 223, 224, 229, 230
Uruguay round, 197
USA, 16, 21, 26, 30, 31, 33, 39, 46, 51, 55, 61, 68, 77, 78, 80, 87, 92, 93, 96, 105, 106, 108, 111, 112, 117, 129, 130, 133, 134, 135, 140, 141, 142, 143, 144, 146, 153, 154, 155, 170, 171, 173, 175, 176, 179, 183, 187, 220, 222, 225, 238, 264, 266, 268, 270, 281, 284, 299, 302, 306, 307, 308
US-Argentina BIT, 293, 300, 301, 306
US-Gambling, 117

Vienna Convention on the Law of Treaties, VCLT, 2, 80, 81, 141, 142, 171, 172, 190, 191, 193, 194, 195, 201, 202, 203, 204, 208, 209, 210, 219, 220, 231, 233, 291, 294, 304, 309
   Article 31, 153, 190, 191, 193, 194, 195, 201, 202, 203, 204, 208, 209, 210, 220, 291, 309
   Article 32, 203, 204

INDEX

Vietnam, 27, 35, 36, 42, 47, 48, 55, 56, 58, 71, 72, 73, 85, 88, 157, 216, 217, 218, 219, 220, 224, 225, 233, 270
Vivendi v. Argentina, 178, 180, 212
voice, 267, 284

Waldock, Humphrey, 203
Weeramantary, Christopher, 202
World Trade Organization, WTO, vii, viii, xii, xiii, xiv, 1, 2, 6, 7, 8, 11, 12, 13, 14, 15, 17, 21, 22, 23, 25, 26, 29, 43, 47, 49, 62, 65, 67, 70, 75, 76, 77, 78, 79, 80, 81, 82, 83, 84, 85, 87, 88, 89, 90, 93, 94, 95, 96, 97, 111, 112, 113, 114, 115, 116, 117, 118, 121, 124, 126, 127, 128, 129, 130, 131, 133, 138, 139, 140, 141, 142, 143, 145, 146, 147, 148, 149, 150, 151, 152, 153, 154, 156, 159, 160, 161, 162, 163, 167, 168, 169, 173, 174, 175, 177, 178, 179, 181, 183, 185, 187, 188, 189, 190, 191, 192, 193, 194, 195, 196, 197, 198, 199, 201, 202, 203, 204, 205, 206, 208, 209, 219, 222, 223, 230, 231, 232, 235, 236, 237, 241, 244, 247, 250, 254, 255, 256, 257, 258, 259, 260, 262, 263, 264, 265, 266, 284, 285, 286, 288, 289, 290, 292, 293, 294, 295, 296, 297, 298, 299, 300, 301, 302, 303, 304, 305, 306, 308, 309, 310, 311
  acquis, 150, 152, 160, 161, 162, 163
  dispute settlement mechanism, 23, 113, 115, 130, 247, 250
  jurisprudence, 150, 151, 154, 156, 159, 161, 173, 177, 185, 192, 259, 294, 295, 296, 299, 300
  panel(s), 4, 72, 76, 79, 80, 81, 82, 83, 87, 88, 89, 103, 113, 114, 115, 116, 139, 141, 155, 173, 174, 179, 181, 184, 185, 187, 188, 189, 192, 193, 194, 195, 197, 198, 201, 204, 205, 207, 208, 254, 255, 256, 262, 263, 264, 265, 266, 296, 297, 301, 302, 303, 304, 306, 307, 308, 309, 310, 311
Wälde, Thomas, 153

Lightning Source UK Ltd.
Milton Keynes UK
UKHW022323020920
369267UK00005B/34